The Age of Empire

THE AGE OF EMPIRE

1875–1914

Eric Hobsbawm

PHOENIX
PRESS

5 UPPER SAINT MARTIN'S LANE
LONDON
WC2H 9EA

A PHOENIX PRESS PAPERBACK

First published in Great Britain
by Weidenfeld & Nicolson in 1987
This paperback edition published in 2000
by Phoenix Press,
a division of The Orion Publishing Group Ltd,
Orion House, 5 Upper St Martin's Lane,
London WC2H 9EA

Copyright © 1987 by E. J. Hobsbawm

A CIP catalogue record for this book
is available from the British Library.

Printed and bound in Great Britain by
Clays Ltd, St Ives plc

ISBN 1 84212 016 6

CONTENTS

MAPS

PREFACE

Though written by a professional historian, this book is addressed not to other academics, but to all who wish to understand the world and who believe history is important for this purpose. Its object is not to tell readers exactly what happened in the world during the forty years before the First World War, though I hope it will give them some idea of the period. If they want to find out more, they can easily do so from the large and often excellent literature, much of which is easily available in English to anyone who takes an interest in history. Some of it is indicated in the guide to Further Reading.

What I have tried to do in this volume, as in the two volumes which preceded it (*The Age of Revolution 1789–1848* and *The Age of Capital 1848–1875*) is to understand and explain the nineteenth century and its place in history, to understand and explain a world in the process of revolutionary transformation, to trace the roots of our present back into the soil of the past and, perhaps above all, to see the past as a coherent whole rather than (as historical specialization so often forces us to see it) as an assembly of separate topics: the history of different states, of politics, of the economy, of culture or whatever. Ever since I began to be interested in history, I have always wanted to know how all these aspects of past (or present) life hang together, and why.

This book is therefore not (except incidentally) a narrative or a systematic exposition, and still less a display of scholarship. It is best read as the unfolding of an argument, or rather, the tracing of a basic theme through the various chapters. Readers must judge whether the attempt is convincing, though I have done my best to make it accessible to non-historians.

There is no way of acknowledging my debts to the many writers whose works I have pillaged, even as I often disagreed with them, and still less my debts to the ideas I have obtained over the years in conversation with colleagues and students. If they recognize their own ideas and observations, they can at least blame me for getting them or the facts wrong, as I have certainly done from time to time. I can, however, acknowledge those who made it possible to pull a long pre-occupation with this period together into a single book. The Collège de France enabled me to produce something like a first draft in the form of a course of thirteen lectures in 1982; I am grateful to this august institution and to Emmanuel Le Roy Ladurie who instigated the invitation. The Leverhulme Trust gave me an Emeritus Fellowship in 1983–5, which allowed me to get research help; the Maison des Sciences de l'Homme and Clemens Heller in Paris, as well as the World Institute for Development Economics Research of the United Nations University and the Macdonnell Foundation, gave me the possibility of a few quiet weeks in 1986 to finish the text. Among the people who assisted me in research I am particularly grateful to Susan Haskins, Vanessa Marshall and Dr Jenna Park. Francis Haskell read the chapter on the arts, Alan Mackay those on the sciences, Pat Thane that on women's emancipation, and preserved me from some, but I am afraid not from all, error. André Schiffrin read the entire manuscript as a friend and exemplar of the educated non-expert to whom this book is addressed. I spent many years lecturing on European history to the students of Birkbeck College, University of London, and I doubt whether I would have been able to envisage a history of the nineteenth century in world history without this experience. So this book is dedicated to them.

OVERTURE

Memory is life. It is always carried by groups of living people, and therefore it is in permanent evolution. It is subject to the dialectics of remembering and forgetting, unaware of its successive deformations, open to all kinds of use and manipulation. Sometimes it remains latent for long periods, then suddenly revives. History is the always incomplete and problematic reconstruction of what is no longer there. Memory always belongs to our time and forms a lived bond with the eternal present; history is a representation of the past.

Pierre Nora, 1984[1]

Merely to recount the course of events, even on a world-wide scale, is unlikely to result in a better understanding of the forces at play in the world today unless we are aware at the same time of the underlying structural changes. What we require first of all is a new framework and new terms of reference. It is these that the present book will seek to provide.

Geoffrey Barraclough, 1964[2]

I

In the summer of 1913 a young lady graduated from secondary school in Vienna, capital of the empire of Austria–Hungary. This was still a fairly unusual achievement for girls in central Europe. To celebrate the occasion, her parents decided to offer her a journey abroad, and since it was unthinkable that a respectable young woman of eighteen should be exposed to danger and temptation alone, they looked for a suitable relative. Fortunately, among the various interrelated families which had advanced westwards to prosperity and education from various small towns in Poland and Hungary during the past generations, there was one which had done unusually well. Uncle Albert had built up a chain of stores in the Levant – Constantinople, Smyrna, Aleppo, Alexandria. In the early twentieth century there was plenty of business to be done in the Ottoman Empire and the Middle East, and Austria had long been central Europe's business window on the orient. Egypt was both a living museum, suitable for cultural self-improvement, and a sophisticated community of the cosmopolitan European middle class, with whom communication was easily possible by means of the French language, which the young lady and her sisters had perfected at a boarding establishment in the neighbourhood of Brussels. It also, of course, contained the Arabs. Uncle Albert was happy to welcome his young relative, who travelled to Egypt on a steamer of the Lloyd Triestino, from Trieste, which was then the chief port of the Habsburg Empire and also, as it happened, the place of residence of James Joyce. The young lady was the present author's future mother.

Some years earlier a young man had also travelled to Egypt, but from London. His family background was considerably more modest. His father, who had migrated to Britain from Russian Poland in the 1870s, was a cabinet-maker by trade, who earned an insecure living in East London and Manchester, bringing up a daughter of his first marriage and eight children of the second, most of them already born in England, as best he could. Except for one son, none of them was gifted for business or drawn to it. Only one of the youngest had the chance to acquire much schooling, becoming a mining engineer in South America, which was then an informal part of the British Empire. All, however, were passionate in the pursuit of English language and culture, and anglicized themselves with enthusiasm. One became an actor, another carried on the family trade, one became a primary school teacher, two others joined the expanding public services in the form of the Post Office. As it happened Britain had recently (1882) occupied Egypt, and so one brother found himself representing a small part of the British Empire, namely the Egyptian Post and Telegraph Service, in the Nile delta. He suggested that Egypt would suit yet another of his brothers, whose main qualification for making his way through life would have served him excellently if he had not actually had to earn a living: he was intelligent, agreeable, musical and a fine all-round sportsman as well as a lightweight boxer of championship standard. In fact, he was exactly the sort of Englishman who would find and hold a post in a shipping office far more easily in 'the colonies' than anywhere else.

That young man was the author's future father, who thus met his future wife where the economics and politics of the Age of Empire, not to mention its social history, brought them together – presumably at the Sporting Club on the outskirts of Alexandria, near which they would establish their first home. It is extremely improbable that such an encounter would have happened in such a place, or would have led to marriage between two such people, in any period of history earlier than the one with which this book deals. Readers ought to be able to discover why.

However, there is a more serious reason for starting the present volume with an autobiographical anecdote. For all of us there is a twilight zone between history and memory; between the past as a generalized record which is open to relatively dispassionate inspection and the past as a remembered part of, or background to, one's own life. For individual human beings this zone stretches from the point where living family traditions or memories begin – say, from the earliest family photo which the oldest living family member can identify or explicate – to the end of infancy, when public and private destinies are recognized as inseparable and as mutually defining one another ('I met him shortly before the end of the war'; 'Kennedy must have died in 1963, because it was when I was still in Boston'). The length of this zone may vary, and so will the obscurity and fuzziness that characterizes it. But there is always such a no-man's land of time. It is by far the hardest part of history for historians, or for anyone else, to grasp. For the present writer, born towards the end of the First World War of parents who were, respectively, aged thirty-three and nineteen in 1914, the Age of Empire falls into this twilight zone.

But this is true not only of individuals, but of societies. The world we live in is still very largely a world made by men and women who grew up in the period with which this volume deals, or in its immediate shadow. Perhaps this is ceasing to be so as the twentieth century draws to its close – who can be certain? – but it was certainly true for the first two-thirds of our century.

Consider, for instance, a list of names of political persons who must be included among the movers and shapers of the twentieth century. In 1914 Vladimir Ilyich Ulyanov (Lenin) was forty-four years old, Joseph Vissarionovich Dzhugashvili (Stalin) thirty-five, Franklin Delano Roosevelt thirty, J. Maynard Keynes thirty-two, Adolf Hitler twenty-five, Konrad Adenauer (maker of the post-1945 German Federal Republic) thirty-eight. Winston Churchill was forty, Mahatma Gandhi forty-five, Jawaharlal Nehru twenty-five, Mao Tse-tung twenty-one, Ho Chi-minh twenty-two, the same age as Josip Broz (Tito) and Francisco Franco Bahamonde (General Franco of Spain), that is two years younger than Charles de Gaulle and nine years younger than Benito Mussolini. Consider figures of significance in the field of culture. A sample from a *Dictionary of Modern Thought* published in 1977 produces the following result:

3

Persons born 1914 and after   23%
Persons active in 1880–1914
    or adult in 1914   45%
Persons born 1900–14   17%
Persons active before 1880   15%

Quite patently men and women compiling such a compendium three-quarters of the way through the twentieth century still considered the Age of Empire as by far the most significant in the formation of the modern thought then current. Whether we agree with their judgment or not, this judgment is historically significant.

Hence not only the relatively few surviving individuals who have a direct link with the years before 1914 face the problem of how to look at the landscape of their private twilight, but so, more impersonally, does everyone who lives in the world of the 1980s, insofar as it has been shaped by the era which led up to the First World War. I mean not that the remoter past is of no significance to us, but that its relation to us is different. When dealing with remote periods we know that we confront them essentially as strangers and outsiders, rather like Western anthropologists setting out to investigate Papuan hill peoples. If they are geographically or chronologically, or emotionally, remote enough, such periods may survive exclusively through the inanimate relics of the dead: words and symbols, written, printed or engraved, material objects, images. Moreover, if we are historians, we know that what we write can be judged and corrected only by other such strangers, to whom 'the past is another country' also. We certainly start with the assumption of our own time, place and situation, including the propensity to reshape the past in our terms, to see what it has sharpened our eye to discern and only what our perspective allows us to recognize. Nevertheless, we go to work with the usual tools and materials of our trade, working on archival and other primary sources, reading an enormous quantity of secondary literature, threading our way through the accumulated debates and disagreements of generations of our predecessors, the changing fashions and phases of interpretation and interest, always curious, always (it is to be hoped) asking questions. But nothing much gets in our way except other contemporaries arguing as strangers about a past which is no longer part of memory. For even what we think we remember about the France of 1789 or the England of George III is what we have learned at second or fifth hand through pedagogues, official or informal.

Where historians try to come to grips with a period which has left surviving eyewitnesses, two quite different concepts of history clash, or, in the best of cases, supplement each other: the scholarly and the existential, archive and personal memory. For everyone is a historian of his or her own consciously lived lifetime inasmuch as he or she comes to terms with it in the mind – an unreliable historian from most points of view, as anyone knows who has ventured into 'oral history', but one whose contribution is essential. Scholars who interview old soldiers or politicians will have already acquired more, and more reliable, information about what happened from print and paper, than their source has in his or her memory, but may nevertheless misunderstand it. And, unlike, say, the historian of the crusades, the historian of the Second World War can be corrected by those who, remembering, shake their head and tell him or her: 'But it was not like that at all.' Nevertheless, both the versions of history which thus confront one another are, in different senses, coherent constructions of the past, consciously held as such and at least potentially capable of definition.

But the history of the twilight zone is different. It is itself an incoherent, incompletely perceived image of the past, sometimes more shadowy, sometimes apparently precise, always transmitted by a mixture of learning and second-hand memory shaped by public and private tradition. For it is still part of us, but no longer quite within our personal reach. It forms something similar to those particoloured ancient maps filled with unreliable outlines and white spaces, framed by monsters and symbols. The monsters and symbols are magnified by the modern mass media, because the very fact that the twilight zone is important to us makes it central also to their preoccupations. Thanks to them such fragmentary and symbolic images have become lasting, at least in the western world: the *Titanic*, which retains all its power to make headlines three-quarters of a century after its sinking, is a striking example. And these images which flash into our mind when it is, for some reason or another, turned to the period which ended in the First World War are far more difficult to detach from a considered interpretation of the period than, say, those images and anecdotes which used to bring non-historians into supposed contact with a remoter past: Drake playing bowls as the Armada approached Britain, Marie-Antoinette's diamond necklace or 'Let them eat cake,' Washington crossing the Delaware. None of these will affect the serious historian for a moment. They are outside us. But can we, even as professionals, be sure that we look at the mythologized images of the Age of Empire with an equally cold eye: the *Titanic*, the San Francisco earthquake, Dreyfus? Patently not, if the centenary of the Statue of Liberty is any guide.

More than any other, the Age of Empire cries out for demystification, just because we – and that includes the historians – are no longer in it, but do not know how much of it is still in us. This does not mean that it calls for debunking or muckraking (an activity it pioneered).

5

I I

The need for some sort of historical perspective is all the more urgent because people in the late twentieth century are indeed still passionately involved in the period which ended in 1914, probably just because August 1914 is one of the most undeniable 'natural breaks' in history. It was felt to be the end of an era at the time, and it is still felt to be so. It is quite possible to argue this feeling away, and to insist on the continuities and enjambments across the years of the First World War. After all, history is not like a bus-line on which the vehicle changes all its passengers and crew whenever it gets to the point marking its terminus. Nevertheless, if there are dates which are more than conveniences for purposes of periodization, August 1914 is one of them. It was felt to mark the end of the world made by and for the bourgeoisie. It marks the end of the 'long nineteenth century' with which historians have learned to operate, and which has been the subject of the three volumes of which this is the last.

No doubt that is why it has attracted historians, amateur and professional, writers on culture, literature and the arts, biographers, the makers of films and television programmes, and not least the makers of fashions, in astonishing numbers. I would guess that in the English-speaking world at least one title of significance – book or article – has appeared on the years from 1880 to 1914 every month for the past fifteen years. Most of them are addressed to historians or other specialists, for the period is not merely, as we have seen, crucial in the development of modern culture, but provides the frame for a large number of passionately pursued debates in history, national or international, mostly initiated in the years before 1914: on imperialism, on the development of labour and socialist movements, on the problem of Britain's economic decline, on the nature and origins of the Russian Revolution – to name but a few. For obvious reasons the best known among these concerns is the question of the origins of the First World War, and it has so far generated several thousand volumes and continues to produce literature at an impressive rate. It has remained alive, because the problem of the origins of world wars has unfortunately refused to go away since 1914. In fact, the link between the past and present concerns is nowhere more evident than in the history of the Age of Empire.

Leaving aside the purely monographic literature, most of the writers on the period can be divided into two classes: the backward lookers and the forward lookers. Each tends to concentrate on one of the two most obvious features of the period. In one sense, it seems extraordinarily remote and beyond return when seen across the impassable

6

canyon of August 1914. At the same time, paradoxically, so much of what is still characteristic of the late twentieth century has its origin in the last thirty years before the First World War. Barbara Tuchman's *The Proud Tower*, a best-selling 'portrait of the world before the war (1890–1914)' is perhaps the most familiar example of the first genre; Alfred Chandler's study of the genesis of modern corporate management, *The Visible Hand*, may stand for the second.

In quantitative terms, and in terms of circulation, the backward lookers almost certainly prevail. The irrecoverable past presents a challenge to good historians, who know that it cannot be understood in anachronistic terms, but it also contains the enormous temptation of nostalgia. The least perceptive and most sentimental constantly try to recapture the attractions of an era which upper- and middle-class memories have tended to see through a golden haze: the so-called 'beautiful times' or *belle époque*. Naturally this approach has been congenial to entertainers and other media producers, to fashion-designers and others who cater to the big spenders. This is probably the version of the period most likely to be familiar to the public through cinema and television. It is quite unsatisfactory, though it undoubtedly catches one highly visible aspect of the period, which, after all, brought such terms as 'plutocracy' and 'leisure class' into the public discourse. One may debate whether it is more or less useless than the even more nostalgic, but intellectually more sophisticated, writers who hope to prove that paradise lost might not have been lost, but for some avoidable errors or unpredictable accidents without which there would have been no world war, no Russian Revolution, or whatever else is held to be responsible for the loss of the world before 1914.

Other historians are more concerned with the opposite of the great discontinuity, namely the fact that so much of what remains characteristic of our times originated, sometimes quite suddenly, in the decades before 1914. They seek these roots and anticipations of our time, which are indeed obvious. In politics, the labour and socialist parties which form the government or chief opposition in most states of western Europe are the children of the era from 1875 to 1914, and so are one branch of their family, the communist parties which govern the regimes of eastern Europe.* So indeed are the politics of governments elected by democratic vote, the modern mass party and nationally organized mass labour union, and modern welfare legislation.

Under the name of 'modernism' the *avant garde* of this period took over most of twentieth-century high cultural output. Even today, when

---

* The communist parties ruling in the non-European world were formed on their model, but after our period.

some *avant gardes* or other schools no longer accept this tradition, they still define themselves in terms of what they reject ('post-modernism'). Meanwhile the culture of everyday life is still dominated by three innovations of this period: the advertising industry in its modern form, the modern mass circulation newspaper or periodical, and (directly or through television) the moving photograph or film. Science and technology may have come a long way since 1875–1914, but in the sciences there is an evident continuity between the age of Planck, Einstein and the young Niels Bohr and the present. As for technology, the petrol-powered road-running automobiles and the flying-machines which appeared in our period, for the first time in history, still dominate our landscapes and townscapes. The telephones and wireless communication invented at that time have been improved but not superseded. It is possible that, in retrospect, the very last decades of the twentieth century may be seen no longer to fit into the framework established before 1914, but for most purposes of orientation it will still serve.

But it cannot be enough to present the history of the past in such terms. No doubt the question of continuity and discontinuity between the Age of Empire and the present still matters, since our emotions are still directly engaged with this section of the historical past. Nevertheless, from the historian's point of view, taken in isolation, continuity and discontinuity are trivial matters. But how are we to situate this period? For, after all, the relation of past to present is central to the preoccupations both of those who write and of those who read history. Both want, or should want, to understand how the past has become the present, and both want to understand the past, the chief obstacle being that it is *not* like the present.

The Age of Empire, though self-contained as a book, is the third and last volume of what has turned out to be a general survey of the nineteenth century in world history – that is, the historians' 'long nineteenth century' which runs from, say, 1776 to 1914. It was not the author's original intention to embark on anything so crazily ambitious. But insofar as three volumes written at intervals over the years and, except for the last, not intentionally conceived as parts of a single project, have any coherence, it is because they share a common conception of what the nineteenth century was about. And insofar as this common conception has succeeded in linking *The Age of Revolution* to *The Age of Capital* and both in turn to *The Age of Empire* – and I hope it has – it should also be helpful in linking the Age of Empire to what came after it.

Essentially the central axis round which I have tried to organize the history of the century is the triumph and transformation of capitalism in the historically specific forms of bourgeois society in its liberal version. The history begins with the decisive double breakthrough of the first industrial revolution in Britain, which established the limitless capacity of the productive system pioneered by capitalism for economic growth and global penetration, and the Franco-American political revolution, which established the leading models for the public institutions of bourgeois society, supplemented by the virtually simultaneous emergence of its most characteristic – and linked – theoretical systems: classical political economy and utilitarian philosophy. The first volume of this history, *The Age of Revolution 1789–1848*, is structured round this concept of a 'dual revolution'.

It led to the confident conquest of the globe by the capitalist economy, carried by its characteristic class, the 'bourgeoisie', and under the banners of its characteristic intellectual expression, the ideology of liberalism. This is the main theme of the second volume, which covers the brief period between the 1848 revolutions and the onset of the 1870s Depression, when the prospects of bourgeois society and its economy seemed relatively unproblematic, because their actual triumphs were so striking. For either the political resistances of 'old regimes', against which the French Revolution had been made, were overcome, or these regimes themselves looked like accepting the economic, institutional and cultural hegemony of a triumphant bourgeois progress. Economically, the difficulties of an industrialization and economic growth limited by the narrowness of its pioneer base were overcome, not least by the spread of industrial transformation and the enormous widening of world markets. Socially, the explosive discontents of the poor during the Age of Revolution were consequently defused. In short, the major obstacles to continued and presumably unlimited bourgeois progress seemed to have been removed. The possible difficulties arising from the inner contradictions of this progress did not yet seem to be cause for immediate anxiety. In Europe there were fewer socialists and social revolutionaries in this period than at any other.

The Age of Empire, on the other hand, is penetrated and dominated by these contradictions. It was an era of unparalleled peace in the western world, which engendered an era of equally unparalleled world wars. It was an era of, in spite of appearances, growing social stability within the zone of developed industrial economies, which provided the small bodies of men who, with almost contemptuous ease, could conquer and rule over vast empires, but which inevitably generated on its outskirts the combined forces of rebellion and revolution that were to engulf it. Since 1914 the world has been dominated by the fear, and sometimes by the reality, of global war and the fear (or hope) of

9

revolution – both based on the historic situations which emerged directly out of the Age of Empire.

It was the era when massive organized movements of the class of wage-workers created by, and characteristic of, industrial capitalism suddenly emerged and demanded the overthrow of capitalism. But they emerged in highly flourishing and expanding economies, and, in the countries in which they were strongest, at a time when probably capitalism offered them slightly less miserable conditions than before. It was an era when the political and cultural institutions of bourgeois liberalism were extended, or about to be extended, to the working masses living in bourgeois societies, including even (for the first time in history) its women, but the extension was at the cost of forcing its central class, the liberal bourgeoisie, on to the margins of political power. For the electoral democracies, which were the inevitable product of liberal progress, liquidated bourgeois liberalism as a political force in most countries. It was an era of profound identity crisis and transformation for a bourgeoisie whose traditional moral foundation crumbled under the very pressure of its own accumulations of wealth and comfort. Its very existence as a class of masters was undermined by the transformation of its own economic system. Juridical persons (i.e. large business organizations or corporations), owned by shareholders, employing hired managers and executives, began to replace real persons and their families owning and managing their own enterprises.

There is no end to such paradoxes. The history of the Age of Empire is filled with them. Indeed, its basic pattern, as seen in this book, is of the society and world of bourgeois liberalism advancing towards what has been called its 'strange death' as it reaches its apogee, victim of the very contradictions inherent in its advance.

What is more, the culture and intellectual life of the period show a curious awareness of this pattern of reversal, of the imminent death of one world and the need for another. But what gave the period its peculiar tone and savour was that the coming cataclysms were both expected, misunderstood and disbelieved. World war would come, but nobody, even the best of the prophets, really understood the kind of war it would be. And when the world finally stood on the brink, the decision-makers rushed towards the abyss in utter disbelief. The great new socialist movements were revolutionary; but for most of them revolution was, in some sense, the logical and necessary outcome of bourgeois democracy, which gave the multiplying many the decision over the diminishing few. And for those among them who expected actual insurrection, it was a battle whose aim, in the first instance, could only be to institute bourgeois democracy as a necessary preliminary to something more advanced. Revolutionaries thus remained within the

Age of Empire, even as they prepared to transcend it.

In the sciences and the arts the orthodoxies of the nineteenth century were being overthrown, but never did more men and women, newly educated and intellectually conscious, believe more firmly in what small *avant gardes* were even then rejecting. If public opinion pollsters in the developed world before 1914 had counted up hope against foreboding, optimists against pessimists, hope and optimism would pretty certainly have prevailed. Paradoxically, they would probably have collected proportionately more votes in the new century, as the western world approached 1914, than they might have done in the last decades of the old. But, of course, that optimism included not only those who believed in the future of capitalism, but also those who looked forward with hope to its supersession.

In itself there is nothing about the historical pattern of reversal, of development undermining its own foundations, which is novel or peculiar to this period as distinct from any other. This is how endogenous historical transformations work. They are still working this way. What is peculiar about the long nineteenth century is that the titanic and revolutionary forces of this period which changed the world out of recognition were transported on a specific, and historically peculiar and fragile vehicle. Just as the transformation of the world economy was, for a crucial but necessarily brief period, identified with the fortunes of a single medium-sized state – Great Britain – so the development of the contemporary world was temporarily identified with that of nineteenth-century liberal bourgeois society. The very extent to which the ideas, values, assumptions and institutions associated with it appeared to triumph in the Age of Capital indicates the historically transient nature of that triumph.

This book surveys the moment in history when it became clear that the society and civilization created by and for the western liberal bourgeoisie represented not the permanent form of the modern industrial world, but only one phase of its early development. The economic structures which sustain the twentieth-century world, even when they are capitalist, are no longer those of 'private enterprise' in the sense businessmen would have accepted in 1870. The revolution whose memory dominates the world since the First World War is no longer the French Revolution of 1789. The culture which penetrates it is no longer bourgeois culture as it would have been understood before 1914. The continent which overwhelmingly constituted its economic, intellectual and military force then, no longer does so now. Neither history in general, nor the history of capitalism in particular, ended in 1914, though a rather large part of the world was, by revolution, moved into a fundamentally different type of economy. The Age of Empire, or, as Lenin called it, Imperialism, was plainly not 'the last stage' of capitalism; but then Lenin never actually claimed that it was. He merely called it, in the earliest version of his influential booklet, 'the latest' stage of capitalism.* And yet one can understand why observers – and not only observers hostile to bourgeois society – might feel that the era of world history through which they lived in the last few decades before the First World War was more than just another phase of development. In one way or another it seemed to anticipate and prepare a world different in kind from the past. And so it has turned out since 1914, even if not in the way expected or predicted by most of the prophets. There is no return to the world of liberal bourgeois society. The very calls to revive the spirit of nineteenth-century capitalism in the late twentieth century testify to the impossibility of doing so. For better or worse, since 1914 the century of the bourgeoisie belongs to history.

* It was renamed 'the highest stage' after his death.

CHAPTER 1

THE CENTENARIAN REVOLUTION

'Hogan is a prophet. . . . A prophet, Hinnissy, is a man that foresees throuble. . . . Hogan is th'happyest man in th'wurruld about today, but tomorrah something is goin' to happen.'

Mr Dooley Says, 1910[1]

I

Centenaries are an invention of the late nineteenth century. Some time between the centennial of the American Revolution (1876) and that of the French Revolution (1889) – both celebrated with the usual international expositions – the educated citizens of the western world became conscious of the fact that this world, born between the Declaration of Independence, the construction of the world's first iron bridge and the storming of the Bastille, was now a century old. How did the world of the 1880s compare with that of the 1780s?*

In the first place, it was now genuinely global. Almost all parts of it were now known and more or less adequately or approximately mapped. With negligible exceptions exploration no longer consisted of 'discovery' but of a form of athletic endeavour, often with strong elements of personal or national competition, typified by the attempt to dominate the most severe and inhospitable physical environments of the Arctic and the Antarctic. Peary of the USA was to win the race to reach the North Pole in 1909 against British and Scandinavian competition; Amundsen of Norway reached the South Pole in 1911, one month ahead of the hapless British Captain Scott. (Neither achievement had or was intended to have the slightest practical consequence.) Railway and steamship had made intercontinental or transcontinental travel a matter of weeks rather than months, except in most of the large land-masses of Africa, continental Asia and parts of the interior of

---

* *The Age of Revolution*, chapter 1, surveys that older world.

South America, and would soon make it a matter of days: with the completion of the Trans-Siberian Railway in 1904 it would be possible to travel from Paris to Vladivostok in fifteen or sixteen days. The electric telegraph now made the communication of information across the entire globe a matter of hours. In consequence men and women from the western world – but not only they – travelled and communicated over large distances with unprecedented facility and in unprecedented numbers. To take simply one illustration which would have been regarded as an absurd fantasy in the age of Benjamin Franklin. In 1879 almost 1 million tourists visited Switzerland. Over 200,000 of them were Americans: the equivalent of more than one in twenty of the entire US population at its first Census (1790).*²

At the same time it was a much more densely populated world. Demographic figures are so speculative, particularly for the late eighteenth century, that numerical precision is both pointless and dangerous, but we shall not be far wrong in supposing that the 1500 million or so human beings who may have been alive in the 1880s represented double the world's population in the 1780s. Much the largest number of them were Asians, as they had always been, but while in 1800 they had constituted almost two-thirds of humanity (according to recent guesses), by 1900 they formed perhaps 55 per cent of it. The next largest block were the Europeans (including Asian Russia, thinly populated). Their numbers had almost certainly more than doubled from, say 200 millions in 1800 to 430 millions in 1900, and what is more, their mass emigration overseas was largely responsible for the most dramatic change in world population, the rise of the Americas from about 30 to nearly 160 millions between 1800 and 1900; and more especially of North America from about 7 to over 80 millions. The devastated continent of Africa, about whose demography we admittedly know little, grew more slowly than any other, perhaps at most by a third in the century. While at the end of the eighteenth century there were perhaps three times as many Africans as Americans (North and Latin), by the end of the nineteenth there were probably substantially more Americans than Africans. The tiny population of the Pacific islands including Australia, though swelled by European migration from a hypothetical 2 millions to perhaps 6, carried little demographic weight.

Yet while in one sense the world was becoming demographically larger and geographically smaller and more global – a planet bound together ever more tightly by the bonds of moving goods and people, of capital and communications, of material products and ideas – in another it was drifting into division. There had been rich and poor

---

* For a fuller account of this process of globalization, see *The Age of Capital*, chapters 3 and 11.

regions, advanced and backward economies and societies, stronger and weaker units of political organization and military force, in the 1780s, as in all other ages of history of which we have record. And it is hardly to be denied that a major gulf separated the great belt of the world which had been the traditional home of class societies and more or less lasting states and cities, operating by means of literate minorities and – happily for the historian – generating written documentation, from the zones to the north and south of them upon which the ethnographers and anthropologists of the late nineteenth and early twentieth centuries concentrated their attention. Nevertheless, within this large belt, which stretched from Japan in the east to the shores of the mid- and North Atlantic and through European conquest into the Americas, and in which the bulk of humanity lived, the disparities, though already large, did not yet seem insurmountable.

In terms of production and wealth, not to mention culture, the differences between the major pre-industrial regions were, by modern standards, remarkably small; say between 1 and 1.8. Indeed a recent estimate calculates that between 1750 and 1800 the *per capita* gross national product in what are today known as the 'developed countries' was substantially the same as in what is now known as the 'Third World', though this is probably due to the enormous size and relative weight of the Chinese Empire (with about a third of the world's population), whose average standard of living may at that stage have actually been superior to that of Europeans.[3] In the eighteenth century Europeans would have found the Celestial Empire a very strange place indeed, but no intelligent observer would have regarded it in any sense as an inferior economy and civilization to Europe's, still less as a 'backward' country. But in the nineteenth century the gap between the western countries, base of the economic revolution which was transforming the world, and the rest widened, at first slowly, later with increasing rapidity. By 1880 (according to the same calculation) the *per capita* income in the 'developed' world was about double that in the 'Third World', by 1913 it was to be over three times as high, and widening. By 1950 (to dramatize the process) the difference was between 1 and 5, by 1970 between 1 and 7. Moreover, the gap between the 'Third World' and the really developed parts of the 'developed' world, i.e. the industrialized countries, began earlier and widened even more dramatically. The *per capita* share of the GNP was already almost twice that in the 'Third World' in 1830, about seven times as high in 1913.*

* The figure measuring the *per capita* share of the GNP is a purely statistical construct: gross national product divided by the number of inhabitants. While it is useful for general comparisons of economic growth between different countries and/or periods, it tells us nothing about the actual

Technology was a major cause of this gap, reinforcing it not merely economically but politically. A century after the French Revolution it was becoming increasingly evident that poorer and backward countries could easily be defeated and (unless they were very large) conquered because of the technical inferiority of their armaments. This was comparatively new. Napoleon's invasion of Egypt in 1798 had pitted against each other French and Mamelouk armies with comparable equipment. The colonial conquests of European forces had been achieved not by miraculous weaponry, but by greater aggressiveness, ruthlessness and, above all, disciplined organization.[4] Yet the industrial revolution, which penetrated warfare in the middle decades of the century (cf. *The Age of Capital*, chapter 4) tilted the balance even further in favour of the 'advanced' world by means of high explosives, machine-guns and steam transport (see chapter 13 below). The half-century from 1880 to 1930 was to be the golden or rather the iron age of gunboat diplomacy for this reason.

We are therefore in 1880 dealing not so much with a single world, as with two sectors combined together into one global system: the developed and the lagging, the dominant and the dependent, the rich and the poor. Even this description is misleading. While the (smaller) first world, in spite of its considerable internal disparities, was united by history and as the common bearer of capitalist development, the (much larger) second world was united by nothing except its relations with, that is to say its potential or actual dependency on, the first. What else, except a common membership of the human race, had the Chinese Empire in common with Senegal, Brazil with the New Hebrides, Morocco with Nicaragua? The second world was united by neither history, culture, social structure nor institutions, nor even by what we today think of as the most salient characteristic of the dependent world, namely mass poverty. For wealth and poverty as social categories apply only to societies stratified in a certain way, and to economies structured in a certain way, and parts of the dependent world were, as yet, neither. All human societies known to history contain some social inequalities (apart from those between the sexes), but if Indian maharajahs visiting the west could be treated as though they were millionaires in the western sense, the big men or chiefs in New Guinea could not be so assimilated, even notionally. And if the common people of any part of the world, when transported away from their homes, were normally turned into workers, and therefore members of the category of 'the poor', it was irrelevant to describe them in this manner in their native habitat. In

---

income or standard of living of anyone in the region or about the distribution of incomes in it, except that, theoretically, in a country with a high *per capita* figure there would be more to distribute than in a country with a low one.

any case, there were favoured parts of the world – notably in the tropics – where nobody needed to lack either shelter, food or leisure. Indeed, there were still small societies in which the concepts of work and leisure had no meaning, and no words for them existed.

If the existence of the two world sectors was undeniable, the boundaries between them were unclear, chiefly because the set of states by and through which the economic – and in our period the political – conquest of the globe was achieved were united by history as well as economic development. They consisted of 'Europe' and not only of those regions, mainly in north-western and central Europe and some of their overseas settlements, which plainly formed the core of world capitalist development. 'Europe' included the southern regions which had once played a major role in early capitalist developments, but had since the sixteenth century become backwaters, and the conquerors of the first great European overseas empires, notably the Italian and Iberian peninsulas. It also included a great eastern border zone where, for more than a thousand years, Christendom – that is to say the heirs and descendants of the Roman Empire* – had fought the periodic invasions of military conquerors from Central Asia. The last wave of these, which had formed the great Ottoman Empire, had been gradually expelled from the enormous areas of Europe it controlled in the sixteenth to eighteenth centuries, and its days in Europe were clearly numbered, though in 1880 it still controlled a substantial belt across the Balkan peninsula (parts of the present Greece, Yugoslavia and Bulgaria and all of Albania) as well as some islands. Much of the reconquered or liberated territories could only be regarded as 'European' by courtesy: in fact, the Balkan peninsula was still currently referred to as the 'Near East': hence South-west Asia came to be known as the 'Middle East'. On the other hand the two states which had done most to push back the Turks were or became great European powers, in spite of the notorious backwardness of all or parts of their peoples and territories: the Habsburg Empire and, above all, the empire of the Russian tsars.

Large parts of 'Europe' were therefore, at best, on the margins of the core of capitalist economic development and bourgeois society. In some, most of the inhabitants clearly lived in a different century from their contemporaries and rulers – as on the Adriatic coasts of Dalmatia or in the Bukovina, where in 1880 88 per cent of the population were

* Between the fifth century AD and 1453 the Roman Empire survived with varying success, with its capital in Byzantium (Istanbul) and Orthodox Christianity as its state religion. The Russian tsar, as his name implies (tsar = Caesar; Tsarigrad, 'city of the emperor', is still the Slav name for Istanbul), considered himself the successor of this empire, and Moscow as 'the third Rome'.

illiterate as against 11 per cent in Lower Austria, part of the same empire.[5] Many educated Austrians shared Metternich's belief that 'Asia begins where the eastern highway leaves Vienna', and most north Italians regarded most south Italians as some kind of African barbarians, but in both monarchies the backward areas formed only part of the state. In Russia the question 'European or Asiatic?' cut much deeper, since virtually the entire zone from Byelorussia and Ukraine eastwards to the Pacific was equally remote from bourgeois society, except for a thin film of the educated. It was indeed the subject of impassioned public debate.

Nevertheless, history, politics, culture and, not least, centuries of overseas and overland expansion against the second world bound even the backward parts of the first world to the advanced ones, if we leave aside a few isolated enclaves of Balkan mountaineers and the like. Russia was indeed backward, though its rulers had systematically looked west for two centuries and acquired control over western border territories such as Finland, the Baltic countries and parts of Poland which were distinctly more advanced. Yet economically Russia was distinctly part of 'the west', inasmuch as her government was clearly engaged on a policy of massive industrialization on the western model. Politically the Tsarist Empire was colonizer rather than colony, and culturally the small educated minority within Russia was one of the glories of nineteenth-century western civilization. Peasants in the Bukovina, in the remotest north-east of the Habsburg Empire*, might still live in the Middle Ages, but its capital, Czernowitz (Cernovtsi), contained a distinguished European university, and its emancipated and assimilated Jewish middle class was anything but medieval. At the other end of Europe Portugal was small, feeble, backward by any contemporary standard, a virtual semi-colony of Britain, and only the eye of faith could detect much in the way of economic development there. Yet Portugal remained not merely a member of the club of sovereign states but a large colonial empire by virtue of her history; she retained her African empire, not only because rival European powers could not decide how to partition it, but because, being 'European', its possessions were not – or not quite – regarded as the mere raw material for colonial conquest.

In the 1880s Europe was not only the original core of the capitalist development which dominated and transformed the world, but by far the most important component of the world economy and of bourgeois society. There has never in history been a more European century, nor will there ever again be such a one. Demographically, the world

* This region became part of Rumania in 1918, and has since 1947 been part of the Ukrainian Soviet Republic.

contained a higher proportion of Europeans at the end of the century than at the beginning – perhaps one in four as against one in five.[6] In spite of the millions the old continent sent to various new worlds, it grew faster. Though the sheer pace and impetus of its industrialization already made America's future as a global economic super-power certain, European industrial output was still more than twice as large as American, and major technological advance still came primarily from east of the Atlantic. Motor cars, cinematography and wireless were first developed seriously in Europe. (Japan was a very slow starter in the modern world economy, though faster off the mark in world politics.)

As for high culture, the world of white settlement overseas still remained overwhelmingly dependent on the old continent; and this was even more obviously so among the tiny educated elites of the non-white societies, insofar as these took 'the west' as their model. Economically, Russia could not begin to compare with the headlong growth and wealth of the USA. Culturally, the Russia of Dostoievsky (1821–81), Tolstoi (1828–1910), Chekhov (1860–1904), of Tchaikovsky (1840–93), Borodin (1834–87) and Rimsky-Korsakov (1844–1908) was a great power, and the USA of Mark Twain (1835–1910) and Walt Whitman (1819–92) was not, even if we throw in Henry James (1843–1916), who had long since emigrated to the more congenial atmosphere of Britain. European culture and intellectual life still belonged mainly to a minority of the prosperous and educated, and was adapted to functioning admirably in and for such a milieu. The contribution of liberalism, and the ideological left beyond it, was to call for the achievements of this elite culture to be made freely accessible to all. The museum and the free library were its characteristic achievements. American culture, more democratic and egalitarian, did not come into its own until the era of mass culture in the twentieth century. For the time being, even in matters so closely geared to technical progress as the sciences, the USA still lagged not only behind the Germans and the British, but even behind the small Netherlands, to judge by the geographical distribution of Nobel prizes in their first quarter-century.

But if part of the 'first world' could have fitted equally well into the zone of dependency and backwardness, virtually the whole of the 'second world' clearly belonged to it, except for Japan, systematically 'westernizing' since 1868 (see *The Age of Capital*, chapter 8), and overseas territories settled by large populations of European descent – in 1880 still primarily from north-western and central Europe – except, of course, for such native populations as they did not succeed in eliminating. It was this dependency – or, more exactly, the inability either to keep out of the way of the trade and technology of the west or to find a substitute for it, or to resist the men armed with its weapons and organization – that put societies which otherwise had nothing in common in the same category as victims of nineteenth-century history against its makers. As a ruthless western wit put it, with a little military oversimplification:

> Whatever happens, we have got
> the Maxim Gun, and they have not.[7]

Compared with this difference, the differences between stone-age societies such as those of the Melanesian islands and the sophisticated and urbanized societies of China, India and the Islamic world, seemed insignificant. What did it matter that their arts were admirable, that the monuments of their ancient cultures were wonderful, and that their (mainly religious) philosophies impressed some western scholars and poets at least as much as, indeed probably more than, Christianity? Basically they were all equally at the mercy of the ships that came from abroad bringing cargoes of goods, armed men and ideas against which they were powerless, and which transformed their universes in ways which suited the invaders, whatever the sentiments of the invaded.

This does not mean that the division between the two worlds was a simple one between industrialized and agricultural countries, between the civilizations of city and countryside. The 'second world' contained cities more ancient than and/or as enormous as the first: Peking, Constantinople. The nineteenth-century capitalist world market generated, within it, disproportionately large urban centres through which the flow of their economic relations was channelled: Melbourne, Buenos Aires, Calcutta, all had about half a million inhabitants each in the 1880s, which was larger than Amsterdam, Milan, Birmingham or Munich, while the three-quarters of a million of Bombay was larger than all but half-a-dozen cities in Europe. Though with a few special exceptions towns were more numerous and played a more significant role in the economies of the first world, the 'developed' world remained surprisingly agricultural. In only six European countries did agriculture employ less than a majority – generally a large majority – of the male population: but these six were, characteristically, the core of the older capitalist development – Belgium, Britain, France, Germany, the Netherlands, Switzerland. However, only in Britain was agriculture the occupation of a smallish minority of about one-sixth; elsewhere it employed between 30 and 45 per cent.[8] There was, indeed, a striking difference between the commercialized and businesslike farming of the 'developed' regions and the agriculture of the backward ones. Danish and Bulgarian peasants had little in common economically by 1880 except an interest in stables and fields. Still, farming, like the ancient handicrafts, was a way of living deeply rooted in the ancient past, as the ethnologists and folklorists of the later nineteenth century knew when they looked for old traditions and 'popular survivals' primarily in the countryside. Even the most revolutionary agriculture still sheltered them.

Conversely, industry was not entirely confined to the first world. Quite apart from the building of an infrastructure (e.g. ports and railways) and extractive industries (mines) in many a dependent and colonial economy, and the presence of cottage industries in many backward rural areas, some industry of the nineteenth-century western type tended to develop modestly in dependent countries such as India even at this early stage, sometimes against strong opposition from metropolitan interests: mainly textiles and food-processing. But even metals penetrated the second world. The great Indian iron and steel firm of Tata began operations in the 1880s. Meanwhile small production by small family artisans or in 'putting-out' workshops remained as characteristic of the 'developed' world as of much of the dependent world. It was about to enter upon a period of crisis, anxiously monitored by German scholars, faced with the competition of factories and modern distribution. But, on the whole, it still survived in considerable strength.

Nevertheless, it is roughly correct to make industry into a criterion of modernity. In the 1880s no country outside the 'developed' world (and Japan, which had joined it) could be described as industrial or even on the way to industrialization. Even those 'developed' countries which were still primarily agrarian, or at any rate not immediately associated in the public mind with factories and forges, were, one might say, already tuned to the wavelength of industrial society and high technology. Apart from Denmark, the Scandinavian countries, for instance, had until recently been notoriously poor and backward. Yet within a few decades they had more telephones per head than any other European region,[9] including Britain and Germany); they won considerably more Nobel prizes in science than the USA; and they were about to become strongholds of socialist political movements specifically organized with the interests of the industrial proletariat in mind.

And, even more obviously, we can describe the 'advanced' world as rapidly urbanizing, and indeed in extreme cases as a world of city-dwellers beyond precedent.[10] In 1800 there had been just seventeen cities in Europe with a population of 100,000 or more, with a total population of under 5 million. By 1890 there were 103 with a total population more than six times as large. What the nineteenth century since 1789 had generated was not so much the giant urban ant-heap with its millions of scurrying inhabitants – though by 1880 three more million-cities had joined London since 1800 (Paris, Berlin and Vienna).

Rather it had generated a widely distributed system of medium and large towns, especially large fairly dense zones or conurbations of such urban and industrial development, gradually eating away the countryside of the region. Some of the more dramatic of these were comparatively new, the product of mid-century heavy industrial development like Tyneside and Clydeside in Great Britain, or only just developing on a massive scale, like the Ruhr in Germany or the Pennsylvania coal–steel belt. These, once again, did not necessarily contain any major cities, unless they also contained capital cities, centres of government administration and other tertiary activities, or major international ports, which also tended to generate unusually large populations. Curiously enough, with the exception of London, Lisbon and Copenhagen, no European state in 1880 contained a city which was both.

II

If it is difficult to describe the economic differences between the two sectors of the world in two or three words, however profound and evident they were, it is not much easier to summarize the political differences between them. There clearly existed a general model of the desirable structure and institutions of a properly 'advanced' country, give or take a few local variations. It should form a more or less homogeneous territorial state, internationally sovereign, large enough to provide the basis of national economic development, enjoying a single set of political and legal institutions of a broadly liberal and representative kind (i.e. it should enjoy a single constitution and the rule of law), but also, at a lower level, it should have a fair degree of local autonomy and initiative. It should be composed of 'citizens', i.e. of the aggregate of the individual inhabitants of its territory who enjoyed certain basic legal and political rights, rather than, say, of corporations or other kinds of groups and communities. Their relations with the national government should be direct and not mediated by such groups. And so on. These were aspirations, and not only for the 'developed' countries (all of which by 1880 conformed to some degree to this model) but for all others who did not wish to cut themselves deliberately off from modern progress. To this extent the liberal–constitutional nation-state as a model was not confined to the 'developed' world. Indeed the largest body of states theoretically operating on this model, generally in the federalist American rather than the centralist French variant, was to be found in Latin America. This consisted at this date of seventeen republics and one empire, which did not survive the 1880s (Brazil). In practice it was notorious that political reality in Latin America, or for that matter in some nominally constitutional monarchies of south east Europe, had little relation to constitutional theory. A very large part of the non-developed world possessed no states of this, or sometimes of any, form. Some of it consisted of the possessions of European powers, directly administered by them: these colonial empires were shortly to be enormously expanded. Some of it, e.g. in the African interior, consisted of political units to which the term 'state' in the then current European sense was not seriously applicable, though other terms then current ('tribes') were not much better. Some of it consisted of sometimes very ancient empires such as the Chinese, the Persian and the Ottoman, which had parallels in European history but were clearly not territorial states ('nation-states') of the nineteenth-century type, and were very obviously (it seemed) obsolescent. On the other hand the same ricketiness, if not always the same antiquity, affected some obsolescent empires which were at least partly or marginally in the 'developed' world, if only because of their, admittedly shaky, status as 'great powers': the Tsarist and the Habsburg empires (Russia and Austria–Hungary).

In terms of international politics (i.e. of the calculations of governments and foreign ministries of Europe), the number of entities treated as sovereign states anywhere in the world was rather modest, by our standards. Around 1875 there were no more than seventeen in Europe (including the six 'powers' – Britain, France, Germany, Russia, Austria–Hungary and Italy – and the Ottoman Empire), nineteen in the Americas (including one virtual 'great power', the USA), four or five in Asia (mainly Japan and the two ancient empires of China and Persia) and perhaps three highly marginal cases in Africa (Morocco, Ethiopia, Liberia). Outside the Americas, which contained the largest collection of republics on the globe, virtually all of these were monarchies – in Europe only Switzerland and (since 1870) France were not – though in the developed countries most of them were constitutional monarchies or at least made official gestures in the direction of some sort of electoral representation. The Tsarist and Ottoman empires – the one on the margins of 'development', the other clearly belonging to the world of the victims – were the only European exceptions. However, apart from Switzerland, France, the USA and possibly Denmark, none of the representative states were based on a democratic (though at this stage exclusively masculine) franchise,* though some nominal white-settler colonies in the British Empire (Australia, New

---

* The disenfranchisement of illiterates, not to mention a tendency to military coups, makes it impossible to describe the Latin American republics as 'democratic' in any sense.

23

Zealand, Canada) were reasonably democratic – indeed they were more so than any other areas apart from some Rocky Mountain states in the USA. However, in such countries outside Europe political democracy assumed the elimination of the former indigenous population – Indians, Aborigines, etc. Where they could not be eliminated by expulsion into 'reservations' or by genocide, they were not part of the political community. In 1890, out of the 63 million inhabitants of the USA only 230,000 were Indians.[11]

As for the inhabitants of the 'developed' world (and the countries seeking or forced to imitate it), the adult males among them increasingly conformed to the minimum criterion of bourgeois society: that of legally free and equal individuals. Legal serfdom no longer existed anywhere in Europe. Legal slavery, abolished almost everywhere in the western and western-dominated world, was in its very last years even in its final refuges, Brazil and Cuba: it did not survive the 1880s. Legal freedom and equality were far from incompatible with real inequality. The ideal of liberal bourgeois society was neatly expressed in Anatole France's ironic phrase: 'The Law in its majestic equality gives every man the same right to dine at the Ritz and to sleep under a bridge.' Still, in the 'developed' world it was now essentially money or the lack of it, rather than birth or differences in legal freedom or status, which determined the distribution of all but the privileges of social exclusiveness. And legal equality did not exclude political inequality either, for not only wealth but *de facto* power counted. The rich and powerful were not merely politically more influential, but could exercise a good deal of extra-legal compulsion, as any inhabitant of such areas as the hinterlands of southern Italy and the Americas knew only too well, not to mention American blacks. Still, there was a clear difference between those parts of the world in which such inequalities were still formally built into the social and political system and those in which they were at least formally incompatible with official theory. It was analogous to the difference between countries in which torture was still a legal form of the judicial process (e.g. the Chinese Empire) and those in which it did not officially exist, though policemen tacitly recognized the distinction between the 'torturable' and the 'non-torturable' classes (to use the novelist Graham Greene's terms).

The clearest distinction between the two sectors of the world was cultural, in the widest sense of the word. By 1880 the 'developed' world consisted overwhelmingly of countries or regions in which the majority of the male and increasingly the female population was literate, in which politics, economics and intellectual life in general had emancipated themselves from the tutelage of the ancient religions, bulwarks of traditionalism and superstition, and which virtually monopolized the sort of science which was increasingly essential for modern technology. By the late 1870s any European country or region with a majority of illiterates could be almost certainly classified as non-developed or backward, and the other way round. Italy, Portugal, Spain, Russia and the Balkan countries were at best on the margins of development. Within the Austrian Empire (omitting Hungary) the Slavs of the Czech lands, the German speakers and the rather less literate Italians and Slovenes represented the advanced parts of the country, the predominantly illiterate Ukrainians, Rumanians and Serbo-Croats the backward regions. Cities with a predominantly illiterate population, as in much of the then 'Third World', would be an even more convincing index of backwardness, since towns were normally much more literate than the countryside. There were some fairly obvious cultural elements in such divergences, for instance the notably greater encouragement of mass education among Protestants and (western) Jews as distinct from Catholic, Muslim and other religions. A poor and overwhelmingly rural country like Sweden with no more than 10 per cent illiteracy in 1850 would be hard to imagine elsewhere than in the Protestant zone of the world (i.e. most of the countries adjoining the Baltic, North Sea and North Atlantic, with extensions into central Europe and North America). On the other hand it also, and visibly, reflected economic development and the social divisions of labour. Among Frenchmen (1901) fishermen were three times more illiterate than workers and domestics, peasants twice as illiterate, persons engaged in trade half as illiterate, public service and the professions evidently the most literate of all. Peasants heading their own enterprise were *less* literate than agricultural workers (though not much), but in the less traditional fields of industry and trade employers were more literate than workers (though not than their office staff).[12] Cultural, social and economic factors cannot be separated in practice.

Mass education, which was by this time secured in the developed countries by increasingly universal primary schooling by or under the supervision of states, must be distinguished from the education and culture of the generally very small elites. Here the differences between the two sectors of that belt of the globe which knew literacy were less, though the higher education of such strata as European intellectuals, Moslem or Hindu scholars and East Asian mandarins had little in common (unless they also adapted to the European pattern). Mass illiteracy, as in Russia, did not preclude an impressive if numerically very restricted minority culture. However, certain institutions typified the zone of 'development' or European domination, notably the essentially secular university, which did not exist outside this zone* and, for

---

* The university was not necessarily yet the modern institution for the advancement of knowledge on the nineteenth-century German model which was then spreading throughout the West.

different purposes, the opera house (see the map in *The Age of Capital*). Both these institutions reflected the penetration of the dominant 'western' civilization.

III

Defining the difference between advanced and backward, developed and non-developed parts of the world is a complex and frustrating exercise, since such classifications are by their nature static and simple, and the reality which is to be fitted into them was neither. Change was the name of the nineteenth century: change in terms of, and to suit the purposes of, the dynamic regions along the shores of the Northern Atlantic seas which were at this time the core of world capitalism. With some marginal and diminishing exceptions, all countries, even the hitherto most isolated, were at least peripherally gripped by the tentacles of this global transformation. On the other hand even the most 'advanced' of the 'developed' countries changed in part by adapting the heritage of an ancient and 'backward' past, and contained layers and patches of society which resisted transformation. Historians rack their brains about the best way to formulate and to present this universal but everywhere different change, the complexity of its patterns and interactions, and its major directions.

Most observers in the 1870s would have been far more impressed by its linearity. In material terms, in terms of knowledge and the capacity to transform nature it seemed so patent that change meant advance that history – at all events modern history – seemed to equal progress. Progress was measured by the ever rising curve of whatever could be measured, or what men chose to measure. Continuous improvement, even of those things which clearly still required it, was guaranteed by historical experience. It seemed hardly credible that little more than three centuries ago intelligent Europeans had regarded the agriculture, military techniques and even the medicine of the ancient Romans as the model for their own, that a bare two centuries ago there could be a serious debate about whether the moderns could ever surpass the achievement of the ancients, and that at the end of the eighteenth century experts could have doubted whether the population of Britain was increasing.

Progress was most evident and undeniable in technology and in its obvious consequence, the growth in material production and communication. Modern machinery was overwhelmingly powered by steam and made of iron and steel. Coal had become overwhelmingly the most important source of industrial energy. It represented 95 per cent of it in Europe (outside Russia). Hill streams in Europe and North America, which had once determined the location of so many early cotton mills – whose very name recalls the significance of water power – once again reverted to rural life. On the other hand the new energy sources, electricity and mineral oil, were not yet of major significance, though by the 1880s large-scale generation of electricity and the internal-combustion engine were both becoming practicable. Even the USA did not claim more than about 3 million electric lights in 1890, and in the early 1880s the most modern European industrial economy, Germany, used less than 400,000 tons of oil per annum.[13]

Modern technology was not only undeniable and triumphant, but highly visible. Its production machines, though not particularly powerful by modern standards – in Britain they averaged less than 20 HP in 1880 – were usually large, being still made mainly of iron, as any visitor to museums of technology can verify.[14] But by far the largest and most powerful engines of the nineteenth century were the most visible and audible of all. These were the 100,000 railway locomotives (200–450 HP), pulling their almost $2\frac{3}{4}$ million carriages and wagons in long trains under banners of smoke. They were part of the most dramatic innovation of the century, undreamed of – unlike air travel – a century earlier when Mozart wrote his operas. Vast networks of shining rails, running along embankments, across bridges and viaducts, through cuttings, through tunnels up to ten miles long, across mountain passes as high as the major Alpine peaks, the railways collectively constituted the most massive effort of public building as yet undertaken by man. They employed more men than any other industrial undertakings. They reached into the centres of great cities, where their triumphal achievements were celebrated in equally triumphal and gigantic railway stations, and into the remotest stretches of the countryside, where no other trace of nineteenth-century civilization penetrated. By the early 1880s (1882) almost 2 billion people a year travelled on them, most of them, naturally, from Europe (72 per cent) and North America (20 per cent).[15] In the 'developed' regions of the west there can by then have been very few men, perhaps even very few of the less mobile women, who had not, at some time in their lives, made contact with the railway. Probably the only other by-product of modern technology, the net of telegraph-lines on their endless succession of wooden poles, about three or four times as great in length as the world's railway system, was more universally known.

The 22,000 steamships of the world in 1882, though probably even more powerful as machines than the locomotives, were not only much less numerous, and visible only to the small minority of humans who went near ports, but in one sense much less typical. For in 1880 they still (but only just) represented less shipping tonnage, even in industrialized Britain, than sailing ships. As for world shipping as a whole, there were in 1880 still almost three tons under the power of wind for every ton under steam-power. This was about to change immediately and dramatically, in the 1880s, in favour of steam. Tradition still ruled on the water, and notably, in spite of the change from timber to iron and from sail to steam, in the matter of building, loading and discharging ships.

How much attention would serious lay observers in the second half of the 1870s have paid to the revolutionary advances of technology which were already incubating or being born at the time: the various kinds of turbines and internal-combustion engines, the telephone, gramophone and incandescent electric light bulb (all just being invented), the motor car, made operational by Daimler and Benz in the 1880s, not to mention cinematography, aeronautics and radio telegraphy which were produced or worked on in the 1890s? Almost certainly they would have expected and predicted important developments in anything connected with electricity, photography and chemical synthesis, which were familiar enough, and they would not have been surprised that technology should succeed in solving so obvious and urgent a problem as the invention of a mobile engine to mechanize road transport. They could not have been expected to anticipate radio waves and radio activity. They would certainly have speculated – when have human beings not done so? – on the prospects of human flight, and would have been hopeful, given the technological optimism of the age. People were certainly hungry for new inventions, the more dramatic the better. Thomas Alva Edison, who set up what was probably the first private industrial development laboratory in 1876 in Menlo Park, New Jersey, became a public hero to Americans with his first phonograph in 1877. But they would certainly not have expected the actual transformations brought about by these innovations in consumer society for in fact, except in the USA, these were to remain relatively modest until the First World War.

Progress was most visible, then, in the capacity for material production and for speedy and massive communication in the 'developed' world. The benefits of this multiplication of wealth almost certainly had not in the 1870s reached the overwhelming majority of the inhabitants of Asia, Africa and all but a part of the southern cone of Latin America. It is not clear how far they had reached the bulk of people in the peninsulas of southern Europe or in the Tsarist Empire. Even in the 'developed' world they were very unevenly distributed as between the 3.5 per cent of the rich, the 13–14 per cent of the middle class and the 82–3 per cent of the labouring classes, to follow the official French classification of the Republic's funerals in the 1870s (see *The Age of Capital*, chapter 12). Nevertheless, some improvement in the condition of the common people in this zone was difficult to deny. The increase in human height, which makes each generation today taller than its parents, had probably begun by 1880 in a number of countries – but by no means everywhere, and in a very modest way compared to the improvement after 1880 or even later. (Nutrition is overwhelmingly the most decisive reason for this growth in human stature.)[16] The average expectation of life at birth was still modest enough in the 1880s: 43–45 years in the main 'developed' zones*, though below 40 in Germany, and 48–50 in Scandinavia.[17] (In the 1960s it was to be about 70 in these countries.) Still, life expectation had pretty certainly risen over the century, though the major fall in infantile mortality, which chiefly affects this figure, was only just beginning.

In short, the highest hope among the poor, even in the 'developed' parts of Europe, was probably still to earn enough to keep body and soul together, a roof over one's head and enough clothes, especially at the most vulnerable ages of their life-cycle, when couples had children below the earning age, and when men and women grew old. In the 'developed' parts of Europe they no longer thought of actual starvation as a possible contingency. Even in Spain the last major famine occurred in the 1860s. However, in Russia famine remained a significant hazard of life: there was to be an important one in 1890–1. In what would later be called the 'Third World' it remained endemic. A substantial sector of prosperous peasants was certainly emerging, as was also in some countries a sector of 'respectable' skilled or otherwise scarce manual workers capable of saving money and buying more than the essentials of life. But the truth is that the only market whose income was such as to tempt entrepreneurs and businessmen was that aimed at the middle incomes. The most notable innovation in distribution was the big-city department store, pioneered in France, America and Britain and just beginning to penetrate Germany. The Bon Marché or Whiteley's Universal Emporium or Wanamakers were not aimed at the labouring classes. The USA, with its vast pool of customers, already envisaged a massive market of medium-range standardized goods, but even there the mass market of the poor (the 'five-and-dime' market) was still left to the petty enterprise which found it worth catering to the poor. Modern mass production and the mass consumer economy had not arrived. They were to arrive very soon.

But progress also seemed evident in what people still liked to call 'moral statistics'. Literacy was plainly on the increase. Was it not a

---

* Belgium, Britain, France, Massachusetts, Netherlands, Switzerland.

measure of the growth of civilization that the number of letters sent in Britain at the outbreak of the wars against Bonaparte was perhaps two per annum for each inhabitant, but about forty-two in the first half of the 1880s? That 186 million copies of newspapers and journals were issued each month in the USA of 1880 compared to 330,000 in 1788? That in 1880 the persons who cultivated science by joining British learned societies were perhaps 44,000, probably fifteen times as many as fifty years earlier?[18] No doubt morality as measured by the very doubtful data of criminal statistics and the wild guesses of those who wished (as so many Victorians did) to condemn non-marital sex showed a less certain or satisfactory trend. But could not the progress of institutions towards liberal constitutionalism and democracy, which was everywhere visible in the 'advanced' countries, be seen as a sign of moral improvement, complementary to the extraordinary scientific and material triumphs of the age? How many would have disagreed with Mandell Creighton, an Anglican bishop and historian, who asserted that 'we are bound to assume, as the scientific hypothesis upon which history has been written, a progress in human affairs'.[19]

In the 'developed' countries, few; though some might note how comparatively recent this consensus was even in these parts of the world. In the remainder of the world most people would not even have understood the bishop's proposition at all, even had they thought about it. Novelty, especially when brought from outside by city folk and foreigners, was something that disturbed old and settled ways rather than something which brought improvement; and indeed the evidence that it brought disturbance was overwhelming, the evidence that it brought improvement was feeble and unconvincing. The world neither progressed nor was it supposed to progress: a point also made forcefully in the 'developed' world by that firm opponent of all the nineteenth century stood for, the Roman Catholic Church (see *The Age of Capital*, chapter 6, 1). At most, if times were bad for reasons other than the vagaries of nature or divinity such as famine, drought and epidemic, one might hope to restore the expected norm of human life by a return to true beliefs which had somehow been abandoned (e.g. the teachings of the Holy Koran) or by a return to some real or putative past of justice and order. In any case old wisdom and old ways were best, and progress implied that the young could teach the old.

'Progress' outside the advanced countries was therefore neither an obvious fact nor a plausible assumption, but mainly a foreign danger and challenge. Those who benefited from it and welcomed it were small minorities of rulers and townsmen who identified with foreign and irreligious values. Those whom the French in North Africa typically called *évolués* – 'persons who had evolved' – were, at this stage, precisely those who had cut themselves off from their past and their people; who were sometimes compelled to cut themselves off (e.g. as in North Africa by abandoning Islamic law) if they were to enjoy the benefits of French citizenship. There were as yet few places, even in the backward regions of Europe adjoining or surrounded by the advanced regions, where countrymen or the miscellaneous urban poor were prepared to follow the lead of the frankly anti-traditionalist modernizers, as many of the new socialist parties were to discover.

The world was therefore divided into a smaller part in which 'progress' was indigenous and another much larger part in which it came as a foreign conqueror, assisted by minorities of local collaborators. In the first, even the mass of ordinary people by now believed that it was possible and desirable and even that in some respects it was taking place. In France no sensible politician campaigning for votes and no significant party described themselves as 'conservative'; in the United States 'progress' was a national ideology; even in imperial Germany – the third great country with universal male suffrage in the 1870s – parties calling themselves 'conservative' won less than a quarter of the votes in general elections in that decade.

But if progress was so powerful, so universal and so desirable, how was this reluctance to welcome it or even to participate in it to be explained? Was it merely the dead weight of the past, which would gradually, unevenly but inevitably, be lifted off the shoulders of those parts of humanity which still groaned under it? Was not an opera house, that characteristic cathedral of bourgeois culture, soon to be erected in Manaus, a thousand miles up the River Amazon, in the midst of the primeval rainforest, out of the profits of the rubber boom – whose Indian victims, alas, had no chance to appreciate *Il Trovatore?* Were not groups of militant champions of the new ways, like the typically named *científicos* in Mexico, already in charge of their country's fate, or preparing to take charge of it like the equally typically named Committee for Union and Progress (better known as the Young Turks) in the Ottoman Empire? Had not Japan itself broken centuries of isolation to embrace western ways and ideas – and to turn itself into a modern great power, as was soon to be demonstrated by the conclusive proof of military triumph and conquest?

Nevertheless, the failure or refusal of most inhabitants of the world to live up to the example set by the western bourgeoisies was rather more striking than the success of the attempts to imitate it. It was perhaps only to be expected that the conquering inhabitants of the first world, still able to overlook the Japanese, should conclude that vast ranges of humanity were biologically incapable of achieving what a minority of human beings with notionally white skins – or, more narrowly, people of north European stock – had alone shown themselves to be capable of. Humanity was divided by 'race', an idea which penetrated the ideology of the period almost as deeply as 'progress', into those whose place in the great international celebrations of progress, the World Expositions (see *The Age of Capital*, chapter 2), was at the stands of technological triumph, and those whose place was in the 'colonial pavilions' or 'native villages' which now supplemented them. Even in the 'developed' countries themselves, humanity was increasingly divided into the energetic and talented stock of the middle classes and the supine masses whose genetic deficiencies doomed them to inferiority. Biology was called upon to explain inequality, particularly by those who felt themselves destined for superiority.

And yet the appeal to biology also dramatized the despair of those whose plans for the modernization of their countries met with the silent incomprehension and resistance of their peoples. In the republics of Latin America, inspired by the revolutions which had transformed Europe and the USA, ideologues and politicians considered the progress of their countries to be dependent on 'Aryanization' – i.e. the progressive 'whitening' of the people through intermarriage (Brazil) or virtual repopulation by imported white Europeans (Argentina). No doubt their ruling classes were white or at least considered themselves so, and the non-Iberian surnames of European descent among their political elites were and are disproportionately frequent. But even in Japan, improbable though this looks today, 'westernization' seemed sufficiently problematic at this period to suggest that it could only be successfully achieved by an infusion of what we would today call western genes (see *The Age of Capital*, chapters 8, 14).

Such excursions into pseudo-scientific quackery (cf. chapter 10 below) dramatize the contrast between progress as a universal aspiration, and indeed reality, and the patchiness of its actual advance. Only some countries seemed to be turning themselves, with varying degrees of speed, into industrial–capitalist economies, liberal–constitutionalist states and bourgeois societies on the western model. Even within countries or communities, the gap between the 'advanced' (who were also, in general, the wealthy) and the 'backward' (who were also, in general, the poor) was enormous, and dramatic, as the comfortable, civilized, assimilated Jewish middle classes and rich of western countries and central Europe were just about to discover when faced with the $2\frac{1}{2}$ millions of their co-religionists who emigrated westwards from their east European ghettos. Could these barbarians really be the *same* people 'as ourselves'?

And was the mass of the interior and exterior barbarians perhaps so great as to confine progress to a minority which maintained civilization only because it was able to keep the barbarians in check? Had it not been John Stuart Mill himself who said, 'Despotism is a legitimate mode of government in dealing with barbarians, provided the end be their improvement'?[20] But there was another, and more profound, dilemma of progress. Whither, in fact, did it lead? Granted that the global conquest of the world economy, the forward march of a triumphant technology and science on which it was increasingly based, were indeed undeniable, universal, irreversible and therefore inevitable. Granted that by the 1870s the attempts to hold them up or even slow them down were increasingly unrealistic and enfeebled, and that even the forces dedicated to conserving traditional societies already sometimes tried to do so with the weapons of modern society, as preachers of the literal truth of the Bible today use computers and broadcasts. Granted even that political progress in the form of representative governments and moral progress in the form of widespread literacy and reading would continue and even accelerate. Would it lead to the advance of civilization in the sense in which the youthful John Stuart Mill had articulated the aspirations of the century of progress: a world, even a country, 'more improved; more eminent in the best characteristics of Man and Society; farther advanced in the road to perfection; happier, nobler, wiser'?[21]

By the 1870s the progress of the bourgeois world had led to a point where more sceptical, even more pessimistic, voices began to be heard. And they were reinforced by the situation in which the world found itself in the 1870s, and which few had foreseen. The economic foundations of advancing civilization were shaken by tremors. After a generation of unparalleled expansion, the world economy was in crisis.

CHAPTER 2

AN ECONOMY CHANGES GEAR

Combination has gradually become the soul of modern commercial systems.

A. V. Dicey, 1905[1]

The object of any amalgamation of capital and production units ... must always be the largest possible reduction in the costs of production, administration and sale, with a view to achieving the highest possible profits by eliminating ruinous competition.

Carl Duisberg, founder of I. G. Farben, 1903–4[2]

There are times when development in all areas of the capitalist economy – in the field of technology, the financial markets, commerce, colonies – has matured to the point where an extraordinary expansion of the world market must occur. World production as a whole will be raised to a new and more all-embracing level. At this point capital begins to enter upon a period of tempestuous advance.

I. Helphand ('Parvus'), 1901[3]

I

A distinguished American expert, surveying the world economy in 1889, the year of the foundation of the Socialist International, observed that it had, since 1873, been marked by 'unprecedented disturbance and depression of trade'. 'Its most noteworthy peculiarity', he wrote,

has been its universality; affecting nations that have been involved in war as well as those which have maintained peace; those which have a stable currency based on gold, and those which have an unstable currency ...; those which live under a system of free exchange of commodities and those whose exchanges are more or less restricted. It has been grievous in old communities like England and Germany, and equally so in Australia, South Africa and California, which represent the new; it has been a calamity exceeding

34

heavy to be borne, alike by the inhabitants of sterile Newfoundland and Labrador, and of the sunny, fruitful sugar-islands of the East and West Indies; and it has not enriched those at the centers of the world's exchanges, whose gains are ordinarily greatest when business is most fluctuating and uncertain.[4]

This view, usually expressed in a less baroque style, was widely shared by contemporary observers, though some later historians have found it difficult to understand. For though the trade cycle which forms the basic rhythm of a capitalist economy certainly generated some very acute depressions in the period from 1873 to the mid-1890s, world production, so far from stagnating, continued to rise dramatically. Between 1870 and 1890 iron output in the five main producing countries more than doubled (from 11 to 23 million tonnes), the production of steel, which now became the convenient index of industrialization as a whole, multiplied twentyfold (from half a million to 11 million tonnes). International trade continued to grow impressively, though admittedly at a less dizzy rate than before. These were the very decades when the American and German industrial economies advanced with giant steps, and industrial revolution extended to new countries such as Sweden and Russia. Several of the overseas countries newly integrated into the world economy boomed as never before – thus, incidentally, preparing an international debt crisis very similar to that of the 1980s, especially as the names of the debtor-states are much the same. Foreign investment in Latin America reached the dizziest heights in the 1880s, as the length of the Argentine railway system doubled in five years and both Argentina and Brazil attracted up to 200,000 immigrants per year. Could such a period of spectacular productive growth be described as a 'Great Depression'?

Historians may doubt it, but contemporaries did not. Were these intelligent, well-informed and troubled Englishmen, Frenchmen, Germans and Americans subject to a collective delusion? It would be absurd to suppose so, even if the somewhat apocalyptic tone of some commentaries might have seemed excessive even at the time. By no means all 'thoughtful and conservative minds' shared Mr Wells' sense of the menace of a mustering of the barbarians from within, rather than as of old from without, for an attack on the whole present organization of society, and even the permanence of civilization itself'.[5] Still, some did, not to mention the growing body of socialists who looked forward to a collapse of capitalism under its insurmountable internal contradictions which the era of depression appeared to demonstrate. The note of pessimism in the literature and philosophy of the 1880s (see pp. 97, 258–9 below) can hardly be entirely understood without this sense of a general economic, and consequently social, malaise.

As for economists and businessmen, what worried even the less apocalyptically minded was the prolonged 'depression of prices, a depression of interest, and a depression of profits', as Alfred Marshall, the future guru of economic theory, put it in 1888.[6] In short, after the admittedly drastic collapse of the 1870s (see *The Age of Capital*, chapter 2), what was at issue was not production but its profitability.

Agriculture was the most spectacular victim of this decline in profits, and indeed some parts of it constituted the most deeply depressed sector of the economy, and the one whose discontents had the most immediate and far-reaching social and political consequences. Its output, vastly increased during previous decades (see *The Age of Capital*, chapter 10), now flooded the world markets, hitherto protected by high transport costs against massive foreign competition. The consequences for agrarian prices, both in European agriculture and in the overseas exporting economies, were dramatic. In 1894 the price of wheat was only a little more than a third of what it had been in 1867 – a splendid bonus for shoppers, but a disaster for the farmers, and farmworkers, who still formed between 40 and 50 per cent of working males in the industrial countries (with the single exception of Britain) and anything up to 90 per cent in the others. In some regions the situation was made worse by coincident scourges, such as the phylloxera infection after 1872, which cut French wine output by two-thirds between 1875 and 1889. The decades of depression were not a good time in which to be a farmer in any country involved in the world market. The reaction of agriculturalists, depending on the wealth and political structure of their countries, ranged from electoral agitation to rebellion, not to mention death by famine, as in Russia in 1891–2. Populism, which swept the USA in the 1890s, had its heart in the wheatlands of Kansas and Nebraska. There were peasant revolts, or agitations treated as such, between 1879 and 1894 in Ireland, Spain, Sicily and Rumania. Countries which did not have to worry about a peasantry because they no longer had one, like Britain, could let their farming atrophy: here two-thirds of the wheat-acreage disappeared between 1875 and 1895. Some countries, like Denmark, deliberately modernized their agriculture, switching to profitable animal products. Other governments, such as the German, but especially the French and American, chose tariffs, which kept up prices.

However, the two commonest non-governmental responses were mass emigration and co-operation, the former mainly by the landless and land-poor, the latter mainly by peasants with potentially viable holdings. The 1880s saw the highest ever rates of overseas migration for the countries of the old emigration (omitting the exceptional case of the

Irish in the decade after the Great Famine) (see *The Age of Revolution*, chapter 8, v), and the real start of mass emigration from such countries as Italy, Spain and Austria–Hungary, to be followed by Russia and the Balkans.* This was the safety valve which kept social pressure below the point of rebellion or revolution. As for co-operation, it provided modest loans for the small peasant – by 1908 more than half of all independent agriculturalists in Germany belonged to such rural mini-banks (pioneered by the Catholic Raiffeisen in the 1870s). Meanwhile societies for the co-operative buying of supplies, co-operative marketing and co-operative processing (notably of dairy products and, in Denmark, bacon-curing) multiplied in various countries. Ten years after 1884, when a law designed to legalize trade unions was seized on by French farmers for their own purposes, 400,000 of them were in almost 2000 such *syndicats*.[7] By 1900 there were 1600 co-operatives manufacturing dairy products in the USA, mostly in the Middle West, and the dairy industry in New Zealand was firmly under the control of farmers' co-operatives.

Business had its own troubles. An era brainwashed into the belief that a rise in prices ('inflation') is an economic disaster may find it difficult to believe that nineteenth-century businessmen were much more worried about a fall in prices – and in an, on the whole, deflationary century, no period was more drastically deflationary than 1873–96, when the level of British prices dropped by 40 per cent. For inflation – within reason – is not only good for debtors, as every householder with a long mortgage knows, but provides an automatic boost for the rate of profit, as goods produced at a lower cost were sold at the higher price-level prevailing when they reached the point of sale. Conversely, deflation cut into the rate of profit. A large expansion of the market could more than offset this – but in fact the market did not grow fast enough, partly because the new technology of industry made enormous increases of output both possible and necessary (at least if plant were to be run at a profit), partly because the number of competitive producers and industrial economies was itself growing, thus vastly increasing the total capacity available, and partly because a mass market for consumer goods was as yet slow to develop. Even for capital goods, the combination of new and improved capacity, more efficient use of the product, and changes in demand could be drastic: the price of iron fell by 50 per cent between 1871/5 and 1894/8.

A further difficulty was that their costs of production were in the short run stickier than prices, for – with some exceptions – wages could

---

* The only part of southern Europe which had significant emigration before the 1880s was Portugal.

not be or were not proportionately reduced, while firms were also saddled with considerable quantities of obsolete or obsolescent plant and equipment or with expensive new plant and equipment which, given low profits, were slower than expected to pay for themselves. In some parts of the world the situation was further complicated by the gradual, but in the short run fluctuating and unpredictable, fall in the price of silver and its exchange rate with gold. So long as both remained stable, as they had for many years before 1872, international payments calculated in the precious metals which formed the basis of world money were simple enough.* When the exchange rate became unstable, business transactions between those whose currencies relied on different precious metals became rather less simple.

What could be done about the depression of prices, profits and interest rates? A sort of monetarism-in-reverse was one solution which, as the enormous and now forgotten contemporary debate on 'bi-metallism' suggests, appealed to many, who attributed the fall in prices primarily to a global shortage of gold, which was increasingly (via the pound sterling, with a fixed gold parity – i.e. the gold sovereign) the exclusive basis of the world payments system. A system based on both gold and silver, which was available in vastly increased quantities especially in America, would surely raise prices through monetary inflation. Currency inflation, which appealed notably to hard-pressed prairie farmers, not to mention the operators of Rocky Mountain silver mines, became a major plank in American populist movements, and the prospect of mankind's crucifixion on a cross of gold inspired the rhetoric of the great people's tribune, William Jennings Bryan (1860–1925). As with Bryan's other favourite causes, such as the literal truth of the Bible and the consequent need to ban the teachings of the doctrines of Charles Darwin, he backed a loser. Banking, big business and governments in the core countries of world capitalism had no intention of abandoning the fixed parity of gold which they regarded in much the same manner as Bryan did the Book of Genesis. In any case, only countries like Mexico, China and India, which did not count, rested primarily on silver.

Governments were more inclined to listen to the very substantial interest groups and bodies of voters who urged them to protect the home producer against the competition of imported goods. For these included not only – as might be expected – the enormous bloc of agriculturalists, but also important bodies of domestic industrialists, seeking to minimize 'overproduction' by at least keeping out the rival foreigner. The Great Depression ended the long era of economic lib-

* Roughly 15 units of silver = 1 unit of gold.

eralism (cf. *The Age of Capital*, chapter 2), at least in the matter of commodity trade.* Starting with Germany and Italy (textiles) in the late 1870s, protective tariffs became a permanent part of the international economic scene, culminating in the early 1890s in the penal tariffs associated with the names of Méline in France (1892) and McKinley in the USA (1890).†

Of all the major industrial countries only Britain held fast to unrestricted free trade, in spite of powerful occasional challenges from protectionists. The reasons were obvious, quite apart from the absence of a large peasantry and therefore of a large built-in protectionist vote. Britain was by far the greatest exporter of industrial products, and had in the course of the century become increasingly export-oriented – probably never more so than in the 1870s and 1880s – much more so than her main rivals, though not more than some advanced economies of much smaller size, such as Belgium, Switzerland, Denmark and the Netherlands. Britain was incomparably the largest exporter of capital, of 'invisible' financial and commercial services, and of transport services. Indeed, as foreign competition encroached on British industry, the City of London and British shipping became more central than ever before to the world economy. Conversely, though this is often forgotten, Britain was by far the largest outlet for the primary exports of the world, and dominated – one might even say constituted – the world market for some of them, such as cane sugar, tea and wheat, of which in 1880 she bought about half of the total traded internationally. In 1881 the British bought almost half of all the world's meat exports and far more wool and cotton (55 per cent of European imports) than anyone else.[9] Indeed, as Britain let her own food production decline during the Depression, her propensity to import became quite extraordinary. By 1905–9 she imported not only 56 per cent of all the cereals she consumed but 76 per cent of all her cheese and 68 per cent of her eggs.[10]

Free trade therefore seemed indispensable, for it allowed primary

---

* The free movement of capital, financial transactions and labour became, if anything, more marked.

† Average level of tariff in Europe 1914[8]

	%		%
United Kingdom	0	Austria–Hungary, Italy	18
Netherlands	4	France, Sweden	20
Switzerland, Belgium	9	Russia	38
Germany	13	Spain	41
Denmark	14	USA (1913)	30[a]

[a] Lowered from 49.5 per cent (1890), 39.9 per cent (1894), 57 per cent (1897), and 38 per cent (1909).

producers overseas to exchange their products for British manufactures, and thus reinforced the symbiosis between the United Kingdom and the underdeveloped world on which British economic power essentially rested. Argentine and Uruguayan *estancieros*, Australian wool-growers and Danish farmers had no interest in encouraging national manufactures, for they did very well out of being economic planets in the British solar system. The costs for Britain were not negligible. As we have seen, free trade meant the readiness to let British agriculture sink if it could not swim. Britain was the only country in which even Conservative statesmen, in spite of the ancient commitment of such parties to protection, were prepared to abandon agriculture. Admittedly the sacrifice was easier, since the finances of the ultra-rich and politically still decisive landowners now rested on the income from urban property and investment portfolios as much as on the rents of cornfields. Might it not also imply a readiness to sacrifice British industry itself, as the protectionists feared? Looking back a century from the deindustrializing Britain of the 1980s, the fear does not seem unrealistic. What capitalism exists to make, after all, is not any particular selection of products but money. Yet while it was already clear that in British politics the opinion of the City of London counted far more than that of provincial industrialists, for the time being City interests did not yet appear to be at odds with those of the bulk of industry. So Britain remained committed to economic liberalism,* and in doing so gave protectionist countries the freedom both to control their home markets and to have plenty of scope for pushing their exports.

Economists and historians have never ceased to argue about the effects of this revival of international protectionism, or, in other words, about the strange schizophrenia of the capitalist world economy. The basic building-blocks of its core in the nineteenth century were increasingly constituted by 'national economies' – the British, German, US, etc. However, in spite of the programmatic title of Adam Smith's great work, *The Wealth of Nations* (1776), the 'nation' as a unit had no clear place in the pure theory of liberal capitalism, whose basic building-blocks were the irreducible atoms of enterprise, the individual or the 'firm' (about which not much was said), moved by the imperative to maximize gains or minimize losses. They operated in 'the market', which, at its limits, was global. Liberalism was the anarchism of the bourgeoisie and, as in revolutionary anarchism, it had no place for the state. Or rather, the state as a factor in the economy existed only as something which interfered with the autonomous and self-acting operations of 'the market'.

* Except in the matter of unrestricted immigration, since the country was one of the first to produce discriminatory legislation against mass influx of (Jewish) foreigners in 1905.

In a way this view made some sense. On the one hand, it seemed reasonable to suppose – particularly after the liberalization of economies in the mid-century (*The Age of Capital,* chapter 2) – that what made such an economy function and grow were the economic decisions of its basic particles. And on the other hand the capitalist economy was, and could not but be, global. It became steadily more so during the nineteenth century, as it extended its operations to ever more remote parts of the planet, and transformed all areas ever more profoundly. Moreover, such an economy recognized no frontiers, for it functioned best where nothing interfered with the free movement of the factors of production. Capitalism was thus not merely international in practice, but internationalist in theory. The ideal of its theorists was an international division of labour which ensured the maximum growth of the economy. Its criteria were global: it was senseless to try to produce bananas in Norway, because they could be produced much more cheaply in Honduras. They waved aside local or regional arguments to the contrary. The pure theory of economic liberalism was obliged to accept the most extreme, even absurd consequences of its assumptions, provided they could be shown to produce globally optimal results. If it could be shown that the entire industrial production of the world should be concentrated in Madagascar (as 80 per cent of its production of watches was concentrated in a small part of Switzerland),[11] or that the entire population of France should transfer itself to Siberia (as a large proportion of Norwegians were actually transferred by migration to the USA),* there was no economic argument against such developments.

What could be shown to be economically wrong about the British quasi-monopoly of global industry in the mid-century, or the demographic development of Ireland, which lost almost half its population between 1841 and 1911? The only equilibrium liberal economic theory recognized was a worldwide one.

But in practice this model was inadequate. The evolving world economy of capitalism was a collection of solid blocs, as well as a fluid. Whatever the origins of the 'national economies' which constituted these blocs – i.e. the economies defined by the frontiers of states – and whatever the theoretical limitations of an economic theory based on them – mainly by theorists in Germany – national economies existed because nation-states existed. It may be true that nobody would think of Belgium as the first industrialized economy on the European continent if Belgium had remained a part of France (as she was before 1815) or a region of the united Netherlands (as she was between 1815 and 1830).

---

* Between 1820 and 1975 the number of Norwegians emigrating to the USA – some 855,000 – was almost as large as the total population of Norway in 1820.[12]

However, once Belgium was a state, both her economic policy and the political dimension of the economic activities of her inhabitants were shaped by this fact. It is certainly true that there were and are economic activities such as international finance which are essentially cosmopolitan and thus escaped from national constraints, insofar as these were effective. Yet even such transnational enterprises took care to attach themselves to a suitably important national economy. The (largely German) merchant banking families thus tended to transfer their headquarters from Paris to London after 1860. And the most international of all great banking houses, the Rothschilds, flourished where they operated in the capital of a major state, and wilted where they did not: the Rothschilds of London, Paris and Vienna remained major forces, but the Rothschilds of Naples and Frankfurt (the firm refused to transfer to Berlin) did not. After the unification of Germany, Frankfurt was no longer enough.

These observations, naturally, apply primarily to the 'developed' sector of the world, i.e. to the states capable of defending their industrializing economies against competition, and not to the remainder of the globe, whose economies were politically or economically dependent on the 'developed' core. Either such regions had no choice, since a colonial power decided what was to happen to their economies, or an imperial economy was in a position to turn them into a banana or coffee republic. Or else, such economies were not usually interested in alternative development choices, since it clearly paid them to turn themselves into specialized producers of primary products for a world market constituted by the metropolitan states. In the world periphery, the 'national economy', insofar as it can be said to have existed, had different functions.

But the developed world was not only an aggregate of 'national economies'. Industrialization and the Depression turned them into a group of *rival* economies, in which the gains of one seemed to threaten the position of others. Not only firms but nations competed. Henceforth the flesh of British readers was made to creep by journalistic exposés of German economic invasion – E. E. Williams' *Made in Germany* (1896) or Fred A. Mackenzie's *American Invaders* (1902).[13] Their fathers had remained calm in the face of (justified) warnings of the technical superiority of foreigners. Protectionism expressed a situation of international economic competition.

But what was its effect? We may take it as established that an excess of generalized protectionism, which seeks to barricade each nation-state economy against the foreigner behind a set of political fortifications, is harmful to world economic growth. This was to be adequately demonstrated between the two world wars. However, in the period

1880–1914 protectionism was neither general nor, with occasional exceptions, prohibitive, and, as we have seen, it was confined to commodity trade and did not affect the movements of labour and international financial transactions. Agricultural protection on the whole worked in France, failed in Italy (where the response was mass migration), and sheltered large-scale agrarians in Germany.[14] Industrial protection on the whole helped to broaden the world's industrial base by encouraging national industries to aim at the domestic markets of their countries, which happened also to be growing by leaps and bounds. Consequently it has been calculated that the global growth of production and commerce between 1880 and 1914 was distinctly higher than it had been during the decades of free trade.[15] Certainly in 1914 industrial production within the metropolitan or 'developed' world was somewhat less unevenly distributed than it had been forty years earlier. In 1870 the four main industrial states had produced almost 80 per cent of total world manufacturing output, but in 1913 they produced 72 per cent of an output which was five times as great.[16] How far protection contributed to this is open to argument. That it cannot have seriously held up growth seems clear.

However, if protectionism was the worried producer's instinctive political reaction to the Depression, it was not the most significant economic response of capitalism to its troubles. This was the combination of economic concentration and business rationalization, or in the American terminology, which now began to set global styles, 'trusts' and 'scientific management'. Both were attempts to widen profit margins, compressed by competition and the fall of prices.

Economic concentration should not be confused with monopoly in the strict sense (control of the market by a single business), or in the more usual wider sense of market control by a handful of dominating firms (oligopoly). Certainly the dramatic examples of concentration which attracted public obloquy were of this kind, generally produced by mergers or market-controlling arrangements between firms which, according to free-enterprise theory, ought to have been cutting each other's throats for the benefit of the consumer. Such were the American 'trusts', which provoked anti-monopolist legislation like the Sherman Anti-Trust Act (1890) of uncertain efficacy, and the German 'syndicates' or 'cartels' – mainly in the heavy industries – which enjoyed government favour. The Rhine-Westphalian Coal Syndicate (1893), which controlled something like 90 per cent of the coal output in its region, or the Standard Oil Company, which in 1880 controlled 90–95 per cent of the oil refined in the USA, were certainly monopolies. So, for practical purposes, was the 'billion-dollar Trust' of United States Steel (1901) with 63 per cent of American steel output. It is also clear

43

that a trend away from unrestricted competition and towards 'the combination of several capitalists who formerly operated singly'[17] became strikingly obvious during the Great Depression, and continued in the new period of global prosperity. A tendency towards monopoly or oligopoly is undeniable in the heavy industries, in industries closely dependent on government orders such as the rapidly growing armaments sector (see pp. 307–9), in industries generating and distributing revolutionary new forms of energy, such as oil and electricity, in transport, and in some mass consumer goods such as soap and tobacco.

However, market control and the elimination of competition were only one aspect of a more general process of capitalist concentration, and were neither universal nor irreversible: in 1914 there was rather more competition in the American oil and steel industries than there had been ten years earlier. To this extent it is misleading in 1914 to speak of what was by 1900 clearly recognized as a new phase of capitalist development, as 'monopoly capitalism'. Still, it does not much matter what we call it ('corporation capitalism', 'organized capitalism', etc.) so long as it is agreed – and it must be – that combination advanced at the expense of market competition, business corporations at the expense of private firms, big business and large enterprise at the expense of smaller; and that this concentration implied a tendency towards oligopoly. This was evident even in so powerful a fortress of old-fashioned small-scale and medium competitive enterprise as Britain. From 1880 on the pattern of distribution was revolutionized. 'Grocer' and 'butcher' now meant not simply a small shopkeeper but increasingly a nationwide or international firm with hundreds of branches. In banking, a handful of giant joint-stock banks with national networks of branches replaced the smaller banks at great speed: Lloyds Bank swallowed 164 of them. After 1900, as has been noted, the old-fashioned – or any – British 'country bank' had become 'a historical curiosity'.

Like economic concentration 'scientific management' (the term itself only came into use around 1910) was the child of the Great Depression. Its founder and apostle, F. W. Taylor (1856–1915), began to evolve his ideas in the problem-racked American steel industry in 1880. It came to Europe from the west in the 1890s. Pressure on profits in the Depression, as well as the growing size and complexity of firms, suggested that the traditional, empirical or rule-of-thumb methods of running business, and especially production, were no longer adequate. Hence the need for a more rational or 'scientific' way of controlling, monitoring and programming large and profit-maximizing enterprises. The task on which 'Taylorism' immediately concentrated its efforts, and with which 'scientific management' was to become identified in the public mind, was how to get more work out of workers. This aim was pursued by three major methods: (1) by isolating each worker from the work group, and transferring the control of the work process from him, her or the group to the agents of management, who told the worker exactly what to do and how much output to achieve in the light of (2) a systematic breakdown of each process into timed component elements ('time and motion study'), and (3) various systems of wage payment which would give the worker an incentive to produce more. Such systems of payment by result spread quite widely, but for practical purposes Taylorism in its literal sense had made virtually no progress before 1914 in Europe – or even in the USA – and only became familiar as a slogan in management circles in the last pre-war years. After 1918 Taylor's name, like that of that other pioneer of mass production, Henry Ford, was to serve as a convenient shorthand label for the rational use of machinery and labour to maximize production, paradoxically among Bolshevik planners as well as among capitalists.

Nevertheless, it is clear that the transformation of the structure of large enterprises, from shop-floor to office and accountancy, made substantial progress between 1880 and 1914. The 'visible hand' of modern corporate organization and management now replaced the 'invisible hand' of Adam Smith's anonymous market. The executives, engineers and accountants therefore began to take over from owner–managers. The 'corporation' or *Konzern* replaced the individual. The typical businessman, at least in big business, was now much more likely to be not a member of the founder's family but a salaried executive, and the man looking over his shoulder was more likely to be a banker or shareholder than a managing capitalist.

There was a third possible way out of business troubles: imperialism. The chronological coincidence between the Depression and the dynamic phase of the colonial division of the globe has often been noticed. How far the two were connected is much debated among historians. In any case, as the next chapter will show, the relation was rather more complex than simple cause and effect. Nevertheless it is quite undeniable that the pressure of capital in search of more profitable investment, as of production in search of markets, contributed to policies of expansion – including colonial conquest. 'Territorial expansion', said an official of the US State Department in 1900, 'is but the by-product of the expansion of commerce.'[18] He was by no means the only person in international business and politics to take such a view.

One final result, or by-product, of the Great Depression must be mentioned. It was also an era of great social agitation. Not only, as we have seen, among farmers, shaken by the seismic tremors of agrarian price collapse, but among the working classes. Why the Great

45

Depression led to a mass mobilization of the industrial working classes in numerous countries, and from the end of the 1880s to the emergence of mass socialist and labour movements in several of them, is not obvious. For, paradoxically, the very price falls which automatically radicalized farmers lowered the cost of living of wage-earners quite markedly, and produced an undoubted improvement in the workers' material standard of life in most industrialized countries. But here we need only note that modern labour movements are also the children of the Depression period. These movements will be considered in chapter 5.

II

From the middle of the 1890s until the Great War, the global economic orchestra played in the major key of prosperity rather than, as hitherto, in the minor key of depression. Affluence based on booming business formed the background to what is still known on the European continent as 'the beautiful era' (*belle époque*). The shift from worry to euphoria was so sudden and dramatic that vulgar economists looked for some special outside force to explain it, a God in the machine, whom they found in the discovery of enormous supplies of gold in South Africa, the last of the great western gold-rushes, the Klondike (1898), and elsewhere. Economic historians have, on the whole, been less impressed by such basically monetarist theses than some late-twentieth-century governments. Still, the speed of the upturn was striking, and almost immediately diagnosed by a particularly sharp-eyed revolutionary, A. L. Helphand (1869–1924) writing under the pen-name Parvus, as indicating the start of a new and lengthy period of tempestuous capitalist advance. In fact, the contrast between the Great Depression and the following secular boom provided the grounds for the first speculations about those 'long waves' in the development of world capitalism, which were later to be associated with the name of the Russian economist Kondratiev. In the meantime it was, at any rate, evident that those who had made gloomy forecasts about the future of capitalism, or even about its imminent collapse, had been wrong. Among the Marxists passionate arguments developed about what this implied for the future of their movements, and whether Marx's doctrines would have to be 'revised'.

Economic historians have tended to fix their attention on two aspects of the era: on its redistribution of economic power and initiative, that is to say on Britain's relative decline and the relative – and absolute – advance of the USA and above all Germany, and on the problem of long- and short-term fluctuations, that is to say primarily on the Kondratiev 'long wave', whose down- and upswing neatly cut our period in half. Interesting though these problems are, they are secondary from the point of view of the world economy.

In principle, it is not really surprising that Germany, its population rising from 45 to 65 millions, and the USA, growing from 50 to 92 millions, should have overhauled Britain, both territorially smaller and less populous. This does not, however, make the triumph of German industrial exports any the less impressive. In the thirty years to 1913 they grew from less than half the British figure to a figure larger than the British. Except in what might be called the 'semi-industrialized countries – i.e. for practical purposes the actual or virtual 'dominions' of the British Empire, including its Latin American economic dependencies – German manufacturing exports had beaten the English all along the line. They were a third larger in the industrial world, and even 10 per cent larger in the undeveloped world. Again, it is not surprising that Britain was unable to maintain the extraordinary position as 'workshop of the world' of c. 1860. Even the USA, at the peak of her global supremacy in the early 1950s – and representing a share of the world population three times as large as the British in 1860 – never achieved 53 per cent of world iron and steel production and 49 per cent of its textile production. Once again, this does not explain precisely why – or even whether – there was a slowing-down in growth and a decline in the British economy, questions which have become the subject of a vast scholarly literature. The important issue is not who, within the growing world economy, grew more and faster, but its global growth as a whole.

As for the Kondratiev rhythm – to call it a 'cycle' in the strict sense of the word is to beg the question – it certainly raises fundamental analytical questions about the nature of economic growth in the capitalist era, or, some students might argue, about the growth of any world economy. Unfortunately, no theory about this curious alternation of phases of economic confidence and uneasiness, together forming a 'wave' of about half a century, is widely accepted. The best-known and most elegant theory about them, that of Josef Alois Schumpeter (1883–1950), associates each 'downturn' with the exhaustion of the profit potential of one set of economic 'innovations', and the new upswing with a new set of innovations, mainly – but not only – seen as technological, whose potential will in turn be exhausted. Thus new industries, acting as 'leading sectors' of economic growth – e.g. cotton in the first industrial revolution, railroads in and after the 1840s – become, as it were, the engines which pull the world economy out of the morass in which it has temporarily been bogged down. The theory is plausible

47

enough, since each of the periods of secular upswing since the 1780s has indeed been associated with the rise of new, and increasingly of technologically revolutionary industries: not least the most extra-ordinary of all such global economic booms, the two and a half decades before the early 1970s. The problem about the upsurge of the later 1890s is that the innovatory industries of that period – broadly speaking, chemical and electrical, or those associated with the new energy sources about to compete seriously with steam – do not as yet seem quite imposing enough to dominate the movements of the world economy. In short, since we cannot adequately explain them, the Kondratiev periodicities cannot help us much. They merely enable us to observe that the period with which this volume deals covers the fall and the rise of a 'Kondratiev wave'; but that is in itself not surprising as the entire modern history of the global economy readily falls into this pattern.

There is, however, one aspect of the Kondratiev analysis which must be relevant to a period of rapid 'globalization' of the world economy. This is the relation between the world's *industrial* sector, which grew by a continuous revolution of production, and the world's *agricultural* output, which grew chiefly by the discontinuous opening of new geo-graphical zones of production, or zones newly specialized in export production. In 1910–13 the western world had, available for consump-tion, almost twice as much wheat as (on average) in the 1870s. But the great bulk of this increase had come from a few countries: the USA, Canada, Argentina and Australia and, in Europe, Russia, Rumania and Hungary. The growth of farm output in western Europe (France, Germany, the United Kingdom, Belgium, the Netherlands, Scan-dinavia) only made up 10–15 per cent of the new supply. So it is not surprising, even if we forget about agrarian catastrophes like the eight years of drought (1895–1902) which killed half Australia's sheep, and new pests like the boll-weevil which attacked the US cotton crop from 1892 onwards, that the rate of growth of world farm production slowed down after the initial bound forward. Then the 'terms of trade' would tend to move in favour of agriculture and against industry, i.e. farmers paid relatively or absolutely less for what they bought from industry, industry relatively or absolutely more for what it bought from agri-culture.

It has been argued that this change in the terms of trade can explain the switch from a striking price fall in 1873–96 to a notable price rise from then until 1914 – and beyond. Perhaps. What is certain is that this change in the terms of trade put pressure on industry's costs of production, and hence on its profitability. Luckily for the 'beauty' of the *belle époque,* the economy was so constructed as to shift this pressure from profits to the workers. The rapid growth in real wages, so characteristic of the Great Depression, slowed down visibly. In France and Britain there was an actual *fall* in real wages between 1899 and 1913. The sullen social tension and outbursts of the last years before 1914 are partly due to this.

What, then, made the world economy so dynamic? Whatever the detailed explanation, clearly the key to the problem is to be found in the central belt of industrializing and industrial countries, increasingly stretching round the temperate northern hemisphere, for they acted as the engine of global growth, both as producers and as markets.

These countries now formed an enormous and rapidly growing, and extending, productive mass at the heart of the world economy. They now included not only the major and minor centres of mid-century industrialization, themselves for the most part expanding at a rate ranging from the impressive to the almost unimaginable – Britain, Germany, the USA, France, Belgium, Switzerland, the Czech lands – but a new range of industrializing regions: Scandinavia, the Netherlands, northern Italy, Hungary, Russia, even Japan. They also formed an increasingly massive body of purchasers for the world's goods and services: a body increasingly living by purchases, i.e. decreasingly dependent on traditional rural economies. The usual nineteenth-century definition of a 'city-dweller' was one who lived in a place of more than 2000 inhabitants. Yet even if we take a slightly less modest criterion (5000), the percentage of Europeans of the 'developed' zone and North Americans who lived in towns had by 1910 risen to 41 (from 19 and 14 respectively in 1850) and perhaps 80 per cent of city-dwellers (as against two-thirds in 1850) lived in towns of over 20,000; of these in turn rather more than half lived in cities of over 100,000 inhabitants, that is to say vast stockpiles of customers.[19]

Moreover, thanks to the price falls of the Depression, these customers had a good deal more money available for spending than before, even allowing for the sag in real wages after 1900. The crucial collective significance of this accumulation of customers, even among the poor, was now recognized by businessmen. If political philosophers dreaded the emergence of the masses, salesmen hailed it. The advertising industry, which first developed as a major force in this period, addressed them. Instalment selling, which is largely a child of this period, was designed to enable people of small income to buy large products. And the revolutionary art and industry of the cinema (see chapter 9 below) grew from nothing in 1895 to displays of wealth beyond the dreams of avarice by 1915, and to products so expensive to make as to beggar the operas of princes, and all on the strength of a public which paid in nickels.

A single figure may illustrate the importance of the world's 'developed' zone at this time. In spite of the remarkable growth of new regions and economies overseas; in spite of the haemorrhage of an unprecedently huge mass emigration, the share of Europeans in the world's population actually rose during the nineteenth century, and its rate of growth accelerated from 7 per cent per year in the first half, 8 per cent in the second, to almost 13 per cent in 1900–13. If we add to this urbanized continent of potential shoppers the USA and some rapidly developing but much smaller overseas economies, we have a 'developed' world of something like 15 per cent of the planet's surface, containing something like 40 per cent of its inhabitants.

These countries thus formed the bulk of the world's economy. Between them they constituted 80 per cent of the international market. What is more, they determined the development of the rest of the world, whose economies grew by supplying foreign needs. What would have happened to Uruguay or Honduras if they had been left to their own devices, we cannot know. (In any case, they were not likely to be: Paraguay had once tried to opt out of the world market and had been massacred back into it – cf. *The Age of Capital*, chapter 4.) What we do know is that the one produced beef because there was a market for it in Britain, and the other bananas, because some Boston traders calculated that Americans would pay money to eat them. Some such satellite economies did better than others, but the better they did, the greater the benefit to the economies of the central core, for whom such growth meant larger and growing outlets for the export of goods and capital. The world merchant marine, whose growth roughly indicates the expansion of the global economy, had remained more or less static between 1860 and 1890. Its size fluctuated between 16 and 20 million tons. Between 1890 and 1914 it almost doubled.

III

How, then, can we sum up the world economy of the Age of Empire?

In the first place, as we have seen, it was a geographically much more broad-based economy than before. Its industrial and industrializing sector was enlarged, in Europe by industrial revolution in Russia and such countries as Sweden and the Netherlands, hitherto little touched by it, outside by developments in North America and, already to some extent, in Japan. The international market in primary products grew enormously – between 1880 and 1913 international trade in these commodities just about tripled – and so, consequently, did both the areas devoted to their production and their integration into the world market. Canada joined the world's major wheat producers after 1900, its crop rising from an annual average of 52 million bushels in the 1890s to one of 200 millions in 1910–13.[20] Argentina became a major wheat exporter at the same time – and every year Italian labourers, nicknamed 'swallows' (*golondrinas*), crossed and recrossed 10,000 miles of Atlantic to gather its harvest. The economy of the Age of Empire was one in which Baku and the Donets Basin became part of industrial geography, when Europe exported both goods and girls to new cities like Johannesburg and Buenos Aires, and when opera houses were built on the bones of dead Indians in rubber-boom towns 1000 miles up the Amazon.

It follows, as already noted, that the world economy was now notably more pluralist than before. Britain ceased to be the only fully indus-trialized, and indeed the only industrial, economy. If we add together the industrial and mining production (including construction) of the four chief national economies, in 1913 the USA provided 46 per cent of this total, Germany 23.5 per cent, Britain 19.5 per cent and France 11 per cent.[21] The Age of Empire, as we shall see, was essentially an age of state rivalry. Moreover, the relations between the developed and the undeveloped worlds were also more varied and complex than in 1860, when half of all exports from Asia, Africa and Latin America had been sent to one country, Great Britain. By 1900 the British share was down to one-quarter, and Third World exports to other West European countries were already larger than those to Britain (31 per cent).[22] The Age of Empire was no longer monocentric.

This growing pluralism of the world economy was to some extent masked by its continued, indeed its increased, dependence on the financial, trading and shipping services of Britain. On the one hand the City of London was, more than ever, the switchboard for the world's international business transactions, so that its commercial and financial services alone earned almost enough to make up for the large deficit in its balance of commodity trade (£137 million against £142 million, in 1906–10). On the other, the enormous weight of Britain's foreign investments and her merchant shipping further reinforced the centrality of the country in a world economy which turned on London and was based on the pound sterling. On the international capital market, Britain remained overwhelmingly dominant. In 1914 France, Germany, the USA, Belgium, the Netherlands, Switzerland and the rest between them had 56 per cent of the world's overseas investments; Britain *alone* had 44 per cent.[23] In 1914 the British steamer fleet alone was 12 per cent larger than all the merchant fleets of all the other European states put together.

In fact, Britain's centrality was for the moment reinforced by the very development of world pluralism. For as the newly industrializing economies bought more primary products from the underdeveloped world, they accumulated between them a fairly substantial deficit in their trade with that world. Britain alone re-established a global balance, by importing more manufactured goods from its rivals, by its own industrial exports to the dependent world, but mainly by its massive invisible income from both its international business services (banking, insurance, etc.) and the income which came to the world's largest creditor from its enormous foreign investments. Britain's relative industrial decline thus reinforced its financial position and wealth. The interests of British industry and of the City, hitherto compatible enough, began to enter into conflict.

The third characteristic of the world economy is at first sight the most obvious: technological revolution. This was, as we all know, the age when the telephone and the wireless telegraph, the phonograph and the cinema, the automobile and the aeroplane, became part of the scenery of modern life, not to mention the domestication of science and high technology by means of such products as the vacuum cleaner (1908) and the only universal medicament ever invented, aspirin (1899). Nor should we forget that most beneficent of all the period's machines, whose contribution to human emancipation was immediately recognized, namely the modest bicycle. And yet, before we hail this impressive crop of innovations as a 'second industrial revolution', let us not forget that it is so only in retrospect. For contemporaries, the major innovation consisted in the updating of the first industrial revolution by improvements in the tried technology of steam and iron: by steel and turbines. Technologically revolutionary industries based on electricity, chemistry and the combustion engine certainly began to play a major role, especially in dynamic new economies. After all, Ford began to manufacture his Model T in 1907. And yet, to take only Europe, between 1880 and 1913 as many miles of railroad were constructed as in the original 'railway age' between 1850 and 1880. France, Germany, Switzerland, Sweden and the Netherlands more or less doubled their railway network in these years. The last triumph of British industry, the virtual monopoly of shipbuilding Britain established between 1870 and 1913, was won by exploiting the resources of the first industrial revolution. As yet the new industrial revolution reinforced rather than replaced the old one.

The fourth characteristic was, as we have already seen, a double transformation in the structure and *modus operandi* of capitalist enterprise. On the one hand there was the concentration of capital, the growth in scale which led men to distinguish between 'business' and 'big business' (*Grossindustrie, Grossbanken, grande industrie ...*), the retreat of the free competitive market, and all the other developments which, around 1900, led observers to grope for general labels to describe what plainly seemed to be a new phase of economic development (see the next chapter). On the other, there was the systematic attempt to rationalize production and the conduct of business enterprise by applying 'scientific methods' not only to technology but to organization and calculation.

The fifth characteristic was an extraordinary transformation in the market for consumer goods: a change in both quantity and quality. With the growth of population, urbanization and real incomes, the mass market, hitherto more or less confined to foodstuffs and clothing, i.e. to basic subsistence needs, began to dominate the industries producing consumer goods. In the long run this was more important than the notable growth in the consumption of the wealthy and comfortable classes, whose demand patterns did not notably change. It was the Ford Model T and not Rolls-Royce which revolutionized the motor industry. At the same time a revolutionary technology and imperialism helped to create a range of novel goods and services for the mass market – from the gas-cookers which multiplied in British working-class kitchens during this period, to the bicycle, the cinema and the modest banana, whose consumption was practically unknown before 1880. One of the most obvious consequences was the creation of mass media which, for the first time, deserved the name. A British newspaper reached a million-copy sale for the first time in the 1890s, a French one around 1900.[24]

All this implied a transformation not only of production, by what now came to be called 'mass production', but also of distribution, including credit-buying (mainly by instalments). Thus the sale of tea in standard quarter-pound packages began in Britain in 1884. It was to make the fortunes of more than one grocery tycoon from the working-class backstreets of big cities, such as Sir Thomas Lipton, whose yacht and money attracted the friendship of King Edward VII, a monarch notoriously drawn to free-spending millionaires. Lipton's branches grew from none in 1870 to 500 in 1899.[25]

It also fitted in naturally with the sixth characteristic of the economy: the marked growth, both absolute and relative, of the tertiary sector of the economy, both public and private – work in offices, shops and other services. To take only the case of Britain, a country which, at its peak, had dominated the world economy with a ridiculously tiny amount of office work: in 1851 there were 67,000 public officials and 91,000 persons in commercial employment out of a total occupied population of about $9\frac{1}{2}$ millions. By 1881 there were already 360,000 in commercial employment – still almost entirely male – though only 120,000 in the public sector. But by 1911 commerce employed almost 900,000, 17 per cent of them women, and the public service had tripled. Commercial employment, as a percentage of the occupied population, had quintupled since 1851. We shall consider the social consequence of this multiplication of white collars and white hands elsewhere.

The final characteristic of the economy I shall note here is the growing convergence between politics and economics, that is to say the growing role of government and the public sector, or what ideologues of a liberal persuasion, like the lawyer A. V. Dicey, saw as the threatening advance of 'collectivism' at the expense of the good old rugged individual or voluntary enterprise. In fact, it was one of the symptoms of that retreat of the competitive free-market economy which had been the ideal – and to some extent the reality – of mid-nineteenth-century capitalism. One way or another, after 1875, there was growing scepticism about the effectiveness of the autonomous and self-correcting market economy, Adam Smith's famous 'hidden hand', without some assistance from state and public authority. The hand was becoming visible in all sorts of ways.

On the one hand, as we shall see (chapter 4), the democratization of politics pushed often reluctant and troubled governments in the direction of policies of social reform and welfare, as well as into political action to defend the economic interests of certain groups of voters, such as protectionism and – somewhat less effectively – measures against economic concentration, as in the USA and Germany. On the other, political rivalries between states and the economic competition between national groups of entrepreneurs fused, thus contributing – as we shall see – both to the phenomenon of imperialism and to the genesis of the First World War. They also led, incidentally, to the growth of industries such as armaments in which the role of government was decisive.

Nevertheless, while the strategic role of the public sector could be crucial, its actual weight in the economy remained modest. In spite of multiplying examples to the contrary – such as the British government's purchase of a stake in the Middle Eastern oil industry and its control of the new wireless telegraphy, both of military significance, the readiness of the German government to nationalize parts of its industry, and, above all, the Russian government's systematic policy of industrialization from the 1890s – neither governments nor public opinion thought of the public sector as other than a sort of minor supplement to the private economy, even allowing for the marked growth in Europe of (mainly local) public management in the field of public utilities and services. The socialists did not share this belief in the supremacy of the private sector, though they gave little if any thought to the problems of a socialized economy. They might have thought of such municipal enterprise as 'municipal socialism', but most of it was undertaken by authorities which had neither socialist intentions nor even sympathies. Modern economies largely controlled, organized and dominated by the state were the product of the First World War. If anything, between 1875 and 1914 the share of public expenditures in the rapidly growing national products of most leading countries tended to fall: and this in spite of the sharp rise in the expenses of preparing for war.[26]

In these ways the economy of the 'developed' world grew and was transformed. Yet what struck contemporaries in the 'developed' and industrial world even more than the evident transformation of their economy was its even more evident success. They plainly lived in flourishing times. Even the labouring masses benefited from this expansion, at least inasmuch as the industrial economy of 1875–1914 was strikingly labour-intensive and appeared to provide an almost unlimited demand for relatively unskilled or rapidly learned work for men and women streaming into city and industry. It was this which allowed the flood of Europeans who emigrated to the USA to fit themselves into an industrial world. Still, if the economy provided work, it did not yet provide more than a modest, and at times minimal, alleviation of the poverty which most labouring people for most of history had regarded as their destiny. In the retrospective mythology of the working classes, the decades before 1914 do not figure as a golden age, as they do in those of the European rich and even of the more modest middle classes. For these, indeed, the *belle époque* was the paradise that was to be lost after 1914. For businessmen and governments after the war 1913 was to be the point of permanent reference, to which they aspired to return from an era of trouble. From the clouded and troubled post-war years, the extraordinary moments of the last pre-war boom appeared in retrospect as the sunny 'normality' to which they both aspired to revert. Vainly. For, as we shall see, the very tendencies in the pre-1914 economy which made the era so golden for the middle classes drove it towards world war, revolution and disruption, and precluded a return to the lost paradise.

CHAPTER 3

THE AGE OF EMPIRE

Only complete political confusion and naive optimism can prevent the recognition that the unavoidable efforts at trade expansion by all civilized bourgeois-controlled nations, after a transitional period of seemingly peaceful competition, are clearly approaching the point where power alone *will decide each nation's share in the economic control of the earth, and hence its people's sphere of activity, and especially its workers' earning potential.*

Max Weber, 1894[1]

'Whin ye get among th'Chinee' ... *says [the Emperor of Germany], 'raymimber that ye ar-re the van guard iv Christyanity' he says, 'an' stick ye'er baynet through ivry hated infidel you see' he says. 'Lave him understand what our westhern civilisation means.... An' if be chance ye shud pick up a little land be th' way, don't lave e'er a Frinchman or Roosshan take it from ye.'*

Mr Dooley's Philosophy, 1900[2]

I

A world economy whose pace was set by its developed or developing capitalist core was extremely likely to turn into a world in which the 'advanced' dominated the 'backward'; in short into a world of empire. But, paradoxically, the era from 1875 to 1914 may be called the Age of Empire not only because it developed a new kind of imperialism, but also for a much more old-fashioned reason. It was probably the period of modern world history in which the number of rulers officially calling themselves, or regarded by western diplomats as deserving the title of, 'emperors' was at its maximum.

In Europe the rulers of Germany, Austria, Russia, Turkey and (in their capacity as lords of India) Britain claimed this title. Two of these (Germany and Britain/India) were innovations of the 1870s. They more than offset the disappearance of the 'Second Empire' of Napoleon III in France. Outside Europe, the rulers of China, Japan, Persia and –

56

perhaps with a larger element of international diplomatic courtesy – Ethiopia and Morocco were habitually allowed this title, while until 1889 an American emperor survived in Brazil. One or two even more shadowy 'emperors' might be added to the list. In 1918 five of these had disappeared. Today (1987) the only titular survivor of this select company of super-monarchs is the ruler of Japan, whose political profile is low and whose political influence is negligible.*

In a less trivial sense, our period is obviously the era of a new type of empire, the colonial. The economic and military supremacy of the capitalist countries had long been beyond serious challenge, but no systematic attempt to translate it into formal conquest, annexation and administration had been made between the end of the eighteenth and the last quarter of the nineteenth century. Between 1880 and 1914 it was made, and most of the world outside Europe and the Americas was formally partitioned into territories under the formal rule or informal political domination of one or other of a handful of states: mainly Great Britain, France, Germany, Italy, the Netherlands, Belgium, the USA and Japan. The victims of this process were to some extent the ancient surviving pre-industrial European empires of Spain and Portugal, the former – in spite of attempts to extend the territory under its control in North-west Africa – more than the latter. However, the survival of the major Portuguese territories in Africa (Angola and Mozambique), which were to outlast other imperialist colonies, was due primarily to the inability of their modern rivals to agree on the exact manner of dividing them among themselves. No similar rivalries saved the relics of the Spanish Empire in the Americas (Cuba, Puerto Rico) and in the Pacific (the Philippines) from the USA in 1898. Nominally most of the great traditional empires of Asia remained independent, though the western powers carved out 'zones of influence' or even direct admin-istration in them which could (as in the Anglo-Russian agreement over Persia in 1907) cover their entire territory. In fact, their military and political helplessness was taken for granted. Their independence rested either on their convenience as buffer-states (as in Siam – now Thailand – which divided the British and French zones in South-east Asia, or Afghanistan; which separated Britain and Russia), on the inability of rival imperial powers to agree on a formula for division, or on their sheer size. The only non-European state which successfully resisted formal colonial conquest when this was attempted was Ethiopia, which held Italy at bay, the weakest of the imperial states.

Two major regions of the world were, for practical purposes, entirely

---

* The Sultan of Morocco prefers the title of 'king'. None of the other surviving mini-sultans in the Islamic world would or could be regarded as 'kings of kings'.

divided up: Africa and the Pacific. No independent states were left at all in the Pacific, now totally distributed among the British, French, Germans, Dutch, USA and – still on a modest scale – Japan. By 1914, except for Ethiopia, the insignificant West African republic of Liberia and that part of Morocco which still resisted complete conquest, Africa belonged entirely to the British, French, German, Belgian, Portuguese and, marginally, Spanish empires. Asia, as we have seen, retained a large and nominally independent area, though the older European empires extended and rounded off their large holdings – Britain by annexing Burma to its Indian empire and establishing or strengthening the zone of influence in Tibet, Persia and the Persian Gulf area, Russia by moving further into Central Asia and (less successfully) Pacific Siberia and Manchuria, the Dutch by establishing firmer control in outlying regions of Indonesia. Two virtually new empires were established by the French conquest of Indochina, initiated in the period of Napoleon III, and by the Japanese at China's expense in Korea and Taiwan (1895) and later more modestly at Russia's expense (1905). Only one major region of the globe remained substantially unaffected by this process of partition. The Americas in 1914 were what they had been in 1875, or for that matter in the 1820s, a unique collection of sovereign republics, with the exception of Canada, the Caribbean islands and parts of the Caribbean littoral. Except for the USA, their political status rarely impressed anyone but their neighbours. It was perfectly understood that economically they were dependencies of the developed world. Yet even the USA, which increasingly asserted its political and military hegemony in this vast area, did not seriously try to conquer and administer it. Its only direct annexations were limited to Puerto Rico (Cuba was allowed an admittedly nominal independence) and a narrow strip along the new Panama Canal, which formed part of another small and nominally independent republic detached from the rather larger Colombia for this purpose by a convenient local revolution. In Latin America economic domination and such political arm-twisting as was necessary was conducted without formal conquest. The Americas, of course, were the only major region of the globe in which there was no serious rivalry between great powers. Except for the British, no European state possessed more than the scattered relics of (mainly Caribbean) eighteenth-century colonial empire, which were of no great economic or other significance. Neither the British nor anyone else saw a good reason for antagonizing the USA by challenging the Monroe Doctrine.*

* This doctrine, first stated in 1823 and subsequently repeated and elaborated by US governments, expressed hostility to any further colonization or political intervention by European powers in the western hemisphere. This was later taken to mean that the USA was the only power with

This partition of the world among a handful of states, which gives the present volume its title, was the most spectacular expression of that growing division of the globe into the strong and the weak, the 'advanced' and the 'backward', which we have already noted. It was also strikingly new. Between 1876 and 1915 about one-quarter of the globe's land surface was distributed or redistributed as colonies among a half-dozen states. Britain increased its territories by some 4 million square miles, France by some 3.5 millions, Germany acquired more than 1 million, Belgium and Italy just under 1 million each. The USA acquired some 100,000, mainly from Spain, Japan something like the same amount from China, Russia and Korea. Portugal's ancient African colonies expanded by about 300,000 square miles; Spain, while a net loser (to the USA), still managed to pick up some stony territory in Morocco and the Western Sahara. Russian imperial growth is more difficult to measure, since all of it was into adjoining territories and continued some centuries of secular territorial expansion of the tsarist state; moreover, as we shall see, Russia lost some territory to Japan. Of the major colonial empires only the Dutch failed, or refused, to acquire new territory, except by extending their actual control over Indonesian islands which they had long formally 'owned'. Of the minor ones, Sweden liquidated its only remaining colony, a West Indian island, by selling it to France, and Denmark was about to do the same – retaining only Iceland and Greenland as dependencies.

What is most spectacular is not necessarily most important. When observers of the world scene in the later 1890s began to analyse what obviously seemed a new phase in the general pattern of national and international development, notably different from the free-trading and freely competing liberal world of the mid-century, they saw the creation of colonial empires merely as one of its aspects. Orthodox observers thought they discerned, in general terms, a new era of national expansion in which (as we have suggested) political and economic elements were no longer clearly separable and the state played an increasingly active and crucial role both at home and abroad. Heterodox observers analysed it more specifically as a new phase of capitalist development, arising out of various tendencies which they discerned in this development. The most influential among these analyses of what was soon called 'imperialism', Lenin's little book of 1916, actually did not consider 'the division of the world among the great powers' until the sixth of his ten chapters.[3]

Nevertheless, if colonialism was merely one aspect of a more general change in world affairs, it was plainly the most immediately striking.

a right to interfere anywhere in that hemisphere. As the USA grew more powerful, the Monroe Doctrine was taken more seriously by European states.

It formed the point of departure for wider analyses, for there is no doubt that the word 'imperialism' first became part of the political and journalistic vocabulary during the 1890s in the course of the arguments about colonial conquest. Moreover that is when it acquired the economic dimension which, as a concept, it has never since lost. That is why references to the ancient forms of political and military aggrandizement on which the term is based are pointless. Emperors and empires were old, but imperialism was quite new. The word (which does not occur in the writings of Karl Marx, who died in 1883) first entered politics in Britain in the 1870s, and was still regarded as a neologism at the end of that decade. It exploded into general use in the 1890s. By 1900, when the intellectuals began to write books about it, it was, to quote one of the first of them, the British Liberal J. A. Hobson, 'on everybody's lips ... and used to denote the most powerful movement in the current politics of the western world'.[4] In short, it was a novel term devised to describe a novel phenomenon. This evident fact is enough to dismiss one of the many schools in the tense and highly charged ideological debate about 'imperialism', namely the one which argues that it was nothing new, perhaps indeed that it was a mere pre-capitalist survival. It was, at any rate, felt to be new and was discussed as a novelty.

The arguments which surround this touchy subject are so impassioned, dense and confused that the first task of the historian is to disentangle them so that the actual phenomenon can be seen for itself. For most of the arguments have not been about what happened in the world of 1875–1914 but about Marxism, a subject which is apt to raise strong feelings; for, as it happens, the (highly critical) analysis of imperialism in Lenin's version was to become central to the revolutionary Marxism of the communist movements after 1917 and to the revolutionary movements of the 'third world'. What has given the debate a special edge is that one side in it appears to have had a slight built-in advantage, for those supporters and opponents of imperialism have been at each other's throats since the 1890s, the word itself has gradually acquired, and is now unlikely to lose, a pejorative colouring. Unlike 'democracy', which even its enemies like to claim because of its favourable connotations, 'imperialism' is commonly something to be disapproved of, and therefore done by others. In 1914 plenty of politicians were proud to call themselves imperialists, but in the course of our century they have virtually disappeared from sight.

The crux of the Leninist analysis (which frankly based itself on a variety of contemporary writers, both Marxian and non-Marxian) was that the new imperialism had economic roots in a specific new phase of capitalism, which, among other things, led to 'the territorial division of the world among the great capitalist powers' into a set of formal and informal colonies and spheres of influence. The rivalries between the capitalist powers which led to this division also engendered the First World War. We need not here discuss the specific mechanisms by which 'monopoly capitalism' led to colonialism – opinions differed on this, even among Marxists – or the more recent extension of such analyses into a more sweeping 'dependency theory' in the later twentieth century. All assume in one way or another that overseas economic expansion and the exploitation of the overseas world were crucial for capitalist countries.

To criticize these theories would not be particularly interesting, and would be irrelevant in the present context. The point to note is simply that non-Marxist analysts of imperialism have tended to argue the opposite of what the Marxists said, and in doing so have obscured the subject. They tended to deny any specific connection between the imperialism of the late nineteenth and twentieth centuries with capitalism in general, or with the particular phase of it which, as we have seen, appeared to emerge in the late nineteenth century. They denied that imperialism had any important economic roots, that it benefited the imperial countries economically, let alone that the exploitation of backward zones was in any sense essential to capitalism, and that it had negative effects on colonial economies. They argued that imperialism did not lead to unmanageable rivalries between the imperial powers, and had no serious bearings on the origin of the First World War. Rejecting economic explanations, they concentrated on psychological, ideological, cultural and political explanations, though usually careful to avoid the dangerous territory of domestic politics, since Marxists also tended to stress the advantages to metropolitan ruling classes of imperialist policies and propaganda which, among other things, counteracted the growing appeal to the working classes of mass labour movements. Some of these counter-attacks have proved powerful and effective, though several of such lines of argument were mutually incompatible. In fact, much of the pioneer theoretical literature of anti-imperialism is not tenable. But the disadvantage of the anti-anti-imperialist literature is that it does not actually explain that conjunction of economic and political, national and international, developments, which contemporaries around 1900 found so striking that they sought a comprehensive explanation for them. It does not explain why contemporaries felt that 'imperialism' at the time was both a novel and historically *central* development. In short, much of this literature amounts to denying facts which were obvious enough at the time and still are.

Leaving Leninism and anti-Leninism aside, the first thing for the historian to re-establish is the obvious fact, which nobody in the 1890s would have denied, that the division of the globe had an economic dimension. To demonstrate this is not to explain everything about the imperialism of the period. Economic development is not a sort of ventriloquist with the rest of history as its dummy. For that matter, even the most single-minded businessman pursuing profit into, say, the South African gold- and diamond-mines, can never be treated exclusively as a money-making machine. He was not immune to the political, emotional, ideological, patriotic or even racial appeals which were so patently associated with imperial expansion. Nevertheless, if an economic connection can be established between the tendencies of economic development in the capitalist core of the globe at this time and its expansion into the periphery, it becomes much less plausible to put the full weight of explanation on motives for imperialism which have no intrinsic connection with the penetration and conquest of the non-western world. And even those which appear to have, such as the strategic calculations of rival powers, must be analysed while bearing the economic dimension in mind. Even today politics in the Middle East, which are far from explicable on simple economic grounds, cannot be realistically discussed without considering oil.

Now the major fact about the nineteenth century is the creation of a single global economy, progressively reaching into the most remote corners of the world, an increasingly dense web of economic transactions, communications and movements of goods, money and people linking the developed countries with each other and with the undeveloped world (see *The Age of Capital*, chapter 3). Without this there was no particular reason why European states should have taken more than the most fleeting interest in the affairs of, say, the Congo basin or engaged in diplomatic disputes about some Pacific atoll. This globalization of the economy was not new, though it had accelerated considerably in the middle decades of the century. It continued to grow – less strikingly in relative terms, but more massively in terms of volume and numbers – between 1875 and 1914. European exports had indeed grown more than fourfold between 1848 and 1875, while they only doubled from then until 1915. But the world's merchant shipping had only risen, between 1840 and 1870, from 10 to 16 million tons, whereas it doubled in the next forty years, as the world's railway network expanded from a little over 200,000 kilometres (1870) to over 1 million kilometres just before the First World War.

This tightening web of transport drew even the backward and previously marginal into the world economy, and created a new interest among the old centres of wealth and development in these remote areas. Indeed, now that they were accessible many of these regions seemed at first sight to be simply potential extensions of the developed world, which were already being settled and developed by men and women of European stock, extirpating or pushing back the native inhabitants, generating cities and doubtless, in due course, industrial civilization: the USA west of the Mississippi, Canada, Australia, New Zealand, South Africa, Algeria, the southern cone of South America. The prediction, as we shall see, was off the mark. Nevertheless, though often remote, such areas were in contemporary minds distinct from those other regions where, for climatic reasons, white settlement was unattractive, but where – to quote a leading imperial administrator of the time – 'the European may come, in small numbers, with his capital, his energy and his knowledge to develop a most lucrative commerce, and obtain products necessary to the use of his advanced civilisation'.[5]

For that civilization now had need of the exotic. Technological development now relied on raw materials which, for reasons of climate or the hazards of geology, were to be found exclusively or profusely in remote places. The internal-combustion engine, that typical child of our period, relied on oil and rubber. Oil still came overwhelmingly from the USA and Europe (Russia and, a long way behind, Rumania) but already the oilfields of the Middle East were the subject of intensive diplomatic confrontation and horse-trading. Rubber was exclusively a tropical product, extracted by the atrocious exploitation of natives in the rainforests of the Congo and the Amazon, the target of early and justified anti-imperialist protest. In due course it was extensively cultivated in Malaya. Tin came from Asia and South America. Non-ferrous metals of previously negligible importance became essential for the steel alloys required by high-speed technology. Some of these were freely available in the developed world, notably the USA, but others were not. The new electrical and motor industries hungered for one of the most ancient metals, copper. Its major reserves, and eventually producers, were in what the late twentieth century called the Third World: Chile, Peru, Zaire, Zambia. And, of course, there was the constant and never satisfied demand for the precious metals which, in this period, turned South Africa into by far the greatest gold-producer in the world, not to mention its wealth of diamonds. Mines were the major pioneers in opening up the world to imperialism, and all the more effective because their profits were sensational enough to justify also the construction of feeder-railways.

Quite apart from the demands of a new technology, the growth of mass consumption in the metropolitan countries produced a rapidly expanding market for foodstuffs. In sheer volume this was dominated by the basic foodstuffs of the temperate zone, grain and meat, now produced cheaply and in vast quantities in several zones of European settlement – in North and South America, Russia and Australasia. But it also transformed the market for the products long and characteristically known (at least in German) as 'colonial goods' and sold by the grocers of the developed worlds: sugar, tea, coffee, cocoa and its derivatives. With rapid transport and conservation, tropical and sub-tropical fruits became available: they made possible the 'banana republic'.

Britons, who had consumed 1.5 lb of tea per head in the 1840s and 3.26 lb in the 1860s, were consuming 5.7 lb in the 1890s – but this represented an average annual import of 224 million lb compared with less than 98 millions in the 1860s and about 40 millions in the 1840s. While the British abandoned what few cups of coffee they had drunk to fill their teapots from India and Ceylon (Sri Lanka), Americans and Germans imported coffee in ever more spectacular quantities, notably from Latin America. In the early 1900s New York families consumed 1 lb of coffee per week. The Quaker beverage and chocolate manufacturers of Britain, happy in dispensing non-alcoholic refreshment, got their raw material from West Africa and South America. The canny Boston businessmen who founded the United Fruit Company in 1885 created private empires in the Caribbean to supply America with the previously insignificant banana. The soap manufacturers, exploiting the market which first demonstrated to the full the capacities of the new advertising industry, looked to the vegetable oils of Africa. Plantations, estates and farms were the second pillar of imperial economies. Metropolitan traders and financiers were the third.

These developments did not change the shape and character of the industrialized or industrializing countries, though they created new branches of big business whose fortunes were closely tied to those of particular parts of the globe, such as the oil companies. But they transformed the rest of the world, inasmuch as they turned it into a complex of colonial and semi-colonial territories which increasingly evolved into specialized producers of one or two primary products for export to the world market, on whose vagaries they were entirely dependent. Malaya increasingly meant rubber and tin, Brazil coffee, Chile nitrates, Uruguay meat, Cuba sugar and cigars. In fact, with the exception of the USA, even the white-settler colonies failed to industrialize (at this stage) because they too were caught in this cage of international specialization. They could become exceedingly prosperous, even by European standards, especially when inhabited by free and, in general, militant European immigrants with political muscle in elected assemblies, whose democratic radicalism could be formidable, though it usually stopped short of including the natives.* A European

---

* In fact, white democracy usually excluded them from the benefits won for white skins, or even refused to consider them as fully human.

wishing to emigrate in the Age of Empire would probably have done better to move to Australia, New Zealand, Argentina or Uruguay than anywhere else, including the USA. All these countries developed labour and radical–democratic parties, or even governments, and ambitious systems of public social welfare and security (New Zealand, Uruguay) long before European states did. But they did so as complements to the European (i.e. essentially British) industrial economy, and hence it did not pay them – or at any rate the interests committed to exporting primary products – to industrialize. Not that the metropoles would have welcomed their industrialization. Whatever the official rhetoric, the function of colonies and informal dependencies was to complement metropolitan economies and not to compete with them.

The dependent territories which did not belong to what has been called (white) 'settler capitalism' did not do so well. Their economic interest lay in the combination of resources with a labour force which, consisting of 'natives', cost little and could be kept cheap. Nevertheless the oligarchies of landowners and compradore traders – local, imported from Europe or both – and, where they had them, their governments, benefited from the sheer length of the period of secular expansion for their region's export staples, interrupted only by short-lived, though sometimes (as in Argentina in 1890) dramatic crises generated by trade cycle, overspeculation, war and peace. However, while the First World War disrupted some of their markets, the dependent producers were remote from it. From their point of view the era of empire, which began in the late nineteenth century, lasted until the Great Slump of 1929–33. All the same, in the course of this period they were to become increasingly vulnerable, as their fortunes were increasingly a function of the price of coffee (which by 1914 already produced 58 per cent of the value of Brazilian and 53 per cent of Colombian exports), of rubber and tin, of cocoa, beef or wool. But until the vertical fall in the price of primary commodities during the 1929 slump, this vulnerability did not seem of much long-term significance compared to the apparently unlimited expansion of exports and credits. On the contrary, as we have seen, before 1914 the terms of trade appeared to be, if anything, running in favour of the primary producers.

Nevertheless, the growing economic significance of such areas for the world economy does not explain why, among other things, there should have been a rush by the leading industrial states to carve up the globe into colonies and spheres of influence. The anti-imperialist analysis of imperialism has suggested various reasons why this should have been so. The most familiar of these, the pressure of capital for more profitable investment than could be ensured at home, investment secure from the rivalry of foreign capital, is the least convincing. Since British capital exports expanded enormously in the last third of the century, and indeed the income from such investments became essential for the British balance of payments, it was natural enough to connect the 'new imperialism' with capital exports, as J. A. Hobson did. But there is no denying that very little indeed of this massive flow went to the new colonial empires: most of British foreign investment went to the rapidly developing and generally old white-settler colonies, soon to be recognized as virtually independent 'dominions' (Canada, Australia, New Zealand, South Africa), and to what might be called 'honorary' dominions such as Argentina and Uruguay, not to mention the USA. Moreover, the bulk of such investment (76 per cent in 1913) took the form of public loans to railways and public utilities which certainly paid better than investment in the British government debt – an average of 5 per cent as against an average of 3 per cent – but were equally certainly less lucrative than the profits of industrial capital at home, except no doubt for the bankers organizing them. They were supposed to be secure rather than high-yield investments. None of this means that colonies were not acquired because some group of investors did not expect to make a killing, or in defence of investments already made. Whatever the ideology, the motive for the Boer War was gold.

A more convincing general motive for colonial expansion was the search for markets. The fact that this was often disappointed is irrelevant. The belief that the 'overproduction' of the Great Depression could be solved by a vast export drive was widespread. Businessmen, always inclined to fill the blank spaces on the map of world trade with vast numbers of potential customers, would naturally look for such unexploited areas: China was one which haunted the imagination of salesmen – what if every one of those 300 millions bought only one box of tin-tacks? – and Africa, the unknown continent, was another. The Chambers of Commerce of British cities in the depressed early 1880s were outraged by the thought that diplomatic negotiations might exclude their traders from access to the Congo basin, which was believed to offer untold sales prospects, all the more so as it was being developed as a paying proposition by that crowned businessman, King Leopold II of the Belgians.[7] (As it happened, his favourite method of exploitation by forced labour was not designed to encourage high *per capita* purchases, even when it did not actually diminish the number of customers by torture and massacre.)

But the crux of the global economic situation was that a number of developed economies simultaneously felt the same need for new markets. If they were sufficiently strong their ideal was 'the open door' on the markets of the underdeveloped world; but if not strong enough, they hoped to carve out for themselves territories which, by virtue of ownership, would give national business a monopoly position or at least a substantial advantage. Partition of the unoccupied parts of the Third World was the logical consequence. In a sense, this was an extension of the protectionism which gained ground almost everywhere after 1879 (see previous chapter). 'If you were not such persistent protectionists,' the British premier told the French ambassador in 1897, 'you would not find us so keen to annex territories.'[8] To this extent the 'new imperialism' was the natural by-product of an international economy based on the rivalry of several competing industrial economies, intensified by the economic pressures of the 1880s. It does not follow that any particular colony was expected to turn into Eldorado by itself, though this is what actually happened in South Africa, which became the world's greatest gold-producer. Colonies might simply provide suitable bases or jumping-off points for regional business penetration. That was clearly stated by an official of the US State Department round the turn of the century, when the USA followed international fashion by making a brief drive for a colonial empire of its own.

At this point the economic motive for acquiring some colonial territory becomes difficult to disentangle from the political action required for the purpose, for protectionism of whatever kind is economy operating with the aid of politics. The strategic motive for colonization was evidently strongest in Britain, which had long-established colonies which were crucially placed to control access to various zones of land and sea believed to be vital to Britain's worldwide commercial and maritime interests or, with the rise of the steamship, which could function as coaling stations. (Gibraltar and Malta were old examples of the first, Bermuda and Aden turned out to be useful examples of the second.) There was also the symbolic or real significance for robbers of getting an appropriate share of loot. Once rival powers began to carve up the map of Africa or Oceania, each naturally tried to safeguard against an excessive portion (or a particularly attractive morsel) going to the others. Once the status of a great power thus became associated with raising its flag over some palm-fringed beach (or, more likely, over stretches of dry scrub), the acquisition of colonies itself became a status symbol, irrespective of their value. Around 1900 even the USA, whose kind of imperialism has never before or since been particularly associated with the possession of formal colonies, felt obliged to follow the fashion. Germany deeply resented the fact that so powerful and dynamic a nation as herself should own so notably smaller a share of colonial territory than the British and the French, though her colonies were of little economic and less strategic interest. Italy insisted on capturing notably unattractive stretches of African desert and mountain in order to back her standing as a great power; and her failure to conquer

Ethiopia in 1896 undoubtedly lowered that standing.

For if great powers were states which acquired colonies, small powers had, as it were, 'no right' to them. Spain lost most of what remained of her colonial empire as a consequence of the Spanish–American War of 1898. As we have seen, plans to partition the remainder of Portugal's African empire between the new colonialists were seriously discussed. Only the Dutch quietly kept their rich and ancient colonies (mainly in South-east Asia), and the King of the Belgians, as we have also seen, was permitted to carve out his private domain in Africa on condition that he allowed it to be accessible to all, because no great power was willing to give others a significant share of the great basin of the Congo river. One ought, of course, to add that there were large tracts of Asia and the Americas where, for political reasons, massive share-outs of territory by European powers were out of the question. In the Americas the situation of the surviving European colonies was frozen by the Monroe Doctrine: only the USA had freedom of action. In most of Asia, the struggle was for spheres of influence in nominally independent states, notably China, Persia and the Ottoman Empire. Exceptions to this were the Russians and the Japanese – the former successful in extending their area in Central Asia but unsuccessful in acquiring chunks of north China, the latter acquiring Korea and Formosa (Taiwan) as a result of a war with China in 1894–5. The main zones of competitive land-grabbing were thus, in practice, in Africa and Oceania.

Essentially strategic explanations of imperialism have thus attracted some historians, who have tried to account for the British expansion in Africa in terms of the need to defend the routes to, and the maritime and terrestrial glacis of, India against potential threats. It is indeed important to recall that, speaking globally, India was the core of British strategy, and that this strategy required control not only over the short sea-routes to the subcontinent (Egypt, the Middle East, the Red Sea, Persian Gulf and South Arabia) and the long sea-routes (the Cape of Good Hope and Singapore), but over the entire Indian Ocean, including crucial sectors of the African coast and its hinterland. British governments were keenly aware of this. It is also true that the disintegration of local power in some areas crucial for this purpose, such as Egypt (including the Sudan), drew the British into establishing a much greater direct political presence than originally intended, and even into actual rule. Yet these arguments do not invalidate an economic analysis of imperialism. In the first place, they underestimate the directly economic incentive to acquire some African territories, of which Southern Africa is the most obvious. In any case the scramble for West Africa and the Congo was primarily economic. In the second place

68

they overlook the fact that India was the 'brightest jewel in the imperial crown' and the core of British global strategic thinking precisely because of her very real importance to the British economy. This was never greater than at this time, when anything up to 60 per cent of British cotton exports went to India and the Far East, to which India was the key – 40–45 per cent went to India alone – and when the international balance of payments of Britain hinged on the payments surplus which India provided. In the third place, the disintegration of indigenous local governments, which sometimes entailed the establishment of European rule over areas Europeans had not previously bothered to administer, was itself due to the undermining of local structures by economic penetration. And, finally, the attempt to prove that nothing in the internal development of western capitalism in the 1880s explains the territorial redivision of the world fails, since world capitalism in this period clearly was different from what it had been in the 1860s. It now consisted of a plurality of rival 'national economies' 'protecting' themselves against each other. In short, politics and economics cannot be separated in a capitalist society, any more than religion and society in an Islamic one. The attempt to devise a purely non-economic expla-nation of the 'new imperialism' is as unrealistic as the attempt to devise a purely non-economic explanation of the rise of working-class parties.

In fact, the rise of labour movements or more generally of democratic politics (see next chapter) had a distinct bearing on the rise of the 'new imperialism'. Ever since the great imperialist Cecil Rhodes observed in 1895 that if one wanted to avoid civil war one must become imperialist,[9] most observers have been aware of so-called 'social imperialism', i.e. of the attempt to use imperial expansion to diminish domestic discontent by economic improvements or social reform or in other ways. There is no doubt at all that politicians were perfectly aware of the potential benefits of imperialism. In some cases – notably Germany – the rise of imperialism has been explained primarily in terms of 'the primacy of domestic politics'. Probably Cecil Rhodes' version of social imperialism, which thought primarily of the economic benefits that empire might bring, directly or indirectly, to the discontented masses, was the least relevant. There is no good evidence that colonial conquest as such had much bearing on the employment or real incomes of most workers in the metropolitan countries,* and the idea that emigration to colonies would provide a safety-valve for overpopulated countries was little more than a demagogic fantasy. (In fact, never was it easier to find

---

* In individual cases empire might be useful. The Cornish miners left the declining tin-mines of their peninsula *en masse* for the goldfields of South Africa, where they earned a great deal of money and died even earlier than usual from lung disease. The Cornish mine-owners, at less risk to their lives, bought themselves into the new tin-mines of Malaya.

somewhere to emigrate to than between 1880 and 1914, and only a tiny minority of emigrants went to anyone's colonies – or needed to.)

Much more relevant was the familiar practice of offering the voters glory rather than more costly reforms: and what was more glorious than conquests of exotic territories and dusky races, especially as these were usually cheaply won? More generally, imperialism encouraged the masses, and especially the potentially discontented, to identify themselves with the imperial state and nation, and thus unconsciously to endow the social and political system represented by that state with justification and legitimacy. And in an era of mass politics (see next chapter) even old systems required new legitimacy. Here again, contemporaries were quite clear about this. The British coronation ceremony of 1902, carefully restyled, was praised because it was designed to express 'the recognition, by a free democracy, of a hereditary crown, *as a symbol of the world-wide dominion of their race*' (my emphasis). In short, empire made good ideological cement.

How effective this specific variant of patriotic flag-waving was is not quite clear, especially in countries where liberalism and the more radical left had acquired strong anti-imperial, anti-military, anti-colonial or more generally anti-aristocratic traditions. There is little doubt that in several countries imperialism was extremely popular among the new middle and white-collar strata, whose social identity largely rested on a claim to be the chosen vehicles of patriotism (see chapter 8 below). There is much less evidence of any spontaneous enthusiasm of the workers for colonial conquests, let alone wars, or indeed of any great interest in the colonies, new or old (except those of white settlement). Attempts to institutionalize pride in imperialism, as by establishing an 'Empire Day' in Britain (1902), largely relied for their success on mobilizing the captive audiences of school-children. (The appeal of patriotism in a more general sense will be considered below.)

Nevertheless, it is impossible to deny that the idea of superiority to, and domination over, a world of dark skins in remote places was genuinely popular, and thus benefited the politics of imperialism. In its great International Expositions (see *The Age of Capital*, chapter 2) bourgeois civilization had always gloried in the triple triumphs of science, technology and manufactures. In the era of empires it also gloried in its colonies. At the end of the century 'colonial pavilions', hitherto virtually unknown, multiplied: eighteen complemented the Eiffel Tower in 1889, fourteen attracted the tourists in Paris in 1900.[11] No doubt this was planned publicity, but like all really successful propaganda, commercial or political, it succeeded because it touched a public nerve. Colonial exhibits were a hit. British jubilees, royal funerals and coronations were all the more impressive because, like ancient Roman triumphs, they displayed submissive maharajahs in jewelled robes – freely loyal rather than captive. Military parades were all the more colourful because they contained turbaned Sikhs, moustached Rajputs, smiling and implacable Gurkhas, Spahis and tall black Senegalese: the world of what was considered barbarism at the service of civilization. Even in Habsburg Vienna, uninterested in overseas colonies, an Ashanti village magnetized the sightseers. The Douanier Rousseau was not the only man to dream of the tropics.

The sense of superiority which thus united the western whites, rich, middle-class and poor, did so not only because all of them enjoyed the privileges of the ruler, especially when actually in the colonies. In Dakar or Mombasa the most modest clerk was a master, and accepted as a 'gentleman' by people who would not even have noticed his existence in Paris or London; the white worker was a commander of blacks. But even where ideology insisted on at least potential equality, it was dissolved into domination. France believed in transforming its subjects in Frenchmen, notional descendants (as school textbooks insisted, in Timbuctoo and Martinique as in Bordeaux) of 'nos ancêtres les gaulois' (our ancestors the Gauls), unlike the British, convinced of the essential and permanent non-Englishness of Bengalis and Yoruba. Yet the very existence of these strata of native évolués underlined the lack of 'evolution' of the great majority. The Churches set out to convert the heathen to various versions of the true Christian faith, except where actively discouraged by colonial governments (as in India) or where the task was clearly impossible (as in Islamic regions).

This was the classic age of massive missionary endeavour.* Missionary effort was by no means an agency of imperialist politics. Often it was opposed to the colonial authorities; pretty well always it put the interests of its converts first. Yet the success of the Lord was a function of imperialist advance. Whether trade followed the flag may still be debated, but there is no doubt at all that colonial conquest opened the way for effective missionary action – as in Uganda, Rhodesia (Zambia and Zimbabwe) and Nyasaland (Malawi). And if Christianity insisted on the equality of souls, it underlined the inequality of bodies – even of clerical bodies. It was something done by whites for natives, and paid for by whites. And though it multiplied native believers, at least half the clergy remained white. As for a coloured bishop, it would require a powerful microscope to detect one anywhere between 1880 and 1914. The Catholic Church did not consecrate its first Asian bishops

* Between 1876 and 1902 there were 119 translations of the Bible, compared to 74 in the previous thirty years and 40 in the years 1816–45. The number of new Protestant missions in Africa during the period 1886–95 was twenty-three or about three times as many as in any previous decade.[12]

until the 1920s, eighty years after observing how desirable such a development would be.[13]

As for the movement most passionately devoted to the equality of all men, it spoke with two voices. The secular left was anti-imperialist in principle and often in practice. Freedom for India, like freedom for Egypt and Ireland, was the objective of the British labour movement. The left never wavered in its condemnation of colonial wars and conquests, often – as in the British opposition to the Boer War – at considerable risk of temporary unpopularity. Radicals revealed the horrors of the Congo, in metropolitan cocoa plantations on African islands, in Egypt. The campaign which led to the great electoral triumph of the British Liberal Party in 1906 was largely waged by public denunciations of 'Chinese slavery' in the South African mines. Yet, with the rarest exceptions (such as Dutch Indonesia), western socialists did little actually to organize the resistance of colonial peoples to their rulers, until the era of the Communist International. Within the socialist and labour movement those who frankly accepted imperialism as desirable, or at least an essential stage in the history of peoples not yet 'ready for self-government', were a minority on the revisionist and Fabian right wing, though many trade union leaders probably thought discussions about colonies were irrelevant, or considered coloured peoples primarily as cheap labour threatening sturdy white workers. Certainly the pressure to ban coloured immigrants, which established the 'White California' and 'White Australia' policies between the 1880s and 1914, came primarily from the working class, and Lancashire unions joined with Lancashire cotton-masters to insist that India must remain deindustrialized. Internationally, socialism before 1914 remained overwhelmingly a movement of Europeans and white emigrants or their descendants (see chapter 5 below). Colonialism remained marginal to their interests. Indeed, their analysis and definition of the new 'imperialist' phase of capitalism, which they detected from the later 1890s, rightly saw colonial annexation and exploitation simply as one symptom and characteristic of that new phase: undesirable, like all its characteristics, but not in itself central. Few were the socialists who, like Lenin, already had their eye fixed on the 'inflammable material' on the periphery of world capitalism.

Insofar as the socialist (i.e. mainly Marxist) analysis of imperialism integrated colonialism into a much wider concept of a 'new phase' of capitalism, it was undoubtedly right in principle, though not necessarily in the details of its theoretical model. It was also sometimes too inclined, as indeed were contemporary capitalists, to exaggerate the economic significance of colonial expansion for metropolitan countries. The imperialism of the late nineteenth century was undoubtedly 'new'. It was the child of an era of competition between rival industrial–capitalist national economies which was new and which was intensified by the pressure to secure and safeguard markets in a period of business uncertainty (see chapter 2 above); in short, it was an era when 'tariff and expansion become the common demand of the ruling class'.[14] It was part of a process of turning away from a capitalism of the private and public policies of *laissez-faire*, which was also new, and implied the rise of large corporations and oligopolies as well as the increased intervention of the state in economic affairs. It belonged to a period when the peripheral part of the global economy became increasingly significant. It was a phenomenon that seemed as 'natural' in 1900 as it would have appeared implausible in 1860. But for this link between the post-1873 capitalism and expansion into the unindustrialized world, it is doubtful whether even 'social imperialism' would have played such part as it did in the domestic politics of states adapting themselves to mass electoral politics. All attempts to divorce the explanation of imperialism from the specific developments of capitalism in the late nineteenth century must be regarded as ideological exercises, though often learned and sometimes acute.

II

This still leaves us with the questions about the impact of western (and from the 1890s Japanese) expansion on the rest of the world, and about the significance of the 'imperial' aspects of imperialism for the metropolitan countries.

The first of these questions can be answered more quickly than the second. The economic impact of imperialism was significant, but, of course, the most significant thing about it was that it was profoundly unequal, for the relationship between metropoles and dependencies was highly asymmetrical. The impact of the first on the second was dramatic and decisive, even without actual occupation, whereas the impact of the second on the first might be negligible, and was hardly ever a matter of life or death. Cuba stood or fell by the price of sugar and the willingness of the USA to import it, but even quite small 'developed' countries – say Sweden – would not have been seriously inconvenienced if all Caribbean sugar had suddenly disappeared from the market, because they did not depend exclusively on that area for sugar. Virtually all the imports and exports of any region in sub-Saharan Africa came from or went to a handful of western metropoles, but metropolitan trade with Africa, Asia and Oceania, while increasing modestly between 1870 and 1914, remained quite marginal. About 80 per cent of European trade throughout the nineteenth century, both exports and imports, was with other developed countries, and the same is true of European foreign investments.[15] Insofar as these were directed overseas, they went mostly to a handful of rapidly developing economies mainly populated by settlers of European descent – Canada, Australia, South Africa, Argentina, etc. – as well as, of course, to the USA. In this sense the age of imperialism looks very different when seen from Nicaragua or Malaya than it does from the point of view of Germany or France.

Among the metropolitan countries imperialism was obviously of greatest importance to Britain, since the economic supremacy of that country had always hinged on her special relationship with the overseas markets and sources of primary products. In fact it is arguable that at no time since the industrial revolution had the manufactures of the United Kingdom been particularly competitive on the markets of industrializing economies, except perhaps during the golden decades of 1850–70. To preserve as much as possible of its privileged access to the non-European world was therefore a matter of life and death for the British economy.[16] In the late nineteenth century it was remarkably successful in doing so, incidentally expanding the area officially or actually under the British monarchy to a quarter of the surface of the globe (which British atlases proudly coloured red). If we include the so-called 'informal empire' of independent states which were in effect satellite economies of Britain, perhaps one-third of the globe was British in an economic, and indeed cultural, sense. For Britain exported even the peculiar shape of her post-boxes to Portugal, and so quintessentially British an institution as Harrods department store to Buenos Aires. But by 1914 much of this zone of indirect influence, especially in Latin America, was already being infiltrated by other powers.

However, not a great deal of this successful defensive operation had much to do with the 'new' imperialist expansion, except that biggest of bonanzas, the diamonds and gold of South Africa. This generated a crop of (largely German) instant millionaires – the Wernhers, Beits, Ecksteins, et al. – most of whom were equally instantly incorporated into British high society, never more receptive to first-generation money if it was splashed around in sufficiently large quantities. It also led to the greatest of colonial conflicts, the South African War of 1899–1902, which eliminated the resistance of two small local republics of white peasant settlers.

Most of Britain's overseas success was due to the more systematic exploitation of Britain's already existing possessions or of the country's special position as the major importer from, and investor in, such areas as South America. Except for India, Egypt and South Africa, most British economic activity was in countries which were virtually independent, like the white 'dominions', or areas like the USA and Latin America, where British state action was not, or could not be, effectively deployed. For in spite of the cries of pain emanating from the Corporation of Foreign Bondholders (established during the Great Depression) when faced with the well-known Latin practice of suspending debt-payment or paying in devalued currency, the government did not effectively back its investors in Latin America, because it could not. The Great Depression was a crucial test in this respect, because, like later world depressions (including the one of the 1970s and 1980s) it led to a major international debt crisis, which put the banks of the metropolis at serious risk. The most the British government could do was to arrange for the great house of Baring to be saved from insolvency in the 'Baring crisis' of 1890, when that bank had, as banks will, ventured too freely into the whirlpools of defaulting Argentinian finance. If it backed investors with diplomacy of force, as it increasingly did after 1905, it was to support them against entrepreneurs of other countries backed by their own governments, rather than against the larger governments of the dependent world.*

In fact, taking the good years with the bad, British capitalists did rather well out of their informal or 'free' empire. Almost half of all Britain's long-term publicly issued capital in 1914 was in Canada, Australia and Latin America. More than half of all British savings were invested abroad after 1900.

Of course Britain took her share of the newly colonialized regions of the world, and, given British strength and experience, it was a larger and probably more valuable share than that of anyone else. If France occupied most of West Africa, the four British colonies in this area controlled 'the denser African populations, the larger productive capacities, and the preponderance of trade'.[17] Yet the British object was not expansion but defence against others encroaching upon territories hitherto, like most of the overseas world, dominated by British trade and British capital.

Did other powers benefit proportionately from their colonial expansion? It is impossible to say, since formal colonization was only one aspect of global economic expansion and competition, and, in the case of the two major industrial powers, Germany and the USA, not a major aspect of it. Moreover, as we have already seen, for no country

---

* There were a few instances of gunboat economics – as in Venezuela, Guatemala, Haiti, Honduras and Mexico – but they do not seriously modify this picture. Of course British governments and capitalists, faced with the choice between local parties or states favouring British economic interests and those hostile to them, would not refrain from backing the side helpful to British profits: Chile against Peru in the 'War of the Pacific' (1879–82), the enemies of President Balmaceda in Chile in 1891. The issue was nitrates.

other than Britain (with the possible exception of the Netherlands) was a special relationship with the non-industrial world economically crucial. All we can say with fair confidence is this. First, the drive for colonies seems to have been proportionately stronger in economically less dynamic metropolitan countries, where it served to some extent as a potential compensation for their economic and political inferiority to their rivals – and, in the case of France, her demographic and military inferiority. Second, in all cases there were particular economic groups – notably those associated with overseas trade and industries using overseas raw materials – pressing strongly for colonial expansion, which they naturally justified by the prospects of national advantage. Third, while some of these groups did rather well out of such expansion – the Compagnie Française de l'Afrique Occidentale paid dividends of 26 per cent in 1913[18] – most of the actual new colonies attracted little capital and their economic results were disappointing.* In short, the new colonialism was a by-product of an era of economic–political rivalry between competing national economies, intensified by protectionism. However, insofar as the metropolitan trade with the colonies almost invariably increased as a percentage of its total trade, that protectionism was modestly successful.

Yet the Age of Empire was not only an economic and political but a cultural phenomenon. The conquest of the globe by its 'developed' minority transformed images, ideas and aspirations, both by force and institutions, by example and by social transformation. In the dependent countries this hardly affected anyone except the indigenous elites, though of course it must be remembered that in some regions, such as sub-Saharan Africa, it was imperialism itself, or the associated phenomenon of Christian missions, which created the possibility of new social elites based on education in the western manner. The division between 'francophone' and 'anglophone' African states today exactly mirrors the distribution of the French and British colonial empires.† Except in Africa and Oceania, where Christian missions sometimes secured mass conversions to the western religion, the great mass of the colonial populations hardly changed their ways of life if they could help it. And, to the chagrin of the more unbending missionaries, what indigenous peoples adopted was not so much the faith imported from the west as those elements in it which made sense to them in terms of their own

---

* France did not even succeed in integrating her new colonies fully into a protectionist system, though in 1913 55 per cent of the French Empire's trade was with the home country. Unable to break the already established economic links of these areas to other regions and metropoles, France had to buy a large share of her needs in colonial products – rubber, skins and leather, tropical timber – via Hamburg, Antwerp and Liverpool.
† Which, after 1918, divided the former German colonies between them.

system of beliefs and institutions, or demands. Just like the sports brought to Pacific islanders by enthusiastic British colonial administrators (so often selected from among the more muscular products of the middle class), colonial religion often looked as unexpected to the western observer as Samoan cricket. This was so even where the faithful nominally followed the orthodoxies of their denomination. But they were also apt to develop their own versions of the faith, notably in South Africa – the one region in Africa where really massive conversions took place – where an 'Ethiopian movement' seceded from the missions as early as 1892 in order to establish a form of Christianity less identified with the whites.

What imperialism brought to the elites or potential elites of the dependent world was therefore essentially 'westernization'. It had, of course, begun to do so long before then. For all governments and elites of countries faced with dependency or conquest it had been clear for several decades that they had to westernize or go under (see *The Age of Capital*, chapters 7, 8, 11). And, indeed, the ideologies which inspired such elites in the era of imperialism dated back to the years between the French Revolution and the mid-nineteenth century, as when they took the form of the positivism of August Comte (1798–1857), a modernizing doctrine which inspired the governments of Brazil, Mexico and the early Turkish Revolution (see pp. 284, 290 below). Elite resistance to the west remained westernizing even when it opposed wholesale westernization on grounds of religion, morality, ideology or political pragmatism. The saintly Mahatma Gandhi, wearing loincloth and bearing a spindle (to discourage industrialization), was not only supported and financed by the owners of mechanized cotton-factories in Ahmedabad* but was himself a western-educated lawyer visibly influenced by western-derived ideology. He is quite incomprehensible if we see in him only a Hindu traditionalist.

In fact, Gandhi illustrates the specific impact of the era of imperialism rather well. Born into a relatively modest caste of traders and money-lenders not previously much associated with the westernized elite which administered India under British superiors, he nevertheless acquired a professional and political education in England. By the late 1880s this was so accepted an option for ambitious young men from his country that Gandhi himself began to write a guide-book to English life for prospective students of modest circumstances such as himself. Written in superb English, it advised them on everything from the journey by P & O steamer to London and how to find lodgings, to ways

---

* 'Ah,' one such patroness is supposed to have exclaimed, 'if Bapuji only knew what it costs to keep him in poverty!'

of meeting the diet requirements of the pious Hindu and how to get used to the surprising western habit of shaving oneself rather than having it done by a barber.[19] Gandhi clearly saw himself neither as an unconditional assimilator nor as an unconditional opponent of things British. As many pioneers of colonial liberation have done since, during their temporary stay in the metropole, he choose to move in western circles which were ideologically congenial – in his case those of British vegetarians, who may safely be taken as being in favour of other 'progressive' causes also.

Gandhi learned his characteristic technique of mobilizing traditionalist masses for non-traditionalist purposes by means of passive resistance, in an environment created by the 'new imperialism'. It was, as one might expect, a fusion of western and eastern elements for he made no secret of his intellectual debt to John Ruskin and Tolstoi. (Before the 1880s the fertilization of Indian political flowers by pollen carried from Russia would have been inconceivable, but by the first decade of the new century it was already common among Indian, as it was to be among Chinese and Japanese radicals.) South Africa, the boom country of diamonds and gold, attracted a large community of modest immigrants from India, and racial discrimination in this novel setting created one of the few situations in which the non-elite Indians were ready for modern political mobilization. Gandhi gained his political experience and won his political spurs as the champion of Indian rights in South Africa. He could hardly as yet have done the same in India itself, where he eventually returned – but only after the outbreak of the 1914 war – to become the key figure in the Indian national movement.

In short, the Age of Empire created both the conditions which formed anti-imperialist leaders and the conditions which, as we shall see (chapter 12 below), began to give their voices resonance. But, of course, it is an anachronism and a misunderstanding to present the history of the peoples and regions brought under the domination and influence of the western metropoles primarily in terms of resistance to the west. It is an anachronism because, with exceptions to be noted below, the era of significant anti-imperial movements begins for most regions at the earliest with the First World War and the Russian Revolution, and a misunderstanding, because it reads the text of modern nationalism – independence, the self-determination of peoples, the formation of territorial states, etc. (see chapter 6 below) – into a historical record which did not yet, and could not yet, contain it. In fact, it was the westernized elites which first made contact with such ideas through their visits to the west and through the educational institutions formed by the west, for that is where they came from. Young Indian students returning from

Britain might bring with them the slogans of Mazzini and Garibaldi, but as yet few of the inhabitants of the Pandjab, let alone of regions like the Sudan, would have the slightest idea of what they could mean.

The most powerful cultural legacy of imperialism was, therefore, an education in western ways for minorities of various kinds: for the favoured few who became literate and therefore discovered, with or without the assistance of Christian conversion, the high road of ambition which wore the white collar of the clergyman, teacher, bureaucrat or office worker. In some regions it also included those who acquired new ways as soldiers and policemen of the new rulers, wearing their clothes, adopting their peculiar ideas of time, place and domestic arrangement. These, of course, were the minorities of potential movers and shakers, which is why the era of colonialism, brief even by the measure of a single human life, has left such lasting effects. For it is a surprising fact that in most parts of Africa the entire experience of colonialism from original occupation to the formation of independent states, fits within a single lifetime – say that of Sir Winston Churchill (1874–1965).

What of the opposite effect of the dependent world on the dominant? Exoticism had been a by-product of European expansion since the sixteenth century, though philosophical observers in the age of Enlightenment had more often than not treated the strange countries beyond Europe and European settlers as a sort of moral barometer of European civilization. Where they were plainly civilized, they could illustrate the institutional deficiencies of the west, as in Montesquieu's *Persian Letters*; where they were not, they were apt to be treated as noble savages whose natural and admirable comportment illustrated the corruption of civilized society. The novelty of the nineteenth century was that non-Europeans and their societies were increasingly, and generally, treated as inferior, undesirable, feeble and backward, even infantile. They were fit subjects for conquest, or at least for conversion to the values of the only *real* civilization, that represented by traders, missionaries and bodies of armed men full of firearms and fire-water. And in a sense the values of traditional non-western societies increasingly became irrelevant to their survival in an age when force and military technology alone counted. Did the sophistication of imperial Peking prevent the western barbarians from burning and looting the Summer Palace more than once? Did the elegance of elite culture in the declining Mughal capital, so beautifully portrayed in Satyajit Ray's *The Chessplayers*, hold up the advancing British? For the average European, such people became objects of contempt. The only non-Europeans they took to were fighters, preferably those who could be recruited into their own colonial armies (Sikhs, Gurkhas, Berber mountaineers, Afghans, Beduin). The Ottoman Empire earned a grudging respect, because even in decline it had an infantry which could resist European armies. Japan came to be treated as an equal when it began to win wars.

And yet the very density of the network of global communication, the very accessibility of foreign lands, directly or indirectly, intensified the confrontation and the intermingling of the western and the exotic worlds. Those who knew and reflected on both were few, though in the imperialist period their number was increased by writers who deliberately chose to make themselves intermediaries between them: writers or intellectuals by vocation and by profession mariners (like Pierre Loti and, greatest of them, Joseph Conrad), soldiers and administrators (like the orientalist Louis Massignon) or colonial journalists (like Rudyard Kipling). But increasingly the exotic became part of everyday education, as in the enormously successful boys' novels of Karl May (1842–1912), whose imaginary German hero ranged through the Wild West and the Islamic east, with excursions into black Africa and Latin America; in the thrillers, whose villains now included inscrutable and all-powerful orientals like Sax Rohmer's Dr Fu Manchu; in the pulp-magazine school stories for British boys, which now included a rich Hindu speaking the baroque Babu–English of the expected stereotype. It could even become an occasional but expected part of everyday experience, as in Buffalo Bill's Wild West show, with its equally exotic cowboys and Indians, which conquered Europe from 1887 on, or in the increasingly elaborate 'colonial villages' or exhibits in the great International Expositions. These glimpses of strange worlds were not documentary, whatever their intention. They were ideological, generally reinforcing the sense of superiority of the 'civilized' over the 'primitive'. They were imperialist only because, as the novels of Joseph Conrad show, the central link between the worlds of the exotic and the everyday was the formal or informal penetration of the Third World by the west. When colloquial language, mainly via various forms of slang, notably that of colonial armies, absorbed words from the actual imperial experience, they often reflected a negative view of its subjects. Italian workers called strike-breakers *crumiri* (after a North African tribe) and Italian politicians called the regiments of docile southern voters marched into elections by local patrons *ascari* (colonial native troops). *Caciques*, the Indian chieftains of Spain's American empire, had become a synonym for any political boss; *caids* (North African indigenous chiefs) provided the term for leaders of criminal gangs in France.

Yet there was a more positive side to this exoticism. Intellectually minded administrators and soldiers – businessmen were less interested in such matters – pondered deeply on the differences between their own societies and those they ruled. They produced both bodies of impressive scholarship about them, especially in the Indian empire, and theoretical reflections which transformed western social sciences. Much of this work was the by-product of colonial rule or intended to assist it, and most of it unquestionably rested on a firm and confident sense of the superiority of western knowledge to any other, except perhaps in the realm of religion, where the superiority of e.g. Methodism to Buddhism was not obvious to impartial observers. Imperialism brought a notable rise in the western interest in, and sometimes the western conversion to, forms of spirituality derived from the orient, or claiming to be so derived.[20] Yet, in spite of post-colonial criticism, this body of western scholarship cannot be dismissed simply as a supercilious depreciation of non-European cultures. At the very least the best of it took them seriously, as something to be respected and from which to derive instruction. In the field of art, and especially the visual arts, western *avant gardes* treated non-western cultures entirely as equals. They were indeed largely inspired by them in this period. This is true not only of arts believed to represent sophisticated civilizations, however exotic (like the Japanese, whose influence on French painters was marked), but of those regarded as 'primitive', and notably those of Africa and Oceania. No doubt their 'primitivism' was their main attraction, but it is undeniable that the *avant-garde* generations of the early twentieth century taught Europeans to see such works as art – often as great art – in its own right, irrespective of its origin.

One final aspect of imperialism must be briefly mentioned: its impact on the ruling and middle classes of the metropolitan countries themselves. In one sense imperialism dramatized the triumph of these classes and the societies created in their image as nothing else could possibly have done. A handful of countries, mainly in north-western Europe, dominated the globe. Some imperialists, to the resentment of the Latins not to mention the Slavs, even liked to stress the peculiar conquering merits of those of Teutonic and especially Anglo-Saxon origins who, whatever their rivalries, were said to have an affinity to each other which still echoes through Hitler's grudging respect for Britain. A handful of men of the upper and middle class within these countries – officers, administrators, businessmen, engineers – exercised that domination effectively. Around 1890 a little over 6000 British officials governed almost 300 million Indians with the help of a little over 70,000 European soldiers, the rank-and-file of whom were, like the much more numerous indigenous troops, mercenaries who took orders, and who indeed were disproportionately drawn from that older reservoir of native colonial fighters, the Irish. The case is extreme, but by no means untypical. Could there be a more extraordinary proof of absolute superiority?

The number of people directly involved in empire was thus relatively small – but their symbolic significance was enormous. When the writer Rudyard Kipling, the bard of the Indian empire, was believed to be dying of pneumonia in 1899, not only the British and the Americans grieved – Kipling had just addressed a poem on 'The White Man's Burden' to the USA on its responsibilities in the Philippines – but the Emperor of Germany sent a telegram.[21]

Yet imperial triumph raised both problems and uncertainties. It raised problems insofar as the contradiction between the rule of metropolitan ruling classes over their empires and their own peoples became increasingly insoluble. Within the metropoles, as we shall see, the politics of democratic electoralism increasingly, and as it seemed inevitably, prevailed or were destined to prevail. Within the colonial empires autocracy ruled, based on the combination of physical coercion and passive submission to a superiority so great as to appear unchallengeable and therefore legitimate. Soldiers and self-disciplined 'proconsuls', isolated men with absolute powers over territories the size of kingdoms, ruled over continents, while at home the ignorant and inferior masses were rampant. Was there not a lesson – a lesson in the sense of Nietzsche's *Will to Power* – to be learned here?

Imperialism also raised uncertainties. In the first place it confronted a small minority of whites – for even the majority of that race belonged to those destined to inferiority, as the new discipline of eugenics unceasingly warned (see chapter 10 below) – with the masses of the black, the brown, perhaps above all the yellow, that 'yellow peril' against which the Emperor William II called for the union and defence of the west.[22] Could world empires, so easily won, so narrowly based, so absurdly easily ruled thanks to the devotion of a few and the passivity of the many, could they last? Kipling, the greatest – perhaps the only – poet of imperialism welcomed the great moment of demagogic imperial pride, Queen Victoria's Diamond Jubilee in 1897, with a prophetic reminder of the impermanence of empires:

> Far-called, our navies melt away;
> On dune and headland sinks the fire:
> Lo, all our pomp of yesterday
> Is one with Nineveh and Tyre!
> Judge of the Nations, spare us yet,
> Lest we forget, lest we forget.[23]

Pomp planned the building of an enormous new imperial capital for India in New Delhi. Was Clemenceau the only sceptical observer who would foresee that it would be the latest of a long series of ruins of imperial capitals? And was the vulnerability of global rule so much greater than the vulnerability of domestic rule over the white masses?

The uncertainty was double-edged. For if empire (and the rule of the ruling classes) was vulnerable to its subjects, though perhaps not yet, not immediately, was it not more immediately vulnerable to the erosion from within of the will to rule, the willingness to wage the Darwinian struggle for the survival of the fittest? Would not the very wealth and luxury which power and enterprise had brought weaken the fibres of those muscles whose constant efforts were necessary to maintain it? Did not empire lead to parasitism at the centre and to the eventual triumph of the barbarians?

Nowhere did such questions sound a more doom-laden echo than in the greatest and most vulnerable of all empires, the one which in size and glory surpassed all empires of the past, and yet in other respects was on the verge of decline. But even the hard-working and energetic Germans saw imperialism as going hand in hand with that 'rentier state' which could not but lead to decay. Let J. A. Hobson give word to these fears: if China were to be partitioned,

> the greater part of Western Europe might then assume the appearance and character already exhibited by tracts of country in the South of England, in the Riviera, and in the tourist-ridden or residential parts of Italy and Switzerland, little clusters of wealthy aristocrats drawing dividends and pensions from the Far East, with a somewhat larger group of professional retainers and tradesmen and a large body of personal servants and workers in the transport trade and in the final stages of production of the more perishable goods: all the main arterial industries would have disappeared, the staple foods and manufactures flowing in as tribute from Africa and Asia.[24]

The bourgeoisie's *belle époque* would thus disarm it. The charming, harmless Eloi of H. G. Wells' novel, living lives of play in the sun, would be at the mercy of the dark Morlocks on whom they depended, and against whom they were helpless.[25] 'Europe', wrote the German economist Schulze-Gaevernitz, '... will shift the burden of physical toil, first agriculture and mining, then the more arduous toil in industry – on to the coloured races, and itself be content with the role of rentier, and in this way, perhaps, pave the way for the economic and later, the political emancipation of the coloured races.'[26]

Such were the bad dreams which disturbed the sleep of the *belle époque*. In them the nightmares of empire merged with the fears of democracy.

83

CHAPTER 4

THE POLITICS OF DEMOCRACY

All those who, by wealth, education, intelligence or guile, have an aptitude for leading a community of men and a chance of doing so – in other words, all the cliques in the ruling class – have to bow to universal suffrage once it is instituted, and also, if occasion requires, cajole and fool it.

Gaetano Mosca, 1895[1]

Democracy is still on trial, but so far it has not disgraced itself; it is true that its full force has not yet come into operation, and this for two causes, one more or less permanent in its effect, the other of a more transient nature. In the first place, whatever be the numerical representation of wealth, its power will always be out of proportion; and secondly, the defective organisation of the newly enfranchised classes has prevented any overwhelming alteration in the pre-existing balance of power.

John Maynard Keynes, 1904[2]

It is significant that none of the modern secular states have neglected to provide national holidays giving occasions for assemblage.

American Journal of Sociology, 1896–73[3]

I

The historical period with which this volume deals began with an international outburst of hysteria among the rulers of Europe and among its terrified middle classes, provoked by the short-lived Commune of Paris in 1871, whose suppression had been followed by massacres of Parisians on a scale which would normally have been inconceivable in civilized nineteenth-century states. Even by our more barbarous standards, the scale is still impressive (cf. *The Age of Capital*, chapter 9). This brief, brutal – and for the time uncharacteristic – unleashing of blind terror by respectable society reflected a fundamental problem of the politics of bourgeois society: that of its democratization.

84

Democracy, as the sagacious Aristotle had observed, was the government of the mass of the people, who were, on the whole, poor. The interests of the poor and the rich, the privileged and the unprivileged, are evidently not the same; even if we assume that they are or can be, the masses are rather unlikely to consider public affairs in the same light and in the same terms as what British Victorian writers called 'the classes', happily still able to identify class political action only with aristocracy and bourgeoisie. This was the basic dilemma of nineteenth-century liberalism (cf. *The Age of Capital*, chapter 6, 1), devoted as it was to constitutions and sovereign elected assemblies, which it did its best to sidestep by being non-democratic, i.e. by excluding the majority of male citizens of states, not to mention the totality of their female inhabitants, from the right to vote and to be elected. Until the period with which this volume deals, its unshakeable foundation was the distinction between what the logical French in Louis Philippe's era had called 'the legal country' and 'the real country' (*le pays légal, le pays réel*). From the moment when the 'real country' began to penetrate the political enclosure of the 'legal' or 'political' country, defended by the fortifications of property and educational qualifications for voting and, in most countries, by institutionalized aristocratic privilege, such as hereditary chambers of peers, the social order was at risk.

What indeed, would happen in politics when the masses of the people, ignorant and brutalized, unable to understand the elegant and salutary logic of Adam Smith's free market, controlled the political fate of states? They would, as likely as not, pursue a road which led to that social revolution whose brief reappearance in 1871 had so terrified the respectable. In its ancient insurrectional form, revolution might no longer seem imminent, but was it not concealed behind any major extension of the franchise beyond the ranks of the propertied and educated? Would this not, as the future Lord Salisbury feared in 1866, inevitably lead to communism?

Yet after 1870 it became increasingly clear that the democratization of the politics of states was quite inevitable. The masses would march on to the stage of politics, whether rulers liked it or not. And this is indeed what happened. Electoral systems based on a wide franchise, sometimes even in theory on universal male suffrage, already existed in the 1870s in France, in Germany (at any rate for the all-German parliament), in Switzerland and in Denmark. In Britain the Reform Acts of 1867 and 1883 almost quadrupled the electorate, which rose from 8 to 29 per cent of men over the age of twenty. Belgium democratized her franchise in 1894, following a general strike for this reform (the increase was from 3.9 to 37.3 per cent of the adult male population), Norway doubled it in 1898 (from 16.6 to 34.8 per cent). In Finland a uniquely extensive democracy (76 per cent of adults) came in with the 1905 revolution; in Sweden the electorate was doubled in 1908 to bring it level with Norway; the Austrian half of the Habsburg Empire received universal suffrage in 1907, and Italy in 1913. Outside Europe the USA, Australia and New Zealand were, of course, already democratic, and Argentina became so in 1912. By later standards this democratization was still incomplete – the usual electorate under universal suffrage was between 30 and 40 per cent of the adult population – but it should be noted that even votes for women was already more than a utopian slogan. They had been introduced on the margins of white-settler territory in the 1890s – in Wyoming (USA), New Zealand and South Australia – and in democratic Finland and Norway between 1905 and 1913.

These developments were viewed without enthusiasm by the governments that introduced them, even when these were committed by ideological conviction to the representation of the people. Readers will already have observed, incidentally, how late even countries we now think of as profoundly and historically democratic, such as the Scandinavian ones, decided to broaden the vote; this is not to mention the Netherlands, which unlike Belgium resisted systematic democratization before 1918 (though their electorate did indeed grow at a comparable rate). Politicians might resign themselves to prophylactic extensions of the vote while they, rather than some extreme left, could still control it. This was probably the case in France and Britain. Among conservatives there were cynics like Bismarck. who had faith in the traditional loyalty – or, as liberals might have claimed, the ignorance and stupidity – of a mass electorate, calculating that universal suffrage would strengthen the right rather than the left. But even Bismarck preferred to run no risks in Prussia (which dominated the German Empire) where he maintained a three-class franchise strongly skewed in favour of the right. This precaution proved to be wise, for the mass electorate turned out to be uncontrollable from above. Elsewhere politicians yielded to popular agitation and pressure, or to the calculations of domestic political conflicts. In both cases they feared that the consequences of what Disraeli had called a 'leap in the dark' might be unpredictable. Certainly the socialist agitations of the 1890s, and the direct and indirect repercussions of the first Russian Revolution, accelerated democratization. Still, whatever the way in which democratization advanced, between 1880 and 1914 most western states had to resign themselves to the inevitable. Democratic politics could no longer be postponed. Henceforth the problem was how to manipulate them.

Manipulation in the crudest sense was still easy. One might, for instance, place strict limits on the political role of assemblies elected by universal suffrage. This was the Bismarckian model, in which the constitutional rights of the German parliament (Reichstag) were minimized. Elsewhere second chambers, sometimes composed of hereditary members as in Britain, voting by special (and weighted) electoral colleges and other analogous institutions put brakes on democratized representative assemblies. Elements of property suffrage were retained, reinforced by educational qualifications (e.g. additional votes for citizens with higher education in Belgium, Italy and the Netherlands, and special seats for universities in Britain). Japan introduced parliamentarism with such limitations in 1890. Such 'fancy franchises', as the British called them, were reinforced by the useful device of gerrymandering or what Austrians called 'electoral geometry' – the manipulation of constituency boundaries to minimize or maximize support for certain parties. Timid or simply cautious voters could be put under pressure by open ballots, especially where powerful landlords or other patrons watched over the scene: Denmark maintained open voting until 1901, Prussia until 1918, Hungary until the 1930s. Patronage, as American city bosses knew well, could deliver voting blocs: in Europe the Italian Liberal Giovanni Giolitti proved to be the master of clientelist politics. The minimum age for voting was elastic: it ranged from twenty in democratic Switzerland to thirty in Denmark, and was often raised somewhat when the right to vote was extended. And there was always the possibility of simple sabotage, by complicating the process of getting on to electoral registers. Thus in Britain it has been estimated that in 1914 about half the working class was *de facto* disenfranchised by such devices.

Nevertheless, such braking devices might slow the movements of the political vehicle towards democracy, but they could not stop its advance. The western world, including after 1905 even tsarist Russia, was plainly moving towards systems of politics based on an increasingly wide electorate dominated by the common people.

The logical consequence of such systems was the political mobilization of the masses for and through elections, that is to say for the purpose of putting pressure on national governments. This implied the organization of mass movements and mass parties, the politics of mass propaganda and the developing mass media – at this stage mainly the newly developing popular or 'yellow' press – and other developments which raised major and novel problems for governments and ruling classes. Unfortunately for the historian, these problems disappear from the scene of open political discussion in Europe, as the growing democratization made it impossible to debate them publicly with any degree of frankness. What candidate wanted to tell his voters that he considered them too stupid and ignorant to know what was best in politics, and that their demands were as absurd as they were dangerous to the future of the country? What statesman, surrounded by reporters carrying his words to the remotest corner tavern, would actually say what he meant? Increasingly politicians were obliged to appeal to a mass electorate; even to speak directly to the masses or indirectly through the megaphone of the popular press (including their opponents' papers). Bismarck had probably never addressed other than an elite audience. Gladstone introduced mass electioneering to Britain (and perhaps to Europe) in the campaign of 1879. No longer would the expected implications of democracy be discussed, except by political outsiders, with the frankness and realism of the debates which had surrounded the British Reform Act of 1867. But as the men who governed wrapped themselves in rhetoric, the serious discussion of politics retreated to the world of the intellectuals and the educated minority public which read them. The era of democratization was also the golden age of a new political sociology: of Durkheim and Sorel, Ostrogorski and the Webbs, Mosca, Pareto, Robert Michels and Max Weber (see pp. 273–4 below).[4]

When the men who governed really wanted to say what they meant, they had henceforth to do so in the obscurity of the corridors of power, the clubs, the private social evenings, the shooting parties or country-house weekends where the members of the elite met each other in a very different atmosphere from that of the gladiatorial comedies of parliamentary debates or public meetings. The age of democratization thus turned into the era of public political hypocrisy, or rather duplicity, and hence also into that of political satire: of Mr Dooley, of bitter, funny and enormously talented cartoon-journals like the German *Simplicissimus* and the French *Assiette au Beurre* or Karl Kraus' *Fackel* in Vienna. For what intelligent observer could overlook the yawning gap between public discourse and political reality, which Hilaire Belloc captured in his epigram of the great Liberal election triumph in 1906:

> The accursed power that rests on privilege
> And goes with women, and champagne, and bridge,
> Broke: and Democracy resumed her reign
> That goes with bridge, and women, and champagne.[5]

But who were the masses who now mobilized for political action? In the first place there were classes of social strata hitherto below and outside the political system, several of which might form rather more heterogeneous alliances, coalitions or 'popular fronts'. The most formidable of these was the working class, now mobilizing in parties and movements on an explicit class basis. These will be considered in the next chapter.

88

There was also that large and ill-defined coalition of discontented intermediate strata uncertain which they feared more, the rich or the proletariat. This was the old petty-bourgeoisie of master artisans and small shopkeepers, undermined by the progress of the capitalist economy, the rapidly increasing new lower-middle class of non-manual and white-collar workers: these constituted the *Handwerkerfrage* and the *Mittelstandsfrage* of German politics during and after the Great Depression. Theirs was a world defined by size, of 'little people' against the 'big' interests, and in which the very word 'little', as in 'the little man', '*le petit commerçant*', '*der kleine Mann*', became a slogan and a rallying call. How many radical–socialist journals in France did not proudly bear this title: *Le Petit Niçois, Le Petit Provençal, La Petite Charente, Le Petit Troyen*? Little, but not too little, for small property needed as much defence against collectivism as big property, and the superiority of the clerk needed to be defended against any confusion with the skilled manual worker, who might have a very similar income; especially as the established middle classes were disinclined to welcome the lower-middle classes as their equals.

This was also, and for good reasons, the political sphere of rhetoric and demagogy *par excellence*. In countries where the tradition of a radical, democratic jacobinism was strong, its rhetoric, strong or flowery, kept the 'little men' on the left, though in France this embodied a heavy dose of national chauvinism and a significant potential of xenophobia. In central Europe its nationalist and especially its anti-Semitic character was unconfined. For Jews could be identified not merely with capitalism, and especially the part of capitalism that impinged on small craftsmen and shopkeepers – bankers, dealers, founders of the new chains of distribution and department stores – but also often with godless socialists and, more generally, with intellectuals who undermined the old and threatened verities of morality and the patriarchal family. From the 1880s on, anti-Semitism became a major component of the organized political movements of 'little men' from the western frontiers of Germany eastwards into the Habsburg Empire, Russia and Rumania. Nor should its significance be under-estimated elsewhere. Who would suspect, from the anti-Semitic convulsions which shook France in the 1890s, the decade of the Panama scandals and the Dreyfus affair,* that there were at this period barely 60,000 Jews in that country of 40 million? (See pp. 158–9, 296 below.)

There was also, of course, the peasantry, which still formed the

---

* Captain Dreyfus of the French general staff was wrongly convicted for espionage on behalf of Germany in 1894. After a campaign to prove his innocence, which polarised and convulsed all France, he was pardoned in 1899 and eventually rehabilitated in 1906. The 'affair' had a traumatic impact throughout Europe.

majority in many countries, the largest economic group in others. Though peasants and farmers from the 1880s on – the era of depression – increasingly mobilized as economic pressure-groups, and indeed joined new organizations for co-operative purchasing, marketing, product processing and credit in impressive masses in countries as different as the USA and Denmark, New Zealand and France, Belgium and Ireland, the peasantry rarely mobilized politically and electorally as a class – assuming that so varied a body can be regarded as a class. Of course no government could afford to neglect the economic interests of so substantial a body of voters as the agricultural cultivators in agrarian countries. Still, insofar as the peasantry mobilized electorally, they did so under non-agricultural banners, even where it was clear that the force of a particular political movement or party, such as the Populists in the USA of the 1890s or the Social-Revolutionaries in Russia (after 1902), rested on the support of farmers or peasants.

If social groups mobilized as such, so did bodies of citizens united by sectional loyalties such as those of religion and nationality. Sectional, because political mass mobilizations on a confessional basis, even in countries of a single religion, were always blocs counterposed to other blocs, either confessional or secular. And nationalist electoral mobilzations (sometimes, as in the case of the Poles and Irish, coinciding with religious ones) were almost always autonomist movements within multinational states. They had little in common with the national patriotism inculcated by states – and sometimes escaping from their control – or with political movements, normally of the right, which claimed to represent 'the nation' against subversive minorities (see chapter 6 below).

However, the rise of politico-confessional mass movements as a general phenomenon was substantially hampered by the ultra-conservatism of the body with much the most formidable capacity to mobilize and organize its faithful, namely the Roman Catholic Church. Politics, parties, elections were part of that miserable nineteenth century which Rome had attempted to banish ever since the Syllabus of 1864 and the Vatican Council of 1870 (see *The Age of Capital*, chapter 14, III). It remained quite unreconciled to it, as witness the proscription of those Catholic thinkers who in the 1890s and 1900s cautiously suggested coming to some sort of terms with contemporary ideas ('Modernism' was condemned by Pope Pius X in 1907). What place could there be for Catholic politics in this infernal world of secular politics, except for total opposition and the specific defence of religious practice, Catholic education and such other institutions of the Church as were vulnerable to the state in its permanent conflict with the Church?

So, while the political potential of Christian parties was enormous, as European history since 1945 was to show,* and while it evidently increased with every extension of the vote, the Church resisted the formation of Catholic political parties formally backed by it, though recognizing, from the early 1890s, the desirability of wresting the working classes away from godless socialist revolution, and, of course, the need to look after its major constituency, the peasants. But, in spite of the Pope's blessing for the Catholics' new concern for social policy (in the Encyclical *Rerum Novarum*, 1891), the ancestors and founders of what were to become the Christian Democratic parties of the second post-war era were viewed with suspicion and periodic hostility by the Church, not only because they also, like 'Modernism', seemed to compromise with undesirable tendencies in the lay world, but also because the Church was ill at ease with the cadres from the new Catholic middle and lower-middle strata, urban and rural, of the expanding economies, who found a scope for action in them. When the great demagogue Karl Lueger (1844–1910) succeeded in the 1890s in founding the first major Christian Social modern mass party, a strongly anti-Semitic lower-middle-class movement which conquererd the city of Vienna, he did so against the resistance of the Austrian hierarchy. (It still survives as the People's Party, which governed independent Austria for most of her history since 1918.)

The Church thus usually backed conservative or reactionary parties of various kinds, or, in Catholic nations subordinate within multinational states, nationalist movements not infected with the secular virus, it kept on good terms with these. Against socialism and revolution, it usually backed anybody. Thus genuine Catholic mass parties and movements were to be found only in Germany (where they had come into being to resist Bismarck's anti-clerical campaigns of the 1870s), in the Netherlands (where all politics took the form of confessional groupings, including the Protestant and the non-religious, organized as vertical blocs, and Belgium (where Catholics and anti-clerical Liberals had formed the two-party system long before democratization).

Even rarer were Protestant religious parties, and where they existed confessional demands usually merged with other slogans: nationalism and liberalism (as in overwhelming by nonconformist Wales), anti-nationalism (as among the Ulster Protestants who opted for union with Britain against Irish Home Rule), liberalism (as in the British Liberal Party, where nonconformity became more powerful as the old Whig aristocrats and important big business interests defected to the Con-

---

* In Italy, France, West Germany and Austria they emerged as, and except for France have remained, major government parties.

servatives in the 1880s.* In eastern Europe, of course, religion in politics was politically indistinguishable from nationalism, including – in Russia – that of the state. The tsar was not merely the head of the Orthodox Church, but mobilized Orthodoxy against revolution. The other great world religions (Islam, Hinduism, Buddhism, Confucianism), not to mention the cults confined to particular communities and people, still operated in an ideological and political universe to which western democratic politics were unknown and irrelevant.

If religion had a vast political potential, national identification was an equally formidable and in practice a more effective mobilizer. When, after the democratization of the British franchise in 1884, Ireland voted for its representatives, the Irish nationalist party captured all Catholic seats in the island. Eighty-five out of 103 members formed a disciplined phalanx behind the (Protestant) leader of Irish nationalism, Charles Stewart Parnell (1846–91). Wherever national consciousness opted for political expression, it became evident that the Poles would vote as Poles (in Germany and Austria), the Czechs as Czechs. The politics of the Austrian half of the Habsburg Empire were paralysed by such national divisions. Indeed, after the riots and counter-riots of Germans and Czechs in the mid-1890s, parliamentarianism broke down completely, since no parliamentary majority was henceforth possible for any government. The grant of universal suffrage in 1907 was not only a concession to pressure, but a desperate attempt to mobilize electoral masses who might vote for non-national parties (Catholic or even socialist) against irreconcilable and squabbling national blocs.

In its extreme form – the disciplined mass party-cum-movement – political mass mobilization remained uncommon. Even among the new labour and socialist movements the monolithic, all-embracing pattern of German Social Democracy was by no means universal (see next chapter). Nevertheless, the elements constituting this new phenomenon could now be discerned almost everywhere. They were, first, the constituent organizations which formed its base. The ideal-typical mass party-cum-movement consisted of a complex of local organizations or branches together with a complex of organizations, each also with local branches, for special purposes, but integrated into a party with wider political objectives. Thus in 1914 the Irish national movement consisted of the United Irish League, which formed its national framework, organized electorally – i.e. in each parliamentary constituency. It organized the electoral congresses, chaired by the president (chairman) of the League and attended not only by its own delegates but also by

* Nonconformity = the dissenting Protestant groups outside the Church of England in England and Wales.

those of the trades councils (city consortia of trade union branches), of the unions themselves, of the Land and Labour Association which represented farmers' interests, of the Gaelic Athletic Association, of mutual aid associations like the Ancient Order of Hibernians, which incidentally linked the island to the American emigration, and of other bodies. This was the cadre of the mobilized which formed the essential link between the nationalist leadership in and out of Parliament, and the mass electorate which defined the outer boundaries of those who supported the cause of Irish autonomy. The activists thus organized could themselves be a very substantial mass: in 1913 the League had 130,000 members out of a total Irish Catholic population of 3 million.[6]

In the second place the new mass movements were ideological. They were more than simple groupings for pressure and action in favour of particular objects, such as the defence of viticulture. Such organized specific-interest groups naturally also multiplied, since the logic of democratized politics required interests to exert pressure on national governments and assemblies in theory sensitive to it. But bodies like the German *Bund der Landwirte* (founded 1893 and almost immediately – 1894 – joined by 200,000 agriculturalists) were not linked to a party, in spite of the Bund's obvious conservative sympathies and its almost total domination by the large landowners. In 1898 it relied on the support of 118 (out of 397) Reichstag deputies who belonged to five distinct parties.[7] Unlike such special-interest groups, however powerful, the new party-cum-movement represented a total vision of the world. It was this, rather than the specific and perhaps changing concrete political programme, that, for its members and supporters, formed something like that 'civic religion' which, for Jean-Jacques Rousseau and for Durkheim and other theorists in the new field of sociology, ought to bind together modern societies: only in this instance it formed a sectional cement. Religion, nationalism, democracy, socialism, the precursor ideologies of inter-war fascism: these held together the newly mobilized masses, whatever material interests their movements also represented.

Paradoxically, in countries of strong revolutionary tradition such as France, the USA and rather more remotely England, the ideology of their own past revolutions allowed old or new elites to domesticate at least part of the new mass mobilization, by strategies long familiar to Fourth of July orators in democratic North America. British Liberalism, which was heir to the Glorious Whig Revolution of 1688 and which did not overlook the occasional appeal to the regicides of 1649 for the benefit of the descendants of the Puritan sects,* succeeded in holding

---

* The Liberal premier Lord Rosebery personally paid for the statue to Oliver Cromwell erected in front of Parliament in 1899.

up the development of a mass Labour Party until after 1914. Moreover the Labour Party (founded 1900), such as it was, sailed in the wake of the Liberals. Republican radicalism in France tried to absorb and assimilate popular mass mobilizations by brandishing the banner of Republic and Revolution against its enemies. And not without success. The slogans 'no enemies on the left' and 'unity of all good Republicans' did much to bind the new popular left to the men of the centre who ran the Third Republic.

In the third place, it follows that the mass mobilizations were, in their way, global. They either shattered the old localized or regional framework of politics, or pushed it to the margin, or integrated it into wider comprehensive movements. In any case national politics in democratized countries left less scope for purely regional parties, even in states with as strongly marked regional differences as Germany and Italy. Thus in Germany the regional character of Hanover (annexed by Prussia as recently as 1866), where anti-Prussian feeling and loyalty to the old Guelph dynasty were still marked, showed itself only by giving a marginally smaller percentage of its vote (85 per cent as against 94–100 per cent elsewhere) to the various nationwide parties.[8] That confessional or ethnic minorities, or for that matter social and economic groups, were sometimes limited to particular geographical areas should not mislead us. In contrast to the electoral politics of the older bourgeois society, the new mass politics were increasingly incompatible with the old localized politics based on the men of local power and influence, known (in the French political vocabulary) as 'notables'. There were still many parts of Europe and the Americas – especially in such areas as the Iberian and Balkan peninsulas, in southern Italy and in Latin America – where *caciques* or patrons, persons of local power and influence, could 'deliver' blocs of client votes to the highest bidder or to even greater patrons. The 'boss' did not even disappear in democratic politics, but there, increasingly, it was the party which made the notable, or at least which saved him from isolation and political impotence, rather than the other way round. Older elites transforming themselves to fit in with democracy might well develop various combinations between the politics of local patronage and influence and those of democracy. And, indeed, the last decades of the old century and the first of the new were filled with complex conflicts between old-style 'notability' and the new political operators, local bosses or other key elements controlling the local party fortunes.

The democracy which thus replaced the politics of notables – insofar as it had already succeeded in doing so – did not substitute 'the people' for patronage and influence, but the organization: that is to say the committees, the party notables, the activist minorities. This paradox was soon noted by realistic observers of politics, who pointed to the crucial role of such committees (or caucuses, in the Anglo-American term) or even to the 'iron law of oligarchy' which Robert Michels believed he could derive from his study of the German Social Democratic Party. Michels also noted the tendency for the new mass movements to venerate leader-figures, though he made too much of it.[9] For the admiration which undoubtedly tended to surround some leaders of national mass movements, and which was embodied on many a modest wall in portraits of Gladstone, the Grand Old Man of Liberalism, or of Bebel, the leader of German social democracy, in our period reflected the cause which united the faithful rather than the man himself. Moreover, there were enough mass movements without charismatic chiefs. When Charles Stewart Parnell fell, in 1891, victim of the complications of his private life and the joint hostility of Catholic and nonconformist morality, the Irish abandoned him without hesitation – and yet no leader aroused more passionate personal loyalties than he, and the Parnell myth long survived the man.

In short, for its supporters the party or movement represented them and acted on their behalf. Thus it was easy for the organization to take the place of its members and supporters, and in turn for its leaders to dominate the organization. Structured mass movements were thus by no means republics of equals. But their combination of organization and mass support gave them an enormous and barely suspected capacity: they were potential states. Indeed, the major revolutions of our century were to replace old regimes, old states and old ruling classes by parties-cum-movements institutionalized as systems of state power. This potential is all the more impressive, since older ideological organizations appeared to lack it. In the west religion, for instance, in this period seemed to have lost the capacity for transforming itself into theocracy, and certainly did not aim to do so.* What victorious Churches established, at least in the Christian world, was clerical regimes operated by secular institutions.

II

Democratization, though advancing, had barely begun to transform politics. Yet its implications, already sometimes explicit, raised the most serious problems for those who governed states and for the classes in whose interests they governed. There was the problem of maintaining the unity, even the existence, of states, which was already urgent in

* The last example of such a transformation is probably the establishment of the Mormon commonwealth in Utah after 1848.

multinational politics confronted with national movements. In the Austrian Empire it was already the central problem of the state, and even in Britain the emergence of mass Irish nationalism shattered the structure of established politics. There were the problems of how to maintain the continuity of sensible policies, as seen by the elites of the country – above all in economic affairs. Would not democracy inevitably interfere with the operations of capitalism, and – as businessmen considered – for the worse? Would it not threaten free trade in Britain, to which all parties were religiously attached? Would it not threaten sound finance and the gold standard, keystone of all respectable economic policy? This last threat seemed urgent in the USA, as the mass mobilization of Populism in the 1890s, which directed its most passionate rhetorical thunderbolts against – to quote its great orator William Jennings Bryan – the crucifixion of mankind on a cross of gold? More generally, and above all, there was the problem of guaranteeing the legitimacy, perhaps the very survival, of society as then constituted, when it faced the menace of mass movements for social revolution. These threats seemed all the more dangerous because of the undeniable inefficiency of parliaments elected by demagogy and riven by irreconcilable party conflicts, and the undoubted corruption of political systems which no longer rested on men of independent wealth, but increasingly on men whose careers and wealth were based on their success in the new politics.

Both these phenomena were impossible to overlook. In democratic states with divided powers, like the USA, government (i.e. the executive branch represented by the presidency) was in some degree independent of the elected parliament, though quite likely to be paralysed by its counterweight. (But the democratic election of presidents introduced another danger.) In the European pattern of representative government, where governments, unless still protected by old-style monarchy, were in theory dependent on elected assemblies, their problems seemed insuperable. In fact, they often came and went like tourist parties in hotels, as one brief parliamentary majority broke down and was succeeded by another. France, mother of European democracies, probably held the record with fifty-two cabinets in the less than thirty-nine years between 1875 and the outbreak of war, of which only eleven lasted twelve months or more. Admittedly, the same names tended to reappear in most of them. Small wonder that the effective continuity of government and policy was in the hands of the permanent, nonelected and invisible functionaries of the bureaucracy. As for corruption, it was probably no greater than in the early nineteenth century, when governments such as the British had shared out the correctly named 'offices of profit under the *Crown*' and lucrative sinecures among their kinsmen and dependants. Yet even when it was not, it was more visible, as self-made politicians cashed in, in one way or another, on the value of their support or opposition to businessmen or other interested parties. It was all the more visible, since the incorruptibility of permanent senior public administrators and judges, now mostly protected, in constitutional countries, against the twin hazards of election and patronage – with the major exception of the USA* – was now generally taken for granted, at least in western and central Europe. Political corruption scandals occurred not only in countries where the sound of money changing hands was not muffled, like France (the Wilson scandal of 1885, the Panama scandal in 1892–3), but even where it was, as in Britain (the Marconi scandal of 1913, in which two such self-made men, Lloyd George and Rufus Isaacs, later Lord Chief Justice and Viceroy of India, were involved).† Parliamentary instability and corruption could, of course, be linked where governments built majorities essentially on what was in effect the buying of votes for political favours which almost inevitably had a financial dimension. As already noted, Giovanni Giolitti in Italy was the master of this strategy.

Contemporaries from the upper ranks of society were acutely aware of the dangers of democratized politics and, more generally, of the growing centrality of 'the masses'. This was not merely a worry of men in public affairs, like the editor of Le Temps and La Revue des Deux Mondes – fortresses of French respectable opinion – who in 1897 published a book characteristically entitled The Organisation of Universal Suffrage: The Crisis of the Modern State,[11] or the thinking Conservative's proconsul and later minister Alfred Milner (1854–1925), who in 1902 called the British Parliament (privately) 'that mob at Westminster'.[12] Much of the pervasive pessimism of bourgeois culture from the 1880s on (see pp. 226, 258–9 below) undoubtedly reflected the sense of leaders abandoned by their former followers of elites whose defences against the masses were crumbling, of the educated and cultured minority (i.e. primarily the children of the well-to-do) invaded by 'those just being emancipated from ... illiteracy or semi-barbarism',[13] or cut off by the rising tide of a civilization geared to these masses.

The new political situation developed only by steps, and unevenly,

* And even here a Civil Service Commission was set up in 1883 to lay the foundations of a Federal Civil Service independent of political patronage. But patronage remained more important in most countries than is conventionally supposed.

† Transactions within a cohesive ruling elite, which would have raised eyebrows among democratic observers and political moralists, were not unusual. At his death in 1895 Lord Randolph Churchill, father of Winston, who had been Chancellor of the Exchequer, owed some £60,000 to Rothschild, who might have been expected to have an interest in the national finances. The size of this debt in our terms is indicated by the fact that this single sum amounted to about 0.4 per cent of the *total* yield of the income tax in Britain in that year.[10]

depending on the domestic history of the various states. This makes a comparative survey of politics in the 1870s and 1880s difficult, and almost pointless. It was the sudden international emergence of mass labour and socialist movements in and after the 1880s (see next chapter) which seemed to place numerous governments and ruling classes in essentially similar predicaments, though we can see retrospectively that they were not the only mass movements which caused governmental headaches. Broadly speaking, in most of the European states of limited constitutions or restricted franchise, the mid-century political predominance of the liberal bourgeoisie (see *The Age of Capital*, chapters 6, I, 13, III) broke down in the course of the 1870s, if not for other reasons, then as a by-product of the Great Depression: in Belgium in 1870, in Germany and Austria in 1879, in Italy in the 1870s, in Britain in 1874. Except for episodic returns to power, they never dominated again. No equally clear political pattern emerged in Europe in the new period, though in the USA the Republican Party, that had led the North to victory in the Civil War, usually continued to win the presidency until 1913. Insofar as insoluble problems or basic challenges of revolution or secession could be kept out of parliamentary politics, statesmen could juggle parliamentary majorities with shifting collections of those who wished to threaten neither state nor the social order. And in most cases they could be kept out, though in Britain the sudden emergence in the 1880s of a solid and militant bloc of Irish nationalists, willing to disrupt the House of Commons and in a position to hold the balance in it, immediately transformed parliamentary politics, and the two parties which had conducted their decorous *pas-de-deux*. Or, at least, it precipitated in 1886 the rush of formerly Whig millionaire noblemen and Liberal businessmen into the Tory Party, which, as the Conservative and Unionist Party (i.e. opposed to Irish autonomy), increasingly developed into the united party of both landed wealth and big business.

Elsewhere the situation, though apparently more dramatic, was actually more manageable. In the restored monarchy of Spain (1874) the fragmentation of the defeated opponents of the system – Republicans on the left, Carlists on the right – enabled Cánovas (1828–97), in power for most of the period 1874–97, to manipulate the politicians and an a-political rural vote. In Germany the weakness of the irreconcilable elements enabled Bismarck to manage well enough in the 1880s, and the moderation of the respectable Slav parties in the Austrian Empire likewise benefited the elegant aristocratic boulevardier Count Taaffe (1833–95, in office 1879–93). The French right, which refused to accept the republic, was a permanent electoral minority, and the army did not challenge civilian authority: hence the republic survived the numerous and colourful crises which shook it (in 1877, in 1885–7, in 1892–3 and in the Dreyfus affair of 1894–1900). In Italy the Vatican's boycott of a secular and anti-clerical state made it easy for Depretis (1813–87) to conduct his policy of 'transformism', i.e. turning opponents into supporters of government.

In truth, the only real challenge to the system were extra-parliamentary – and insurrection from below did not, for the moment, need to be taken seriously in constitutional countries, while armies, even in Spain, the classic territory of *pronunciamentos*, kept quiet. And where, as in the Balkans and Latin America, both insurrection and armed men in politics remained familiar parts of the scenery, they were so as parts of the system, rather than as potential challenges to it.

Yet this situation was unlikely to last. And when governments found themselves confronting the rise of apparently irreconcilable forces in politics, their first instinct, more often than not, was to coerce. Bismarck, the master of manipulating the politics of a limited franchise, was at a loss in the 1870s when facing what he regarded as an organized mass of Catholics owing loyalty to a reactionary Vatican 'beyond the mountains' (hence the term 'ultramontane'), and declared anti-clerical war against them (the so-called *Kulturkampf* or cultural struggle of the 1870s). Faced with the rise of the Social Democrats, he outlawed the party in 1879. Since a return to straightforward absolutism appeared impossible, and indeed unthinkable – the banned Social Democrats were allowed to put up electoral candidates – he failed in both cases. Sooner or later – in the case of the socialists, after his fall in 1889 – governments had to live with the new mass movements. The Austrian emperor, whose capital was captured by the demagogy of the Social Christians, refused three times to accept their leader, Lueger, as mayor of Vienna, before resigning himself to the inevitable in 1897. In 1886 the Belgian government suppressed with military force the wave of strikes and riots by Belgian workers – among the most miserable in western Europe – and gaoled socialist leaders, whether they were involved in the disturbances or not. Yet seven years later it conceded a sort of universal suffrage after an effective general strike. Italian governments shot down Sicilian peasants in 1893 and Milanese workers in 1898. Yet after the fifty corpses of Milan, they changed course. Broadly speaking, the 1890s, the decade of the emergence of socialism as a mass movement, mark the turning-point. An era of new political strategies began.

Generations of readers who have grown up since the First World War may find it surprising that no government seriously envisaged the abandonment of constitutional and parliamentary systems at this time. For *after* 1918 liberal constitutionalism and representative democracy were indeed to retreat on a broad front, though partly restored after 1945. In our period this was not the case. Even in tsarist Russia the defeat of the 1905 revolution did not lead to the total abolition of elections and parliament (the Duma). Unlike 1849 (see *The Age of Capital*, chapter 1), there was no simple return to reaction, even if at the end of his period of power Bismarck played with the idea of suspending or abolishing the constitution. Bourgeois society may have been uneasy about where it was going, but it was confident enough, and not least because the worldwide economic surge forward hardly encouraged pessimism. Even politically moderate opinion (unless it had diplomatic or financial interests to the contrary) looked forward to a Russian revolution, which was generally expected to turn a blot on European civilization into a decent bourgeois–liberal state, and indeed within Russia the 1905 revolution, unlike that of October 1917, was enthusiastically supported by middle classes and intellectuals. Other insurrectionaries were insignificant. Governments remained remarkably cool during the anarchist epidemic of assassinations in the 1890s, to which two monarchs, two presidents and one prime minister fell victim,* and after 1900 nobody seriously bothered about anarchism outside Spain and parts of Latin America. At the outbreak of war in 1914 the French Minister of the Interior did not even bother to arrest the (mainly anarchist and anarcho-syndicalist) revolutionaries and anti-militarist subversives regarded as dangers to the state, of whom his police had long compiled a list for just such a purpose.

But if (unlike the decades after 1917) bourgeois society as a whole did not feel seriously and immediately threatened, neither had its nineteenth-century values and historic expectations been seriously undermined as yet. Civilized behaviour, the rule of law and liberal institutions were still expected to continue their secular progress. There was plenty of barbarism left, especially (so the 'respectable' were convinced) among the lower orders and of course among the now fortunately colonized 'uncivilized' peoples. There were still states, even in Europe, such as the Tsarist and Ottoman empires, where the candles of reason flickered dimly or were unlit. Yet the very scandals which convulsed national or international opinion indicate how high expectations of civility were in the bourgeois world in times of peace: Dreyfus (refusal to enquire into a single miscarriage of justice), Ferrer in 1909 (the execution of one Spanish educationalist wrongly accused of leading a wave of riots in Barcelona), Zabern in 1913 (twenty demonstrators locked up for a night by the German army in an Alsatian town). From

---

* King Umberto of Italy, the Empress Elizabeth of Austria, Presidents Sadi Carnot of France and McKinley of the USA, and Premier Cánovas of Spain.

the late twentieth century we can only look back with melancholy incredulity upon a period when massacres such as occur almost daily in the world today were believed to be a monopoly of Turks and tribesmen.

III

The ruling classes therefore opted for the new strategies, even as they did their best to limit the impact of mass opinion and mass electorates on their own and state interests, and on the formation and continuity of high policy. Their major target was the labour and socialist movement which suddenly emerged internationally as a mass phenomenon around 1890 (see next chapter). As it turned out, it was to prove easier to come to terms with than the nationalist movements which emerged in this period, or, which if already on the scene, entered a new phase of militancy, autonomism or separatism (see chapter 6 below). As for the Catholics, they were, unless identified with some autonomist nationalism, relatively easy to integrate, since they were socially conservative – this was so even in the case of the rare Social Christian parties such as Lueger's – and usually content with the safeguarding of specific Church interests.

Bringing labour movements into the institutionalized game of politics was difficult, insofar as employers, faced with strikes and unions, were distinctly slower than politicians to abandon the policy of the strong fist for that of the velvet glove, even in pacific Scandinavia. The growing power of big business was particularly recalcitrant. In most countries, notably in the USA and Germany, employers as a class were never reconciled to unions before 1914, and even in Britain, where they had long been accepted in principle, and often in practice, the 1890s saw a counter-offensive of employers against unions, even as government administrators pursued policies of conciliation and the Liberal Party leaders did what they could to reassure and captivate the labour vote. It was also difficult politically, where the new parties of labour refused all compromise with the bourgeois state and system nationally – they were rarely as intransigent in the field of local government – as those adhering to the Marxist-dominated International of 1889 tended to do. (Non-revolutionary or non-Marxist labour politics raised no such problem.) But by 1900 it had become clear that a moderate or reformist wing had emerged in all the socialist mass movements; indeed, even among the Marxists it had found its ideologue in Eduard Bernstein, who argued that 'the movement was everything, the final aim nothing', and whose tactless demand for a revision of Marxist theory caused scandal, outrage and impassioned debate in the socialist world after 1897. Meanwhile, the politics of mass electoralism, of which even the most Marxist parties were enthusiastic champions, since it allowed their armies to grow with maximum visibility, could not but quietly integrate these parties into the system.

Socialists could certainly not yet be brought into governments. They could not even be expected to tolerate 'reactionary' politicians and governments. Yet a policy of bringing at least the moderate representatives of labour into broader alignments in favour of reform, the union of all democrats, republicans, anti-clericals or 'men of the people', especially against mobilized enemies of these good causes, had good chances of success. It was systematically pursued in France from 1899 under Waldeck Rousseau (1846–1904), architect of a government of republican union against the enemies who were so clearly challenging it in the Dreyfus affair; in Italy by Zanardelli, whose 1903 government relied on support from the extreme left, and later by Giolitti, the great fudger and conciliator. In Britain – after some difficulties in the 1890s – the Liberals in 1903 made an electoral pact with the young Labour Representation Committee which enabled it to enter Parliament in some force in 1906 as the Labour Party. Elsewhere a common interest in widening the suffrage drew together socialists and other democrats, as in Denmark, where in 1901 – for the first time anywhere in Europe – a government counted and could rely on the support of a socialist party.

The reason for these overtures from the parliamentary centre to the extreme left was usually not the need for socialist support, for even large socialist parties were minority groups which in most cases could easily have been frozen out of the parliamentary game, as communist parties of comparable size were in Europe after the Second World War. German governments kept the most formidable of all such parties in the cold by a so-called *Sammlungspolitik* (politics of broad union), i.e. by assembling majorities from the guaranteed anti-socialist conservatives, Catholics, and liberals. It was rather the desire to exploit the possibilities of domesticating these wild beasts of the political forest, which sensible men in the ruling classes soon discerned. The strategy of the soft embrace had varying results, and the intransigence of employers given to coercion and provoking mass industrial confrontations did not make it any easier, but on the whole it worked, at least inasmuch as it succeeded in splitting mass labour movements into a moderate and a radical wing of irreconcilables – generally a minority – and isolating the latter.

However, democracy would be the more easily tameable, the less acute its discontents. The new strategy thus implied a readiness to venture into programmes of social reform and welfare, which undermined the classic mid-century liberal commitment to governments which kept out of the field reserved for private enterprise and self-help. The British jurist, A. V. Dicey (1835–1922), saw the steamroller of collectivism, which had been in motion since 1870, flattening the landscape of individual liberty into the centralized and levelling tyranny of school meals, health insurance and old age pensions. And in a sense he was right. Bismarck, logical as always, had already decided in the 1880s to cut the ground from under socialist agitation by an ambitious scheme of social insurance, and he was to be followed on this road by Austria and the British Liberal governments of 1906–14 (old age pensions, public labour exchanges, health and unemployment insurance), and even, after several hesitations, France (old age pensions, 1911). Curiously enough, the Scandinavian countries, now the 'welfare states' *par excellence*, were slow off the mark and several countries made only nominal gestures in this direction, the USA of Carnegie, Rockefeller and Morgan none at all. In that paradise of free enterprise even child labour remained uncontrolled by federal law, though by 1914 laws nominally prohibiting it (in theory) existed even in Italy, Greece and Bulgaria. Workmen's compensation laws for accidents, generally available by 1905, were of no interest to Congress and were condemned as unconstitutional by the courts. With the exception of Germany such social welfare schemes were modest until the last years before 1914, and even in Germany they visibly failed to halt the growth of the socialist party. Nevertheless, the trend, notably faster in the Protestant countries of Europe and in Australasia than elsewhere, was established.

Dicey was also right in stressing the inevitable growth in the role and weight of the state apparatus, once the ideal of state non-intervention was abandoned. By modern standards bureaucracy remained modest, though it grew at a rapid rate – nowhere more so than Great Britain, where government employment tripled between 1891 and 1911. In Europe, around 1914, it ranged from a low of about 3 per cent of the labour force in France – a somewhat surprising fact – to a high of 5.5–6 per cent in Germany and – an equally surprising fact – Switzerland.[14] For comparison, in the EEC countries of the 1970s it formed between 10 and 13 per cent of the occupied population.

But could not the loyalties of the masses be acquired without expensive social policies which might cut into the profits of entrepreneurs on whom the economy depended? As we have seen, it was believed not only that imperialism could pay for social reform but that it was also popular. As it turned out, war, or at least the prospects of successful war, had an even greater built-in demagogic potential. The British Conservative government used the South African War (1899–1902) to sweep away its Liberal opponents in the 'Khaki election' of 1900, and

American imperialism mobilized the popularity of guns successfully for war against Spain in 1898. Indeed the ruling elites of the USA, headed by Theodore Roosevelt (1858–1919, President in 1901–9), had just discovered the gun-toting cowboy as symbol of true Americanism, freedom and native white tradition against the invading hordes of low-class immigrants and the uncontrollable big city. That symbol has been extensively exploited ever since.

However, the problem was wider than this. Could the regimes of states and ruling classes be given a new legitimacy in the minds of democratically mobilized masses? Much of the history of our period consists of attempts to answer this question. The task was urgent, because the ancient mechanisms of social subordination were often clearly breaking down. Thus the German Conservatives – essentially the party of electors loyal to the large landed proprietors and nobles – lost half of their share of the total vote between 1881 and 1912, for the simple reason that 71 per cent of their vote came from villages of less than 2000 inhabitants, which housed a declining share of the population, and only 5 per cent from big cities over 100,000, into which Germans were pouring. The old loyalties might still work on the estates of the Pomeranian *junkers** where the Conservatives held on to almost half the vote, but even in Prussia as a whole they could only mobilize 11–12 per cent of electors.[15] The situation of that other master-class, the liberal bourgeoisie, was even more dramatic. It had triumphed by shattering the social cohesion of ancient hierarchies and communities, by choosing the market against human relations, *Gesellschaft* against *Gemeinschaft* – and when the masses entered the political stage pursuing their own concerns, they were hostile to all that bourgeois liberalism stood for. Nowhere was this more obvious than in Austria, where the Liberals by the end of the century were reduced to a small isolated rump of city-dwelling comfortable middle-class Germans and German Jews. The municipality of Vienna, their fortress in the 1860s, was lost to radical democrats, anti-Semites, the new Christian Social party and eventually the Social Democrats. Even in Prague, where this bourgeois nucleus could claim to represent the interests of the small and diminishing German-speaking minority of all classes (some 30,000, and by 1910 a mere 7 per cent of the population), they could hold the loyalties neither of the German-nationalist (*völkisch*) students and petty-bourgeoisie, nor of the Social Democratic or politically passive German workers, nor even of a proportion of the Jews.[16]

And what of the state itself, normally still represented by monarchs? It might be quite new, and lacking all relevant historical precedent as

* Pomerania, an area along the Baltic north-east of Berlin, is now part of Poland.

in Italy and the new German Empire, not to mention Rumania and Bulgaria. Its regimes might be the product of recent defeat, revolution and civil war as in France, Spain and for that matter post-Civil War USA, not to mention the ever-changing regimes of Latin American republics. In old-established monarchies – even in the Britain of the 1870s – republican agitations were, or appeared to be, far from negligible. National agitations gathered strength. Could the state's claim on the loyalty of all its subjects or citizens be taken for granted?

This was consequently the moment when governments, intellectuals and businessmen discovered the political significance of irrationality. Intellectuals wrote, but governments acted. 'Whoever sets himself to base his political thinking on a re-examination of the working of human nature, must begin by trying to overcome his own tendency to exaggerate the intellectuality of mankind': thus wrote the British political scientist Graham Wallas in 1908, conscious that he was also writing the epitaph of nineteenth-century liberalism.[17] Political life thus found itself increasingly ritualized and filled with symbols and publicity appeals, both overt and subliminal. As the ancient ways – mainly religious – of ensuring subordination, obedience and loyalty were eroded, the now patent need for something to replace them was met by the *invention* of tradition, using both old and tried evokers of emotion such as crown and military glory and, as we have seen (see previous chapter), new ones such as empire and colonial conquest.

Like horticulture, this development was a mixture of planting from above and growth – or at any rate readiness for planting – from below. Governments and ruling elites certainly knew what they were doing when they instituted new national festivals, like the Fourteenth of July in France (in 1880), or developed the ritualization of the British monarchy which has become increasingly hieratic and byzantine since it began in the 1880s.[18] Indeed, the standard commentator of the British constitution, after the franchise extension of 1867, distinguished lucidly between the 'efficient' parts of it by which government was actually carried on and the 'dignified' parts whose function was to keep the masses happy while they were being governed.[19] The masses of marble and towering masonry with which states anxious to confirm their legitimacy – notably the new German Empire – filled their open spaces had to be planned by authority, and were so planned, to the financial rather than artistic benefit of numerous architects and sculptors. British coronations were now, quite consciously, organized as politico-ideological operations for the attention of the masses.

Yet they did not create the demand for emotionally satisfying ritual and symbolism. They rather discovered and filled a void left by the political rationalism of the liberal era, by the new need to address the masses and by the transformation of these masses themselves. In this respect the invention of traditions ran parallel to the commercial discovery of the mass market and of mass spectacle and entertainment, which belongs to the same decades. The advertising industry, though pioneered in the USA after the Civil War, for the first time came into its own. The modern poster was born in the 1880s and 1890s. A common frame of social psychology (the psychology of 'the crowd' became a flourishing topic for both French professors and American advertising gurus) bound together the annual Royal Tournament (initiated in 1880), a public display of the glory and drama of the British armed forces, and the illuminations on the seafront of Blackpool, playground of the new proletarian holiday-makers; Queen Victoria and the Kodak girl (product of the 1900s), the Emperor William's monuments to Hohenzollern rulers and Toulouse-Lautrec's posters for famous variety artists.

Official initiatives naturally succeeded best where they exploited and manipulated spontaneous and undefined grassroots emotion, or integrated themes from unofficial mass politics. The Fourteenth of July in France established itself as a genuine national day because it mobilized both the people's attachment to the Great Revolution and the demand for an institutionalized carnival.[20] The German government, countless tons of marble and masonry to the contrary, failed to establish the Emperor William I as father of the nation, but cashed in on the unofficial nationalist enthusiasm which erected 'Bismark columns' by the hundred after the death of the great statesman, whom the Emperor William II (reigned 1888–1918) had sacked. Conversely, unofficial nationalism was welded to the 'Little Germany' it had so long opposed, by military might and global ambition: as witness the triumph of 'Deutschland Uber Alles' over more modest national anthems, and of the new Prusso-German black-white-red flag over the old black-red-gold of 1848 – both of which triumphs occurred in the 1890s.[21]

Political regimes thus conducted a silent war for the control of the symbols and rites of belonging to the human race within their frontiers, not least through their control of the public school system (especially the primary schools, the essential basis in democracies for 'educating our masters'* in the 'right' spirit) and, generally where the Churches were politically unreliable, through the attempt to control the great ceremonies of birth, marriage and death. Of all such symbols, perhaps the most powerful were music, in its political forms of the national anthem and the military march – both played for all they were worth

* The phrase is that of Robert Lowe in 1867.[22]

in this age of J. P. Sousa (1854–1932) and Edward Elgar (1857–1934)† – and above all the national flag. In the absence of monarchies, the flag itself could become the virtual embodiment of state, nation and society, as in the USA where the practice of worshipping the flag as a daily ritual in the country's schools spread from the end of the 1880s until it became universal.[24]

Lucky the regime which could rely on mobilizing universally acceptable symbols, such as the British monarch, who even began his annual appearance at that festival of the proletariat, the football Cup Final, thus underlining the convergence between mass public ritual and mass spectacle. In this period, both public and political ceremonial spaces, for instance around the new German national monuments, and the new sports halls and stadia, which could also double as political areas, began to multiply. Elderly readers may recall speeches by Hitler in Berlin's Sportspalast (sport palace). Lucky the regime which could at least associate itself with some great cause for which there was mass grassroots support, like revolution and republic in France and the USA.

For states and governments competed for symbols of togetherness and emotional loyalty with the unofficial mass movements, which might devise their own counter-symbols such as the socialist 'Internationale', when the former anthem of revolution, the 'Marseillaise', had been taken over by the state.[25] Though the German and Austrian socialist parties are usually cited as the extreme examples of such separate communities, counter-societies and counter-culture (see next chapter), they were in fact only incompletely separatist since they remained linked to official culture by their faith in education (i.e. the public school system), in reason and science, and in the values of the (bourgeois) arts – the 'classics'. They were, after all, the heirs of the Enlightenment. It was religious and nationalist movements which rivalled the state by setting up rival school systems on linguistic or confessional bases. Still, all mass movements tended, as we have seen in the Irish case, to form a complex of associations and counter-communities around centres of loyalty which rivalled the state.

IV

Did the political societies and ruling classes of western Europe succeed in managing these potentially or actually subversive mass mobilizations? On the whole, in the period up to 1914, they did, except in Austria, that conglomerate of nationalities all of whom looked elsewhere

† Between 1890 and 1910 there were more musical settings of the British national anthem than ever before or since.[23]

for their future prospects, and which was now held together only by the longevity of her ancient emperor Francis Joseph (reigned 1848–1916), by the administration of a sceptical and rationalist bureaucracy, and by being less undesirable than any alternative fate for a number of the national groups. By and large, they let themselves be integrated into the system. For most states of the bourgeois and capitalist west – the situation in other parts of the world was, as we shall see, very different (see chapter 12 below) – the period from 1875 and 1914, and certainly from 1900 to 1914, was, in spite of alarums and excursions, one of political stability.

ovements rejecting the system, like socialism, were caught in its web, or else – if sufficiently powerless – they could even be used as catalysts of a majority consensus. This was the function of 'reaction' in the French Republic perhaps, of anti-socialism in imperial Germany: nothing united as much as a common enemy. Even nationalism could sometimes be managed. Welsh nationalism served to strengthen Liberalism, its champion Lloyd George becoming government minister and chief demagogic container and conciliator of democratic radicalism and labour. Irish nationalism, after the dramas of 1879–91, appeared to have been tranquillized by agrarian reform and political dependence on British Liberalism. Pan-German extremism was reconciled to 'Little Germany' by the militarism and imperialism of William's empire. Even the Flemings in Belgium still remained within the fold of the Catholic party, which did not challenge the existence of the unitary bi-national state. The irreconcilables of the ultra-right and the ultra-left could be isolated. The great socialist movements announced the inevitable revolution, but they had other things with which to occupy themselves at present. When war broke out in 1914 most of them joined their governments and ruling classes in patriotic union. The major west European exception actually proves the rule. For the British Independent Labour Party, which continued to oppose the war, did so because it shared the long pacific tradition of Britain nonconformity and bourgeois Liberalism – which actually made Britain the *only* country from whose cabinet in August 1914 Liberal ministers resigned from such motives.*

The socialist parties which accepted the war often did so without enthusiasm, and chiefly because they feared to be abandoned by their followers, who flocked to the colours with spontaneous zeal. In Britain, which had no conscription, 2 millions were to volunteer for military service between August 1914 and June 1915, melancholy proof of the success of the politics of integrating democracy. Only where the effort

---

* John Morley, biographer of Gladstone and John Burns, former labour leader.

to make the poor citizen identify with nation and state had hardly begun to be seriously pursued, as in Italy, or where it could hardly succeed, as among the Czechs, did the masses in 1914 remain indifferent or hostile to the war. The mass anti-war movement did not seriously begin until much later.

Since political integration succeeded, regimes therefore faced only the immediate challenge of direct action. Such forms of unrest certainly spread, above all in the last years before the war. But they constituted a challenge to public order rather than to the social system, given the absence of revolutionary or even pre-revolutionary situations in the central countries of bourgeois society. The riots of southern French wine-growers, the mutiny of the 17th Regiment sent against them (1907), violent quasi-general strikes in Belfast (1907), Liverpool (1911) and Dublin (1913), a general strike in Sweden (1908), even the 'tragic week' of Barcelona (1909), were insufficient by themselves to shake the foundations of political regimes. They were indeed serious, not least as symptoms of the vulnerability of complex economies. In 1912 the British Prime Minister Asquith, in spite of the British gentleman's proverbial impassivity, wept as he announced the government's retreat before a general strike of coal-miners.

Such phenomena are not to be underestimated. Even if contemporaries did not know what was to come after, they often had the sense, in these last pre-war years, of society trembling as under seismic shocks before greater earthquakes. These were years when wisps of violence hung in the air over the Ritz hotels and country houses. They underlined the impermanence, the fragility, of the political order in the *belle époque*.

But let us not overestimate them either. So far as the core countries of bourgeois society were concerned, what destroyed the stability of the *belle époque*, including its peace, was the situation in Russia, the Habsburg Empire and the Balkans, and not in western Europe or even Germany. What made the British political situation dangerous on the eve of the war was not the rebellion of the workers, but the division within the ranks of the rulers, a constitutional crisis as the ultra-conservative Lords resisted the Commons, the collective refusal of officers to obey the orders of a liberal government committed to Irish Home Rule. No doubt such crises were in part due to the mobilization of labour, for what the Lords resisted blindly and vainly was the intelligent demagogy of Lloyd George, designed to keep 'the people' within the framework of the system of their rulers. And yet the last and gravest of such crises was provoked by the political commitment of the Liberals to (Catholic) Irish autonomy and of Conservatives to the armed refusal of Ulster Protestant ultras to accept it. Parliamentary democracy, the stylized game of politics, was – as we still know in the 1980s – powerless to control such a situation.

All the same in the years between 1880 and 1914 ruling classes discovered that parliamentary democracy, in spite of their fears, proved itself to be quite compatible with the political and economic stability of capitalist regimes. The discovery, like the system itself, was new – at least in Europe. It proved disappointing to social revolutionaries. For Marx and Engels had always seen the democratic republic, though plainly 'bourgeois', as the ante-chamber of socialism, since it permitted, and even encouraged, the political mobilization of the proletariat as a class, and of the oppressed masses under the leadership of the proletariat. It would thus, whether it liked to or not, favour the eventual victory of the proletariat in its confrontation with the exploiters. And yet, after the end of our period, a very different note was to be heard among their disciples. 'A democratic republic', argued Lenin in 1917, 'is the best possible political shell for capitalism, and therefore, once capitalism has gained control of this very best shell ... it establishes its power so securely, so firmly, that *no* change, either of persons, of institutions, or of parties in the bourgeois–democratic republic, can shake it.'[26] As always, Lenin was concerned not so much with political analysis in general, as with finding effective arguments for a specific political situation, in this instance against the provisional government of revolutionary Russia and for Soviet power. In any case, we are not concerned with the validity of his claim, which is highly debatable, not least because it fails to distinguish between the economic and social circumstances which have safeguarded states from social upheaval, and the institutions which have helped them to do so. We are concerned with its plausibility. Before 1880 such a claim would have seemed equally implausible to either supporters or opponents of capitalism insofar as they were committed to political activity. Even on the political ultra-left, so negative a judgment on 'the democratic republic' would have been almost inconceivable. Behind Lenin's judgment of 1917 there stood the experience of a generation of western democratization, and especially of the last fifteen years before the war.

But was not the stability of this marriage between political democracy and a flourishing capitalism the illusion of a passing era? What strikes us, in retrospect, about the years from 1880 to 1914 is both the fragility and the restricted scope of such a combination. It was and remained confined to a minority of prosperous and flourishing economies in the west, generally in states with a lengthy history of constitutional government. Democratic optimism, a belief in historical inevitability, might make it look as though its universal progress could not be halted. But it was not, after all, to be the universal model of the future. In 1919 the whole of Europe west of Russia and Turkey was systematically reorganized into states on the democratic model. Yet how many democracies remained in the Europe of 1939? As fascism and other dictatorships rose, the opposite case to Lenin's was widely argued, not least by Lenin's followers. Capitalism must inevitably abandon bourgeois democracy. This was equally wrong. Bourgeois democracy was reborn from its ashes in 1945, and has since remained the favourite system for capitalist societies sufficiently strong, economically flourishing and socially unpolarized or divided to afford so politically advantageous a system. But this system operates effectively in very few of the more than 150 states which form the United Nations of the late twentieth century. The progress of democratic politics between 1880 and 1914 foreshadowed neither its permanence nor its universal triumph.

CHAPTER 5

WORKERS OF THE WORLD

I got to know a shoemaker called Schröder.... Later he went to America.... He gave me some newspapers to read and I read a bit because I was bored, and then I got more and more interested.... They described the misery of the workers and how they depended on the capitalists and landlords in a way that was so lively and true to nature that it really amazed me. It was as though my eyes had been closed before. Damn it, what they wrote in those papers was the truth. *All my life up to that day was proof of it.*

A German labourer, *c.* 1911[1]

They [the European workers] feel that great social changes must come soon; that the curtain has been rung down on the human comedy of government by, of and for the classes; that the day of democracy is at hand and that the struggles of the toilers for their own shall take precedence over those wars between nations which mean battles without cause between working men.

Samuel Gompers, 1909[2]

A proletarian life, a proletarian death, and cremation in the spirit of cultural progress.

Motto of the Austrian Workers' Funeral Association, 'The Flame'[3]

I

Given the inevitable extension of the electorate, the majority of electors were bound to be poor, insecure, discontented, or all of those things. They could not but be dominated by their economic and social situation and the problems arising from it; in other words, by the situation of their class. And the class whose numbers were most visibly growing as the wave of industrialization engulfed the west, whose presence became ever more inescapable, and whose class consciousness seemed most directly to threaten the social, economic and political system of modern societies, was the proletariat. These were the people the young Winston

Churchill (then a Liberal cabinet minister) had in mind when he warned Parliament that, if the system of Conservative–Liberal two-party politics broke down, it would be replaced by class politics.

The number of people who earned their living by manual labour for a wage was indeed increasing in all countries flooded or even lapped by the tidal wave of western capitalism, from the ranches of Patagonia and the nitrate mines of Chile to the frozen gold-mines of north-eastern Siberia, scene of a spectacular strike and massacre on the eve of the Great War. They were to be found wherever modern cities required building work or the municipal services and public utilities which had become indispensable in the nineteenth century – gas, water, sewage – and wherever the network of ports and railways and telegraphs stretched which bound the economic globe together. Mines were to be found in remote spots throughout the five continents. By 1914 even oilfields were exploited on a significant scale in North and Central America, in eastern Europe, South-east Asia and the Middle East. More significantly, even in predominantly agrarian countries urban markets were supplied with manufactured food, drink, stimulants and elementary textiles by cheap labour working in a sort of industrial establishment, and in some – India is a case in point – fairly significant textile and even iron and steel industries were developing. Yet the number of wage-workers multiplied most spectacularly, and formed recognized classes of such labour, chiefly in the countries of old-established industrialization, and in the growing number of countries which, as we have seen, entered their period of industrial revolution between the 1870s and 1914, that is to say mainly in Europe, North America, Japan and some of the areas of white mass settlement overseas.

They grew mainly by transfer from the two great reservoirs of pre-industrial labour, the handicrafts and the agricultural countryside, which still held the majority of human beings. By the end of the century urbanization had probably advanced more rapidly and massively than ever before, and important currents of migration – for instance from Britain and east European Jewry – came from towns, though sometimes small ones. These could and did transfer from one kind of non-agricultural work to another. As for the men and women who fled from the land (to use the then current term, *Landflucht*), relatively few of them had the chance to go into agriculture, even if they wanted to.

On the one hand, the modernizing and modernized farming of the west required relatively fewer permanent hands than before, though considerable use was made of seasonal migrant labour, often from far away, for whom farmers did not have to take responsibility when the working season ended: the *Sachsengänger* from Poland in Germany, the

Italian 'swallows' in Argentina,* the train-jumping hobo transients and even, already, the Mexicans, in the USA. In any case agricultural progress means fewer people farming. In 1910 New Zealand, which had no industry worth mentioning and lived entirely by means of extremely efficient agriculture, specializing in livestock and dairy products, had 54 per cent of her population living in towns, and 40 per cent (or twice the proportion of Europe without Russia) employed in tertiary occupations.[5]

Meanwhile the unmodernized agriculture of the backward regions could no longer provide enough land for the would-be peasants whose numbers multiplied in the villages. What most of them wanted, when they emigrated, was certainly not to end up their lives as labourers. They wanted to 'make America' (or wherever they went), hoping to earn enough after a few years to buy themselves a holding, a house and the respect of the neighbours as a man of means, in some Sicilian, Polish or Greek village. A minority returned, but most stayed, to fill the constructional gangs, the mines, the steel mills, and the other activities of the urban and industrial world which needed hard labour and little else. Their daughters and brides went into domestic service.

At the same time machine and factory production cut the ground from under the considerable masses who had, until the late nineteenth century, made most familiar urban consumer goods – clothing, footwear, furniture and the like – by handicraft methods, ranging from those of the proud master artisan to those of the sweated workshop or attic seamstress. If their numbers did not appear to fall dramatically, their share of the labour force did, in spite of the spectacular increase in the output of their products. Thus in Germany the number of people engaged in shoe-making sank only slightly between 1882 and 1907 from c. 400,000 to c. 370,000 – but the consumption of leather doubled between 1890 and 1910. Plainly most of this additional output was produced in the c. 1500 larger plants (whose numbers had tripled since 1882, and who now employed almost six times as many workers as then), rather than in the small workshops employing no workers or less than ten workers, whose numbers had fallen by 20 per cent and which now employed only 63 per cent of people engaged in shoe-making as against 93 per cent in 1882.[6] In rapidly industrializing countries, the pre-industrial manufacturing sector thus also provided a small, but by no means negligible, reserve for the recruitment of the new workers.

On the other hand, the number of proletarians in the industrializing economies also grew at so impressive a rate because of the apparently

---

* It is said that they refused to take harvesting jobs in Germany, since travel from Italy to South America was cheaper and easier, while wages were higher.[4]

limitless appetite for labour in this period of economic expansion, and not least for the sort of pre-industrial labour that was now prepared to pour into their expanding sectors. Insofar as industry still grew by a sort of marriage between manual dexterity and steam technology, or – as in building – had not yet seriously changed its methods, the demand was for old craft skills, or skills adapted from old crafts like smiths and locksmiths to new machine-making industries. This was significant, since trained craft journeymen, an established pre-industrial body of wage-workers, often formed the most active, educated and self-confident element in the developing proletariat of early economies: the leader of the German Social Democratic Party was a wood-turner (August Bebel), of the Spanish Socialist Party a printer (Iglesias).

Insofar as industrial labour was unmechanized and required no particular skills, it was not only within reach of most raw recruits, but, being labour-intensive, multiplied the numbers of such workers as output rose. To take two obvious examples: both construction, which built the infrastructure of production, transport and the rapidly expanding giant cities, and coal-mining, which produced the basic form of energy for this period – steam – generated vast armies. The constructional industry in Germany grew from about half a million in 1875 to almost 1.7 million in 1907, or from about 10 per cent to almost 16 per cent of the labour force. In 1913 no less than a million and a quarter men in Britain (800,000 in Germany, 1907) hacked, shovelled, hauled and lifted the coal that kept the economies of the world going. (In 1985 the equivalent numbers were 197,000 and 137,500.) On the other hand, mechanization, seeking to replace manual skill and experience by sequences of specialized machines or processes, served by more or less unskilled labour, welcomed the cheapness and helplessness of green workers – and nowhere more so than in the USA, where the old pre-industrial skills were in any case in short supply and not much wanted on the shop-floor. ('The will to be skilled is not general,' said Henry Ford.)[7]

As the nineteenth century drew to a close, no industrial, industrializing or urbanizing country could fail to be aware of these historically unprecedented, apparently anonymous and rootless masses of labouring people who formed a growing and, it seemed, an inevitably rising proportion of its people: probably, one day soon, a majority. For the diversification of industrial economies, notably by the rise of tertiary occupations – offices, shops and services – was only just beginning, except in the USA where tertiary workers already outnumbered blue-collar workers. Elsewhere the contrary development seemed to predominate. Cities, which in pre-industrial times had been primarily inhabited by people in the tertiary sector, for even their handicraftsmen were also generally shopkeepers, became centres of manufacture. By the end of the nineteenth century something like two-thirds of the occupied population in big cities (i.e. cities over 100,000 inhabitants) were in industrial occupations.[8]

As men looked back from the end of the century they would be struck chiefly by the advance of the armies of industry, and within each town or region, as like as not, by the advance of industrial specialization. The typical industrial city, which was usually a town of between 50,000 and 300,000 – of course at the beginning of the century any city over 100,000 would have been considered very large – tended to evoke a monochrome image, or at best two or three associated hues: textiles in Roubaix or Lodz, Dundee or Lowell, coal, iron and steel alone or in combination in Essen, or Middlesbrough, armaments and shipbuilding in Jarrow and Barrow, chemicals in Ludwigshafen or Widnes. In this respect it differed from the size and variety of the new multi-million megalopolis, whether or not this was a capital city. Though some of the great capitals were also important industrial centres (Berlin, St Petersburg, Budapest) usually capitals occupied no central position in the pattern of a country's industry.

What is more, though these masses were heterogeneous and far from uniform, the tendency for more and more of them to work as parts of large and complex firms, in plants ranging from hundreds to many thousands, appeared to be universal, especially in the new centres of heavy industry. Krupp in Essen, Vickers in Barrow, Armstrong in Newcastle, measured the size of the labour force in their individual plants in tens of thousands. Those who worked in these giant factories and yards were a minority. Even in Germany the mean number of people employed in units with more than ten workers in 1913 was only 23-4,[9] but they were an increasingly visible and potentially formidable minority. And, whatever the historian can establish in retrospect, for contemporaries the mass of workers was large, was indisputably growing, and threw a dark shadow over the established ordering of society and politics. What indeed would happen if, as a class, they organized politically?

This is precisely what happened, on a European scale, suddenly and with extraordinary speed. Wherever democratic and electoral politics allowed it, mass parties based on the working class, for the most part inspired by an ideology of revolutionary socialism (for all socialism was by definition seen as revolutionary) and led by men – and even sometimes by women – who believed in such an ideology, appeared on the scene and grew with startling rapidity. In 1880 they barely existed, with the major exception of the German Social Democratic Party, recently (1875) unified and already an electoral force to be reckoned with. By 1906 they were so much taken for granted that a German scholar could publish a book on the topic 'Why is there no socialism in the USA?'[10] The existence of mass labour and socialist parties was already the norm: it was their absence which seemed surprising.

In fact, by 1914 there were mass socialist parties even in the USA, where the party's candidate in 1912 polled almost a million votes, and in Argentina, where the party had 10 per cent of the vote in 1914, while in Australia an admittedly quite non-socialist Labour Party already formed the federal government in 1912. As for Europe, socialist and labour parties were serious electoral forces almost everywhere where conditions permitted. They were indeed minorities, but in some states, notably Germany and Scandinavia, they were already the largest national parties, with up to 35–40 per cent of the total vote – and every extension of the right to vote revealed the industrial masses ready to choose socialism. And they not only voted, but organized in gigantic armies: the Belgian Labour Party in its small country had 276,000 members in 1911, the great German SPD had more than a million, and the less directly political workers' organizations, linked with such parties and often founded by them, were even more massive – trade unions and co-operative societies.

Not all the armies of labour were as large, solid and disciplined as in northern and central Europe. But even where workers' parties consisted rather of groups of activist irregulars, or local militants, ready to lead mobilizations when they occurred, the new labour and socialist parties had to be taken seriously. They were a significant factor in national politics. Thus the French party, whose membership in 1914 – 76,000 – was neither united nor large, nevertheless elected 103 deputies by virtue of its 1.4 million votes. The Italian party, with an even more modest membership – 50,000 in 1914 – had almost a million who voted for it.[11] In short, labour and socialist parties were almost everywhere growing at a rate which, depending on one's point of view, was extremely alarming or marvellous. Their leaders cheered themselves with triumphant extrapolations of the curve of past growth. The proletariat was destined – one had only to look at industrial Britain and the record of national censuses over the years – to become the great majority of the people. The proletariat was joining its parties. It was only a question of time, according to systematic and statistically minded German socialists, before these parties would pass the magic figure of 51 per cent of votes, which, in democratic states, must surely be a decisive turning-point. Or, as the new anthem of world socialism put it: 'The Internationale will be the human race.'

We need not share this optimism, which proved to be misplaced. Nevertheless, in the years before 1914 it was patent that even the most miraculously successful parties still had vast reserves of potential support to mobilize, and that they were indeed mobilizing it. And it is natural that the extraordinary rise of socialist labour parties since the 1880s should give their members and supporters, as well as their leaders, a sense of excitement, of marvellous hope, of the historic inevitability of their triumph. Never before had there been such an age of hope for those who laboured with their hands in factory, workshop and mine. In the words of a Russian socialist song: 'Out of the dark past, the light of the future shines forth brightly.'

II

This remarkable upsurge of working-class parties was, at first sight, rather surprising. Their power lay essentially in the elementary simplicity of their political appeal. They were the parties of all manual workers who laboured for wages. They represented this class in its struggles against the capitalists and their states, and their object was to create a new society, which would begin with the emancipation of the workers by their own action, and which would emancipate the entire human race, except for an increasingly tiny minority of the exploiters. The doctrine of Marxism, formulated as such between Marx's death and the end of the century, increasingly dominated the majority of the new parties, because the clarity with which it enunciated these propositions gave it an enormous power of political penetration. It was enough to know that all workers must join or support such parties, for history itself guaranteed their future victory.

This assumed that a class of workers existed sufficiently numerous and homogeneous to recognize itself in the Marxist image of 'the proletariat', and sufficiently convinced of the validity of the socialist analysis of its situation and its tasks, of which the first was to form proletarian parties and, whatever else they did, engage in political action. (Not all revolutionaries agreed with this primacy of politics, but for the moment we can leave aside this anti-political minority, which was mainly inspired by ideas then associated with anarchism.)

But practically all observers of the working-class scene were agreed that 'the proletariat' was very far from being a homogeneous mass, even within single nations. Indeed, before the rise of the new parties people had habitually talked of 'the working classes' in the plural rather than the singular.

The divisions within the masses whom socialists classified under the heading of 'the proletariat' were indeed so great that one might have expected them to stand in the way of any practical assertion of a single unified class consciousness.

The classic proletariat of the modern industrial factory or plant, often still a smallish though rapidly growing minority, was far from identical with the bulk of manual workers who laboured in small workshops, in rural cottages or city back-rooms or in the open air, with the labyrinthine jungle of wage-work which filled the cities and – even leaving aside farming – the countryside. Industries, crafts or other occupations, often extremely localized and with the most geographically restricted horizons, did not see their problems and situation as the same. How much was there in common between, say, the exclusively male boilermakers and the, in Britain, mainly female cotton weavers, or, within the same port cities, between skilled workers in shipyards, dockers, the garment workers and the builders? These divisions were not only vertical but horizontal: between craftsmen and labourers, between 'respectable' people and occupations (who respected themselves and were respected) and the rest, between labour aristocracy, lumpenproletariat and those in between, or indeed between different strata of skilled crafts, where the typographical compositor looked down on the bricklayer, and the bricklayer on the house-painter. There were, moreover, not only divisions but rivalries between equivalent groups each seeking to monopolize a particular kind of work: rivalries exasperated by technological developments which transformed old processes, created new ones, made old skills irrelevant and dissolved the clear traditional definitions of what 'rightly' belonged to the functions of, say, the locksmith or the farrier. Where employers were strong and workers weak, management, through machines and command, imposed its own division of labour, but elsewhere skilled workers might engage in those embittered 'demarcation disputes' which flickered through the British shipyards, notably in the 1890s, often throwing workers uninvolved in these inter occupational strikes into uncontrollable and undeserved idleness.

And in addition to all these there were the even more obvious differences of social and geographical origin, of nationality, language, culture and religion, which could not but emerge as industry recruited its rapidly growing armies from all corners of its own country, and indeed, in this era of massive international and trans-oceanic migration, from abroad. For what, from one point of view, looked like a concentration of men and women in a single 'working class', could be seen from another as a gigantic scattering of the fragments of societies, a diaspora of old and new communities. Insofar as these divisions kept workers apart, they were obviously useful to, and indeed encouraged by, employers – notably in the USA, where the proletariat consisted largely of a variety of immigrant foreigners. Even so militant a body as the Western Federation of Miners in the Rocky Mountains risked being torn apart by the fights between the skilled and Methodist Cornishmen, specialists of the hard rocks, who were to be found wherever on the globe metal was commercially mined, and the less skilled Catholic Irish, who were to be found wherever strength and hard labour was needed on the frontiers of the English-speaking world.

Whatever the other differences within the working class, there was no doubt at all that differences of nationality, religion and language divided it. The classic case of Ireland is tragically familiar. But even in Germany Catholic workers resisted the appeal of social democracy far more than Protestant ones, and in Bohemia Czech workers resisted integration in a pan-Austrian movement dominated by workers of German speech. The passionate internationalism of the socialists – the workers, Marx told them, had no country, only a class – appealed to labour movements, not only because of its ideal, but also because it was often the essential precondition of their operation. How otherwise could workers be mobilized as such in a city like Vienna, where a third of them were Czech immigrants, or in Budapest, where the skilled operatives were Germans, the rest Slovaks or Magyars? The great industrial centre of Belfast showed, and still shows, what could happen when workers identified primarily as Catholics and Protestants, and not as workers, or even as Irishmen.

Fortunately the appeal to internationalism or, what was almost the same in large countries, to inter-regionalism, was not entirely ineffective. Differences of language, nationality and religion did not by themselves make the formation of a unified class consciousness impossible, especially when national groups of workers did not compete, for each had their niche in the labour market. They created major difficulties only where such differences expressed, or symbolized, severe group conflicts which cut across class lines, or differences within the working class which seemed to be incompatible with the unity of all workers. Czech workers were suspicious of German workers not as workers but as members of a nation which treated Czechs as inferior. Catholic Irish workers in Ulster were not likely to be impressed by appeals to class unity, when they saw Catholics increasingly excluded between 1870 and 1914 from the skilled jobs in industry which therefore became a virtual monopoly of Protestant workers, with the approval of their unions. Even so, the force of class experience was such that the worker's alternative identification with some other group in plural working classes – as Pole, as Catholic or whatever – narrowed rather than replaced class identification. A person felt himself to be a worker, but a specifically Czech, Polish or Catholic worker. The Catholic Church, in spite of its deep hostility to class division and conflict, was obliged to form, or at least to tolerate, labour unions, even Catholic trade unions – at this period generally not very large – though it would have preferred joint organizations of employers and employed. What alternative identifications really excluded was not class consciousness as such but *political* class consciousness. Thus there was a trade union movement, and the usual tendencies to form a party of labour, even on the sectarian battlefield of Ulster. But the unity of the workers was possible only insofar as the two issues which dominated existence and political debate were excluded from discussion: religion and Home Rule for Ireland, on which Catholic and Protestant, Orange and Green workers could not agree. Some kind of trade union movement and industrial struggle was possible under these circumstances, but not – except within each community, and then only feebly or intermittently – a party based on class identification.

Add to these factors which stood in the way of labour class consciousness and organization, the heterogeneous structure of the industrial economy itself, as it developed. Here Britain was quite exceptional, since a strong non-political class feeling and labour organization already existed. The sheer antiquity – and archaism – of this country's pioneer industrialization had allowed a rather primitive, largely decentralized trade unionism, mainly of craft unions, to sink roots into the basic industries of the countries, which – for a number of reasons – developed less through machinery replacing labour than through a marriage of manual operations and steam power. In all the great industries of the former 'workshop of the world' – in cotton, mining and metallurgy, the construction of machines and ships (the last industry dominated by Britain) – a nucleus of labour organization, mainly along craft or occupational lines, existed, capable of transformation into mass unionism. Between 1867 and 1875 trade unions had actually acquired a legal status and privileges so far-reaching that militant employers, conservative governments and judges did not succeed in reducing or abolishing them until the 1980s. Labour organization was not merely present and accepted, but powerful, expecially in the workplace. This exceptional, indeed unique, power of labour was to create growing problems for the British industrial economy in the future, and indeed even during our period major difficulties for industrialists who wished to mechanize or administer it out of existence. Before 1914 they failed in the most crucial cases, but for our purposes it is sufficient simply to note the anomaly of Britain in this respect. Political pressure might help in reinforcing workshop strength, but it did not, in effect, have to take its place.

Elsewhere the situation was rather different. Broadly speaking effective trade unions only functioned on the margins of modern and especially large-scale industry: in workshops, on work-sites or in small and medium enterprises. Organization might in theory be national, but in practice it was extremely localized and decentralized. In countries like France and Italy its effective groupings were alliances of small local unions grouped round local labour halls. The French national trade union federation (CGT) required only a minimum of *three* local unions to constitute a national union.[12] In the large plants of modern industry unions were negligible. In Germany the strength of social democracy and its 'Free Trade Unions' was not to be found in the heavy industries of Rhineland and Ruhr. In the USA unionism in the great industries was virtually eliminated during the 1890s – it would not return until the 1930s – but it survived in small-scale industry and among the craft unions of the building trade, protected by the localism of the market in the large cities, where rapid urbanization, not to mention the politics of graft and municipal contracting, gave it greater scope. The only real alternative to the local union of small knots of organized labour, to the (mainly skilled) craft union, was the occasional and rarely permanent mobilization of masses of workers in intermittent strikes, but this also was mainly local.

There were only some striking exceptions, among which the miners stand out by their very difference from the carpenters and cigar-makers, the locksmith-mechanics, the printers and the rest of the journeymen artisans who formed the normal working-class cadre of the new proletarian movements. In one way or another these masses of muscular men, labouring in darkness, often living with their families in separate communities as forbidding and harsh as their pits, bound together by the solidarity of work and community and by the hardness and danger of their toil, showed a marked tendency to engage in collective struggle: even in France and the USA coal-miners formed at least intermittently powerful unions.* Given the size of the mining proletariat, and its marked regional concentrations, its potential – and in Britain its actual – role in labour movements could be formidable.

Two other, partly overlapping, sectors of non-craft unionism also deserve attention: transport and public employment. Employees of the state were still – even in France, the later stronghold of public service unions – excluded from labour organization, and this notably retarded the unionization of railways, which were frequently state-owned.

* As is indicated in the German miners' doggerel, roughly translatable as:

> Bakers can bake their bread alone
> Joiners can do their work at home:
> But wherever miners stand,
> Mates brave and true must be at hand.[13]

However, even private railways proved difficult to organize, outside large and thinly populated land-spaces, where their indispensability gave some of those employed on them considerable strategic leverage: especially the engine drivers and train crews. Railway companies were by far the largest enterprises in the capitalist economy, and were virtually impossible to organize except over the whole of what might be an almost nationwide network: in the 1890s the London and North-western Railway Company, for instance, controlled 65,000 workers over a system of 7000 kilometres of line and 800 stations.

By contrast, the other key sector of transport, the maritime, was extraordinarily localized in and around the sea-ports, where, in turn, the entire economy tended to pivot on it. Here, therefore, any strike in the docks tended to turn into a general transport strike which might grow into a general strike. The economic general strikes which multiplied in the first years of the new century* – and were to lead to impassioned ideological debates within the socialist movement – were thus mainly strikes in port cities: Trieste, Genoa, Marseilles, Barcelona, Amsterdam. These were giant battles, but unlikely to lead as yet to permanent mass union organization, given the heterogeneity of an often unskilled labour force. But while rail and sea transport were so different, they had in common their crucial strategic importance for national economies, which could be paralysed by their cessation. As labour movements grew, governments were increasingly conscious of this potential strangulation, and considered possible counter-measures: the decision by the French government to break a general rail strike in 1910 by conscripting 150,000 railwaymen, i.e. putting them under military discipline, is the most drastic example.[14]

However, private employers also recognized the strategic role of the transport sector. The counter-offensive against the wave of British unionization in 1889–90 (which had itself been launched by seamen's and dockers' strikes) began with a battle against the Scottish railwaymen and a series of battles against the massive but unstable unionization of great sea-ports. Conversely, the labour offensive on the eve of the world war planned its own strategic striking force, the Triple Alliance of coal-miners, railwaymen and the transport workers' federation (i.e. the port employees). Transport was now clearly seen as a crucial element in the class struggle.

It was more clearly seen than another zone of confrontation which was, shortly, to prove even more crucial: the great and growing metal industries. For here the traditional force of labour organization, the skilled workers of craft background and with stubborn craft unions met

---

* Brief general strikes in favour of the democratization of voting rights were a different matter.

123

the great modern factory, which set out to reduce them (or most of them) to semi-skilled operators of increasingly specialized and sophisticated machine-tools and machines. Here, on the rapidly moving frontier of technological advance, the conflict of interest was clear. While peace lasted, by and large, the situation favoured management, but after 1914 it is not surprising that the cutting edge of labour radicalization would be found everywhere in the great armament plants. Behind the metalworkers' turn to revolution during and after the world war we discern the preparatory tensions of the 1890s and 1900s.

The working classes were thus neither homogeneous nor easy to unite into a single coherent social group – even if we leave aside the agricultural proletariat, which labour movements also sought to organize and mobilize, in general with indifferent success.* Yet they were being unified. But how?

III

One powerful way was through ideology carried by organization. Socialists and anarchists carried their new gospel to masses hitherto neglected by almost all agencies except their exploiters and those who told them to be quiet and obedient: and even primary schools (where they reached them) were mainly content to inculcate the civic duties of religion, while organized Churches themselves, apart from a few plebeian sects, were slow to move into proletarian territory, or ill-suited to deal with populations so different from the structured communities of ancient rural or city parishes. Workers were unknown and forgotten people in proportion as they were a new social group. How unknown, scores of writings by middle-class social explorers and observers testify; how forgotten, any reader of the letters of the painter Van Gogh, who went into the Belgian coalfield as an evangelist, can judge. The socialists were often the first to come to them. Where conditions were right, they impressed on the most varied groups of workers – from craft journeymen or vanguards of militants to entire working communities of outworkers or miners – a single identity: that of 'the proletarian'. In 1886 the cottagers in the Belgian valleys round Liège, traditionally manufacturing guns, had no politics. They lived ill-paid lives varied for the

* Except in Italy, where the Federation of Land Workers was by far the largest union, and the one which laid the base for the later communist influence in central and parts of southern Italy. Possibly in Spain anarchism may have had comparable influence among landless labourers from time to time.

males among them only by pigeon-fancying, fishing and cock-fighting. From the moment the 'Workers' Party' arrived on the scene, they converted to it *en masse*: 80–90 per cent of the Val de Vesdre henceforth voted socialist, and even the last ramparts of local Catholicism were breached. The people of the Liègois found themselves sharing an identification and a faith with the weavers of Ghent, whose very language (Flemish) they could not understand, and thereby with all who shared the ideal of a single, universal working class. This message of the unity of all who worked and were poor was brought into the remotest corners of their countries by the agitators and propagandists. But they also brought *organization*, the structured collective action without which the working class could not exist as a class, and through organization they acquired that cadre of spokesmen who could articulate the feelings and hopes of men and women who were unable to do so themselves. These possessed or found the words for the truths they felt. Without this organized collectivity, they were only poor labouring folk. For the ancient corpus of wisdom – proverbs, sayings, songs – which formulated the *Weltanschauung* of the labouring poor of the pre-industrial world was no longer enough. They were a *new* social reality, requiring new reflection. This began at the moment when they understood their new spokesmen's message: You are a class, you must show that you are. Hence, in extreme cases, it was enough for the new parties merely to enunciate their name: 'the workers' party'. Nobody except the militants of the new movement brought this message of class consciousness to the workers. It unified all those who were prepared to recognize this great truth across all differences among them.

But people were prepared to recognize it, because the gap which separated those who were, or were becoming, workers from the rest, including other branches of the socially modest 'little people', was widening, because the working-class world was increasingly separate, and, not least, because the conflict between those who paid wages and those who lived by them was an increasingly dominant existential reality. This was plainly the case in places virtually created by and for industry like Bochum (4200 inhabitants in 1842, 120,000 in 1907, of whom 78 per cent were workers, 0.3 per cent 'capitalists') or Middlesbrough (6000 in 1841, 105,000 in 1911). In these centres, mainly of mining and heavy industry, which mushroomed in the second half of the century, perhaps even more than in the textile mill-towns which had been the typical centres of industry earlier, men and women might live without regularly even seeing any member of the non-wage-earning classes who did not in some way command them (owner, manager, official, teacher, priest), except for the small artisans and shopkeepers and publicans who served the modest needs of the poor, and who, dependent on their clientele, adjusted to the proletarian environment.* Bochum's consumer production contained, apart from the usual bakers, butchers and brewers, a few hundred seamstresses, and forty-eight milliners, but only eleven laundresses, six hat- and cap-makers, eight furriers – and, significantly, no single person making that characteristic status symbol of the middle and upper classes, gloves.[15]

Yet even in the great city, with its miscellaneous and increasingly diversified services and social variety, functional specialization, supplemented in this period by town-planning and property-development, separated the classes, except on such neutral territories as parks, railway stations and the structures of entertainment. The old 'popular quarter' declined with the new social segregation: in Lyon, La Croix-Rousse, ancient stronghold of the riotous silk-weavers descending into the city centre, was in 1913 described as a quarter of 'small employees' – 'the bee-swarm of workers has left the plateau and its slopes of access'.[16] Workers moved from the old city to the other bank of the Rhône and its factories. Increasingly the grey uniformity of new working-class quarters, extruded from the central city areas, took over: Wedding and Neukölln in Berlin, Favoriten and Ottakring in Vienna, Poplar and West Ham in London – counterparts to the rapidly developing segregated middle- and lower-middle-class quarters and suburbs. And if the much discussed crisis of the traditional craft sector drove some groups among the master artisans to the anti-capitalist and anti-proletarian radical right, as in Germany, it could also, as in France, intensify their anti-capitalist jacobinism or republican radicalism. As for their journeymen and apprentices, it could hardly fail to convince them that they were now no more than proletarians. And was it was not natural for the hard-pressed proto-industrial cottage-industries, often, like the handloom weavers, symbiotic with the early stages of the factory system, to identify with the proletarian situation? Localized communities of this kind, in various hilly regions of central Germany, Bohemia or elsewhere, became natural strongholds of the movement.

All workers were, for good reasons, apt to be convinced of the injustice of the social order, but the crux of their experience was their relation with employers. The new socialist labour movement was inseparable from the discontents of the workplace, whether or not expressed in strikes and (more rarely) organized trade unions. Time and again the rise of a local socialist party is inseparable from a particular group of locally central workers, whose mobilization it released or reflected. In Roanne (France) the weavers formed the core of the Parti Ouvrier;

---

* The role of taverns as meeting-places for unions and socialist party branches, and of tavern-keepers as socialist militants, is familiar in several countries.

when weaving in the region organized in 1889–91 the rural cantons suddenly switched their politics from 'reaction' to 'socialism' and industrial conflict passed over into political organization and electoral activity. Yet, as the example of British labour in the middle decades of the century shows, there was no necessary connection between the willingness to strike and organize, and the identification of the class of employers (the 'capitalists') as the major political adversary. Indeed, traditionally a common front had united those who laboured and produced, workers, artisans, shopkeepers, bourgeois against the idle and against 'privilege' – the believers in progress (a coalition which also crossed class boundaries) against 'reaction'. Yet this alliance, largely responsible for the earlier historic and political force of liberalism (see *The Age of Capital*, chapter 6, 1) crumbled, not only because electoral democracy revealed the divergent interests of its various components (see pp. 88–90 above), but because the class of employers, increasingly typified by size and concentration – as we have seen, the key word 'big', as in big business, *grande industrie, grand patronat, Grossindustrie,* appears more frequently[17] – became more visibly integrated into the undifferentiated zone of wealth, state power and privilege. It joined the 'plutocracy' which Edwardian demagogues in Britain liked to excoriate – a 'plutocracy' which, as the era of depression gave way to the intoxicating surge of economic expansion, increasingly flaunted itself, visibly and through the new mass media. The British government's chief labour expert claimed that newspapers and the motor car, in Europe a monopoly of the rich, made the contrast between rich and poor inescapable.[18]

But as the political fight against 'privilege' merged with the hitherto separate fight at and around the place of employment, the world of the manual worker was increasingly separated from those above it by the growth, rapid and striking in some countries, of the tertiary sector of the economy which generated a stratum of men and women who worked without getting their hands dirty. Unlike the ancient petty-bourgeoisie of small craftsmen and shopkeepers which could be seen as a transitional zone or no-man's land between labour and bourgeoisie, these new lower-middle classes separated the two, if only because the very modesty of their economic situation, often little better than those of well-paid workers, made them stress precisely what separated them from manual labour and what they hoped they had or thought they ought to have, in common with their social superiors (see chapter 7). They formed a layer isolating the workers below them.

If economic and social developments thus favoured the formation of a class consciousness of all manual workers, a third factor virtually forced unification on them: the national economy and the nation-state, both increasingly intertwined. The nation-state not only formed the framework of the citizen's life, established its parameters, and determined the concrete conditions and the geographical limits of the workers' struggle, but its political, legal and administrative interventions were more and more central to working-class existence. The economy increasingly operated as an integrated system, or rather one in which a trade union could no longer function as an aggregage of loosely linked local units, concerned in the first instance only with local conditions, but was compelled to adopt a national perspective, at least for its own industry. In Britain the novel phenomenon of organized *national* labour conflicts appears for the first time in the 1890s, while the spectre of national transport and coal strikes became a reality in the 1900s. Correspondingly industries began to negotiate nationwide collective agreements, which had been practically unknown before 1889. By 1910 they were quite usual.

The growing tendency among trade unions, especially socialist ones, to organize workers in comprehensive bodies each covering a single national industry ('industrial unionism') reflected this sense of the economy as an integrated whole. 'Industrial unionism' as an aspiration recognized that 'the industry' had ceased to be a theoretical classification for statisticians and economists and was now becoming a nationwide operational or strategic concept, the economic framework of trade union struggle, however localized. Fiercely attached though British coal-miners were to the autonomy of their coalfield or even their pit, conscious of the specificity of their problems and customs, South Wales and Northumberland, Fife and Staffordshire, they found themselves for this reason inevitably drawn together between 1888 and 1908 into national organization.

As for the state, its electoral democratization imposed the class unity its rulers hoped to avoid. The fight for the extension of citizen rights itself inevitably took on a class tinge for workers, since the central question at issue (at least for men) was the right to vote of the *propertyless* citizen. A property qualification, however modest, had to exclude primarily a large part of workers. Conversely, where general voting rights had not yet been achieved, at least in theory, the new socialist movements inevitably made themselves the major champions of universal suffrage, launching or threatening gigantic demonstration general strikes in its favour – in Belgium 1893 and twice thereafter, in Sweden in 1902, in Finland in 1905 – which both demonstrated and reinforced their power to mobilize the newly converted masses. Even deliberately anti-democratic electoral reforms might reinforce national class consciousness if, as in Russia after 1905, they formed working-class electors into a separate (and underrepresented) electoral compartment or *curia*. But electoral activities, into which socialist parties characteristically plunged, to the horror of anarchists who saw them as diverting the movement from revolution, could not but give the working class a single national dimension, however divided it was in other respects.

But more than this: the state unified the class, since increasingly any social group had to pursue its political aims by exerting pressure on the *national* government, in favour of or against the legislation and administration of *national* laws. No class had a more consistent and continuous need for positive state action on economic and social matters, to compensate for the inadequacies of their unaided collective action; and the more numerous the national proletariat, the more (reluctantly) sensitive politicians were to the demands of so large and dangerous a body of voters. In Britain the old mid-Victorian trade unions and the new labour movement divided, in the 1880s, essentially on the issue of the demand for an Eight-Hour Day to be established *by law* and not by collective bargaining. That is to say a law universally applicable to *all* workers, by definition a *national* law, and even, as the Second International thought, fully conscious of the significance of the demand, an international law. The agitation did indeed generate what is probably the most visceral and moving institution asserting working-class internationalism, the annual May Day demonstrations, inaugurated in 1890. (In 1917 the Russian workers, at last free to celebrate it, even jumped their own calendar in order to demonstrate on precisely the same day as the rest of the world.)*[19] And yet the force of working-class unification within each nation inevitably replaced the hopes and theoretical assertions of working-class internationalism, except for a noble minority of militants and activists. As the behaviour of most national working classes in August 1914 demonstrated, the effective framework of their class consciousness was, except at brief moments of revolution, the state and the politically defined nation.

IV

It is neither possible nor necessary here to survey the full range of geographical, ideological, national, sectional or other variations, actual or potential, on the general theme of the formation of the working classes of 1870–1914 as conscious and organized social groups. It was quite plainly not yet taking place, to any significant extent, among that

---

* As we know, in 1917 the Russian (Julian) calendar was still thirteen days behind our (Gregorian) calendar: hence the familiar puzzle of the October Revolution, which occurred on 7 November.

part of humanity whose skins were a different shade of colour, even when (as in India and, of course, Japan) industrial development was already undeniable. This advance of class organization was chronologically uneven. It accelerated rapidly in the course of two short periods. The first major leap forward occurred between the end of the 1880s and in the early years of the 1890s, years marked both by the re-establishment of a labour International (the 'Second', to distinguish it from Marx's International of 1864–72) and by that symbol of working-class hope and confidence, May Day. These were the years when socialists first appeared in significant numbers in the parliaments of several countries, while even in Germany, where their party was already strong, the force of the SPD more than doubled between 1887 and 1893 (from 10.1 to 23.3 per cent). The second period of major advance falls some time between the Russian Revolution of 1905, which greatly influenced it, especially in central Europe, and 1914. The massive electoral advance of labour and socialist parties was now assisted by the spread of a democratized suffrage which allowed it to be effectively registered. At the same time waves of labour agitation produced a major advance in the strength of organized trade unionism. While the details varied enormously with national circumstances, these two waves of rapid labour advance are to be found, in one way or another, almost everywhere.

Yet the formation of a working-class consciousness cannot be simply identified with the growth of organized labour movements, though there are examples, particularly in central Europe and in some industrially specialized zones, where the identification of the workers with their party and movement was almost total. Thus in 1913 an analyst of elections in a central German constituency (Naumburg-Merseburg) expressed surprise that only 88 per cent of workers had voted for the SPD: plainly here the equation 'worker = Social Democrat' was assumed to be the norm.[20] But this case was as yet neither typical nor even usual. What was increasingly usual, whether or not workers identified with 'their' party, was a non-political class identification, a conscious membership of a separate workers' world which included but went far beyond the 'class party'. For it was based on a separate life experience, a separate manner and style of living which emerged, across the regional variations of speech and custom, in shared forms of social activity (for instance, versions of sport specifically identified with proletarians as a class, as association football came to be in Britain from the 1880s), or even class-specific and novel kinds of clothing, such as the proverbial worker's peaked cap.

Still, without the simultaneous appearance of 'the movement', even the non-political expressions of class consciousness would have been neither complete nor even fully conceivable: for it was through the movement that the plural 'working classes' were fused into the singular 'working class'. But, in turn, the movements themselves, insofar as they became mass movements, were imbued with the workers' non-political but instinctive distrust of all who did not get their hands dirty in labour. This pervasive *ouvrierisme* (as the French called it) reflected reality in mass parties, for these, as distinct from small or illegal organizations, were overwhelmingly composed of manual workers. The 61,000 members of the Social Democratic Party in Hamburg in 1911–12 contained only thirty-six 'authors and journalists' and *two* members of the higher professions. Indeed only 5 per cent of its members were non-proletarian, and half of these consisted of innkeepers.[21] But distrust of non-workers did not exclude the admiration for great teachers from a different class such as Karl Marx himself, nor for a handful of socialists of bourgeois origin, founding fathers, national leaders and orators (two functions which were often hard to distinguish) or 'theorists'. And indeed in their first generation the socialist parties attracted admirable middle-class figures of great gifts who deserved such admiration: Victor Adler in Austria (1852–1918), Jaurès in France (1859–1914), Turati in Italy (1857–1932), Branting in Sweden (1860–1925).

What then was 'the movement' which, in extreme cases, could be virtually coextensive with the class? Everywhere it included the most basic and universal organization of workers, the trade union, though in different forms and varying strength. It also frequently included co-operatives, mainly in the form of shops for workers, occasionally (as in Belgium) as the central institution of the movement.* In countries of mass socialist parties it might include virtually every association in which workers participated, from cradle to grave – or rather, given their anti-clericalism, to the crematorium, which 'the advanced' strongly favoured as being better suited to the age of sciences and progress.[22] These might range from the 200,000 members of the German Federation of Worker Choirs in 1914 and the 130,000 members of the Workers' Cycling Club 'Solidarity' (1910) to the Worker Stamp Collectors and Worker Rabbit Breeders, whose traces are still occasionally found in the suburban inns of Vienna. But in essence all these were subordinate to, or part of, or at least closely linked with, the political party which was its essential expression, almost always called either Socialist (Social Democratic), and/or even more simply 'Workers' or 'Labour' party. Labour movements which were without organized class

---

* While workers' co-operation was closely linked with labour movements, and in fact often formed a bridge between the 'utopian' ideals of pre-1848 socialism and the new socialism, this was not the case with the most flourishing part of co-operation, that of peasants and farmers, except in parts of Italy.

parties or which were opposed to politics, though they represented an old strain of utopian or anarchist ideology on the left, were almost invariably weak. They represented shifting cadres of individual militants, evangelists, agitators and potential strike-leaders rather than mass structures. Except in the Iberian world, always out of phase with other European developments, anarchism nowhere in Europe became the majority ideology of even weak labour movements. Except in Latin countries, and – as the revolution of 1917 revealed – in Russia, anarchism was politically negligible.

The great majority of these working-class parties, Australasia being the major exception, envisaged a fundamental change in society, and consequently called themselves 'socialist', or were judged to be on the way to doing so, like the British Labour Party. Before 1914 they wanted to have as little as possible to do with the politics of the ruling class, and still less with government, until the day when labour itself formed its own government, and presumably would set about the great transformation. Labour leaders tempted into compromises with middle-class parties and governments were execrated unless they kept very quiet, as J. R. MacDonald did about the electoral arrangement with the Liberals, which first gave the British Labour Party significant parliamentary representation in 1906. (For understandable reasons the parties' attitude to local government was rather more positive.) Perhaps the chief reason why so many of such parties ran up the red flag of Karl Marx was that he, more than any other theorist of the left, told them three things which seemed equally plausible and encouraging: that no foreseeable improvement within the present system would change the basic situation of workers as workers (their 'exploitation'); that the nature of capitalist development, which he analysed at length, made the overthrow of the present society and its replacement by a new and better society quite uncertain; and that the working class, organized in class-parties, would be the creator and inheritor of this glorious future. Marx thus provided workers with the certainty, akin to that once given by religion, that science demonstrated the historical inevitability of their eventual triumph. In these respects Marxism was so effective that even Marx's opponents within the movement largely adopted his analysis of capitalism.

Thus both the orators and the ideologists of these parties and their adversaries generally took it for granted that they wanted a social revolution, or that their activities implied one. Yet what exactly did this phrase mean, except that the change from capitalism to socialism, from a society based on private property and enterprise to one based on 'the common ownership of the means of production, distribution and exchange',[23] would indeed revolutionize life, though the exact nature and content of the socialist future was surprisingly little discussed, and remained unclear – except that what was bad now would be good then. The nature of revolution was the issue which dominated the debates on proletarian politics throughout this period.

What was at issue was not faith in a total transformation of society, even though there were many leaders and militants who were much too busy with immediate struggles to take much interest in the remoter future. It was rather that, by a left-wing tradition which reached back beyond Marx and Bakunin to 1789 or even 1776, revolutions hoped to achieve fundamental social change by means of sudden, violent, insurrectionary transfers of power. Or, in a more general and millennial sense, that the great change whose inevitability was established ought to be more imminent than it actually appeared to be in the industrial world, or indeed than it had seemed in the depressed and discontented 1880s, or in the hopeful surges of the early 1890s. Even then the veteran Engels, who looked back to the Age of Revolution when barricades could be expected to go up every twenty years or so, and who had indeed taken part in revolutionary campaigns, gun in hand, warned that the days of 1848 were gone for good. And, as we have seen, from the middle 1890s on the idea of an imminent collapse of capitalism seemed quite implausible. What then was there to do for the armies of the proletariat, mobilized in their millions under the red flag?

On the right of the movement there were some who recommended concentrating on the immediate improvements and reforms which the working class might win from governments and employers, leaving the remoter future to take care of itself. Revolt and insurrection were in any case not on the agenda. Even so, few labour leaders born after, say, 1860 abandoned the idea of the New Jerusalem. Eduard Bernstein (1850–1932), a self-made socialist intellectual who suggested incautiously, not only that Karl Marx's theories should be revised in the light of a flourishing capitalism ('revisionism'), but also that the putative socialist end was less important than the reforms to be won on the way, was massively condemned by labour politicians whose interest in actually overthrowing capitalism was sometimes extremely faint. The belief that the present society was intolerable made sense to working-class people, even when, as an observer of a German socialist congress in the 1900s noted, their militants 'kept a loaf or two ahead of capitalism'.[24] The ideal of a new society was what gave the working class hope.

All the same, how was the new society to be brought about in times when the collapse of the old system looked far from imminent? Kautsky's embarrassed description of the great German Social Democratic Party as 'a party which, while revolutionary, does not make a revolution'[25] sums up the problem. Was it enough to maintain, as the SPD did, a commitment to nothing less than social revolution in theory, a stance of undeviating opposition, periodically to measure the growing strength of the movement in elections and rely on the objective forces of historical development to bring about its inevitable triumph? Not if it meant, as to often it did in practice, that the movement adjusted itself to operating within the framework of the system it could not overthrow. The intransigent front, or so many a radical or militant felt, concealed compromise, passivity, the refusal to order the mobilized armies of labour into action, and the suppression of the struggles which spontaneously welled up among the masses, in the miserable name of organizational discipline.

What the ill-assorted, but after 1905 growing, radical left of rebels, grassroots trade union militants, intellectual dissidents and revolutionaries rejected was thus the mass proletarian parties, which they saw as inevitably reformist and bureaucratized by virtue of engaging in certain kinds of political action. The arguments against them were much the same whether the prevailing orthodoxy was Marxist, as it usually was on the continent, or anti-Marxist in the Fabian manner as in Britain. Instead, the radical left preferred to rely on direct proletarian action which bypassed the dangerous bog of politics, ideally culminating in something like a revolutionary general strike. 'Revolutionary syndicalism', which flourished in the last ten years before 1914, suggests by its very name this marriage between all-out social revolutionaries and decentralized trade union militancy, which was, in varying degrees, associated with anarchist ideas. It flourished, outside Spain, mainly as an ideology of a few hundred or thousand proletarian union militants and a few intellectuals, during the second phase of the movement's growth and radicalization which coincided with considerable and internationally widespread labour unrest, and considerable uncertainty in the socialist parties about what exactly they could or ought to be doing.

Between 1905 and 1914 the typical revolutionary in the west was likely to be some kind of revolutionary syndicalist who, paradoxically, rejected Marxism as the ideology of parties which used it as an excuse for not trying to make revolution. This was a little unfair to the shades of Marx, for the striking thing about the western mass proletarian parties which ran up his banner on their flagpoles was how modest the role of Marx actually was in them. The basic beliefs of their leaders and militants were often indistinguishable from those of the non-Marxist working-class radical or jacobin left. They all believed equally in the struggle of reason against ignorance and superstition (that is to say clericalism); in the struggle of progress against the dark past; in science, in education, in democracy and in the secular trinity of Liberty, Equality and Fraternity. Even in Germany, where almost one in three citizens voted for a Social Democratic Party which had declared itself formally Marxist in 1891, the *Communist Manifesto* before 1905 was published in editions of a mere 2000–3000 copies and the most popular ideological work in workers' libraries was one whose title is self-explanatory: *Darwin versus Moses*.[26] Actually, even native Marxist intellectuals were scarce. The leading 'theorists' of Germany were imported from the Habsburg Empire, like Kautsky and Hilferding, or from the tsar's empire, like Parvus and Rosa Luxemburg. For from Vienna and Prague eastwards, Marxism and Marxist intellectuals were in abundant supply. And in these regions Marxism had retained its revolutionary impulse undiluted, and the link between Marxism and revolution was obvious, if only because the prospects of revolution were immediate and real.

And here, indeed, lay the key to the pattern of labour and socialist movements; as of so much else in the history of the fifty years before 1914. They emerged in the countries of the dual revolution, and indeed in the zone of western and central Europe in which every politically minded person looked back on the greatest of revolutions, that of France in 1789, and any city-dweller born in the year of Waterloo was quite likely in the course of a lifetime of sixty years to have lived through at least two or even three revolutions at first or second hand. The labour and socialist movement saw itself as the lineal continuation of this tradition. The Austrian Social Democrats celebrated March Day (anniversary of the victims of the Vienna revolution of 1848) before they celebrated the new May Day. Yet social revolution was rapidly retreating from its original zone of incubation. And in some ways the very emergence of massive, organized and above all disciplined class-parties accelerated its retreat. The organized mass meeting, the carefully planned mass demonstration or procession, the election campaign, replaced rather than prepared riot and insurrection. The sudden upsurge of 'red' parties in the advanced countries of bourgeois society was indeed a worrying phenomenon for its rulers: but few of them actually expected to see the guillotine erected in their capitals. They could recognize such parties as bodies of radical opposition within a system which, nevertheless, provided room for improvement and conciliation. These were not, or not yet, or no longer, societies in which, in spite of rhetoric to the contrary, much blood flowed.

What kept the new parties committed to the complete revolution of society, at least in theory, and the masses of ordinary workers committed to them, was certainly not the inability of capitalism to bring them some improvement. It was that, so far as most workers who hoped for improvement could judge, all significant amelioration came primarily through their action and organization as a class. Indeed, in some respects the decision to choose the road of collective improvement foreclosed other options. In the regions of Italy where poor landless farm labourers chose to organize in unions and co-operatives, they did not choose the alternative of mass emigration. The stronger the sense of a working-class community and solidarity, the stronger the social pressures to keep within it, though they did not exclude – especially for groups like the miners – the ambition to give one's children the schooling that would keep them out of the pit. What lay behind the socialist convictions of working-class militants and the approval of their masses was, more than anything, the segregated world imposed on the new proletariat. If they had hope – and their organized members were indeed proud and hopeful – it was because they had hope in the movement. If 'the American dream' was individualist, the European worker's was overwhelmingly collective.

Was this revolutionary? Almost certainly not in the insurrectionary sense, to judge by the behaviour of the majority of the strongest of all revolutionary socialist parties, the German SPD. But there was in Europe a vast semi-circular belt of poverty and unrest in which revolution actually was on the agenda, and – at least in one part of it – actually broke out. It stretched from Spain through large parts of Italy, via the Balkan peninsula into the Russian Empire. Revolution migrated from western to eastern Europe in our period. We shall consider the fortunes of the revolutionary zone of the continent and the globe below. Here we can only note that in the east Marxism retained its original explosive connotations. After the Russian Revolution it returned to the west as well as expanding into the east as the quintessential ideology of social revolution, which it was to remain for so much of the twentieth century. Meanwhile the gap in communication between socialists speaking the same theoretical language widened almost without their being aware of it, until its width was suddenly revealed by the outbreak of war in 1914, when Lenin, long the admirer of German social democratic orthodoxy, discovered that its chief theorist was a traitor.

V

Even though socialist parties in most countries, in spite of national and confessional divisions, plainly seemed to be on the way to mobilize the majority of their working classes, it was undeniable that, except for Great Britain, the proletariat was not – socialists confidently claimed 'not yet' – anything like a majority of the population. As soon as socialist parties acquired a mass basis, ceasing to be propagandist and agitational sects, bodies of cadres or scattered local strongholds of converts, it thus became evident that they could not confine their attention exclusively to the working class. The intensive debate on 'the agrarian question' which began among Marxists in the middle 1890s reflects precisely this discovery. While 'the peasantry' was no doubt destined to fade away (as Marxists argued, correctly, since this has virtually happened in the later twentieth century), what could or ought socialism to offer meanwhile to the 36 per cent in Germany, the 43 per cent in France who lived by agriculture (1900), not to mention the European countries which were, as yet, overwhelmingly agrarian? The need to widen the appeal of socialist parties from the purely proletarian could be formulated and defended in various ways, from simple electoral calculations or revolutionary considerations to general theory ('Social Democracy is the party of the proletariat ... but ... it is simultaneously a party of social development, envisaging the development of the entire social body from the present capitalist stage to a higher form').[27] It could not be denied, since the proletariat could almost everywhere be outvoted, isolated, or even repressed by the united force of other classes.

But the very identification between party and proletariat made the appeal to other social strata more difficult. It stood in the way of the political pragmatists, the reformists, the Marxist 'revisionists', who would have preferred to broaden socialism from a class-party into a 'people's party', for even practical politicians ready to leave doctrine to a few comrades classified as 'theorists' appreciated that the almost existential appeal to the workers as workers was what gave the parties their real force. What is more, the political demands and slogans specifically tailored to proletarian measurements – such as the Eight-Hour Day and socialization – left other strata indifferent, or even risked antagonizing them by the implied threat of expropriation. Socialist labour parties rarely had much success in breaking out of the large but separate working-class universe within which their militants, and quite often their masses, actually felt quite comfortable.

And yet the appeal of such parties sometimes went far beyond the working classes; and even those mass parties most uncompromisingly identifying themselves with one class patently mobilized support from other social strata. There were, for instance, countries in which socialism, in spite of its ideological lack of rapport with the rural world, captured large areas of the countryside – and not only the support of those who might be classified as 'rural proletarians': as in parts of southern France, of central Italy and of the USA, where the most solid stronghold of the Socialist Party was, surprisingly, to be found among the Bible-punching poor white farmers of Oklahoma – with a vote of more than 25 per cent for its 1912 presidential candidate in the twenty-three most rural counties of that state. Equally remarkable, small artisans and shopkeepers were notably overrepresented in the membership of the Italian Socialist Party, compared to their numbers in the total population.

There were, no doubt, historical reasons for this. Where the political tradition of the (secular) left – republican, democratic, jacobin or the like – was old and strong, socialism might seem a logical extension of it – today's version, as it were, of that declaration of faith in the eternal great causes of the left. In France, where it was clearly a major force, those grassroots intellectuals of the countryside and champions of republican values, the primary school teachers, were much attracted to socialism, and the major political grouping of the Third Republic paid its respects to the ideals of its electorate by naming itself Republican Radical and Radical Socialist Party in 1901. (It was patently neither radical nor socialist.) Yet socialist parties drew strength, as well as political ambiguity, from such traditions only because, as we have seen, they shared them, even when they were no longer felt to be sufficient. Thus in states where the franchise was still restricted, their militant and effective combat for democratic voting rights won support from other democrats. As the parties of the least privileged, it was natural that they should now be seen as standard-bearers of that fight against inequality and 'privilege' which had been central to political radicalism since the American and French revolutions; all the more so since so many of its former standard-bearers had, like the liberal middle class, joined the forces of privilege themselves.

Socialist parties benefited even more clearly by their status as the unqualified opposition to the rich. They stood for a class which was, without exception, poor, though not necessarily very poor by contemporary standards. They denounced exploitation, wealth and its growing concentration with unceasing passion. Others who were poor and felt exploited, though not proletarian, might well find such a party congenial.

Thirdly, socialist parties were, almost by definition, parties devoted to that key concept of the nineteenth century, 'progress'. They stood, especially in their Marxist form, for the inevitable forward march of history towards a better future, whose precise content might be unclear, but which would certainly see the continued and accelerated triumph of reason and education, science and technology. When Spanish anarchists speculated about their utopia, it was in terms of electricity and automatic waste-disposal machines. Progress, if only as a synonym of hope, was the aspiration of those who had little or nothing, and the new rumblings of doubt about its reality or desirability in the world of bourgeois and patrician culture (see below) augmented its plebeian and politically radical associations, at least in Europe. There can be no doubt that socialists benefited from the prestige of progress among all who believed in it, especially among those brought up in and imbued with the tradition of liberalism and the Enlightenment.

Finally, and paradoxically, being both outsiders and in permanent opposition (at least until the revolution) gave them an advantage. In their first capacity they clearly attracted much more than the statistically expectable support from minorities whose position in society was in some degree anomalous, such as, in most European countries, the Jews even when they were comfortably bourgeois, and in France the Protestant minority. In their second capacity, unsullied by the contamination of ruling classes, they might in multinational empires attract oppressed nations, which might for this reason rally to red banners, to which they gave a distinct national tinge. This was notably so, as we shall see in the next chapter, in the Tsarist Empire, the most dramatic case being that of the Finns. For this reason the Finnish Socialist Party, which polled 37 per cent of the vote as soon as the law allowed it to, rising to 47 per cent in 1916, became *de facto* the national party of its country.

The support of nominally proletarian parties could therefore extend considerably beyond the proletariat. Where this was so, it could easily turn such parties into parties of government in suitable circumstances; and indeed after 1918 it did so. However, to join the system of 'bourgeois' governments meant to abandon the status of revolutionaries or even radical oppositionists. Before 1914 this was not quite unthinkable, but certainly it was publicly inadmissible. The first socialist who joined a 'bourgeois' government, even with the excuse of unity in defence of the republic against the imminent threat of reaction, Alexandre Millerand (1899) – he subsequently became President of France – was solemnly drummed out of the national and international movement. Before 1914 no serious socialist politician was fool enough to make his mistake. (In fact, in France the Socialist Party did not join a government until 1936.) On the face of it the parties remained pure and uncompromising until the war.

One last question must, however, be asked. Can one write the story of the working classes in our period simply in terms of their class organizations (not necessarily socialist ones) or of that generic class consciousness expressed in the lifestyles and behaviour patterns in the ghetto-world of the proletariat? Only to the extent that they felt and behaved in some way as members of such a class. Such consciousness could extend very far, into entirely unexpected quarters, such as the ultra-pious Chassidic weavers of ritual Jewish prayer-shawls in a lost corner of Galicia (Kolomea) who went on strike against their employers with the help of the local Jewish socialists. And yet a great many of the poor, and especially the very poor, did not think of themselves or behave as 'proletarians', or find the organizations and modes of action of the movement applicable or relevant to them. They saw themselves as belonging to the eternal category of the poor, the outcast, the unlucky or the marginal. If they were immigrants into the big city from the countryside or some foreign region, they might live in a ghetto which could overlap with the working-class slum, but was more likely to be dominated by the street, the market, the innumerable petty ways, legal or non-legal, in which poor families kept body and soul together, only some of which were in any real sense wage-work. What counted for them was not union or class-party, but neighbours, family, patrons who could do favours or provide jobs, otherwise avoiding rather than pressuring public authorities, priests, people from the same place in the old country, anybody and anything that made life in a new and unknown environment possible. If they belonged to the old urban inner-city plebs, the admiration of anarchists for their underworlds and half-worlds would not make them more proletarian or political. The world of Arthur Morrison's *A Child of the Jago* (1896) or of Aristide Bruant's song *Belleville-Ménilmontant* is not that of class consciousness, except insofar as the sense of resentment against the rich is shared by both. The ironic, shoulder-shrugging, accepting, utterly a-political world of English music-hall song,* which had its golden age in these years, is closer to that of the conscious working class, but its themes – mothers-in-law, wives, no money for the rent – belonged to any community of nineteenth-century urban underdogs.

We should not forget these worlds. In fact, they are not forgotten because, paradoxically, they attracted the artists of the time more than the respectable and monochrome and especially the provincial world of the classical proletariat. But neither should we counterpose it to the proletarian world. The culture of the plebeian poor, even the world of the traditional outcasts, shaded over into that of class consciousness where both coexisted. Both recognized one another, and where class consciousness and its movement were strong, as in, say, Berlin or the great sea-port of Hamburg, the pre-industrial miscellaneous world of poverty fitted into it, and even the pimps, thieves and fences would pay their respects to it. They had nothing independent to contribute to it, though anarchists thought differently. They certainly lacked the

---

* As Gus Elen sang:

> With a ladder and some glasses
> You could see the Hackney Marshes
> If it wasn't for the houses in between.

permanent militancy, let alone the commitment, of the activist – but so, as every activist knew, did the great bulk of ordinary working-class people anywhere. There is no end to the complaints of the militants about this dead weight of passivity and scepticism. Insofar as a conscious working class, which found expression in its movement and party, was emerging in this period, the pre-industrial plebs were drawn into its sphere of influence. And insofar as they were not, they must be left out of history, because they were not its makers but its victims.

CHAPTER 6

WAVING FLAGS: NATIONS AND NATIONALISM

'Scappa, che arriva la patria' (*Run away, the fatherland is coming*).
Italian peasant woman to her son[1]

*Their language has become complex, because now they read. They read books –
or at any rate they learn to read out of books. ... The word and the idiom of the
literary language tend and the pronunciation suggested by its spelling tends to
prevail over the local usage.*

H. G. Wells, 1901[2]

*Nationalism ... attacks democracy, demolishes anti-clericalism, fights socialism
and undermines pacifism, humanitarianism and internationalism. ... It declares
the programme of liberalism finished.*

Alfredo Rocco, 1914[3]

I

If the rise of working-class parties was one major by-product of the
politics of democratization, the rise of nationalism in politics was
another. In itself it was plainly not new (see *The Age of Revolution*, *The
Age of Capital*). Yet in the period from 1880 to 1914 nationalism took a
dramatic leap forward, and its ideological and political content was
transformed. Its very vocabulary indicates the significance of these
years. For the word 'nationalism' itself first appeared at the end of the
nineteenth century to describe groups of right-wing ideologists in
France and Italy, keen to brandish the national flag against foreigners,
liberals and socialists and in favour of that aggressive expansion of their
own state which was to become so characteristic of such movements.
This was also the period when the song 'Deutschland Über Alles'
(Germany above all others) replaced rival compositions to become the
actual national anthem of Germany. Though it originally described

only a right-wing version of the phenomenon, the word 'nationalism' proved to be more convenient than the clumsy 'principle of nationality' which had been part of the vocabulary of European politics since about 1830, and so it came to be used also for all movements to whom the 'national cause' was paramount in politics: that is to say for all demanding the right to self-determination, i.e. in the last analysis to form an independent state, for some nationally defined group. For the number of such movements, or at least of leaders claiming to speak for such movements, and their political significance, increased strikingly in our period.

The basis of 'nationalism' of all kinds was the same: the readiness of people to identify themselves emotionally with 'their' nation' and to be politically mobilized as Czechs, Germans, Italians or whatever, a readiness which could be politically exploited. The democratization of politics, and especially elections, provided ample opportunities for mobilizing them. When states did so they called it 'patriotism', and the essence of the original 'right-wing' nationalism, which emerged in already established nation-states, was to claim a monopoly of patriotism for the extreme political right, and thereby brand everyone else as some sort of traitor. This was a new phenomenon, for during most of the nineteenth century nationalism had been rather identified with liberal and radical movements and with the tradition of the French Revolution. But elsewhere nationalism had no necessary identification with any colour in the political spectrum. Among the national movements still lacking their own states we shall encounter those identifying with the right or the left, or indifferent to either. And indeed, as we have suggested, there were movements, and not the least powerful, which mobilized men and women on a national basis, but, as it were, by accident, since their primary appeal was for social liberation. For while in this period national identification clearly was or became a major factor in the politics of states, it is quite mistaken to see the national appeal as incompatible with any other. Nationalist politicians and their opponents naturally liked to suggest that one kind of appeal excluded the other, as wearing one hat excludes wearing another at the same time. But, as a matter of history, and observation, this is not so. In our period it was perfectly possible to become simultaneously a class-conscious Marxian revolutionary and an Irish patriot, like James Connolly, who was to be executed in 1916 for leading the Easter Rising in Dublin.

But of course, insofar as parties in the countries of mass politics competed for the same body of supporters, these had to make mutually exclusive choices.

The new working-class movements, appealing to their potential constituency on grounds of class identification, soon realized this, insofar as they found themselves competing, as was usually the case in multi-national regions, against parties which asked proletarians and potential socialists to support them as Czechs, Poles or Slovenes. Hence their preoccupation as soon as they actually became mass movements, with 'the national question'. That virtually every Marxist theorist of importance, from Kautsky and Rosa Luxemburg, via the Austro-Marxists, to Lenin and the young Stalin, took part in the impassioned debates on this subject during this period, suggests the urgency and centrality of this problem.[4]

Where national identification became a political force, it therefore formed a sort of general substratum of politics. This makes its multifarious expressions extremely difficult to define, even when they claimed to be specifically nationalist or patriotic. As we shall see, national identification almost certainly became more widespread in our period, and the significance of the national appeal in politics grew. However, what was almost certainly more important was a major set of mutations within political nationalism, which was to have profound consequences for the twentieth century.

Four aspects of this mutation must be mentioned. The first, as we have already seen, is the emergence of nationalism and patriotism as an ideology taken over by the political right. This was to find its extreme expression between the wars in fascism, whose ideological ancestors are to be found here. The second is the assumption, quite foreign to the liberal phase of national movements, that national self-determination up to and including the formation of independent sovereign states applied not just to some nations which could demonstrate economic, political and cultural viability, but to any and all groups which claimed to be a 'nation'. The difference between the old and the new assumption is illustrated by the difference between the twelve rather large entities envisaged as constituting 'the Europe of nations' by Giuseppe Mazzini, the great prophet of nineteenth-century nationalism, in 1857 (see *The Age of Capital*, chapter 5, 1), and the twenty-six states – twenty-seven if we include Ireland – which emerged from President Wilson's principle of national self-determination at the end of the First World War. The third was the growing tendency to assume that 'national self-determination' could not be satisfied by any form of autonomy less than full state independence. For most of the nineteenth century, the majority of demands for autonomy had not envisaged this. Finally, there was the novel tendency to define a nation in terms of ethnicity and especially in terms of language.

Before the middle 1870s there had been states, mainly in the western half of Europe, which saw themselves as representing 'nations' (e.g. France, Britain or the new Germany and Italy), and states which, though based on some other political principle, were regarded as representing the main body of their inhabitants on grounds which could be thought of as something like national (this was true of the tsars, who certainly enjoyed the loyalty of the Great Russian people as both Russian and Orthodox rulers). Outside the Habsburg Empire and perhaps the Ottoman Empire, the numerous nationalities within the established states did not constitute much of a political problem, especially once a German and an Italian state had been established. There were, of course, the Poles, divided between Russia, Germany and Austria but never losing sight of the restoration of an independent Poland. There were, within the United Kingdom, the Irish. There were various chunks of nationalities which, for one reason or another, found themselves outside the frontiers of the relevant nation-state to which they would much have preferred to belong, though only some created political problems, e.g. the inhabitants of Alsace–Lorraine, annexed by Germany in 1871. (Nice and Savoy, handed over by what was to become Italy to France in 1860, showed no marked signs of discontent.)

There is no doubt that the number of nationalist movements increased considerably in Europe from the 1870s, though in fact much fewer new national states were established in Europe in the last forty years before the First World War than in the forty years preceding the formation of the German Empire, and those established were not very significant: Bulgaria (1878), Norway (1907), Albania (1913).* There were now 'national movements' not only among peoples hitherto considered 'unhistorical' (i.e. who had never previously possessed an independent state, ruling class or cultural elite), such as Finns and Slovaks, but among peoples about whom hardly anybody except folklore enthusiasts had previously thought at all, such as Estonians and Macedonians. And within long-established nation-states regional populations now began to mobilize politically as 'nations'; this happened in Wales, where a Young Wales movement was organized in the 1890s under the leadership of a local lawyer of whom much more was to be heard in future, David Lloyd George, and in Spain, where a Basque National Party was formed in 1894. And about the same time Theodor Herzl launched Zionism among the Jews, to whom the sort of nationalism it represented had hitherto been unknown and meaningless.

Many of these movements did not yet have much support among the people for whom they claimed to speak, though mass emigration now gave many more members of backward communities the powerful incentive of nostalgia to identify with what they had left behind,

* The states established or internationally recognized in 1830–71 included Germany, Italy, Belgium, Greece, Serbia and Rumania. The so-called 'Compromise' of 1867 also amounted to the grant of very far-reaching autonomy by the Habsburg Empire to Hungary.

and opened their minds to new political ideas. Nevertheless, mass identification with a 'nation' almost certainly grew, and the political problem of nationalism probably became more difficult to manage for both states and non-nationalist competitors. Probably most observers of the European scene in the early 1870s felt that, after the period of Italian and German unification and the Austro–Hungarian compromise, the 'principle of nationality' was likely to be less explosive than it had been. Even the Austrian authorities, asked to include a question on language in their censuses (a step recommended by the International Statistical Congress of 1873), though unenthusiastic, did not say no. However, they thought, one had to give time for the hot national tempers of the past ten years to cool down. They thought they could safely assume that this would have happened by the census of 1880. They could not have been more spectacularly mistaken.[5]

However, what proved to be significant in the long run was not so much the degree of support for the national cause achieved at the time among this or that people, as the transformation of the definition and programme of nationalism. We are now so used to an ethnic–linguistic definition of nations that we forget that this was, essentially, invented in the later nineteenth century. Without going at length into the matter, it is enough to recall that the ideologists of the Irish movement did not begin to tie the cause of the Irish nation to the defence of the Gaelic language until some time after the foundation of the Gaelic League in 1893; that the Basques did not base their national claims on their language (as distinct from their historic *fueros* or constitutional privileges) until the same period; that the impassioned debates about whether Macedonian is more like Bulgarian than it is like Serbo-Croat were among the last arguments used to decide which of those two people they should unite with. As for the Zionist Jews, they went one better by identifying the Jewish nation with Hebrew, a language which no Jews had used for ordinary purposes since the days of the Babylonian captivity, if then. It had just (1880) been invented as a language for everyday use – as distinct from a sacred and ritual tongue or a learned *lingua franca* – by a man who began the process of providing it with a suitable vocabulary by inventing a Hebrew term for 'nationalism', and it was learned as a badge of Zionist commitment rather than as a means for communication.

This does not mean that language had previously been unimportant as a national issue. It was one criterion of nationality among several others; and, in general, the less prominent it was, the stronger was the identification of the masses of a people with its collectivity. Language was not an ideological battleground for those who merely talked it, if only because the exercise of control over what language mothers talked with children, husbands with wives, and neighbours with each other, was virtually impossible. The language which most Jews actually spoke, namely Yiddish, had virtually no ideological dimension until the non-Zionist left took it up, nor did most Jews who spoke it mind that many authorities (including those of the Habsburg Empire) refused even to accept it as a separate language. Millions chose to become members of the American nation, which obviously had no single ethnic basis, and learned English as a matter of necessity or convenience, without reading any essential element of a national soul or a national continuity into their efforts to speak the language. Linguistic nationalism was the creation of people who wrote and read, not of people who spoke. And the 'national languages' in which they discovered the essential character of their nations were, more often than not, artefacts, since they had to be compiled, standardized, homogenized and modernized for contemporary and literary use, out of the jigsaw puzzle of local or regional dialects which constituted non-literary languages as actually spoken. The major written national languages of old nation-states or literate cultures had gone through this phase of compilation and 'correction' long since: German and Russian in the eighteenth, French and English in the seventeenth century, Italian and Castilian even earlier. For most languages of smaller linguistic groups the nineteenth century was the period of the great 'authorities' who established the vocabulary and 'correct' usage of their idiom. For several – Catalan, Basque, the Baltic languages – it was the turn of the nineteenth and twentieth centuries.

Written languages are closely, though not necessarily, linked with territories and institutions. The nationalism which established itself as the standard version of the national ideology and programme was essentially territorial, since its basic model was the territorial state of the French Revolution, or at any rate the nearest thing to complete political control over a clearly defined territory and its inhabitants which was available in practice. Once again Zionism provides the extreme example, just because it was so clearly a borrowed programme which had no precedent in, or organic connection with, the actual tradition which had given the Jewish people permanence, cohesion and an indestructible identity for some millennia. It asked them to acquire a territory (inhabited by another people) – for Herzl it was not even necessary that that territory should have any historic connection with the Jews – as well as a language they had not spoken for millennia.

The identification of nations with an exclusive territory created such problems over large areas of the world of mass migration, and even of the non-migratory world, that an alternative definition of nationality was developed, notably in the Habsburg Empire and among the Jewish diaspora. It was here seen as inherent, not in a particular piece of the map to which a body of inhabitants were attached, but in the members of such bodies of men and women as considered themselves to belong to a nationality, wherever they happened to live. As such members, they would enjoy 'cultural autonomy'. Supporters of the geographical and human theories of 'the nation' were locked in embittered argument, notably in the international socialist movement and between Zionists and Bundists among the Jews. Neither theory was particularly satisfactory, though the human theory was more harmless. At all events it did not lead its supporters to create a territory first and squeeze its inhabitants into the right national shape afterwards: or, in the words of Pilsudski, the leader of the newly independent Poland after 1918: 'It is the state which makes the nation and not the nation the state.'[6]

As a matter of sociology, the non-territorialists were almost certainly right. Not that men and women – give or take a few nomadic or diaspora peoples – were not deeply attached to some piece of land they called 'home', especially considering that for most of history the great majority of them belonged to that most rooted part of humanity, those who live by agriculture. But that 'home territory' was no more like the territory of the modern nation than the word 'father' in the modern term 'fatherland' was like a real parent. The 'homeland' was the locus of a *real* community of human beings with real social relations with each other, not the imaginary community which creates some sort of bond between members of a population of tens – today even of hundreds – of millions. Vocabulary itself proves this. In Spanish *patria* did not become coterminous with Spain until late in the nineteenth century. In the eighteenth it still meant simply the place or town where a person was born.[7] *Paese* in Italian ('country') and *pueblo* in Spanish ('people') can and do still mean a village as well as the national territory or its inhabitants.* Nationalism and the state took over the associations of kin, neighbours and home ground, for territories and populations of a size and scale which turned them into metaphors.

But, of course, with the decline of the real communities to which people had been used – village and kin, parish and *barrio*, gild, confraternity or whatever – a decline which occurred because they clearly no longer encompassed, as they once had done, most contingencies of people's lives, their members felt a need for something to take their place. The imaginary community of 'the nation' could fill this void.

It found itself attached, and inevitably so, to that characteristic phenomenon of the nineteenth century, the 'nation-state'. For as a matter of politics, Pilsudski was right. The state not only made the

* The force of the German television serial *Heimat* lay precisely in marrying the characters' experience of the 'little fatherland' (to use the Spanish term) – the Hunsrück mountain – to their experience of the 'big fatherland', Germany.

nation, but *needed* to make the nation. Governments now reached down directly to each citizen on their territory in everyday life, through modest but omnipresent agents, from postmen and policemen to teachers and (in many countries) railway employees. They might require his, and eventually even her, active personal commitment to the state: in fact their 'patriotism'. Authorities in an increasingly democratic age, who could no longer rely on the social orders submitting spontaneously to their social superiors in the traditional manner, or on traditional religion as an effective guarantee of social obedience, needed a way of welding together the state's subjects against subversion and dissidence. 'The nation' was the new civic religion of states. It provided a cement which bonded all citizens to their state, a way to bring the nation-state directly to each citizen, and a counterweight to those who appealed to other loyalties over state loyalty – to religion, to nationality or ethnicity not identified with the state, perhaps above all to class. In constitutional states, the more the masses were drawn into politics by elections, the more scope there was for such appeals to be heard.

Moreover, even non-constitutional states now learned to appreciate the political force of being able to appeal to their subjects on grounds of nationality (a sort of democratic appeal without the dangers of democracy), as well as on grounds of their duty to obey the authorities sanctioned by God. In the 1880s even the Russian tsar, faced with revolutionary agitations, began to apply the policy vainly suggested to his grandfather in the 1830s, namely to base his rule not only on the principles of autocracy and orthodoxy, but also on nationality: i.e. on appealing to Russians as Russians.[8] Of course in one sense practically all nineteenth-century monarchs had to put on national fancy-dress, since hardly any of them were natives of the countries they ruled. The (mostly) German princes and princesses who became rulers or rulers' consorts of Britain, Greece, Rumania, Russia, Bulgaria, or whatever other country needed crowned heads, paid their respect to the principle of nationality by turning themselves into Britons (like Queen Victoria) or Greeks (like Otto of Bavaria) or learning some other language which they spoke with an accent, even though they had far more in common with the other members of the international princes' trade union – or rather family, since they were all related – than with their own subjects.

What made state nationalism even more essential was that both the economy of a technological era and the nature of its public and private administration required mass elementary education, or at least literacy. The nineteenth century was the era when oral communication broke down, as the distance between authorities and subjects increased, and mass migration put days or weeks of travel between even mothers and sons, bridegrooms and brides. From the state's point of view, the school had a further and essential advantage: it could teach all children how to be good subjects and citizens. Until the triumph of television, there was no medium of secular propaganda to compare with the classroom.

Hence, in educational terms, the era from 1870 to 1914 was above all, in most European countries, the age of the primary school. Even in notoriously well-schooled countries the number of primary school teachers multiplied. It trebled in Sweden and rose almost as much in Norway. Relatively backward countries caught up. The number of primary school children in the Netherlands doubled; in the United Kingdom (which had had no public educational system before 1870) it trebled; in Finland it increased thirteenfold. Even in the illiterate Balkans the number of children in elementary schools quadrupled and the number of teachers almost trebled. But a national, i.e. an overwhelmingly state-organized and state-supervised, educational system required a national language of instruction. Education joined the law courts and bureaucracy (see *The Age of Capital*, chapter 5) as a force which made language into the primary condition of nationality.

States therefore created 'nations', i.e. national patriotism and, at least for certain purposes, linguistically and administratively homogenized citizens, with particular urgency and zeal. The French republic turned peasants into Frenchmen. The Italian kingdom, following D'Azeglio's slogan (see *The Age of Capital*, chapter 5, 11), did its best, with mixed success, to 'make Italians' through school and military service, after having 'made Italy'. The USA made a knowledge of English a condition for American citizenship and, from the end of the 1880s on, began to introduce actual worship under the new civic religion – the only one permitted under an agnostic constitution – in the form of a daily ritual of homage to the flag in every American school. The Hungarian state did its best to turn all its multinational inhabitants into Magyars; the Russian state pressed the russification of its lesser nationalities – i.e. it tried to give Russian the monopoly of education. And where multi-nationality was sufficiently recognized to permit elementary or even secondary education in some other vernacular (as in the Habsburg Empire), the state language inevitably enjoyed a decisive advantage at the highest levels of the system. Hence the significance, for non-state nationalities, of the struggle for a university of their own, as in Bohemia, Wales or Flanders.

For state nationalism, real or (as in the case of the monarchs) invented for convenience, was a double-edged strategy. As it mobilized some inhabitants, it alienated others – those who did not belong, or wish to belong, to the nation identified with the state. In short, it helped to define the nationalities excluded from the official nationality by separating out those communities which, for whatever reason, resisted the official public language and ideology.

II

But why should some have resisted, where so many others did not? After all, there were quite substantial advantages for peasants – and even more for their children – in becoming Frenchmen, or indeed for anyone who acquired a major language of culture and professional advancement in addition to their own dialect or vernacular. In 1910 70 per cent of German immigrants to the USA, who arrived there, on average after 1900, with $41 in their pockets,[9] had become English-speaking American citizens, though they had plainly no intention of ceasing to speak and feel German.[10] (To be fair, few states really tried to stop the private life of a minority language and culture, so long as it did not challenge the public supremacy of the official state-nation.) It might well be that the unofficial language could not effectively compete with the official one, except for purposes of religion, poetry and community or family sentiment. Hard though it may be to believe today, there were passionately national Welshmen who accepted a lesser place for their ancient Celtic tongue in the century of progress, and some who envisaged an eventual natural euthanasia* for it. There were, indeed, many who chose to migrate not from one territory but from one class to another; a voyage which was apt to mean a change of nation or at least a change of language. Central Europe became full of German nationalists with obviously Slav names, and Magyars whose names were literal translations of German or adaptations of Slovak ones. The American nation and English language were not the only ones which, in the era of liberalism and mobility, issued a more or less open invitation for membership. And there were plenty who were happy to accept such invitations, all the more so when they were not actually expected to deny their origins by doing so. 'Assimilation' for most of the nineteenth century was far from a bad word: it was what vast numbers of people hoped to achieve, especially among those who wanted to join the middle classes.

One obvious reason why members of some nationalities refused to 'assimilate' was because they were not allowed to become full members of the official nation. The extreme case is that of the native elites in European colonies, educated in the language and culture of their masters so that they could administer the colonials on the Europeans' behalf, but patently not treated as their equals. Here a conflict was

---

* The term is actually used by a Welsh witness to the 1847 parliamentary committee on Welsh education.

bound to erupt sooner or later, all the more so since western education actually provided a specific language for articulating their claims. Why, wrote an Indonesian intellectual in 1913 (in Dutch), should Indonesians be expected to celebrate the centenary of the liberation of the Netherlands from Napoleon? If he were a Dutchman, 'I would not organise an independence celebration in a country where the independence of the people has been stolen.'[11]

Colonial peoples were an extreme case, since it was clear from the outset that, given the pervasive racism of bourgeois society, no amount of assimilation would turn men with dark skins into 'real' Englishmen, Belgians or Dutchmen, even if they had as much money and noble blood and as much taste for sports as the European nobility – as was the case with many an Indian rajah educated in Britain. And yet, even within the zone of white skins, there was a striking contradiction between the offer of unlimited assimilation to anyone who proved his or her willingness and ability to join the state-nation and the rejection of some groups in practice. This was particularly dramatic for those who had hitherto assumed, on highly plausible grounds, that there were no limits to what assimilation could achieve: the middle-class, westernized, cultivated Jews. That is why the Dreyfus case in France, the victimization of a single French staff officer for being Jewish, produced so disproportionate a reaction of horror – not only among Jews but among all liberals – and led directly to the establishment of Zionism, a territorial state nationalism for Jews.

The half-century before 1914 was a classic era of xenophobia, and therefore of nationalist reaction to it, because – even leaving aside global colonialism – it was an era of massive mobility and migration and, especially during the Depression decades, of open or concealed social tension. To take a single example: by 1914 something like 3.6 millions (or almost 15 per cent of the population) had permanently left the territory of inter-war Poland, not counting another half-million *a year* of seasonal migrants.[12] The consequent xenophobia did not only come from below. Its most unexpected manifestations, which reflected the crisis of bourgeois liberalism, came from the established middle classes, who were not likely actually ever to meet the sort of people who settled on New York's Lower East Side or who lived in the harvest-labourers' barracks in Saxony. Max Weber, glory of open-minded German bourgeois scholarship, developed so passionate an animus against the Poles (whom he, correctly, accused German landowners of importing *en masse* as cheap labour) that he actually joined the ultra-nationalist Pan-German League in the 1890s.[13] The real systematization of race-prejudice against 'Slavs, Mediterraneans and Semites' in the USA is to be found among the native white, preferably

Protestant anglophone-born middle and upper classes, which even, in this period, invented their own heroic nativist myth of the white Anglo-Saxon (and fortunately non-unionized) cowboy of the wide open spaces, so different from the dangerous antheaps of the swelling great cities.*

In fact, for this bourgeoisie the influx of the alien poor dramatized and symbolized the problems raised by the expanding urban proletariat, combining as they did the characteristics of internal and external 'barbarians', which threatened to swamp civilization as respectable men knew it (see p. 35 above). They also dramatized, nowhere more than in the USA, the apparent inability of society to cope with the problems of headlong change, and the unpardonable failure of the new masses to accept the superior position of the old elites. It was in Boston, the centre of the traditional white, Anglo-Saxon, Protestant bourgeoisie, both educated and wealthy, that the Immigration Restriction League was founded in 1893. Politically the xenophobia of the middle classes was almost certainly more effective than the xenophobia of the labouring classes, which reflected cultural frictions between neighbours and the fear of low-wage competition for jobs. Except in one respect. It was sectional working-class pressure which actually excluded foreigners from labour markets, since for employers the incentive to import cheap labour was almost irresistible. Where exclusion kept the stranger out entirely, as did the bans on non-white immigrants in California and Australia, which triumphed in the 1880s and 1890s, this produced no national or communal friction, but where it discriminated against a group already on the spot, such as Africans in white South Africa or Catholics in Northern Ireland, it was naturally apt to do so. However, working-class xenophobia was rarely very effective before 1914. All things considered, the greatest international migration of people in history produced surprisingly little by way of anti-foreign labour agitations even in the USA, and sometimes virtually none, as in Argentina and Brazil.

Nevertheless, bodies of immigrants into foreign countries were very likely to discover national sentiments, whether or not they were met by local xenophobia. Poles and Slovaks would become conscious of themselves as such, not only because once they left their home villages they could no longer take themselves for granted as people who did not require any definition, and not only because the states they moved to imposed some new definition on them, classifying people who had hitherto thought of themselves as Sicilians or Neapolitans, or even as

---

* The three members of the north-eastern elite who are chiefly responsible for this myth (which, incidentally, extruded the people chiefly responsible for the cowboy culture and vocabulary, the Mexicans) were Owen Wister (author of *The Virginian*, 1902), the painter Frederick Remington (1861–1909;) and the later President, Theodore Roosevelt.[14]

natives of Lucca or Salerno, as 'Italians' on arrival in the USA. They needed their community for mutual aid. From whom could migrants into new, strange, unknown lives expect help except kin and friends, people from the old country? (Even regional migrants within the same country would usually stick together.) Who could even understand him or, more to the point, her – for women's domestic sphere left them more monoglot than men? Who could give them shape as a community rather than a mere heap of foreigners, except, in the first instance, some body like their Church which, even though in theory universal, was in practice national, because its priests came from the same people as their congregations and Slovak priests had to talk Slovak to them, whatever the language in which they celebrated the mass? In this manner 'nationality' became a real network of personal relations rather than a merely imaginary community, simply because, far from home, every Slovene actually had a potential personal connection with every other Slovene when they met.

Moreover, if such populations were to be organized in any manner for the purpose of the new societies in which they found themselves, it had to be done in ways which allowed communication. Labour and socialist movements, as we have seen, were internationalist, and even dreamed, as liberals had done (*The Age of Capital*, chapter 3, I, IV), of a future in which all would talk a single world language – a dream still surviving in small groups of Esperantists. Eventually, as Kautsky still hoped in 1908, the entire body of educated humanity would be fused into a single language and nationality.[15] Yet in the meantime they faced the problem of the Tower of Babel: unions in Hungarian factories might have to issue strike-calls in four different languages.[16] They soon discovered that nationally mixed branches did not work well, unless members were already bilingual. International movements of labouring people *had to be* combinations of national or linguistic units. In the USA the party which in effect became the workers' mass party, the Democrats, necessarily developed as an 'ethnic' coalition.

The greater the migration of peoples and the more rapid the development of cities and industry which threw uprooted masses against each other, the greater the basis for national consciousness among the uprooted. Hence, in the case of new national movements, exile was often their main place of incubation. When the future President Masaryk signed the agreement which was to create a state uniting Czechs and Slovaks (Czechoslovakia) he did so in Pittsburgh, for the mass basis of an organized Slovak nationalism was to be found in Pennsylvania rather than in Slovakia. As for the backward mountain peoples of the Carpathians known in Austria as Ruthenes, who were also to be joined to Czechoslovakia from 1918 to 1945, their nationalism had no organized expression whatever except among emigrants to the USA.

The mutual aid and protection of emigrants may have contributed to the growth of nationalism in their nations, but is not enough to explain it. However, insofar as it rested on an ambiguous and double-edged nostalgia for the old ways emigrants had left behind, it had something in common with a force which undoubtedly fostered nationalism at home, especially in the smaller nations. This was neo-traditionalism, a defensive or conservative reaction against the disruption of the old social order by the advancing epidemic of modernity, capitalism, cities and industry, not forgetting the proletarian socialism which was their logical outcome.

The traditionalist element is obvious enough in the support of the Catholic Church for such movements as Basque and Flemish nationalism, or indeed many nationalisms of small peoples which were, almost by definition, rejected by liberal nationalism as incapable of forming viable nation-states. The right-wing ideologues who now multiplied also tended to develop a taste for traditionally rooted cultural regionalism such as the Provençal *félibrige*. In fact, the ideological ancestors of most of the separatist–regionalist movements in late-twentieth-century western Europe (Breton, Welsh, Occitan, etc.) are to be found on the pre-1914 intellectual right. Conversely, among these small peoples neither the bourgeoisies nor the new proletariat usually found mini-nationalism to their taste. In Wales the rise of Labour undermined the Young Wales nationalism which had threatened to take over the Liberal Party. As for the new industrial bourgeoisie, it could be expected to prefer the market of a large nation or world to the provincial constriction of a small country or region. Neither in Russian Poland nor in the Basque country, two disproportionately industrialized regions of larger states, did indigenous capitalists show enthusiasm for the national cause, and the demonstratively franco-centred bourgeoisie of Ghent was a permanent provocation to Flemish nationalists. Though this lack of interest was not quite universal, it was strong enough to mislead Rosa Luxemburg into supposing that there was no bourgeois base for Polish nationalism.

But, even more frustrating to traditionalist nationalists, the most traditionalist of all classes, the peasantry, also showed only a faint interest in nationalism. The Basque-speaking peasants showed little enthusiasm for the Basque National Party, founded in 1894 to defend all that was ancient against the incursion of Spaniards and godless workers. Like most other such movements, it was primarily an urban middle- and lower-middle-class body.[17]

In fact, the advance of nationalism in our period was largely a phenomenon carried by these middle strata of society. Hence there is much point to the contemporary socialists who called it 'petty-bourgeois'. And its connection with these strata helps to explain the three novel characteristics we have already observed: its shifts to linguistic militancy, to a demand for independent states rather than lesser kinds of autonomy, and to the political right and ultra-right.

For the lower-middle classes rising from a popular background, career and vernacular language were inseparably welded together. From the moment that society rested on mass literacy, a spoken language had to be in some sense official – a medium of bureaucracy and instruction – if it was not to sink into the half-world of purely oral communication ocasionally dignified with the status of an exhibit in a folklore museum. *Mass*, i.e. primary, education was the crucial development, since it was possible only in a language which the bulk of the population could be expected to understand.* Education in a totally foreign language, alive or dead, is possible only for a select and sometimes exiguous minority which can afford the considerable time, expense and effort to acquire sufficient command of it. Bureaucracy, again, was a crucial element, both because it decided the official status of a language and because, in most countries, it provided the largest body of employment requiring literacy. Hence the endless petty struggles which disrupted the politics of the Habsburg Empire from the 1890s, about the language in which street signs were to be written in areas of mixed nationality, and about such matters as the nationality of particular assistant postmasters or railway station masters.

But only political power could transform the status of lesser languages or dialects (which, as everyone knows, are just languages without an army and police force). Hence the pressures and counter-pressures behind the elaborate linguistic censuses of the period (e.g., most notably, those of Belgium and Austria in 1910), on which the political claims of this or that idiom depended. And hence, at least in part, the political mobilization of nationalists for language at the very moment when, as in Belgium, the number of bilingual Flemings grew very strikingly or, as in the Basque country, the use of the Basque language was virtually dying out in the rapidly growing cities.[18] For political pressure alone could win a place for what were in practice 'uncompetitive' languages as a medium of education or written public communication. This, and

* The prohibition of the use of Welsh, or some local language or patois in the classroom, which left such traumatic traces in the memories of local scholars and intellectuals, was due not to some kind of totalitarian claims by the dominant state-nation, but almost certainly to the sincere belief that no adequate education was possible except in the state language, and that the person who remained a monoglot would inevitably be handicapped as a citizen and in his or her professional prospects.

this alone, made Belgium officially bilingual (1870) and Flemish a compulsory subject in the secondary schools of Flanders (as late as 1883). But once the unofficial language had thus won official standing, it automatically created a substantial political constituency of vernacular literates for itself. The 4.8 million pupils in the primary and secondary schools of Habsburg Austria in 1912 obviously contained a great many more potential and actual nationalists than the 2.2 millions of 1874, not to mention the 100,000 or so extra teachers who now instructed them in various rival languages.

And yet in multilingual societies those educated in the vernacular, and able to use this education for professional advancement, probably still felt themselves to be inferior and unprivileged. For while they were in practice at an advantage in competing for the lesser jobs, because they were much more likely to be bilingual than the snobs of the elite language, they might justifiably feel that they were at a disadvantage in the search for the top jobs. Hence the pressure to extend vernacular teaching from primary to secondary education, and eventually to the crown of a full educational system, the vernacular university. In both Wales and Flanders the demand for such a university was intensely, and exclusively, political for this reason. In fact in Wales the national university (1893) actually became for a while the first and *only* national institution of a people whose small country had no administrative or other existence distinct from England. Those whose first language was an unofficial vernacular would almost certainly still be excluded from the higher ranges of culture and private or public affairs, unless as speakers of the official and superior idiom in which they would certainly be conducted. In short, the very fact that new lower-middle and even middle classes had been educated in Slovene or Flemish emphasized that the major prizes and the top status still went to those who spoke French or German, even if they did not bother to learn the lesser language.

Yet more political pressure was needed to overcome this built-in handicap. In fact, what was needed was political *power*. To put it bluntly, people had to be compelled to use the vernacular for purposes for which they would normally have found it preferable to use another language. Hungary insisted on magyarized schooling, even though every educated Hungarian, then as now, knew perfectly well that a knowledge of at least one internationally current language was essential for all except the most subaltern functions in Hungarian society. Compulsion, or government pressure amounting to it, was the price paid for turning Magyar into a literary language which could serve all modern purposes in its own territory, even if nobody could understand a word of it outside. Political power alone – in the last analysis state power – could hope to achieve such results. Nationalists, especially those whose livelihood and career prospects were tied up with their language, were unlikely to ask whether there were other ways in which languages might develop and flourish.

To this extent linguistic nationalism had a built-in bias towards secession. And, conversely, the call for an independent state territory seemed increasingly inseparable from language, so that we find the official commitment to Gaelic entering Irish nationalism (in the 1890s) even though – perhaps actually because – most of the Irish were quite satisfied to speak only English, and Zionism invented Hebrew as an everyday language, because no other language of the Jews committed them to the construction of a territorial state. There is room for interesting reflections about the varied fate of such essentially political efforts at linguistic engineering, for some were to fail (like the reconversion of the Irish to Gaelic) or half-fail (like the construction of a more Norwegian Norwegian – Nynorsk), while others were to succeed. However, before 1914 they generally lacked the required state power. In 1916 the number of actual everyday speakers of Hebrew was no more than 16,000.

But nationalism was linked to the middle strata in another way, which gave both it and them a twist towards the political right. Xenophobia appealed readily to traders, independent craftsmen and some farmers threatened by the progress of the industrial economy, especially, once again, during the hard-pressed years of the Depression. The foreigner came to symbolize the disruption of old ways and the capitalist system which disrupted them. Thus the virulent political anti-Semitism which we have observed spreading across the western world from the 1880s had little to do with the actual number of Jews against whom it was directed: it was as effective in France, where there were 60,000 among 40 millions, in Germany where there were half a million among 65 millions, as in Vienna where they formed 15 per cent of the population. (It was not a political factor in Budapest, where they formed a quarter of it). This anti-Semitism took aim rather against the bankers, entrepreneurs and others who were identified with the ravages of capitalism among the 'little men'. The typical cartoon image of the capitalist in the *belle époque* was not just a fat man in a top hat smoking a cigar, but one with a Jewish nose – because the fields of enterprise in which Jews were prominent competed with small shopkeepers and gave or refused credit to farmers and small artisans.

Anti-Semitism, the German socialist leader Bebel therefore felt, was 'the socialism of idiots'. Yet what strikes us about the rise of political anti-Semitism at the end of the century is not so much the equation 'Jew = capitalist', which was not implausible in large parts of east-central Europe, but its association with *right-wing* nationalism. This was not only due to the rise of socialist movements which systematically combated the latent or overt xenophobia of their supporters, so that a deeply rooted dislike of foreigners and Jews in those quarters tended to be rather more shamefaced than in the past. It marked a distinct shift of the nationalist ideology to the right in the major states, especially in the 1890s, when we can see, for instance, the old mass organizations of German nationalism, the *Turner* (gymnastic associations), veer from the liberalism inherited from the 1848 revolution to an aggressive, militarist and anti-Semitic posture. This is when the banners of patriotism became so much a property of the political right that the left found trouble in grasping them, even where patriotism was as firmly identified with revolution and the cause of the people as was the French tricolour. To brandish the national name and flag, they felt, risked contamination from the ultra-right. Not until the days of Hitler did the French left recover the full use of jacobin patriotism.

Patriotism shifted to the political right, not only because its former ideological stablemate, bourgeois liberalism, was in disarray, but because the international situation which had apparently made liberalism and nationalism compatible no longer held good. Up to the 1870s – perhaps even up to the Congress of Berlin of 1878 – it could be claimed that one nation-state's gain was not necessarily another's loss. Indeed, the map of Europe had been transformed by the creation of two major new nation-states (Germany and Italy) and the formation of several minor ones in the Balkans, without either war or intolerable disruption of the international state system. Until the Great Depression something very like global free trade, while perhaps benefiting Britain rather more than others, had been in the interest of all. Yet from the 1870s on such claims ceased to ring true, and as a global conflict came, once more, to be considered as a serious, if not an impending possibility, the sort of nationalism which saw other nations frankly as menace or victims gained ground.

It both bred and was encouraged by the movements of the political right which emerged out of the crisis of liberalism. Indeed the men who first called themselves by the novel name of 'nationalists' were frequently stimulated into political action by the experience of their state's defeat in war, like Maurice Barrès (1862–1923) and Paul Deroulède (1846–1914) after the German victory over France in 1870–1, and Enrico Corradini (1865–1931) after Italy's even more galling defeat at the hands of Ethiopia in 1896. And the movements they founded, which brought the word 'nationalism' into the general dictionaries, were quite deliberately set up 'in reaction against the democracy then in government', i.e. against parliamentary politics.[19] The French movements of this kind remained marginal, like the Action Française (est. 1898) which lost itself in a politically irrelevant monarchism and in vituperative prose. The Italian ones eventually merged with fascism after the First World War. They were characteristic of a new breed of political movements built on chauvinism, xenophobia and, increasingly, the idealization of national expansion, conquest and the very act of war.

Such nationalism lent itself exceptionally well to expressing the collective resentments of people who could not explain their discontents precisely. It was the foreigners' fault. The Dreyfus case gave French anti-Semitism a special edge, not only because the accused was a Jew (what business had an alien in the French general staff?) but because his alleged crime was espionage on behalf of Germany. Conversely, the blood of 'good' Germans curdled at the thought that their country was being systematically 'encircled' by the alliance of its enemies, as their leaders frequently reminded them. Meanwhile the English were getting ready to celebrate the outbreak of the world war (like other belligerent peoples) by an outburst of anti-alien hysteria which made it advisable to change the German family name of the royal dynasty to the Anglo-Saxon 'Windsor'. No doubt every native citizen, apart from a minority of internationalist socialists, a few intellectuals, cosmopolitan businessmen and the members of the international club of aristocrats and royals, felt the appeal of chauvinism to some extent. No doubt almost all, including even many socialists and intellectuals, were so deeply imbued with the fundamental racism of nineteenth-century civilization (see *The Age of Capital*, chapter 14, II, and pp. 253–4 below) that they were also indirectly vulnerable to the temptations which come from believing one's own class or people to have a built-in natural superiority over others. Imperialism could not but reinforce these temptations among members of imperial states. Yet there is little doubt that those who responded most eagerly to the nationalist bugles were to be found somewhere between the established upper classes of society and the peasants and proletarians at the bottom.

For this widening body of middle strata, nationalism also had a wider and less instrumental appeal. It provided them with a collective identity as the 'true defenders' of the nation which eluded them as a class, or as aspirants to the full bourgeois status they so much coveted. Patriotism compensated for social inferiority. Thus in Britain, where there was no compulsory military service, the curve of volunteer recruitment of working-class soldiers in the imperialist South African War (1899–1902) simply reflects the economic situation. It rose and fell with unemployment. But the curve of recruitment for lower-middle-class and white-collar youths clearly reflected the appeals of patriotic propaganda. And, in a sense, patriotism in uniform could bring its social rewards. In Germany it provided the potential status as reserve officer for boys who had undergone secondary education to the age of sixteen, even if they went no further. In Britain, as the war was to show, even clerks and salesmen in the service of the nation could become officers and – in the brutally frank terminology of the British upper class – 'temporary gentlemen'.

III

Yet, nationalism between the 1870s and 1914 cannot be confined to the kind of ideology which appealed to the frustrated middle classes or the anti-liberal (and anti-socialist) ancestors of fascism. For it is beyond question that in this period governments and parties or movements which could make, or imply, a national appeal were likely to enjoy an extra advantage; and conversely those which could not or would not were to some extent handicapped. It is quite undeniable that the outbreak of war in 1914 produced genuine, if sometimes shortlived, outbursts of mass patriotism in the main belligerent countries. And in multinational states working-class movements organized on an all-state basis fought and lost a rearguard action against disintegration into separate movements based on the workers of each nationality. The labour and socialist movement of the Habsburg Empire thus fell apart before the empire itself did.

Nevertheless, there is a major difference between nationalism as an ideology of nationalist movements and flag-waving governments, and the broader appeal of nationality. The first did not look beyond the establishment or aggrandizement of 'the nation'. Its programme was to resist, expel, defeat, conquer, subject or eliminate 'the foreigner'. Anything else was unimportant. It was enough to assert the Irishness, Germanness or Croatianness of the Irish, German or Croatian people in an independent state of their own, belonging exclusively to them, to announce its glorious future and to make every sacrifice to achieve it.

It was this which, in practice, limited its appeal to a cadre of impassioned ideologists and militants, to shapeless middle classes searching for cohesion and self-justification, to such groups (again, mainly among the struggling 'little men') as could ascribe all their discontents to the damned foreigners – and, of course, to governments which welcomed an ideology which told citizens that patriotism was enough.

But for most people nationalism alone was not enough. This is, paradoxically, most evident in the actual movements of nationalities which had not yet achieved self-determination. The national movements which gained genuine mass support in our period – and by no means all which wanted it had achieved it – were almost invariably those which combined the appeal of nationality and language with some more powerful interest or mobilizing force, ancient or modern. Religion was one. Without the Catholic Church the Flemish and Basque movements would have been politically negligible, and nobody doubts that Catholicism gave consistency and mass strength to the nationalism of Irish and Poles ruled by rulers of a different faith. In fact, during this period the nationalism of the Irish Fenians, originally a secular, indeed anti-clerical, movement appealing to Irishmen across confessional frontiers, became a major political force precisely by letting Irish nationalism identify itself essentially with the Catholic Irish.

More surprisingly, as we have already suggested, parties whose original and primary object was international class and social liberation found themselves becoming the vehicles of national liberation also. The re-establishment of an independent Poland was achieved, not under the leadership of any of the numerous nineteenth-century parties devoted exclusively to independence, but under leadership coming from the Second International's Polish Socialist Party. Armenian nationalism shows the same pattern, as indeed does Jewish territorial nationalism. What made Israel was not Herzl or Weizmann, but (Russian-inspired) labour Zionism. And while some such parties were, justifiably, criticized within international socialism because they put nationalism a long way before social liberation, this cannot be said of other socialist, or even Marxist, parties which found themselves to their surprise to be the representative of particular nations: the Finnish Socialist Party, the Mensheviks in Georgia, the Jewish Bund in large areas of eastern Europe – in fact, even the rigidly non-nationalist Bolsheviks in Latvia. Conversely, nationalist movements became aware of the desirability of spelling out, if not a specific social programme, then at least a concern with economic and social questions. Characteristically it was in industrialized Bohemia, torn between Czechs and Germans both drawn to labour movements,* that movements specifically describing themselves as 'national socialist' emerged. The Czech national socialists eventually became the characteristic party of independent Czechoslovakia, and provided its last President (Beneš). The German national socialists inspired a young Austrian who took their name and their combination of anti-Semitic ultra-nationalism with a vague populist social demagogy into post-war Germany: Adolf Hitler.

---

* The Social Democrats polled 38 per cent of Czech votes in the first democratic election – 1907 – and emerged as the largest party.

Nationalism therefore became genuinely popular essentially when it was drunk as a cocktail. Its attraction was not just its own flavour, but its combination with some other component or components which, it was hoped, would slake the consumers' spiritual and material thirst. But such nationalism, though genuine enough, was neither as militant nor as single-minded, and certainly not as reactionary, as the flag-waving right would have wanted it to be.

The Habsburg Empire, about to disintegrate under the various national pressures, paradoxically illustrates the limitations of national-ism. For though most of its people were, by the early 1900s, unques-tionably conscious of belonging to some nationality or other, few of them thought that this was incompatible with support for the Habsburg monarchy. Even after the outbreak of war national independence was not a major issue, and a decided hostility to the state was to be found only in four of the Habsburg nations, three of which could identify with national states beyond their borders (the Italians, the Rumanians, the Serbs and the Czechs). Most of the nationalities did not visibly wish to break out of what middle- and lower-middle-class zealots liked to call 'the prison of peoples'. And when, in the course of the war, discontent and revolutionary feelings really mounted, it took the form, in the first instance, not of movements for national independence but for social revolution.[20]

As for the western belligerents, in the course of the war anti-war feeling and social discontent increasingly overlaid, but without destroy-ing, the patriotism of the mass armies. The extraordinary international impact of the Russian revolutions of 1917 is comprehensible only if we bear in mind that those who had gone to war willingly, even enthusiastically, in 1914 were moved by the idea of patriotism which could not be confined within nationalist slogans: for it included a sense of what was due to citizens. These armies had not gone to war out of a taste for fighting, for violence and heroism, or to pursue the uncon-ditional national egoism and expansionism of the nationalism of the right. And still less out of hostility to liberalism and democracy.

On the contrary. The domestic propaganda of all belligerents with mass politics demonstrates, in 1914, that the point to stress was not glory and conquest, but that 'we' were the victims of aggression, or of a policy of aggression, that 'they' represented a mortal threat to the values of freedom and civilization which 'we' embodied. What is more, men and women would not be successfully mobilized for the war unless they felt that the war was more than a plain armed combat: that in some sense the world would be better for 'our' victory and 'our' country would be – to use Lloyd George's phrase – 'a land fit for heroes to live in'. The British and French governments thus claimed to defend democracy and freedom against monarchical power, militarism and barbarism ('the Huns'), while the German government claimed to defend the values of order, law and culture against Russian autocracy and barbarism. The prospects of conquest and imperial aggrandizement could be advertised in colonial wars, but not in the major conflicts – even if they occupied foreign ministries behind the scenes.

The German, French and British masses who marched to war in 1914 did so, not as warriors or adventurers, but as citizens and civilians. Yet this very fact demonstrates both the necessity of patriotism for governments operating in democratic societies and its force. For only the sense that the cause of the state was genuinely their own could mobilize the masses effectively: and in 1914 the British, French and Germans had it. They were so mobilized, until three years of unparalleled massacre and the example of revolution in Russia taught them that they had been mistaken.

CHAPTER 7

WHO'S WHO OR THE UNCERTAINTIES OF THE BOURGEOISIE

In its widest possible sense ... a man's Self is the sum-total of what he can call his, not only his body and his psychic powers, but his clothes and his house, his wife and children, his ancestors and friends, his reputation and works, his lands and horses and yacht and bank-account.

William James[1]

With an immense zest ... they begin shopping. ... They plunge into it as one plunges into a career; as a class they talk, think and dream possessions.

H. G. Wells, 1909[2]

The College is founded by the advice and counsel of the Founder's dear wife ... to afford the best education for women of the Upper and Upper Middle Classes.

From the Foundation Deed of Holloway College, 1883

I

Let us now turn to those whom democratization appeared to threaten. In the century of the conquering bourgeoisie, members of the successful middle classes were sure of their civilization, generally confident and not usually in financial difficulties, but only very late in the century were they physically *comfortable*. Until then they had lived well enough, surrounded by a profusion of decorated solid objects, encased in large quantities of textiles, able to afford what they regarded as suitable to persons of their standing and unsuitable to those below them, and consuming food and drink in substantial, and probably in excessive, quantities. The food and drink, in some countries at least, were excellent: *cuisine bourgeoise*, in France at least, was a term of gastronomic praise. Elsewhere, at least, they were copious. An ample supply of servants compensated for the discomfort and impracticability of their

165

houses. But it could not conceal them. It was only quite late in the century that bourgeois society developed a style of life and the suitable material equipment actually designed to fit the requirements of the class which was supposed to form its backbone: men in business, the free professions or the higher ranks of public service and their families, who did not necessarily aspire to or expect the status of aristocracy or the material rewards of the very rich, but who were well above the zone where buying one thing meant forgoing others.

The paradox of the most bourgeois of centuries was that its life-styles became 'bourgeois' only late, that this transformation was pioneered on its fringes rather than at its centre, and that, as a specifically bourgeois way and style of living, it triumphed only momentarily. That is perhaps why the survivors looked back to the era before 1914 so often and so nostalgically as the *belle époque*. Let us begin the survey of what happened to the middle classes in our period by considering this paradox.

That new lifestyle was the suburban house and garden, which has long ceased to be specifically 'bourgeois' except as an index of aspiration. Like so much else in bourgeois society it came from the classic country of capitalism, Great Britain. We may first detect it in the garden suburbs constructed by architects like Norman Shaw in the 1870s for comfortable, though not particularly wealthy, middle-class households (Bedford Park). Such colonies, generally intended for rather richer strata than their British equivalents, developed on the outskirts of central European cities – the Cottage-Viertel in Vienna, Dahlem and the Grunewald-Viertel in Berlin – and eventually moved socially downwards into the lesser or lower-middle-class suburbs or the unplanned labyrinth of 'pavilions' on the fringes of great cities, and eventually, via speculative builders and socially idealistic town-planners into the semi-detached streets and colonies intended to recapture the village and small-town spirit (*Siedlungen* or 'settlements' was to be the significant German term for them) of some municipal housing for the more comfortable workers later in the twentieth century. The ideal middle-class house was no longer seen as part of a city street, a 'town house' or its substitute, an apartment in a large building fronting a city street and pretending to be a palace, but an urbanized or rather suburbanized country house ('villa' or even 'cottage') in a miniature park or garden, surrounded by greenery. It was to prove an enormously powerful ideal of living, though not applicable as yet within most non-Anglo-Saxon cities.

The 'villa' differed from its original model, the country house of nobility and gentry, in one major respect, apart from its more modest (and reducible) scale and cost. It was designed for the convenience of private living rather than social status-striving and role-playing. Indeed, the fact that such colonies were largely single-class communities, topographically isolated from the rest of society, made it easier to concentrate on the comforts of life. This isolation developed even when it was not intended: the 'garden cities' and 'garden suburbs' designed by socially idealistic (Anglo-Saxon) planners went the same way as the suburbs specifically built to remove the middle classes from their inferiors. And this exodus in itself indicated a certain abdication of the bourgeoisie from its role as a ruling class. 'Boston', the local rich told their sons around 1900, 'holds nothing for you except heavy taxes and political misrule. When you marry, pick out a suburb to build a house in, join the Country Club, and make your life center about your club, your home, and your children.'[3]

But this was the very opposite of the function of the traditional country house or château, or even of its bourgeois rival or imitator, the great capitalist's mansion – the Krupps' Villa Hügel, or the Bankfield House and Belle Vue of the Akroyds and Crossleys, who dominated the smoky lives of the woollen town of Halifax. Such establishments were the engine-casings of power. They were designed to demonstrate the resources and prestige of a member of a ruling elite to other members and to the inferior classes, and to organize the business of influence and ruling. If cabinets were made in the country house of the Duke of Omnium, John Crossley of Crossleys Carpets at least invited forty-nine of his colleagues on the Halifax Borough Council for three days to his house in the Lake District on the occasion of his fiftieth birthday, and entertained the Prince of Wales on the occasion of the inauguration of Halifax town hall. In such houses private life was inseparable from public life with recognized and, as it were, diplomatic and political public functions. The requirements of these took precedence over home comforts. One does not imagine that the Akroyds would have built themselves a grand stairway painted with scenes from classical mythology, a painted banqueting hall, a dining room, library and suite of nine reception rooms, or for that matter a servants' wing designed for twenty-five domestics, primarily for their family use.[4] The country gentleman could no more avoid exercising his power and influence in his county than the local business magnate could avoid doing so in Bury or Zwickau. Indeed, so long as he lived in the city, by definition an image of the urban social hierarchy, even the average member of the bourgeoisie could hardly avoid indicating – nay, underlining – his place in it by the choice of his address, or at least of the size of his apartment and the storey it occupied in the building, the degree of servitude he could command, the formalities of his costume and social intercourse. The Edwardian stockbroker's family which a dissident son recalled later in life was inferior to the Forsytes, because their house did not quite overlook Kensington Gardens, but it was not so far away as to lose status. The London Season was beyond it, but the mother was formally 'At Home' on regular afternoons, and organized evening receptions with a 'Hungarian band' hired from Whiteleys Universal Store, as well as giving or attending almost daily dinner parties at the required time, during the months of May and June.[5] Private life and the public presentation of status and social claims could not be distinct.

The modestly rising middle classes of the pre-industrial period were mostly excluded from such temptations by their inferior, if respectable, social status or their puritan and pietist convictions, not to mention by the imperatives of capital accumulation. It was the bonanza of mid-nineteenth-century economic growth which put them within the reach of the successful, but which at the same time imposed a public lifestyle patterned on that of the older elites. Yet at this moment of triumph four developments encouraged the formation of a less formal, a more genuinely private and privatized lifestyle.

The first, as we have seen, was the democratization of politics which undermined the public and political influence of all but the very grandest and most formidable of bourgeois. In some cases the (mainly liberal) bourgeoisie was forced *de facto* to withdraw altogether from a politics dominated by mass movements or a mass of voters which refused to recognize their 'influence' when it was not actually directed against them. The culture of *fin de siècle* Vienna, it has been argued, was largely that of a class and a people – the middle-class Jews – who were no longer allowed to be what they wanted, namely German liberals, and who would not have found many followers even as a non-Jewish liberal bourgeoisie.[6] The culture of the Buddenbrooks and of their author Thomas Mann, himself the son of a patrician in an ancient and proud city of Hanseatic traders, is that of a bourgeoisie which has withdrawn from politics. The Cabots and the Lowells in Boston were far from extruded from national politics, but they were to lose control of Boston politics to the Irish. From the 1890s the paternalist 'factory culture' of northern England broke down, a culture in which workers might be trade unionists, but would celebrate the anniversaries of their employers, whose political colours they followed. One of the reasons why a Labour Party emerged after 1900 is that the men of influence in the working-class constituencies, the local bourgeoisie, had refused to give up the right to nominate local 'notables', i.e. people like themselves for Parliament and council in the 1890s. Insofar as the bourgeoisie retained its political power, it was henceforth by mobilizing influence rather than followers.

The second was a certain loosening of the links between the triumphant bourgeoisie and the puritan values which had been so useful for capital accumulation in the past and by means of which the class had so often identified itself and marked its distance from the idle and dissolute aristocrat and the lazy and drunken labourers. In the established bourgeoisie the money had already been made. It might come, not directly from its source, but as a regular payment produced by pieces of paper which represented 'investments' whose nature might be obscure, even when they did not originate in some remote region of the globe, far from the Home Counties round London. Frequently it was inherited, or distributed to non-working sons and female relatives. A good deal of the late-nineteenth-century bourgeoisie consisted of a 'leisure class' whose name was invented at this time by a maverick American sociologist of considerable originality, Thorstein Veblen, who wrote a 'Theory' about it.[7] And even some of those who actually made money did not have to spend too much time at it, at all events if they did so in (European) banking, finance and speculation. In Britain, at any rate, these left plenty of time for other pursuits. In short, spending became at least as important as earning. The spending did not have to be as lavish as that of the ultra-rich, of whom there was indeed plenty in the *belle époque*. Even the relatively less affluent learned how to spend for comfort and enjoyment.

The third was the loosening of the structures of the bourgeois family, which was reflected in a certain emancipation of the women in it (which will be considered in the next chapter), and the emergence of the age-groups between adolescence and marriage as a separate and more independent category of 'youth', which in turn had a powerful impact on the arts and literature (see chapter 9 below). The words 'youth' and 'modernity' sometimes became almost interchangeable; and if 'modernity' meant anything, it meant a change of taste, décor and style. Both these developments became noticeable among the established middle classes in the second half of the century, and obvious in its last two decades. They not only affected that form of leisure which took the form of tourism and holidays – as Visconti's *Death in Venice* rightly shows, the grand hotel by beach or mountain, which now entered its period of glory, was dominated by the image of its women guests – but they greatly increased the role of the bourgeois home as a setting for its women.

The fourth was the substantial growth of those who belonged, or claimed to belong, or aspired passionately to belong, to the bourgeoisie: in short, of the 'middle class' as a whole. A certain idea of an essentially domestic lifestyle was one of the things that bound all its members together.

II

At the same time democratization, the rise of a self-conscious working class and social mobility created a novel problem of social identity for those who belonged or wished to belong to some layer or other of these 'middle classes'. The definition of 'the bourgeoisie' is notoriously difficult (see *The Age of Capital*, chapter 13, III, IV), and it became no easier as democracy and the rise of labour movements led those who belonged to the bourgeoisie (whose name became an increasingly dirty word) to deny their existence as a class in public, if not to deny the existence of classes altogether. In France it was held that the Revolution had abolished classes, in Britain that classes, not being closed castes, did not exist, in the increasingly vocal field of sociology that social structure and stratification were too complex for such simplifications. In America the danger seemed to be not so much that the masses might mobilize themselves as one class and identify their exploiters as another, as that, in pursuit of their constitutional right to equality, they might declare themselves to belong to the middle class, thus diminishing the advantages (other than the unanswerable facts of wealth) of belonging to an elite. Sociology, as an academic discipline a product of the period 1870–1914, still suffers from endless and inconclusive debates about social class and status, due to the fondness of its practitioners for reclassifying the population in a manner most suitable to their ideological convictions.

Moreover, with social mobility and the decline of traditional hierarchies establishing who belonged and did not belong to a 'middle rank' or 'estate' of society, the boundaries of this intermediate social zone (and the area within it), became hazy. In countries used to the older classification, like Germany, elaborate distinctions were now drawn between a *Bürgertum* of bourgeoisie, in turn divided into a *Besitzbürgertum* based on the ownership of property and a *Bildungsbürgertum* based on the access to bourgeois status by means of higher education, and a *Mittelstand* ('middle estate') below it, which in turn looked down on the *Kleinbürgertum* or petty-bourgeoisie. Other languages of western Europe merely manipulated the shifting and imprecise categories of a 'big' or 'upper', a 'petty' or 'lower' middle class/bourgeoisie, with an even more imprecise space between them. But how to determine who could claim to belong to any of these?

The basic difficulty lay in the growing number of those who claimed bourgeois status in a society in which, after all, the bourgeoisie formed the top social stratum. Even where the old landed nobility had not been eliminated (as in America) or deprived of its *de jure* privileges (as in republican France), its profile in developed capitalist countries was now distinctly lower than before. Even in Britain, where it had maintained both a very prominent political presence and much the greatest wealth in the middle decades of the century, it was relatively falling back. In 1858–79, of the British millionaires who died, four-fifths (117) had still been landowners; in 1880–99 only a little more than a third were, and in 1900–14 the percentage was even lower.[8] Aristocrats were a majority in almost all British cabinets before 1895. After 1895 they never were. Titles of nobility were far from despised, even in countries which officially had no place for them: rich Americans, who could not acquire them for themselves, were quick to buy them in Europe by subsidized marriage for their daughters. Singer sewing-machines became the Princess de Polignac. Nevertheless, even ancient and deep-rooted monarchies conceded that money was now as useful a criterion of nobility as blue blood. The Emperor William II 'considered it as one of his duties as a ruler to meet the wishes of millionaires for decorations and patents of nobility, but made their grant conditional on the making of charitable gifts in the public interest. Perhaps he was influenced by English models.'[9] Well might the observer think so. Of the 159 peerages created in Britain between 1901 and 1920 (omitting those given to the armed services), sixty-six were given to businessmen – about half of these to industrialists – thirty-four to the professions, overwhelmingly the lawyers, and only twenty to men of landed background.[10]

But if the line between bourgeoisie and aristocracy was hazy, the boundaries between the bourgeoisie and its inferiors were also far from clear. This did not so much affect the 'old' lower-middle class or petty-bourgeoisie of independent artisans, small shopkeepers and their like. Their scale of operations placed them firmly on a lower level, and indeed opposed them to the bourgeoisie. The French Radicals' programme was a series of variations on the theme 'small is beautiful': 'the word "petit" constantly recurs in the congresses of the Radical party'.[11] Its enemy were *les gros* – big capital, big industry, big finance, big merchants. The same attitude, with a nationalist, right-wing and anti-Semitic twist rather than a republican and left-wing one, was to be found among their German equivalents, more hard-pressed by an irresistible and rapid industrialization from the 1870s onward. Seen from above, not only their littleness but their occupations debarred them from higher status, unless, exceptionally, the size of their wealth wiped out the memory of its origin. Still, the dramatic transformation of the distributive system, especially from the 1880s on, made some revisions necessary. The word 'grocer' still carries a note of contempt among the upper-middle classes, but in Britain of our period a Sir Thomas Lipton (who made his money from packets of tea), a Lord Leverhulme (who made it from soap) and a Lord Vestey (who made it from frozen meat) acquired titles and steam yachts. However, the real difficulty arose with the enormous expansion of the tertiary sector – of employment in public and private offices – that is to say of work which was both clearly subaltern and remunerated by wages (even if they were called 'salaries'), but which was also clearly non-manual, based on formal educational qualifications, if relatively modest ones, and above all carried out by men – and even some women – most of whom specifically refused to consider themselves as part of the working-class and aspired, often at great material sacrifice, to the style of life of middle-class respectability. The line between this new 'lower-middle class' of 'clerks' (*Angestellte, employés*) and the higher ranges of the professions, or even of large business increasingly employing salaried executives and managers, raised novel problems.

Leaving aside these new lower-middle classes themselves, it was clear that the new entrants to the middle class or claimants to middle-class status were now rapidly increasing in numbers, which posed practical problems of demarcation and definition, made more difficult by the uncertainty of the theoretical criteria for such definition. What constituted 'the bourgeoisie' was always more difficult to determine than what, in theory, defined a nobility (e.g. birth, hereditary title, land-ownership) or a working class (e.g. the wage-relationship and manual labour). Still (see *The Age of Capital*, chapter 13), the mid-nineteenth-century criteria were fairly explicit. Except for senior salaried state servants, members of this class would be expected to possess capital or an investment income and/or act as independent profit-making entrepreneurs employing labour or as members of a 'free' profession which was a form of private enterprise. Significantly 'profits' and 'fees' were included under the same heading for purposes of the British income tax. Yet with the changes mentioned above, these criteria became far less useful for distinguishing the members of the 'real' bourgeoisie – both economically and above all socially – in the very considerable mass of 'the middle classes', not to mention the even larger body of those aspiring to this status. They did not all possess capital; but neither, at least initially, did many men of undoubted bourgeois status who substituted higher education for it as an initial resource (*Bildungsbürgertum*): and their number was increasing substantially. The number of doctors in France, more or less stable at around 12,000 between 1866 and 1886, had risen to 20,000 by 1911; in Britain the number of doctors rose from 15,000 to 22,000, of architects from 7000 to 11,000 between 1881 and 1901: in both countries the rise was much faster than the growth of the adult population. They were not all entrepreneurs and employers (except of servants).[12] But who could deny bourgeois status to those senior salaried managers who were an increasingly essential part of large business enterprise at a time when, as a German expert pointed out in 1892, 'the intimate, purely private character of the old small businesses' simply could no longer apply to such large undertakings?'[13]

The great majority of all these middle classes, at least insofar as most of them were the product of the era since the dual revolution (see *The Age of Revolution*, Introduction), had one thing in common: social mobility, past or present. Sociologically, as a French observer noted in Britain, the 'middle classes' consisted 'essentially of families in the process of rising socially', and the bourgeoisie of those who 'had arrived' – whether at the top or at some conventionally defined plateau.[14] But such snapshots could hardly give an adequate image of a process of movement which could only be seized, as it were, by a sociological equivalent of that recent invention, the moving picture or film. The 'new social strata' whose advent Gambetta saw as the essential content of the regime of the French Third Republic – he was no doubt thinking of men like himself, making their way without business and property to influence and income through democratic politics – did not stop moving even when recognized as 'arrived'.[15] Conversely, did not 'arrival' change the character of the bourgeoisie? Could membership of this class be denied to the members of their second and third generations who lived leisured lives on the family wealth; who sometimes reacted against the values and activities which still constituted the essence of their class?

Such problems do not at our period concern the economist. An economy based on profit-making private enterprise, such as unquestionably dominated the developed countries of the west, does not require its analysts to speculate about what individuals exactly constitute a 'bourgeoisie'. From the economist's point of view Prince Henckel von Donnersmarck, the second-richest man in imperial Germany (after Krupp), was functionally a capitalist, since nine-tenths of his income came from the ownership of coal-mines, industrial and banking shares, partnerships in real-estate developments, not to mention 12–15 million Marks earning interest. On the other hand for the sociologist and the historian his status as a hereditary aristocrat is far from irrelevant. The problem of defining the bourgeoisie *as a group of men and women*, and the line between these and the 'lower-middle classes', therefore has no direct bearing on the analysis of capitalist development at this stage (except for those who believe that the system depends on the personal motivations of individuals as private entrepreneurs,* though of course it reflects structural changes in the capitalist

---

* There were indeed thinkers who argued that growing bureaucratization, the increasing unpopularity of entrepreneurial values and other such factors would undermine the role of the

economy, and may throw light on its forms of organization.

III

Establishing recognizable criteria was thus urgent for the contemporary members or would-be members of the bourgeoisie or middle class, and in particular for those whose money alone was insufficient to buy a status of assured respect and privilege for themselves and their offspring. Three major ways of establishing such membership became increasingly important in our period – at any rate in countries in which uncertainty about 'who was who' already arose.* All required to fulfil two conditions: they had clearly to distinguish members of the middle classes from the working classes, peasants and others engaged in manual labour, and they had to provide a hierarchy of exclusiveness, without closing the possibility of climbing the steps of this social stairway. A middle-class lifestyle and culture was one such criterion, leisure activity, and especially the new invention of sport, was another; but the chief indicator of social membership increasingly became, and has remained, formal education.

Its major function was not utilitarian, in spite of the potential financial returns from trained intelligence and specialized knowledge in an age increasingly based on scientific technology, and in spite of its opening careers a little more widely for meritocratic talent, especially in the expanding industry of education itself. What counted was the demonstration that adolescents were able to postpone earning a living. The content of education was secondary, and indeed the vocational value of the Greek and Latin on which British 'public school' boys spent so much of their time, of the philosophy, letters, history and geography which filled 77 per cent of the hours in French lycées (1890), was negligible. Even in practical-minded Prussia the classical *Gymnasien* in 1885 contained almost three times as many pupils as the more 'modern' and technically minded *Realgymnasien* and *Ober-Realschulen*. Moreover, the cost of providing such an education for a child was itself a social marker. One Prussian official, who calculated it with German thoroughness, spent 31 per cent of his income on his three sons' education over a period of thirty-one years.[16]

Formal education, preferably crowned by some certificate, had hith-

---

private entrepreneur, and thereby of capitalism. Max Weber and Joseph Schumpeter held such opinions among contemporaries.

*The publication of reference works about persons of status in the nation – as distinct from guides to membership of royal and noble families such as the *Almanach de Gotha* – began in this period. The British *Who's Who* (1897) was perhaps the first.

erto been irrelevant to the rise of a bourgeoisie, except for those learned professions inside and outside public service which it was the main function of universities to train, in addition to providing an agreeable environment for the drinking, whoring and sporting activities of young gentlemen, to whom actual examinations were quite unimportant. Few nineteenth-century businessmen were graduates of anything. The French *polytechnique* at this period did not especially attract the bourgeois elite. A German banker, giving advice to a budding industrialist in 1884, dismissed theory and university education, which he considered merely 'a means of enjoyment for times of rest, like the cigar after lunch'. His advice was to get into practical business as soon as possible, look for a financial backer, observe the USA, and gain experience, leaving higher education to the 'scientifically trained technician', whom the entrepreneur would find useful. From a business point of view this was plain common sense, though it left the technical cadres dissatisfied. German engineers bitterly demanded 'a social position corresponding to the engineer's significance in life'.[17]

Schooling provided above all a ticket of admission to the recognized middle and upper zones of society and a means of socializing the entrants into the ways which would distinguish them from the lower orders. Even the minimum school-leaving age for this type of entry – around sixteen years – guaranteed boys in some countries with military conscription classification as potential officer-material. Increasingly, secondary education to the age of eighteen or nineteen became usual among the middle classes, normally followed by university or higher professional training. The numbers involved remained small, though they increased somewhat in secondary education and much more dramatically in higher education. Between 1875 and 1912 the number of German students more than tripled, of French students (1875–1910) more than quadrupled. However, in 1910 still less than 3 per cent of the French age-groups between twelve and nineteen attended secondary schools (77,500 in all), and only 2 per cent stayed for the final examination, which half of them passed.[18] Germany, with a population of 65 millions, entered the First World War with a corps of something like 120,000 reserve officers, or about 1 per cent of the men between the ages of twenty and forty-five.[19]

Modest though these numbers were, they were much larger than the usual size of older ruling classes – e.g. the 7000 persons who in the 1870s owned 80 per cent of all privately held land in Britain, let alone the 700 or so families which constituted the British peerage. They were certainly too large for the formation of those informal, personal networks by means of which the bourgeoisie earlier in the nineteenth century had been able to structure itself, partly because the economy was highly localized, partly because religious and ethnic minority groups which developed a particular affinity for capitalism (French Protestants, Quakers, Unitarians, Greeks, Jews, Armenians) generated webs of mutual trust, kinship and business transactions which stretched over entire countries, continents and oceans.* At the very peak of the national and international economy such informal networks could still operate, since the number of people involved was tiny, and some parts of business, especially banking and finance, were increasingly concentrated in a handful of financial centres (generally also the actual capital cities of major nation-states). Around 1900 the British banking community, which *de facto* controlled the world's financial business, consisted of a few score families with houses in a small area of London, who knew each other, frequented the same clubs and social circles, and intermarried.[20] The Rhine-Westphalian steel syndicate, which constituted most of the German steel industry, consisted of twenty-eight firms. The largest of all trusts, United States Steel, was formed in informal talks between a handful of men and finally took shape during after-dinner conversations and at golf.

The genuine big bourgeoisie, old or new, therefore had no great difficulty in organizing itself as an elite, since it could use methods very similar to those used by aristocracies, or even – as in Great Britain – the actual mechanisms of aristocracy. Indeed, where possible their aim increasingly was to crown business success by joining the class of the nobility, at least via their sons and daughters, and, if not, at least by an aristocratic lifestyle. It is a mistake to see this simply as an abdication of bourgeois before old aristocratic values. For one thing, socialization through elite (or any) schools had been no more important for traditional aristocracies than for bourgeoisies. Insofar as it became so, as in British 'public schools', it assimilated aristocratic values to a moral system designed for a bourgeois society and for its public service. For another, the test of aristocratic values now increasingly became a profligate and expensive style of life which required above all *money*, never mind where it came from. Money therefore became its criterion. The genuinely traditional landed nobleman, insofar as he could not maintain such a lifestyle and the activities associated with it, found himself exiled into a fading provincial world, loyal, proud but socially marginal, like the characters in Theodore Fontane's *Der Stechlin* (1895) that powerful elegy on ancient Brandenburg *junker* values. The big

---

* The reasons for this affinity have been much discussed, notably in our period by German scholars (e.g. Max Weber and Werner Sombart). Whatever the explanation – and all that such groups have in common is self-conscious minority status – the fact remains that small groups of this kind, such as the British Quakers, had turned themselves almost completely into bodies of bankers, merchants and manufacturers.

bourgeoisie used the mechanism of aristocracy, as of any elite selection, for its own purposes.

The real test of schools and universities as socializers was for those who were climbing up the social ladder, not for those who had already arrived at the top. It transformed the son of a nonconformist Salisbury gardener into a Cambridge don, and *his* son, via Eton and King's College, into the economist John Maynard Keynes, so obviously a member of a confident and polished elite that we are still amazed to think of his mother's childhood milieu among provincial Baptist tabernacles – and yet, to the end, a proud member of his class, of what he later called the 'educated bourgeoisie'.[21]

No wonder that the kind of schooling which offered the probability, perhaps even the certainty, of bourgeois status expanded to meet the rising number who had acquired wealth but not status (like grandfather Keynes), those whose own bourgeois status traditionally depended on education, such as the sons of impecunious Protestant clergymen and the more liberally rewarded professions, and the masses of lesser 'respectable' parents ambitious for their children. Secondary education, the essential gate of entry, grew. The number of its pupils multiplied by anything between two (Belgium, France, Norway, Netherlands) and five (Italy). The number of students in universities, which offered a guarantee of middle-class membership, approximately tripled in most European countries between the late 1870s and 1913. (In the previous decades it had remained more or less stable.) In fact, by the 1880s, German observers were becoming worried about admitting more university students than the middle class sectors of the economy could accommodate.

The problem of the genuine 'upper-middle class' – say, the sixty-eight 'large industrialists' who from 1895 to 1907 joined the five who were already in the top class of taxpayers in Bochum (Germany)[22] – was that such general educational expansion did not provide sufficiently exclusive badges of status. Yet at the same time the big bourgeoisie could not formally separate itself from its inferiors, because its structure had to be kept open to new entrants – that was the nature of its being – and because it needed to mobilize, or at least conciliate, the middle and lower-middle classes against the increasingly mobilized working classes. Hence the insistence of non-socialist observers that the 'middle class' was not merely growing but was of enormous size. The redoubtable Gustav von Schmoller, chieftain of German economists, thought they formed a quarter of the population,[23] but he included among it not only the new 'officials, managers and technicians on good, but moderate, salaries' but also foremen and skilled workers. Sombart similarly estimated it at 12.5 million against 35 million workers.[24]

These were essentially calculations of potentially antisocialist voters. A generous estimate could hardly go very far beyond the 300,000 who are reckoned to have constituted the 'investing public' in late Victorian and Edwardian Britain.[25] In any case the actual members of the established middle classes were far from opening their arms to the lower orders even when these wore collars and ties. An English observer, more characteristically, dismissed the lower-middle classes as belonging with the workers to 'the world of the board schools'.[26]

Within systems of open entry, circles of informal but definite exclusiveness thus had to be established. This was easiest in a country like England, which lacked public primary education until 1870 (school attendance was not compulsory for another twenty years), public secondary education until 1902, and any significant university education outside the two ancient universities of Oxford and Cambridge.* Numerous strikingly misnamed 'public schools' were founded for the middle classes from the 1840s on, on the model of the nine ancient foundations recognized as such in 1870, and already (especially Eton) nurseries of the nobility and gentry. By the early 1900s they had expanded to a list of – depending on the degree of exclusiveness or snobbery – anything between 64 and some 160 more or less expensive schools claiming such status, and deliberately training their pupils as members of a ruling class.[27] A body of similar private secondary schools, mainly in the north-eastern USA, also prepared the sons of good, or at any rate rich, families for the final polish of private elite universities.

Within these, as within the large body of German university students, even more exclusive groups were recruited by private associations such as the student *Korps* or the more prestigious Greek Letter fraternities – whose place in the old English universities was taken by the residential 'colleges'. The late-nineteenth-century bourgeoisies were thus a curious combination of educationally open and closed societies: open, since entry was available by virtue of money, or even (through scholarships or other provisions for poor students) merit, but closed insofar as it was clearly understood that some circles were considerably more equal than others. The exclusiveness was purely social. German *Korps* students, beery and scarred, duelled because this proved that they were (unlike the lower orders) *satisfaktionsfähig*, i.e. gentlemen and not plebeians. The subtle gradations of status among British private schools were established by what schools were prepared to engage in sporting contests against each other – i.e. whose sisters were suitable marriage partners. The body of American elite universities, at least in the east, was actually

---

* The Scottish system was somewhat more comprehensive, but Scots graduates who wanted to make their way in the world found it advisable to take a further degree or examination at Oxbridge, as Keynes' father did after a London degree.

defined by the social exclusiveness of sports: they played each other in the 'Ivy League'.

For those who were on the way up into the big bourgeoisie, these mechanisms of socialization guaranteed unquestioned membership for their sons. Academic education for daughters was optional, and outside liberal and progressive circles still not guaranteed. But it also had some distinct practical advantages. The institution of 'old boys' (*Alte Herren*, alumni), which developed rapidly from the 1870s on, demonstrated that the products of an educational establishment formed a network which might be national or even international but it also bonded younger generations to the older. In short, it gave social cohesion to a heterogeneous body of recruits. Here also sport provided much of the formal cement. By these means a school, a college, a *Korps* or fraternity – revisited and often financed by their alumni – formed a sort of potential mafia ('friends of friends') for mutual aid, not least in business, and in turn the network of such 'extended families' of people whose equivalent economic and social status could be assumed, provided a grid of potential contacts beyond the range of local or regional kin and business. As the guide to American college fraternities put it, observing the vast growth of alumni associations – Beta Theta Phi had alumni chapters in 16 cities in 1889 but 110 in 1912 – they formed 'circles of cultivated men who would not otherwise know each other'.[28]

The practical potential of such networks in a world of national and international business may be indicated by the fact that one such American fraternity (Delta Kappa Epsilon) boasted six senators, forty congressmen, a Cabot Lodge and *the* Theodore Roosevelt in 1889, while in 1912 it also included eighteen New York bankers (including J. P. Morgan), nine figures of substance from Boston, three directors of Standard Oil and persons of comparable weight in the Middle West. It would certainly not be to the disadvantage of the future entrepreneur from, say, Peoria to undergo the rigours of initiation into Delta Kappa Epsilon at a suitable Ivy League college.

All this was of economic as well as social importance, as capitalist concentration developed, and purely local or even regional industry lacking a tie to wider networks atrophied, like the rapidly dying 'country banks' in Great Britain. Yet while the formal and informal schooling system was convenient for the established economic and social elite, it was essential chiefly for those who wanted to join it, or to have their 'arrival' certified by the assimilation of their children. School was the ladder by which children of the more modest members of the middle strata climbed higher; for even in the most meritocratic educational systems few sons of actual peasants and even fewer of workers got further than the bottom rungs.

IV

The relative ease with which the 'upper ten thousand' (as they came to be called) could establish exclusiveness did not solve the problem of the upper hundred thousands who filled the ill-defined space between the top people and the populace, and even less, the problem of the much larger 'lower-middle class', often barely a financial hair's breadth above the better-paid skilled workers. They certainly belonged to what British social observers called the 'servant-keeping class' – 29 per cent of the population in a provincial city like York. In spite of the fact that the number of domestic servants stagnated or even declined from the 1880s on, and therefore did not keep pace with the growth of the middle strata, middle- or even lower-middle-class aspiration without domestic service was still hardly conceivable, except in the USA. To this extent the middle class was still a class of masters (cf. *The Age of Capital*), or rather of mistresses over some labouring girl. They certainly gave their sons, and even increasingly their daughters, a secondary education. Insofar as this qualified men for reserve-officer status (or 'temporary gentlemen' officers in the British mass armies of 1914) it also stamped them as potential masters over other men. Yet a large and growing number of them were no longer 'independent' in the formal sense, but were themselves receivers of wages from employers, even if these were euphemistically called by some other name. Side by side with the old bourgeoisie of entrepreneurs or independent professionals, and those recognizing only the orders of God or the state, there now grew up the new middle class of salaried managers, executives and technical experts in the capitalism of state corporations and high technology: the public and private bureaucracy whose rise Max Weber monitored. Side by side with and overshadowing the old petty-bourgeoisie of independent artisans and small shopkeepers, there now grew up the new petty-bourgeoisie of office, shop and subaltern administration. These were indeed numerically very large strata, and the gradual shift from primary and secondary to tertiary economic activities promised to increase their size. In the USA they were, by 1900, already larger than the actual working class, though this was exceptional.

These new middle and lower-middle classes were too numerous and often, as individuals, too insignificant, their social environments too unstructured and anonymous (especially in the big city), and the scale on which economics and politics operated was too vast for them to count as persons or families, in the way in which the 'upper-middle class' or 'haute-bourgeoisie' could. No doubt this had always been so in the big city, but in 1871 less than 5 per cent of Germans lived in cities of 100,000 or more, whereas in 1910 over 21 per cent did so.

Increasingly, then, the middle classes were identifiable not so much as individuals who 'counted' as such, but by collective recognition signs: by the education they had received, the places they lived in, their lifestyles and practices which indicated their situation to others who were, as individuals, equally unidentifiable. For the recognized middle classes these normally implied a combination of income and education and a certain visible distance from popular origins, as indicated, for instance, by the habitual use of the standard national language of culture and the accent which indicated class, in social intercourse with other than inferiors. The lower-middle classes, old or new, were clearly separate and inferior because of 'insufficient income, mediocrity of culture or closeness to popular origins'.[29] The main objective of the 'new' petty-bourgeoisies was to demarcate themselves as sharply as possible from the working classes – an aim which, generally, inclined them to the radical right in politics. Reaction was their form of snobbery.

The main body of the 'solid', undoubted middle class was not large: in the early 1900s less than 4 per cent of people dying in the United Kingdom left behind them more than £300 worth of property (including houses, furniture, etc.). Yet even though a more than comfortable middle-class income – say £700–1000 a year – was perhaps ten times as high as a good working-class income, it could not compare with the really rich, let alone the super-rich. The gap was enormous, between the established, recognizable and prosperous upper-middle class and what now came to be called the 'plutocracy', which represented what a late Victorian observer called 'the visible obliteration of the conventional distinction between the aristocracies of birth and money'.[30]

Residential segregation – more likely than not in a suitable suburb – was one way of structuring such masses of the comfortable into a social grouping. Education, as we have seen, was another. Both were tied together by a practice which became essentially institutionalized in the last quarter of the old century: sport. Formalized about this time in Britain, which provided the model and vocabulary for it, it spread like wildfire to other countries. At its start its modern form was essentially associated with the middle class, and not necessarily even the upper class. Young aristocrats might, as in Britain, try their hand at any form of physical prowess, but their special field was exercise connected with riding and killing, or at least attacking, animals and people: hunting, shooting, fishing, horse-races, fencing and the like. Indeed in Britain the word 'sports' was originally confined to such pursuits, the games and physical contests now called 'sports' being classified as 'pastimes'. The bourgeoisie, as usual, not only adopted but transformed noble ways of life. Aristocrats also, characteristically, took to notably expensive forms of pursuit such as the newly invented motor car, which was correctly described in the Europe of 1905 as 'the toy of millionaires and the conveyance of the moneyed class'.[31]

The new sports also made their way into the working classes, and even before 1914 some were enthusiastically practised by workers – there were perhaps half a million football players in Britain – and passionately watched and followed by vast multitudes. This fact provided sport with a built-in class criterion, amateurism, or rather the prohibition or strict caste segregation of the 'professionals'. No amateur could genuinely excel in sport unless able to devote far more time to it than members of the labouring classes could, unless they were paid. The sports which became most characteristic of the middle classes, such as lawn tennis, rugby football, American football, still a game of college students, in spite of some strain, or the as yet undeveloped winter sports, stubbornly rejected professionalism. The amateur ideal, which had the additional advantage of uniting middle class and nobility, was enshrined in the new institution of the Olympic Games (1896), brainchild of a French admirer of the British public school system, which was built round its playing-fields.

That sport was seen as an important element in the formation of a new governing class on the model of the public-school-trained British bourgeois 'gentleman' is evident from the role of schools in introducing it to the continent. (The future professional football clubs were more often works teams of expatriate British firms and their staff.) That it had a patriotic, even militarist aspect is also clear. But it also served to create new patterns of middle-class life and cohesion. Lawn tennis, invented in 1873, rapidly became the quintessential game of middle-class suburbs, largely because it was bisexual, and therefore provided a means for 'the sons and daughters of the great middle class' to meet partners not introduced via the family but certain to be of comparable social position. In short, they widened the narrow circle of middle-class family and acquaintance, and, through the network of interacting 'lawn tennis subscription clubs', created a social universe out of self-contained household cells. 'The parlour of home soon dwindled into an insignificant spot.'[32] The triumph of tennis is inconceivable without both suburbanization and the growing emancipation of the middle-class woman. Alpinism, the new sport of cycling (which became the first mass working-class spectator sport on the continent) and the later winter sports, preceded by skating, also benefited substantially from the attraction between the sexes, and incidentally played a significant role in women's emancipation for this reason (see below, pp. 205, 207).

Golf clubs were to play an equally important role in the (Anglo-Saxon) masculine world of middle-class professional men and businessmen. We have already encountered an early business deal concluded on a golf course. The social potential of this game, played on large, expensively constructed and maintained pieces of real estate by members of clubs designed to exclude socially and financially unacceptable outsiders, struck the new middle classes like a sudden revelation. Before 1889 there had only been two 'golf links' in all of Yorkshire (West Riding): between 1890 and 1895 twenty-nine of them were opened.[33] In fact, the extraordinary speed with which all forms of organized sport conquered bourgeois society between 1870 and the early 1900s suggests that it filled a social need for considerably more than open-air exercise. Paradoxically, in Britain at least, an industrial proletariat and a new bourgeoisie or middle class emerged as self-conscious groups at about the same time, defining themselves, against each other, by ways and styles of collective living and action. Sport, a middle-class creation transformed into two obviously class-identified wings, was one of the major ways of doing so.

V

So three major developments marked the middle classes of the pre-1914 decades socially. At the lower end, the number of those with some claim to membership of this middle group grew. These were the non-manual employees who, at the margin, were distinguished from workers who might earn as much as they only by the would-be formality of their working dress (the 'black-coated' or, as the Germans said, 'stiff-collared' proletariat), and by a would-be middle-class style of living. At the upper end the line between employers, upper professionals and higher managers, salaried executives and senior officials, grew hazy. All of them were (realistically) grouped together as 'Class 1' when the British Census in 1911 first attempted to record the population by class. At the same time the bourgeois leisure class of men and women who lived off profits at second hand – the puritan tradition echoes through the British Inland Revenue's classification of 'unearned income' – grew much larger. Relatively fewer bourgeois were now engaged in actually 'earning', and the available accumulations of profit to be distributed among their relatives were now much greater. Above all there were the super-rich, the plutocrats. There were, after all, already more than 4000 (dollar) millionaires in the USA of the early 1890s.

To most of these the pre-war decades were kind; to the more favoured they were extraordinarily generous. The new lower-middle class got little enough in material terms, for their incomes might not be higher than the skilled artisan's, though measured by the year rather than by the week or the day, and workers did not have to spend so much 'to keep up appearances'. However, their status placed them unquestionably above the labouring masses. In Britain the males among them could even think of themselves as 'gentlemen', a term originally devised for the landed gentry, but, in the era of the bourgeoisie, drained of its specific social content and opened to anyone who did not actually perform manual labour. (It was never applied to workers.) Most of them thought of themselves as having done better than their parents, and hoped for even better prospects for their own children. This probably did little to diminish the sense of helpless resentment against those above and below them, which seemed so characteristic of this class.

Those who belonged to the unquestioned world of the bourgeoisie had very little indeed to complain about, for an exceptionally agreeable life, now conducted in an exceptionally agreeable lifestyle, was at the disposal of anyone with a few hundred pounds sterling a year, which was far below the threshold of the big money. The great economist Marshall thought (in *Principles of Economics*) that a professor could live a suitable life on £500 a year,[34] an opinion confirmed by his colleague, the father of John Maynard Keynes, who managed to save £400 a year out of an income (salary plus inherited capital) of £1000, which enabled him to run a Morris-wallpapered home with three regular servants and a governess, to take two holidays a year – a month in Switzerland cost the couple £68 in 1891 – and to indulge his passions for stamp collecting, butterfly hunting, logic and, of course, golf.[35] There was no difficulty in finding ways to spend a hundred times as much per year, and the ultra-rich of the *belle époque* – American multi-millionaires, Russian grand dukes, South African gold magnates and assorted international financiers – rushed to compete in spending as lavishly as they could. But one did not have to be a tycoon to enjoy some very palatable sweets of life, for in 1896, for example, a 101-piece dinner service decorated with one's own monogram could be bought retail in London for less than £5. The international grand hotel, born of the railway in mid-century, reached its apogee in the last twenty years before 1914. Many of them still bear the name of the most famous of contemporary chefs, César Ritz. These palaces might be frequented by the super-rich, but they were not primarily built for them, since the super-rich still constructed or rented their own palatial establishments. They aimed at the middling-rich and the comfortably off. Lord Rosebery dined at the new Hotel Cecil, but not on the standard dinner of 6 shillings a head. The activities aimed at the really wealthy were priced on a different scale. In 1909 a set of golf clubs and bag would cost one and a half pounds sterling in London, while the basic price for the new Mercedes car was £900. (Lady Wimborne and her son owned two of them, plus two Daimlers, three Darracqs and two Napiers.)[36]

Small wonder that the pre-1914 years live on in the folklore of the bourgeoisie as an era of golden days. Or that the sort of leisure class which attracted most public attention was the one which engaged in (Veblen again) 'conspicuous consumption' to establish the person's status and wealth, not so much against the lower orders, too far in the depths to be even noticed, but in competition with other tycoons. J. P. Morgan's answer to the question how much it cost to run a yacht ('If you have to ask, you can't afford it'), and John D. Rockefeller's, equally apocryphal, remark when told that J. P. Morgan had left $80 million at his death ('And we all thought he was rich'), indicate the nature of the phenomenon. There was plenty of it in those gold-plated decades when art-dealers like Joseph Duveen convinced billionaires that only a collection of old masters could put the seal on their status, when no successful grocer was complete without a huge yacht, no mining speculator without a string of race-horses and a (preferably British) country palace and grouse-moor, and when the sheer quantity and variety of food wasted – and indeed even the quantities consumed – in an Edwardian weekend beggar the imagination.

In fact, however, as already suggested the largest body of leisure subsidized by private incomes probably took the form of non-profit-making activities by the wives, sons and daughters, and sometimes other relatives, of well-heeled families. This, as we shall see, was an important element in the emancipation of women (see chapter 8 below): Virginia Woolf regarded 'a room of one's own', i.e. £500 a year, as essential for this purpose, and the great Fabian partnership of Beatrice and Sidney Webb rested on £1000 a year settled on her at her marriage. Good causes, ranging from campaigns for peace and sobriety through social service for the poor – this was the era of slum 'settlements' by middle-class activists – to the support of the uncommercial arts, bene-fited from unpaid help and financial subsidy. The history of the early-twentieth-century arts is full of such subsidies: Rilke's poetry was made possible by the generosity of an uncle and a succession of noble ladies, Stefan George's poetry and Karl Kraus' social criticism, like Georg Lukacs' philosophy, by the family business, which also allowed Thomas Mann to concentrate on the literary life before it became lucrative. In the words of E. M. Forster, another beneficiary of a private income : 'In came the dividends, up went the lofty thoughts.' They rose in and out of villas and apartments furnished by the 'arts-and-crafts' movement which adapted the methods of the medieval artisan for those who could pay, and among 'cultivated' families for whom, given the right accent and income, even hitherto unrespectable occupations became what the Germans called *salonfähig* (acceptable in family drawing rooms). Not the least curious development of the ex-puritan middle class is its readiness, at the end of the century, to let its sons and daughters go on the professional stage, which acquired all the symbols of public recognition. After all, Sir Thomas Beecham, the heir to Beecham's Pills, chose to spend his time as a professional conductor of Delius (son of the Bradford woollen trade) and of Mozart (who had had no such advantages).

VI

And yet, could the age of the conquering bourgeoisie flourish, when large tracts of the bourgeoisie itself found themselves so little engaged in the generation of wealth, and drifting so rapidly and so far away from the puritan ethic, the values of work and effort, accumulation through abstention, duty and moral earnestness, which had given them their identity, pride and ferocious energy? As we have seen in chapter 3, the fear – nay, the shame – of a future as parasites haunted them. Leisure, culture, comfort were all very well. (The gross public flaunting of wealth by luxurious waste was still greeted with considerable reserve by a Bible-reading generation which recalled the worship of the golden calf.) But was not the class that had made the nineteenth century its own, withdrawing from its historic destiny? How, if at all, could it combine the values of its past and its present?

The problem was hardly yet visible in the USA, where the dynamic entrepreneur felt no discernible twinges of uncertainty, though some were worried about their public relations. It was among the old New England families dedicated to university-educated public and pro-fessional services, such as the Jameses and the Adamses, that men and women distinctly ill at ease in their society were to be found. The most that can be said of American capitalists is that some of them earned money so fast and in such astronomic quantities that they were forcibly brought up against the fact that mere capital accumulation in itself is not an adequate aim in life for human beings, even bourgeois ones.*
However, most American businessmen were not in the class of the admittedly unusual Carnegie, who gave away $350 million to a variety of excellent causes and people all over the world, without visibly affecting his style of life in Skibo Castle, or Rockefeller, who imitated Carnegie's new device of the philanthropic foundation, and was to give

---

* 'The amassing of wealth is one of the worst species of idolatry – no idol more debasing than the worship of money.... To continue much longer overwhelmed by business care and with most of my thoughts wholly on the way to make money in the shortest time, must degrade me beyond the hope of permanent recovery' – Andrew Carnegie.[37]

away even more before his death in 1937. Philanthropy on this scale, like art collecting, had the incidental advantage that it retrospectively softened the public outlines of men whose workers and business rivals remembered them as merciless predators. For most of the American middle class getting rich, or at least well-off, was still a sufficient aim in life and an adequate justification of their class and of civilization.

Nor can we detect much of a crisis of bourgeois confidence in the smaller western countries entering upon their era of economic transformation – such as the 'pillars of society' in the provincial Norwegian shipbuilding town about whom Henrik Ibsen wrote a celebrated and eponymous play (1877). Unlike capitalists in Russia, they had no reason to feel that the entire weight and morality of a traditionalist society, from grand dukes to muzhiks, was dead against them; not to mention their exploited workers. On the contrary. Still, even in Russia, where we find surprising phenomena in literature and life like the successful businessman who is ashamed of his triumphs (Lopakhin in Chekhov's *Cherry Orchard*), and the great textile magnate and art-patron who finances Lenin's Bolsheviks (Savva Morozov), rapid industrial progress brought self-assurance. Paradoxically what was to turn the February Revolution of 1917 into the October Revolution, or so it has been persuasively argued, was the conviction, acquired by Russian employers in the previous twenty years, that 'there can be no other economic order in Russia besides capitalism', and that Russian capitalists were strong enough to force their workers back into line.*

There were no doubt plenty of businessmen and successful professional men in the developed parts of Europe who still felt the wind of history in their sails, even though it was increasingly difficult to overlook what was happening to two of the masts which had traditionally carried these sails: the owner-managed firm, and the male-centred family of its proprietor. The conduct of big business by salaried functionaries or the loss of independence of formerly sovereign entrepreneurs in cartels were indeed, as a German economic historian noted with relief at the time, 'still a long way from socialism'.[39] But the mere fact that private business and socialism could be so linked shows how far from the accepted idea of private enterprise the new economic structures of our period seemed. As for the erosion of the bourgeois family, not least by the emancipation of its female members, how could it fail to undermine the self-definition of a class which rested so largely on its maintenance (see *The Age of Capital*, chapter 13, II) – a class for

---

* As a moderate industrialist leader put it on 3 August 1917: 'We must insist ... that the present revolution is a bourgeois revolution [voice: 'Correct'], that a bourgeois order at the current time is inevitable, and since inevitable, should lead to a completely logical conclusion: those persons who rule the country ought to think and act in a bourgeois manner.'[38]

which respectability equated with 'morality' and which depended so crucially on the perceived conduct of its women?

What made the problem particularly acute, at all events in Europe, and dissolved the firm contours of the nineteenth-century bourgeoisie, was a crisis in what, except for some self-consciously pietist Catholic groups, had long been its identifying ideology and allegiance. For the bourgeoisie had believed, not only in individualism, respectability and property, but also in progress, reform and a moderate liberalism. In the eternal political battle among the upper strata of nineteenth-century societies, between the 'parties of movement' or 'progress' and the 'parties of order', the middle classes had unquestionably stood, in their great majority, for movement, though by no means insensitive to order. Yet, as we shall see below, progress, reform and liberalism were all in crisis. Scientific and technical progress, of course, remained unquestioned. Economic progress still seemed a safe bet, at any rate after the doubts and hesitations of the Depression, even though it generated organized labour movements usually led by dangerous subversives. Political progress, as we have seen, was a far more problematic concept in the light of democracy. As for the situation in the field of culture and morality, it seemed increasingly puzzling. What was one to make of Friedrich Nietzsche (1844–1900) or Maurice Barrès (1862–1923), who in the 1900s were the gurus of the children of those who had navigated their intellectual seas by the beacons of Herbert Spencer (1820–1903) or Ernest Renan (1820–92)?

The situation became even more puzzling intellectually with the rise to power and prominence in the bourgeois world of Germany, a country in which middle-class culture had never taken kindly to the lucid simplicities of the rationalist eighteenth-century Enlightenment, which penetrated the liberalism of the original countries of the dual revolution, France and Great Britain. Germany was unquestionably a giant in science and learning, in technology and economic development, in civility, culture and the arts and not least in power. Probably, taken all in all, it was the most impressive national success story of the nineteenth century. Its history exemplified progress. But was it really liberal? And even insofar as it was, where did what *fin de siècle* Germans called liberalism fit in with the accepted verities of the mid-nineteenth century? German universities even refused to teach economics as that subject was now universally understood elsewhere (see below, pp. 270, 271). The great German sociologist Max Weber came from an impeccably Liberal background, considered himself a lifelong bourgeois Liberal, and indeed was very much a Liberal of the left by German standards. Yet he was also an impassioned believer in militarism, imperialism and – at least for a time – sufficiently tempted by right-wing nationalism to join the Pan-German League. Or consider the domestic literary wars of the brothers Mann: Heinrich,* a classical rationalist, francophile man of the left, Thomas, a passionate critic of western 'civilization' and liberalism, to which (in a familiar Teutonic manner) he counterposed an essentially German 'culture'. Yet Thomas Mann's entire career, and certainly his reactions to the rise and triumph of Hitler, demonstrate that his roots and his heart were in the nineteenth-century liberal tradition. Which of the two brothers was the real 'Liberal'? Where did the *Bürger* or German bourgeois stand?

Moreover, as we have seen, bourgeois politics themselves became more complex and divided, as the supremacy of Liberal parties crumbled during the Great Depression. Former Liberals shifted to Conservatism, as in Britain, Liberalism divided and declined, as in Germany, or lost support to left and right as in Belgium and Austria. What exactly did it mean to be a Liberal or even a liberal under these circumstances? Need one be an ideological or political liberal at all? After all, by the 1900s there were enough countries in which the typical member of the entrepreneurial and professional classes would be frankly on the right of the political centre. And, below them, there were the swelling ranks of the new middle and lower-middle classes, with their resentful and built-in affinity for a frankly anti-liberal right.

Two issues of increasing urgency underlined this erosion of old collective identities: nationalism/imperialism (see chapters 3 and 6 above) and war. The liberal bourgeoisie had certainly not been enthusiasts for imperial conquest, although (paradoxically) its intellectuals were responsible for the way the largest imperial possession of all – India – was administered (see *The Age of Revolution*, chapter 8, iv). Imperial expansion could be reconciled with bourgeois liberalism, but not, as a rule, comfortably. The most vocal bards of conquest were usually found further to the right. On the other hand the liberal bourgeoisie had been opposed in principle to neither nationalism nor war. However, they had seen 'the nation' (including their own) as a temporary phase in the evolution towards a truly global society and civilization, and were sceptical of the claims to national independence of what they regarded as obviously unviable or small peoples. As for war, though sometimes necessary, it was something to be avoided, which aroused enthusiasm only among the militarist nobility or the uncivilized. Bismarck's (realistic) observation that the problems of Germany would only be solved by 'blood and iron' was deliberately meant to shock a mid-nineteenth-century bourgeois liberal public, and in the 1860s it had done so.

* Probably, and unfairly, known outside Germany chiefly for having written the book on which Marlene Dietrich's film *Blue Angel* was based.

It is evident that in the era of empires, extending nationalism and approaching war, these sentiments were no longer in tune with the political realities of the world. A man who in the 1900s repeated what in the 1860s or even the 1880s would have been regarded as the merest common sense of bourgeois experience, would in 1910 find himself out of sympathy with much of his times. (Bernard Shaw's plays after 1900 get some of their comic effects by such confrontations.)[40] Under the circumstances one might have expected realistic middle-class Liberals to evolve the usual circuitous rationalizations of positions half-changed, or to remain silent. Indeed that is what British Liberal government ministers did as they committed the country to war while pretending, perhaps even to themselves, that they were not. But we also find something more.

As bourgeois Europe moved in growing material comfort towards its catastrophe, we observe the curious phenomenon of a bourgeoisie, or at least a significant part of its youth and its intellectuals, which plunged willingly, even enthusiastically, into the abyss. Everyone knows of the young men – there is much less evidence before 1914 of prospective bellicosity among young women – who hailed the outbreak of the First World War like people who have fallen in love. 'Now God be thanked who has matched us with this hour,' wrote the normally rational Fabian socialist and Cambridge Apostle, the poet Rupert Brooke. 'Only war', wrote the Italian futurist Marinetti, 'knows how to rejuvenate, accelerate and sharpen the human intelligence, to make more joyful and air the nerves, to liberate us from the weight of daily burdens, to give savour to life and talent to imbeciles.' 'In the life of camps and under fire', wrote a French student, '... we shall experience the supreme expansion of the French force that lies within us.'[41] But plenty of older intellectuals were also to greet the war with manifestos of delight and pride which some lived long enough to regret. The fashion, in the years before 1914, for rejecting an ideal of peace, reason and progress for an ideal of violence, instinct and explosion has often been observed. An influential book on British history during those years has called it 'The Strange Death of Liberal England'.

One might extend the title to western Europe. Amid the physical comforts of their newly civilized existence, the middle classes of Europe were uneasy (though this was not yet true of the businessmen of the New World). They had lost their historic mission. The most heartfelt and unqualified songs in praise of the benefits of reason, science, education, enlightenment, freedom, democracy and the progress of humanity which the bourgeoisie had once been proud to exemplify, now came (as we shall see below) from those whose intellectual formation belonged to an earlier era and had not kept up with the times. It was the working classes and not the bourgeoisie whom Georges Sorel, a brilliant and rebellious intellectual eccentric, warned against 'The Illusions of Progress' in a book published under that title in 1908. Looking backwards and forwards, the intellectuals, the young, the politicians of the bourgeois classes, were by no means convinced that all was or would be for the best. However, one important part of the upper and middle classes of Europe retained a firm confidence in future progress, for it was based on the recent and spectacular improvement in their situation. It consisted of the women, and especially the women born since about 1860.

CHAPTER 8

THE NEW WOMAN

In Freud's opinion it is true that woman gains nothing by studying, and that on the whole woman's lot will not improve thereby. Moreover, women cannot equal man's achievement in the sublimation of sexuality.

Minutes of the Vienna Psychoanalytical Society, 1907[1]

My mother left school at 14. She had to go into service rightaway, on some farm.... Later she went to Hamburg as a servant girl. But her brother was allowed to learn something, he became a locksmith. When he lost his job they even let him start a second apprenticeship with a painter.

Grete Appen on her mother, born 1888[2]

The restoration of woman's self-respect is the gist of the feminist movement. The most substantial of its political victories can have no higher value than this – that they teach women not to depreciate their own sex.

Katherine Anthony, 1915[3]

I

It may seem absurd, at first sight, to consider the history of half the human race in our period in the context of that of the western middle classes, a relatively small group even within the countries of 'developed' and developing capitalism. Yet it is legitimate, insofar as historians concentrate their attention on changes and transformations in the condition of women, for the most striking of these, 'women's emancipation', was at this period pioneered and still almost entirely confined to the middle and – in a different form – the statistically less significant upper strata of society. It was modest enough at this time, even though the period produced a small but unprecedented number of women who were active, and indeed extraordinarily distinguished, in fields previously confined entirely to men: figures like Rosa Luxemburg, Madame Curie, Beatrice Webb. Still, it was large enough to produce

not simply a handful of pioneers, but – within the bourgeois milieu –
a novel species, the 'new woman' about whom male observers speculated and argued from the 1880s onwards, and who was the protagonist
of 'progressive' writers: Henrik Ibsen's Nora and Rebecca West,
Bernard Shaw's heroines, or rather anti-heroines.

In the condition of the great majority of the world's women, those
who lived in Asia, Africa, Latin America and the peasant societies of
southern and eastern Europe, or indeed in most agrarian societies, there
was as yet no change whatever. There was little enough change in the
condition of most women of the labouring classes anywhere, except, of
course, in one crucial respect. From 1875 on women in the 'developed'
world began to have notably fewer children.

In short, this part of the world was now visibly experiencing the so-
called 'demographic transition' from some variant of the old pattern –
speaking very roughly high birth-rates balanced by high death-rates –
to the familiar modern pattern of low birth-rates offset by low mortality.
Just how and why this transition came about is one of the major puzzles
which confront historians of population. Historically speaking, the
sharp decline in fertility in the 'developed' countries is quite novel.
Incidentally, the failure of fertility and mortality to decline together in
most of the world accounts for the spectacular explosion in the global
population since the two world wars, for while mortality has fallen
dramatically, partly through improvements in the standard of living,
partly through a revolution in medicine, the birth-rate in most of the
Third World remains high, or is only beginning to decline after the lag
of a generation.

In the west the declines in birth- and death-rates were better co-
ordinated. Both obviously affected the lives and feelings of women –
for the most striking development affecting death was the sharp fall in
the mortality of babies below one year, which also became unmistakable
in the last decades before 1914. In Denmark, for instance, infant
mortality had averaged about 140 per 1000 live births in the 1870s,
but it stood at 96 in the last five years before 1914; in the Netherlands
the equivalent figures were almost 200 and a little over 100. (For
comparison: in Russia infant mortality remained at about 250 per 1000
in the early 1900s, compared to about 260 in the 1870s.) Nevertheless,
it is reasonable to suppose that having fewer children in a lifetime was
a more notable change in women's lives than having more of their
children survive.

A lower birth-rate can be ensured either by women marrying later,
by more of them staying unmarried (always assuming no rise in illegit-
imacy) or by some form of birth-control which, in the nineteenth
century overwhelmingly meant abstention from sex or *coitus interruptus*.

(In Europe we can leave aside mass infanticide.) In fact, the rather peculiar west European pattern of marriage, which had prevailed over several centuries, had used all these, but especially the first two. For, unlike the usual marriage pattern in non-western countries, where girls married young and hardly any of them remained unmarried, pre-industrial western women tended to marry late – sometimes in their late twenties – and the proportion of bachelors and spinsters was high. Hence, even during the period of rapid population increase in the eighteenth and nineteenth centuries, the European birth-rate in the 'developed' or developing countries of the west was lower than in the twentieth century Third World, and the rate of demographic growth, however amazing by past standards, was more modest. Nevertheless, and in spite of a general, but not universal, tendency for a higher proportion of women to marry, and to do so at a younger age, the birth-rate dropped: i.e. deliberate birth-control must have spread. The passionate debates on this emotionally explosive issue, which was more freely discussed in some countries than in others, are less significant than the massive and (outside the relevant bedrooms) silent decisions of armies of couples to limit the size of their families.

In the past such decisions had been overwhelmingly part of the strategy of maintaining and extending family resources which, given that most Europeans were country people, meant safeguarding the transmission of land from one generation to the next. The two most startling examples of nineteenth-century control of progeny, post-rev-olutionary France and post-famine Ireland, were primarily due to the decision of peasants or farmers to prevent the dissipation of family holdings by cutting down the number of heirs with possible claims to share in them: in the French case by reducing the number of children; in the case of the much more pious Irish by reducing the number of men and women in a position to have children with such claims by raising the average age at marriage to an all-time European peak, by multiplying bachelors and spinsters, preferably in the prestigious form of the religiously celibate, and, of course, by exporting spare offspring *en masse* across the seas as emigrants. Hence the rare examples, in a century of population growth, of a country (France) whose population remained barely more than stable, and another (Ireland) whose popu-lation actually fell.

The new forms of controlling family size were almost certainly not due to the same motives. In the cities they were undoubtedly stimulated by the desire for a higher standard of living, particularly among the multiplying lower-middle classes, whose members could not afford both the expense of a large brood of small children and the wider range of consumer goods and services which now became available; for in the nineteenth century nobody, other than the indigent old, was poorer than a couple with a low income and a houseful of small children. But it was probably also due to the changes which at this time made children an increasing burden on parents, as they went to school or training for a lengthening period during which they remained economically dependent. Prohibitions on child labour and the urbanization of work reduced or eliminated the modest economic value which children had for parents, e.g. on farms where they could make themselves useful.

At the same time birth-control indicated significant cultural changes, both towards children and in respect of what men and women expected from life. If children were to do better than their parents – and for most people in the pre-industrial era this had been neither possible nor desirable – then they had to be given a better chance in life, and smaller families made it possible to devote more time, care and resources to each. And, just as one aspect of a world of change and progress was to open the chance of social and professional improvement from one generation to the next, so it might also teach men and women that their own lives did not just have to replicate their parents'. The moralists shook their heads over the French, with their single-child or double-child families; but there can be no doubt that in the privacy of pillow-talk it suggested new possibilities to husbands and wives.*

The rise of birth-control thus indicates a certain penetration of new structures, values and expectations into the sphere of western labouring women. Nevertheless, most of them were only marginally affected. Indeed they were largely outside 'the economy', conventionally defined to consist of those who declared themselves as having an employment or 'occupation' (other than domestic labour in the family). In the 1890s something like two-thirds of all males were thus classified as 'occupied' in the 'developed' countries of Europe and the USA, while something like three-quarters of females – in the USA 87 per cent of them – were not.† More precisely, 95 per cent of all married men between the ages of eighteen and sixty were 'occupied' in this sense (e.g. in Germany), whereas only 12 per cent of all married women were in the 1890s, though half the unmarried and about 40 per cent of the widowed were.

Pre-industrial societies are not entirely repetitive, even in the country-side. Conditions of life change, and even the pattern of women's existence does not remain the same through the generations, though one

* The French example was still cited by Sicilians who decided to enter on family limitation in the 1950s and 1960s, or so I am informed by two anthropologists who are enquiring into the subject, P. and J. Schneider.

† A different classification might have produced very different figures. Thus the Austrian half of the Habsburg monarchy counted 47.3 per cent of occupied women, compared to the economically not dissimilar Hungarian half which counted just under 25 per cent. These percentages are based on total population, including children and the old.[4]

would hardly expect to see any dramatic transformations over a period of fifty years except as the result of climatic or political catastrophe or the impact of the industrial world. For most rural women outside the 'developed' zone of the world, that impact was still quite small. What characterized their lives was the inseparability of family functions and labour. They were conducted in a single setting in which most men and women carried out all their sexually differentiated tasks – whether in what we today consider the 'household' or in 'production'. Farmers needed wives for farming as well as cooking and bearing children, handicraft masters and small shopkeepers needed them to conduct their trades. If there were some occupations which collected together men without women for lengthy periods – say as soldiers or sailors – there were no purely female occupations (except perhaps prostitution and the public entertainments assimilated to it) which were not normally carried out for most of the time in the setting of some household: for even unmarried men and women who were hired out as servants or agricultural labourers 'lived in'. Insofar as the bulk of the world's women continued to live in this manner, shackled by double labour and inferiority to men, there is little to be said about them that could not have been said in the days of Confucius, Mohammed or the Old Testament. They were not outside history, but they were outside the history of nineteenth-century society.

There was indeed a large and growing number of labouring women whose patterns of life had been or were being transformed – not necessarily for the better – by economic revolution. The first aspect of this revolution which transformed them had been what is now called 'proto-industrialization', the striking growth of cottage and putting-out industries for sale in wider markets. Insofar as this continued to be carried out in a setting which combined household and outside production, it did not change the position of women, though certain kinds of cottage manufacture were specifically feminine (e.g. lace-making or straw-plaiting) and therefore provided rural women with the comparatively rare advantage of a means of earning a little cash independent of men. However, what cottage industries achieved more generally was a certain erosion of the conventional differences between men's and women's work and above all a transformation in family structure and strategy. Households could be set up as soon as two people reached working age; children, a valuable addition to the family labour force, could be engendered without considering what would happen next to the plot of land on which their future as peasants depended. The complex and traditional mechanisms for maintaining a balance over the next generation between people and the means of production on which they depended, by controlling the age and choice of marriage partners, family size and inheritance, broke down. The consequences for demographic growth have been much discussed, but what is relevant here are the more immediate consequences for the life-histories and life-patterns of women.

As it happens, by the late nineteenth century proto-industries, whether male, female or combined, were falling victim to more large-scale manufacture, as indeed was handicraft production in the indus-trialized countries (see pp. 114–15 above). Globally speaking 'domestic industry', whose problems therefore increasingly preoccupied social investigators and governments, was still substantial. It included perhaps 7 per cent of all industrial employment in Germany, perhaps 19 per cent in Switzerland, as much as 34 per cent in Austria in the 1890s.[5] Such industries, known as 'sweated industries', even expanded under certain circumstances, with the aid of small-scale mechanization which was new (notably the sewing-machine), and notoriously underpaid and exploited labour. However, they increasingly lost their character as 'family manufacture' as their labour force became more and more feminized and, incidentally, compulsory schooling deprived them of child labour, which was usually an integral part of them. As the traditional 'proto-industrial' occupations were swept away – hand-loom weaving, framework knitting etc. – most domestic industry ceased to be a family enterprise and became merely a kind of underpaid work which women could do in cottages, garrets and back-yards.

Domestic industry at least enabled them to combine paid work with some supervision of household and children. That is why so many married women who needed to earn money, but remained chained to kitchens and small children, found themselves doing such work. For the second and major effect of industrialization on the position of women was much more drastic: it separated the household from the place of work. And in doing so it largely excluded them from the publicly recognized economy – the one in which people were paid wages – and compounded their traditional inferiority to men by a new economic dependence. Peasants, for instance, could hardly exist as peasants without wives. Farm work required the woman as well as the man. It was absurd to regard the household income as earned by one sex rather than both, even though one sex was considered as dominant. But in the new economy the household income was typically and increasingly earned by specifiable people who went out to work and came back from factory or office at regular intervals with money, which was distributed to other family members who, equally clearly, did *not* earn it directly even if their contribution to the household was essential in other ways. Those who brought back money were not necessarily only men, even though the main 'bread-winner' was typically a male; but those who found it difficult to bring back money from outside were typically the married women.

Such a separation of household and place of work logically entailed a pattern of sexual–economic division. For the woman it meant that her role as a household manager became her primary function, especially where family earnings were irregular or tight. This may explain the constant complaints from middle-class sources about the inadequacies of working-class women in this respect: such complaints do not appear to have been common in the pre-industrial era. Of course, except among the rich, this produced a new kind of complementarity between husbands and wives. Nevertheless, she no longer brought home income.

The main bread-winner had to aim at earning an income sufficient to maintain all his dependants. His earnings (for he was typically a male) ought therefore ideally to be fixed at a level which did not require any other contribution to produce a family wage sufficient to keep all. Conversely, the income of other family members was conceived of as at best complementary, and this reinforced the traditional belief that women's (and of course children's) work was inferior and low-paid. After all, the woman needed to be paid less since she did not have to earn the family income. Since better-paid men would have their wages reduced by the competition of low-paid women, the logical strategy for them was to exclude such competition if possible, thus pressing women further into economic dependence or permanent low-wage occupations. At the same time, from the woman's point of view, dependence became the optimum economic strategy. By far her best chance of getting a good income lay in attaching herself to a man who was capable of bringing it home, since her own chance of earning such a living was usually minimal. Apart from the higher reaches of prostitution, which were no easier to reach than Hollywood stardom in later days, her most promising career was marriage. But marriage made it exceedingly difficult for her to go out to earn a living even had she wanted to, partly because domestic work and looking after children and husband tied her to the household, partly because the very assumption that a good husband was by definition a good bread-winner intensified the conventional resistance, by both men and women, to the wife's work. The fact that she could be seen not to need to work was the visible proof, before society, that the family was not pauperized. Everything conspired to keep the married woman a dependant. Women habitually went to work until they married. They were very often obliged to go to work when widowed or abandoned by their husbands. But they did not usually do so when married. In the 1890s only 12.8 per cent of German married women had a recognized occupation. In Britain (1911) only about 10 per cent had one.[6]

Since a great many adult male bread-winners could plainly not bring home an adequate family income by themselves, the paid labour of women and children was, in fact, only too often essential to the family budget. Moreover, since women and children were notoriously cheap labour and easy to brow-beat, especially since most female labour consisted of young girls, the economy of capitalism encouraged their employment wherever possible – i.e. where not prevented by the resistance of the men, by law, by convention, or by the nature of certain physically taxing jobs. There was thus a great deal of women's work even according to the narrow criteria of the censuses, which in any case almost certainly substantially understated the amount of 'occupied' married women, since much of their paid work would not be reported as such or would not be distinguished from the domestic tasks with which it overlapped: the taking in of lodgers, part-time work as domestic cleaners, laundresses and the like. In Britain 34 per cent of women over the age of ten were 'occupied' in the 1880s and 1890s – compared with 83 per cent of the men, and in 'industry' the proportion of women ranged from 18 per cent in Germany to 31 per cent in France.[7] Women's work in industry was at the beginning of our period still overwhelmingly concentrated in a few typically 'female' branches, notably textiles and clothing but increasingly also food manufacture. However, the majority of women earning an income as individuals did so in the service sector. The number and proportion of domestic servants, curiously enough, varied very greatly. It was probably larger in Britain than anywhere else – probably nearly twice as high as in France or Germany – but from the end of the century it began to fall quite notably. In the extreme case of Britain, where the number had doubled between 1851 and 1891 (from 1.1 to 2 millions) it remained stable for the rest of the period.

Taking it all in all, we can see nineteenth-century industrialization – using the word in its widest sense – as a process which tended to extrude women, and particularly married women, from the economy officially defined as such, namely that in which only those who received an individual cash income counted as 'occupied': the sort of economics which included the earnings of prostitutes in the 'national income', at least in theory, but not the equivalent but unpaid conjugal or extra-conjugal activities of other women, or which counted paid servants as 'occupied' but unpaid domestic work as 'unoccupied'. It produced a certain masculinization of what economics recognized as 'labour', just as in the bourgeois world where the prejudice against women working was far greater and more easily applied (see *The Age of Capital*, chapter 13, II) it produced a masculinization of business. In pre-industrial times women who themselves looked after estate or enterprise were recognized, though not common. In the nineteenth century they were increasingly considered as freaks of nature, except at the inferior social levels where poverty and the general lowness of the lower orders made it impossible to regard the large numbers of female shopkeepers and market-women, inn- and lodging-house-keepers, small traders and moneylenders as quite so 'unnatural'.

If the economy was thus masculinized, so was politics. For as demo- cratization advanced, and as the right to vote – both locally and nationally – was extended after 1870 (see pp. 85–6 above) women were systematically excluded. Thus politics became essentially a man's affair, to be discussed in the inns and cafés where men gathered or at meetings attended by them, while the women were confined to that part of life which was private and personal, for which alone nature fitted them (or so it was argued). This also was a relative innovation. In the popular politics of pre-industrial society, which ranged from the pressure of village opinion through riots in favour of the old 'moral economy' to revolutions and barricades, poor women at least had not only a part but a recognized role. It had been the women of Paris who marched on Versailles to express the people's demand for controlled food-prices to the king in the French Revolution. In the era of parties and general elections they were pushed into the background. If they exerted any influence at all, it was only through their men.

In the nature of things these processes affected, more than any others, the women of the new classes most typical of the nineteenth century: the middle and working classes. Peasant women, the daughters and wives of small craftsmen, shopkeepers and the like went on much as before, except insofar as they or their menfolk themselves were drawn into the new economy. In the nature of things the differences between women in the new situation of economic dependency and in the old situation of inferiority were in practice not very large. In both men were the dominant sex, women second-class human beings: since they had no citizen rights at all one cannot even call them second-class citizens. In both most of them worked, whether they were paid for it or not.

Both working- and middle-class women saw their position begin to change quite substantially for economic reasons in these decades. In the first place both structural transformations and technology now altered and greatly increased the scope for women's employment as wage-earners. The most striking change, apart from the decline of domestic service, was the rise of occupations which are now primarily feminine: employment in shops and offices. Female shop-assistants in Germany rose from 32,000 in 1882 (under one-fifth of the total) to

174,000 in 1907 (or about 40 per cent of the total) in 1907. In Britain central and local government employed 7000 women in 1881 but 76,000 in 1911; the number of 'commercial and business clerks' had risen from 6000 to 146,000 – a tribute to the typewriter.[8] The growth of elementary education expanded teaching, a (subaltern) profession which in a number of countries – the USA and increasingly Britain – became strikingly feminized. Even in France in 1891 for the first time more women than men were recruited into that ill-paid and devoted army of the 'black hussars of the Republic';[9] for women could teach boys, but it was unthinkable that men should undergo the temptations of teaching the growing number of schoolgirls. Some of these new openings benefited the daughters of workers or even peasants; more of them benefited the daughters of the middle classes and the old or new lower-middle classes, attracted in particular to posts which had a certain social respectability or could (at the cost of depressing their wage-levels) be considered as working 'for pocket-money'.*

A change in the social position and expectations of women became obvious in the last decades of the nineteenth century, though the more visible aspects of women's emancipation were still largely confined to women of the middle classes. Among these we need not pay too much attention to the most spectacular aspect, the active, and in countries like Britain dramatic, campaign of the organized female 'suffragists' and 'suffragettes' for the women's right to vote. As an independent women's movement it was not of major significance except in a few countries (notably the USA and Britain), and even there it did not begin to achieve its objects until after the First World War. In countries like Britain, where suffragism became a significant phenomenon, it measured the public strength of organized feminism, but in doing so it also revealed its major limitation, an appeal primarily confined to the middle class. Votes for women were, like other aspects of female emancipation, strongly supported on principle by the new labour and socialist parties, which actually provided by far the most favourable environment in which emancipated women could take part in public life, at least in Europe. However, while this new socialist left (unlike parts of the old, and strongly masculine, radical–democratic and anti-clerical left) overlapped with suffragist feminism and was sometimes attracted to it, it could not but observe that most working-class women laboured under disabilities which were more urgent than political disenfranchisement, which were not likely to be automatically removed

---

* 'Ware-house girls and clerks come from better-class families and are therefore more frequently subsidised by their parents.... In a few trades, such as typewriting, clerical trades and shop-assistants ... we find the modern phenomenon of a girl working for pocket money.'[10]

by the right to vote, and which were not in the forefront of the minds of most middle-class suffragists.

II

In retrospect the movement for emancipation seems natural enough, and even its acceleration in the 1880s is not very surprising at first sight. Like the democratization of politics, a greater degree of equal rights and opportunities for women was implicit in the ideology of the liberal bourgeoisie, however inconvenient and inopportune it might appear to patriarchs in their private lives. The transformations within the bourgeoisie after the 1870s inevitably provided more scope for its women, and especially its daughters, for, as we have seen, it created a substantial leisure class of females of independent means, irrespective of marriage, and a consequent demand for non-domestic activities. Moreover, when a growing number of bourgeois males were no longer required to do productive work, and many of them engaged in cultural activities, which tough businessmen had been inclined to leave to the females of the family, the gender differences could not but seem attenuated.

Moreover, some degree of women's emancipation was probably *necessary* for middle-class fathers, because by no means all middle-class families, and practically no lower-middle-class families, were sufficiently well-off to keep their daughters in comfort if they did not marry and did not work either. This may explain the enthusiasm of many middle-class men, who would not have admitted women to their clubs or professional associations, for educating their daughters to envisage a certain independence. All the same, there is no reason at all to doubt the genuine convictions of liberal fathers in these matters.

The rise of labour and socialist movements as major movements for the emancipation of the unprivileged unquestionably encouraged women seeking their own freedom: it is no accident that they formed one-quarter of the membership of the (small and middle-class) Fabian Society – founded 1883. And, as we have seen, the rise of an economy of services and other tertiary occupations provided a wider range of jobs for women, while the rise of a consumer economy made them into the central target for the capitalist market.

We need not, therefore, spend much time in discovering reasons for the emergence of the 'new woman', although it is as well to remember that the reasons may not have been quite so simple as they appear at first sight. There is, for instance, no good evidence that in our period woman's position was much changed by her increasingly central econ-

omic significance as wielder of the shopping basket, which the advertising industry, now entering upon its first age of glory, recognized with
its usual ruthless realism. It had to focus on women in an economy
which discovered mass consumption even among the fairly poor,
because money was to be made out of the person who decided most
household purchases. She had to be treated with greater respect, at
least by this mechanism of capitalist society. The transformation of the
distributive system – multiple shops and department stores gaining on
corner shop and market, mail-order catalogues on pedlars – institutionalized this respect, through deference, flattery, display and adver-
tisement.

However, bourgeois ladies had long been treated as valuable customers, while most of the expenditure of the relatively or absolutely
poor still went on necessities or was fixed by custom. The range of
what were now considered household necessities widened, but personal
luxuries for women such as toiletries and changing fashions were still
confined chiefly to the middle classes. Women's market power did not
yet contribute much to the change in their status, and especially not
among the middle classes, where it was not new. One might even argue
that the techniques which advertisers and journalists found to be most
effective tended, if anything, to perpetuate traditional stereotypes of
women's behaviour. On the other hand the women's market generated
a substantial number of new jobs for women professionals, many of
whom were also, and for obvious reasons, actively interested in
feminism.

Whatever the complexities of the process, there is no doubt about
the striking change in the position and aspiration of women, at all
events in the middle classes, during the decades before 1914. The most
obvious symptom of this was the remarkable expansion in the secondary
education for girls. In France the number of boys' lycées remained
roughly stable at 330–340 during our entire period, but the number of
girls' establishments of the same kind grew from none in 1880 to 138
in 1913, and the number of girls in them (c. 33,000) had reached a third
of that of the boys. In Britain, where there was no national secondary
system before 1902, the number of boys' schools climbed from 292 to
1904/5 to 397 in 1913/14, but the number of girls' schools from 99 to a
comparable figure (349).* By 1907/8 in Yorkshire the number of girls
in secondary schools was roughly equal to that of boys: but what is
perhaps more interesting is that by 1913/14 the number of girls staying
on in the nation's state secondary schools past the age of sixteen was

---

* The number of co-educational schools, almost certainly of inferior status, grew more modestly
from 184 to 281.

very much *larger* than that of boys.[11]

Not all countries showed a comparable zeal for the formal education of (middle- and lower-middle class) girls. It advanced far more slowly in Sweden than in the other Scandinavian countries, hardly at all in the Netherlands, little enough in Belgium and Switzerland, while in Italy, with 7500 pupils, it was quite negligible. Conversely by 1910 about a quarter of a million girls received secondary education in Germany (vastly more than in Austria) and, somewhat surprisingly, in Russia it had reached this figure by 1900. It grew much more modestly in Scotland than in England and Wales. University education for women showed less unevenness, except for the quite remarkable expansion in tsarist Russia, where it grew from less than 2000 in 1905 to 9300 in 1911 – and of course the USA where total numbers (56,000 in 1910) which had not quite doubled since 1890, were not really comparable to other university systems. In 1914 numbers in Germany, France and Italy were between 4500 and 5000, in Austria 2700. It is to be noted that women were admitted to university study in Russia, the USA and Switzerland from the 1860s, but in Austria not until 1897 and in Germany not until 1900–8 (Berlin). Outside medicine, only 103 women had graduated in German universities by 1908, the year in which the first woman was appointed as a university teacher in that country (at the Commercial Academy in Mannheim). National differences in the progress of women's education have not attracted any great interest among historians so far.[12]

Even if all these girls (with the exception of the handful who penetrated the male institutions of the university) did not receive the same education, or one as good, as boys of the same age, the mere fact that formal secondary education for middle-class women became familiar, and in some countries already almost normal in certain circles, was quite unprecedented.

The second, less quantifiable symptom of a significant change in the position of (young) women is the greater freedom of movement in society they acquired, both in their own right as individuals and in their relations with men. This was of particular importance for girls of the 'respectable' families, subject to the strongest conventional restraints. The practice of casual social dancing in public places available regularly for this purpose (i.e. neither in the home nor at formal balls organized for special occasions) reflects this loosening of conventions. By 1914 the more unshackled youth in the western big cities and resorts was already familiar with sexually provocative rhythmic dances of dubious but exotic origin (the Argentinian tango, the syncopated steps of American blacks), practised in night-clubs or, in a way even more shocking, in hotels at tea-time or between courses of dinner.

This implied freedom of movement not only in the social but in the literal sense. For though women's fashions did not dramatically express emancipation until after the First World War, the disappearance of the armours of textiles and whalebone which enclosed the female figure in public was already anticipated by the loose and flowing garments which the vogues of intellectual aestheticism in the 1880s, art nouveau and pre-1914 haute-couture at the end of the period popularized. And here the escape of middle-class women from the twilit or lamplit cocoon of the bourgeois interior into the open air is significant, for it also implied, at least on certain occasions, escape from the movement-inhibiting confinement of clothes and corsets (and also their substitution after 1910 by the novel, more flexible, brassiere). It is no accident that Ibsen symbolized the liberation of his heroine by a draught of fresh air into the Norwegian home. Sport not only made it possible for young men and women to meet as partners outside the confines of household and kinship. Women, if in small numbers, were members of the new touring clubs and mountaineering clubs, and that great engine of freedom, the bicycle, emancipated the female proportionately more than the male, since she had more need of free movement. It gave more freedom even than that enjoyed by the horsewomen of the aristocracy, who were still obliged by feminine modesty, at substantial physical risk to themselves, to ride sidesaddle. How much additional freedom did middle-class women acquire through the growing, and sexually skewed, practice of holidays in summer resorts – winter sports, except for bisexual skating, were in their infancy – where they were only occasionally joined by husbands who otherwise remained in their city offices?* At all events mixed bathing now, in spite of all efforts to the contrary, inevitably revealed more of the body than Victorian respectability would have regarded as tolerable.

How far this increased freedom of movement meant greater sexual liberty for middle-class women is difficult to establish. Sex without marriage was certainly still confined to a minority of consciously emancipated girls of this class, almost certainly also seeking other expressions of liberation, political or otherwise. As a Russian woman recalls, in the period after 1905, 'It became very difficult for a "progressive" girl to refuse advances without long explanations. The provincial lads were not very demanding, simple kisses were enough, but the university students from the capital ... could not easily be turned down. "Are you old-fashioned, Fräulein?" And who wanted to be old-fashioned?'[13] How large these communities of emancipated young women were is

* Readers interested in psychoanalysis may have noted the role played by holidays in the progress of patients in Sigmund Freud's case-book.

unknown, though almost certainly they were largest in tsarist Russia, negligible in size in the Mediterranean countries,* and probably quite significant in north-western Europe (including Britain) and the cities of the Habsburg Empire. Adultery, which was pretty certainly the most widespread form of extra-marital sex for middle-class women, may or may not have increased with their self-confidence. There is all the difference between adultery as a form of utopian dream of liberation from a confined life, as in the standard Madame Bovary version of nineteenth-century novels, and the relative freedom of French middle-class husbands and wives, so long as conventions were kept up, to have lovers, as presented in nineteenth-century French boulevard plays. (Both, incidentally, were primarily written by men.) However, nine-teenth-century adultery, like most nineteenth-century sex, resists quantification. All that can be said with any confidence is that this form of behaviour was commonest in aristocratic and fashionable circles, and in the large cities where (with the help of discreet and impersonal institutions such as hotels) appearances could be more easily kept up.†

However, if the quantitative historian is at a loss, the qualitative historian cannot fail to be struck by the growing recognition of female sensuality in the strident masculine statements about women during this period. Many of these are attempts to reassert, in literary and scientific terms, the superiority of men in active and intellectual achieve-ment and the passive and, as it were supplementary, function of women in the relation between the sexes. Whether or not these appear to express a fear of women's ascendancy, as perhaps in the Swedish dramatist Strindberg and the unbalanced young Austrian Otto Weininger's *Sex and Character* (1903), which went through twenty-five editions in twenty-two years, seems secondary. The philosopher Nietz-sche's endlessly quoted injunction to men not to forget the whip when they went to woman (*Thus Spake Zarathustra*, 1883)[14] was actually no more 'sexist' than the praise of women of Weininger's contemporary and admirer Karl Kraus. To insist, like Kraus, that 'what is not given to woman is just what ensures that man makes use of his gifts'[15] or, like the psychiatrist Möbius (1907), that 'cultural man alienated from nature' needed natural woman as his counterpart, could suggest (as for Möbius) that all higher educational establishments for women should be destroyed, or (as for Kraus) it could suggest no such thing. The basic attitude was similar. There was, however, an unmistakable and novel

* This may explain the disproportionate role of Russian émigré women in the progressive and labour movements of a country like Italy.

† These observations apply exclusively to the middle and upper classes. They do not apply to the pre- and post-marital sexual behaviour of women of the peasantry and urban labouring classes, who, of course, constituted the majority of all women.

insistence that women as such had powerful erotic interests: for Kraus 'the *sensuality* [my emphasis] of women is the source to which man's intellectuality [*Geistigkeit*] goes for renewal'. *Fin de siècle* Vienna, that remarkable laboratory of modern psychology, provides the most sophisticated and unconstrained recognition of female sexuality. Klimt's portraits of Viennese ladies, not to mention of women in general, are images of persons with powerful erotic concerns of their own rather than merely images of the sexual dreams of men. It would be very improbable if they did not reflect something of the sexual reality of the Habsburg middle and upper classes.

The third symptom of change was the notably greater public attention given to women as a group having special interests and aspirations as individuals. No doubt business nostrils were the first to catch the scent of a special women's market – for instance, for the women's pages of the new mass dailies addressed to the lower-middle class, and the girls' and women's periodicals for the newly literate – but even the market appreciated the publicity value of treating women not only as consumers but as achievers. The great Anglo-French International exhibition of 1908 caught the tone of the time not only by combining the sales efforts of exhibitors with celebrations of empire and the first custom-built Olympic stadium, but with a centrally placed Palace of Women's Work including a historic exhibit on distinguished women who had died before the 1900s of 'royal, noble and of simple origins' (sketches of the young Victoria, the manuscript of *Jane Eyre*, Florence Nightingale's Crimean carriage, etc.) and displays of needlework, arts-and-crafts, book illustration, photography and the like.* Nor should we overlook the emergence of women as individual achievers in competitive efforts of which sport, once again, provides a striking example. The institution of a women's singles at Wimbledon within six years of that of the men's singles and also, with about the same time-lag, in the French and US tennis championships, was a more revolutionary innovation in the 1880s than is easy to recognize today. For respectable, even married, women to appear in such public roles unattached to families and men, would have been virtually inconceivable even two decades earlier.

---

* It is, however, typical of the time that 'the women artists preferred for the most part to show their work in the Fine Arts Palace'. And that the Women's Industrial Council complained to *The Times* of the intolerable conditions under which the thousand or so women employed at the Exhibition worked.[16]

III

For obvious reasons it is easier to document the conscious and campaigning movement for women's emancipation, and the women who actually succeeded in penetrating the hitherto masculine preserves of life. Both consist of articulate and, by their very rarity, recorded minorities of western middle- and upper-class women – all the better documented since their very efforts, or in some cases their very existence, aroused resistance and debate. The very visibility of these minorities detracts attention from the groundswell of historical change in the social position of women, which historians can only apprehend obliquely. Indeed, even the conscious development of the movement for emancipation is not entirely seized by concentrating on its militant spokespeople. For an important section of it, and almost certainly the majority of those who took part in it outside Britain, America and possibly Scandinavia and the Netherlands, did not do so by identifying with specifically feminine movements, but by identifying with woman's liberation as part of wider movements of general emancipation, such as the labour and socialist movements. Nevertheless, these minorities must be briefly surveyed.

As already suggested, the specifically feminist movements were small: in many continental countries their organizations consisted of a few hundred or at best one or two thousand individuals. Their members were overwhelmingly drawn from the middle class, and their identification with the bourgeoisie, and in particular with the bourgeois liberalism whose extension to the second sex they stood for, gave them such strength as they had and determined their limitations. Below the level of the prosperous and educated bourgeoisie, votes for women, access to higher education, the right to go out to work and to join the professions, and the fight for male legal status and rights (especially property rights) were unlikely to rouse as much crusading fervour as other issues. Nor should we forget that the relative freedom of middle-class women to campaign for such demands rested, in Europe at least, on passing the burdens of domestic work to a much larger group of women, their servants.

The limitations of middle-class western feminism were not only social and economic but also cultural. The form of emancipation to which their movements aspired, namely to be treated legally and politically like man and to take part as individuals, irrespective of sex, in the life of society, assumed a transformed pattern of social life which was already far removed from the traditional 'woman's place'. To take an extreme case: emancipated Bengali men, who wished to show their westernization by bringing their wives out of seclusion and 'into the drawing room', produced unexpected tensions with and among their women-folk, since it was quite unclear to these women what they gained in return for the certain loss of the subaltern, but very real autonomy in that section of the household which was unquestionably *theirs*.[17] A clearly defined 'women's sphere' – whether of women singly in their household relations or of women collectively as part of a community – might strike progressives as a mere excuse for keeping women down, as indeed, among other things, it evidently was. And of course it increasingly became so with the weakening of traditional social structures.

Yet within its limits it had given women such individual and collective resources as they had, and these were not entirely negligible: for instance, they were the perpetuators and formers of language, culture and social values, the essential makers of 'public opinion', the acknowledged initiators of certain kinds of public action (e.g. the defence of the 'moral economy'), and not least, the persons who had not only learned to manipulate their men, but to whom, in some subjects and in some situations, men were *expected* to defer. The rule of men over women, however absolute in theory, was no more unrestricted and arbitrary in collective practice than the rule of absolute monarchs by divine right was an unlimited despotism. This observation does not justify one form of rule rather than the other, but it may help to explain why many women who, for want of anything better, had learned over the generations to 'work the system' were relatively indifferent to liberal middle-class demands which appeared to offer no such practical advantages. After all, even within the bourgeois liberal society, middle-class and petty-bourgeois Frenchwomen, far from foolish and not often given to gentle passivity, did not bother to support the cause of women's suffrage in large numbers.

Since times were changing and the subordination of women was universal, overt and proudly advertised by men, this still left plenty of room for movements of feminine emancipation. Yet insofar as these were likely to gain support among the mass of women in this period, it was paradoxically *not* as specifically feminist movements, but as women's components within movements of universal human emancipation. Hence the appeal of the new social revolutionary and socialist movements. They were specifically committed to women's emancipation – the most popular exposition of socialism by the leader of the German Social Democratic Party was, significantly, August Bebel's *Woman and Socialism*. Indeed, socialist movements provided much the most favourable public environment for women, other than entertainers and a few very favoured daughters of the elite, to develop their personalities and talents. But more than this, they promised a total transformation of society which, as realistic women well knew, would be required to change the ancient pattern of the relation between the sexes.*

To this extent the real political choice for the mass of European women lay not between feminism and mixed political movements, but between the Churches (notably the Catholic Church) and socialism. The Churches, fighting a powerful rearguard action against nineteenth-century 'progress' (cf. *The Age of Capital*, chapter 6, 1), defended such rights as women possessed in the traditional order of society, and with all the more zeal inasmuch as both the body of their faithful and, in many respects, their actual personnel were being dramatically fem-inized: by the end of the century there were almost certainly far more female religious professionals than at any time since the Middle Ages. It is hardly an accident that the best-known Catholic saints of the period since the mid-nineteenth century were women: St Bernadette of Lourdes and St Teresa of Lisieux – both canonized in the early twentieth century – and that the Church gave notable encouragement to the cult of the Virgin Mary. In Catholic countries the Church provided wives with powerful, and resented, weapons against husbands. Much of anti-clericalism therefore had a marked tinge of anti-feminine hostility, as in France and Italy. On the other hand the Churches championed women at the cost of also committing their pious supporters to accept their traditional subordination, and to condemn the female eman-cipation which the socialists offered.

Statistically the women who opted for the defence of their sex through piety enormously outnumbered those who opted for liberation. Indeed, while the socialist movement attracted an *avant garde* of exceptionally able women from the start – mainly, as might be expected, from the middle and upper classes – there is not much sign before 1905 of any significant female membership in labour and socialist parties. In the 1890s not more than fifty women at any time, or 2–3 per cent, were members of the admittedly not very large Parti Ouvrier Français.[18] When they were recruited in larger numbers, as in Germany after 1905, it was largely as wives, daughters or (as in Gorki's famous novel) mothers of socialist men. Before 1914 there is no equivalent to, say, the Austrian Social Democratic Party of the mid-1920s, almost 30 per cent of whose members were women, or the British Labour Party in the 1930s, about 40 per cent of whose individual membership was female, though in Germany the percentage was already substantial.[19] The percentage of women organized in labour unions remained consistently small: negligible in the 1890s (except for Britain), normally not more

---

* It does not follow that this transformation would take the form only of the social revolution anticipated by the socialist and anarchist movements.

than 10 per cent in the 1900s.* However, as women did not have the vote in the vast majority of countries, the most convenient index of their political sympathies is not available to us, and further speculation is idle.

Most women thus remained outside any form of the movement for emancipation. Moreover, even many of those whose lives, careers and opinions showed that they cared intensely about breaking the traditional cage of 'the woman's sphere' showed little enthusiasm for the more orthodox campaigns of the feminists. The early period of women's emancipation produced a remarkable crop of eminent women, but some of the most distinguished among them (e.g. Rosa Luxemburg or Beatrice Webb) saw no reason to confine their talents to the cause of any one sex. It is true that public recognition was now somewhat easier: from 1891 the British reference book *Men of the Time* changed its title to *Men and Women of the Time,* and public activity for women's causes or for those commonly regarded as of special interest to women (e.g. children's welfare) was itself now apt to bring some public prominence. Nevertheless, the road of the woman in a man's world remained hard, success implied quite exceptional efforts and endowments, and the numbers of those who succeeded was modest.

By far the largest proportion of them practised activities recognized as being compatible with traditional femininity, such as in the performing arts and (for middle-class women, especially married ones) writing. Much the largest number of British 'women of the time' recorded in 1895 were authors (forty-eight) and stage figures (forty-two).[21] In France Colette (1873–1954) was both. Before 1914 one woman had already won a Nobel prize for literature (Selma Lagerlöf of Sweden, 1909). Professional careers now also opened, for instance in education with the great growth of secondary and higher education for girls, or – certainly in Britain – in the new journalism. In our period politics and public campaigning on the left became another promising option. The largest percentage of prominent British women in 1895 – one-third – came under the heading 'Reformers, Philanthropists etc.' In fact, socialist and revolutionary politics offered opportunities

* Percentage of women among organized trade unionists 1913:[20]

Country	Percentage
UK	10.5
Germany	9
Belgium (1923)	8.4
Sweden	5
Switzerland	11
Finland	12.3

unequalled elsewhere, as a number of women from tsarist Russia, operating in a variety of countries (Rosa Luxemburg, Vera Zasulich, Alexandra Kollontai, Anna Kuliscioff, Angelica Balabanoff, Emma Goldman), and a few in other countries (Beatrice Webb in Britain, Henrietta Roland-Holst in the Netherlands) showed.

In this it differed from conservative politics which in Britain – though hardly anywhere else – held the loyalty of many an aristocratic lady feminist,* but offered no such possibilities; and it differed from liberal party politics, in which politicians were also at this time essentially male. Nevertheless, the relative ease with which women could make their mark in public life is symbolized by the award of the Nobel peace prize to one (Bertha von Suttner, 1905). The hardest task was undoubtedly that of the woman who braved the entrenched resistance, institutional and informal, of men in the organized professions, in spite of the small but rapidly expanding bridgehead they had established in medicine: 20 doctors in the England and Wales of 1881, 212 in 1901, 447 in 1911. This is some measure of the extraordinary achievement of Marie Sklodkowska-Curie (another product of the Tsarist Empire), who won two Nobel prizes for science in this period (1903, 1911). These luminaries do not measure the participation of women in a male world, which could be very impressive, allowing for the tiny numbers involved: one thinks of the role of a handful of emancipated British women in the revival of the labour movement after 1888: of Annie Besant and Eleanor Marx, and the itinerant propagandists who did so much to form the young Independent Labour Party (Enid Stacy, Katherine Conway, Caroline Martyn). Nevertheless, while almost all such women were supporters of women's rights and, particularly in Britain and the USA, most were strong supporters of the political feminist movement, they devoted only marginal attention to it.

Those who did concentrate on it were normally committed to political agitation, since they demanded rights which, like the vote, required political and legal changes. They could hardly expect much from conservative and confessional parties, and their relation with liberal and radical ones, with whom the ideological affinities of middle-class feminism lay, were sometimes difficult, especially in Britain where it was Liberal governments which stood in the way of the strong suffragist movement in 1906–14. Occasionally (as among the Czechs and Finns) they were associated with opposition movements of national liberation. Within the socialist and labour movements females were encouraged to concentrate on their own sex, and many socialist fem-

---

* The Directory of the feminist *Englishwoman's Year-Book* (1905) included 158 titled ladies, including thirty duchesses, marchionesses, viscountesses and countesses. This comprised a quarter of the British duchesses.[22]

inists did so, not only because the exploitation of working women so obviously called for action, but also because they discovered the need to fight for the rights and interests of women within their own movement, in spite of its ideological commitment to equality. For the difference between a small *avant garde* of progressive or revolutionary militants and a mass labour movement was that the latter consisted primarily not just of men (if only because the bulk of the wage-earning and even more of the organized working class was masculine), but of men whose attitude to women was traditional, and whose interests as trade unionists were to exclude low-paid competitors from men's work. And women were the quintessential form of cheap labour. However, within the labour movements these issues were muted and to some extent defused by the multiplication of women's organizations and committees within them, particularly after 1905.

Of the political issues of feminism, the right to vote in parliamentary elections was much the most prominent. Before 1914 it had not been won anywhere nationally except in Australasia, Finland and Norway, though it existed in a number of states of the USA and to a limited extent in local government. Women's suffrage was not an issue which mobilized important movements of women or played a major role in national politics except in the USA and Britain, where it had very substantial support among women of the upper and middle class, and among the political leaders and activists of the socialist movement. The agitations were dramatized by the tactics of direct action of the Women's Social and Political Union (the 'suffragettes'), in the period 1906–14. However, suffragism should not tempt us to overlook the extensive political organization of women as pressure-groups for other causes either of special interest to their sex – such as the campaigns against the 'white slave traffic' (which led to the Mann Act of 1910 in the USA) – or concerning such issues as peace and anti-alcoholism. If they were, alas, unsuccessful in the first endeavour, their contribution to the triumph of the second, the eighteenth amendment to the US constitution (Prohibition), was crucial. Nevertheless, outside the USA, Britain, the Low Countries and Scandinavia, the independent political activities of women (except as part of labour) remained of minor importance.

IV

Yet there was another strand of feminism twining its way through political and non-political debates about women: sexual liberation. This was a touchy subject, as witness the persecution of women who publicly propagated so respectably backed a cause as birth-control – Annie Besant, deprived of her children for this reason in 1877, Margaret Sanger and Marie Stopes later. But, above all, it did not fit readily into the texture of any movement. The upper-class world of Proust's great novel or the Paris of independent and often well-heeled lesbians like Natalie Barney accepted sexual freedom, orthodox or heterodox, with ease, so long as appearances were kept up where necessary. But – as witness Proust – it did not associate sexual liberation with social or private happiness, or social transformation; nor (except for a much lower *bohème* of artists and writers attracted to anarchism) did it welcome the prospect of such transformation. Conversely social revolutionaries were certainly committed to sexual freedom of choice for women – the sexual utopia of Fourier, admired by Engels and Bebel, had not been entirely forgotten – and such movements attracted the anti-conventional, utopians, bohemians and counter-cultural propagandists of all kinds, including those who wished to assert the right to sleep with anyone in any way they pleased. Homosexuals like Edward Carpenter and Oscar Wilde, champions of sexual toleration like Havelock Ellis, liberated women of varying tastes like Annie Besant and Olive Schreiner, gravitated in the orbit of the small British socialist movement of the 1880s. Free unions without marriage certificates were not only accepted, but, where anti-clericalism was particularly impassioned, virtually mandatory. Yet, as Lenin's later brushes with female comrades too preoccupied with the sexual question show, opinions were divided about what 'free love' should mean and how central a concern of the socialist movement it should be. An advocate of the unlimited liberation of instincts like the psychiatrist Otto Grosz (1877–1920), criminal, drug-addict and early disciple of Freud, who made his way through the intellectual and artistic milieux of Heidelberg (not least through his lovers the Richthofen sisters, lovers or wives of Max Weber, D. H. Lawrence and others), through Munich, Ascona, Berlin and Prague, was a Nietzschean with scant sympathy for Marx. Though he was hailed by some of the pre-1914 bohemian anarchists – but opposed as an enemy of morals by others – and favoured anything that would destroy the existing order, he was an elitist who can hardly be fitted into any political framework. In short, as a programme sexual liberation raised more problems than it offered solutions. Outside the *avant garde bohème* its programmatic appeal was small.

One major problem it raised, or drew attention to, was the precise nature of woman's future in society given equal rights, opportunities and treatment. The crux here was the future of the family, which hinged on woman as mother. It was easy to conceive of women emancipated from the burdens of the household, which the middle and upper classes (especially in Britain) had largely shed by means of servants and by sending their male offspring to boarding-schools from an early age. American women, in a country already short of servants, had long advocated – and now began to achieve – the labour-saving technological transformation of the home. Christine Frederick, in the *Ladies Home Journal* of 1912, even brought 'scientific management' into the home (see above, pp. 44–5). Gas cookers began to spread, not very fast, from 1880, electric cookers, more rapidly, from the last pre-war years. The term 'vacuum cleaner' appears in 1903 and electric irons were pushed on a sceptical public from 1909, but their triumph lay in the inter-war future. Laundries – not as yet in the home – were mechanized: the value of washing-machine production in the US quintupled between 1880 and 1910.[23] Socialists and anarchists, equally enthusiastic about technological utopia, favoured more collective arrangements, and also concentrated on infant schools, crèches and public provision of cooked food (of which school meals were an early example), which would enable women to combine motherhood with work and other activities. Yet this did not entirely solve the problem.

Would not women's emancipation imply the replacement of the existing nuclear family by some other human grouping? Ethnography, which flourished as never before, demonstrated that this was far from the only type of family known to history – the Finnish anthropologist Westermarck's *History of Human Marriage* (1891) ran through five editions by 1921 and was translated into French, German, Swedish, Italian, Spanish and Japanese – and Engels' *Origin of the Family, Private Property and the State* (1884) drew the required revolutionary conclusions. Yet though the utopian–revolutionary left experimented with new forms of communal units, whose most lasting product was to be the *kibbutz* of Jewish settlers in Palestine, it is safe to say that most socialist leaders and an even more overwhelming majority of their supporters, not to mention less 'advanced' persons, conceived of the future in terms of a transformed but still essentially nuclear family. However, opinions differed about the woman who made marriage, housekeeping and motherhood her primary career. As Bernard Shaw pointed out to an emancipated female correspondent, woman's emancipation was chiefly about *her*.[24] In spite of some defence of home and hearth by the moderates of socialism (e.g. the German 'revisionists'), left-wing theorists generally felt that woman's emancipation would come through outside employment or interests, which they therefore encouraged strongly. And yet the problem of combining emancipation and motherhood was not to be easily solved.

A large number, and probably the majority, of the emancipated middle-class women who opted for a career in a man's world at this time solved it by childlessness, refusal to marry, often (as in Britain) virtual celibacy. This was not only a reflex of hostility to men, sometimes disguised as a sense of female superiority to the other sex, such as could be found on the fringes of the Anglo-Saxon suffrage movement. Nor was it simply a by-product of the demographic fact that the excess of women – $1\frac{1}{3}$ million in Britain in 1911 – precluded marriage for many. Marriage was indeed still a career to which even many non-manual working women looked forward, abandoning their school-teaching or office-employment on their wedding day, even when they did not have to. It reflected the very real difficulty of combining two demanding occupations, at a time when only exceptional resources and help made this practicable. In their absence a worker–feminist like Amalie Ryba-Seidl (1876–1952) had to abandon her lifelong militancy in the Austrian Socialist party for five years (1895–1900) in order to bear her husband three children,[25] and, by our standards more inexcusably, Bertha Philpotts Newall (1877–1932), a distinguished and neglected historian, felt she had to resign as Mistress of Girton College, Cambridge, as late as 1925, because 'her father needs her and she feels she must go'.[26] But the cost of self-abnegation was high and women who opted for a career, like Rosa Luxemburg, knew that it had to be paid and that they were paying it.[27]

How far, then, had the condition of women been transformed in the half-century before 1914? The problem is not how to measure but how to judge changes which, by any standards, were substantial for a vast number, perhaps for most women in the urban and industrial west, and dramatic for a minority of middle-class women. (But it is worth repeating that all these together formed only a small percentage of the female half of the human race.) By the simple and elementary standards of Mary Wollstonecraft, who asked for the same rights for both sexes, there had been a major breakthrough in women's access to occupations and professions hitherto maintained as male monopolies, and often bitterly defended in the teeth of common sense and even bourgeois convention, as when male gynaecologists argued the special *un*suitability of women to treat specifically female diseases. By 1914 few women had advanced through the gap, but in principle the way was now open. In spite of appearances to the contrary, women were on the verge of a massive victory in the long struggle for equal citizen rights, symbolized by the vote. However bitterly contested before 1914, less than ten years later women could vote in national elections for the first time in Austria, Czechoslovakia, Denmark, Germany, Ireland, the Netherlands, Norway, Poland, Russia, Sweden, the United Kingdom and the USA.* It is evident that this remarkable change was the

* In fact in Europe women were excluded from the vote only in the Latin countries, including France, in Hungary, the more backward parts of east and south-east Europe – and in Switzerland.

culmination of pre-1914 struggles. As for equal rights before the (civil) law, the balance-sheet was rather less positive, in spite of the removal of some of the more flagrant inequalities. In the matter of equality of earnings, there had been no significant advance. With negligible exceptions women could still expect to earn much less than men for the same work, or to occupy jobs which, being seen as 'women's jobs', were for that reason low-paid.

One might say that, a century after Napoleon, the Rights of Man of the French Revolution had been extended to women. Women were on the verge of equal citizen rights, and, however grudgingly and narrowly, careers were now open to their talent as well as to men's. In retrospect it is easy to recognize the limitations of these advances, as it is easy to recognize those of the original Rights of Man. They were welcome, but they were not enough, especially not for the vast majority of women whom poverty and marriage kept dependent.

But even for those for whom the progress of emancipation was unquestionable – women of the established middle classes (though probably not of the new and old petty-bourgeoisie or lower-middle classes) and young women of working age before marriage – it posed a major problem. If emancipation meant emergence from the private and often separate sphere of family, household and personal relations to which women had so long been confined, could they, how could they, retain those parts of their femininity which were not simply roles imposed on them by males in a world designed for males? In other words, how could women compete as women in a public sphere formed by and in terms suited to a differently designed sex?

Probably there is no permanent answer to this question, faced in different ways by every generation which takes the position of women in society seriously. Each answer, or set of answers, may be satisfactory only for its own historical conjuncture. What was the answer of the first generations of western urban women which plunged into the era of emancipation? We know a good deal about the vanguard of politically active or culturally articulate prominent pioneers, but little about the inactive and inarticulate. All we know is that the women's fashions which swept the emancipated sectors of the west after the First World War, and which took up themes anticipated in the milieux of 'the advanced' before 1914, notably the artistic bohemias of great cities, combined two very different elements. On the one hand the post-war 'jazz generation' demonstratively took over the public use of cosmetics, which had previously been the characteristic of women whose exclusive function was to please men: prostitutes and other entertainers. They now displayed parts of the body, starting with the legs, which nine-teenth-century conventions of female sexual modesty had kept shielded from the concupiscent eyes of males. On the other hand post-war fashions were to do their best to minimize the secondary sexual characteristics which distinguished women from men most visibly, by cutting and eventually cropping traditionally long hair, and making their chests look as flat as was physically possible. Like the short skirts, the abandoned corsets, the new-found ease of movement, all these were signs of, and calls for, freedom. They could not have been tolerated by an older generation of fathers, husbands or other holders of traditional patriarchal authority. What else did they indicate? Perhaps, as in the triumph of the 'little black dress', invented by Coco Chanel (1883–1971), pioneer of the professional businesswoman, they also reflected the requirements of women who needed to combine work and public informality with elegance. But we can only speculate. Yet it is hard to deny that the signs of emancipated fashion pointed in opposite and not always compatible directions.

Like so much else in the world between the wars, the post-1918 fashions of women's liberation were first pioneered in the pre-war *avant gardes*. More precisely, they flourished in the bohemian quarters of the great cities: Greenwich Village, Montmartre and Montparnasse, Chelsea, Schwabing. For the ideas of bourgeois society, including its ideological crises and contradictions, found characteristic, if often puzzling and puzzled expressions, in its arts.

CHAPTER 9

THE ARTS TRANSFORMED

They [French politicians of the left] were very ignorant about art ... but they all pretended more or less to some knowledge of it, and often they really loved it.... One of them would be a playwright; another would scrape on the violin; another would be a besotted Wagnerian. And they all collected Impressionist pictures, read decadent books, and prided themselves on a taste for some ultra-aristocratic art.

Romain Rolland, 1915[1]

It is among such men, with cultivated intellects, sensitive nerves, and bad digestion, that we find the prophets and disciples of the gospel of Pessimism.... Accordingly Pessimism is not a creed which is likely to exert much influence on the strong, practical, Anglo-Saxon race, and we can only discern some faint traces of it in the tendency of certain very limited cliques of so-called Aestheticism to admire morbid and selfconscious ideals, both in poetry and painting.

S. Laing, 1885[2]

The past is necessarily inferior to the future. That is how we wish it to be. How could we acknowledge any merit in our most dangerous enemy? ... This is how we deny the obsessing splendour of the dead centuries, and how we cooperate with the victorious Mechanics that hold the world firm in its web of speed.

F. T. Marinetti, the futurist, 1913[3]

I

Perhaps nothing illustrates the identity crisis through which bourgeois society passed in this period better than the history of the arts from the 1870s to 1914. It was the era when both the creative arts and the public for them lost their bearings. The former reacted to this situation by a flight forward into innovation and experiment, increasingly linked to utopianism or pseudo-theory. The latter, unless converted by fashion and snob-appeal, murmured defensively that they 'didn't know about art, but they knew what they liked', or retreated into the sphere of 'classic' works whose excellence was guaranteed by the consensus of generations. Yet the very concept of such a consensus was itself under fire. From the sixteenth until the end of the nineteenth century, about a hundred ancient sculptures embodied what all agreed to be the highest achievements of plastic art, their names and reproductions familiar to every educated western person: the Laocoön, the Apollo Belvedere, the Dying Gladiator, the Boy Removing a Thorn, the Weeping Niobe and various others. Virtually all were forgotten in the two generations after 1900, except perhaps the Venus de Milo, singled out after discovery early in the nineteenth century by the conservatism of the authorities of the Louvre museum in Paris, which has retained its popularity to this day.

Moreover, from the end of the nineteenth century the traditional kingdom of high culture was undermined by an even more formidable enemy: the arts appealing to the common people and (with the partial exception of literature) revolutionized by the combination of technology and the discovery of the mass market. The cinema, the most extraordinary innovation in this field, together with jazz and its various offspring, had not yet triumphed: but by 1914 it was very much present and ready to conquer the globe.

It is, of course, unwise to exaggerate the divergence between public and creative artists in high or bourgeois culture at this period. In many respects the consensus between them remained in being, and the works of people who considered themselves innovators, and met with resistance as such, were absorbed into the corpus of what was both 'good' and 'popular' among the cultured public, but also, in diluted or selected form, among much wider strata of the population. The accepted repertoire of the late-twentieth-century concert-hall includes the work of composers of this period as well as the eighteenth- and nineteenth-century 'classics' which form its main stock: Mahler, Richard Strauss, Debussy, and various figures of mainly national eminence (Elgar, Vaughan Williams, Reger, Sibelius). The international operatic repertoire was still being extended (Puccini, Strauss, Mascagni, Leoncavallo, Janáček, not to mention Wagner, whose triumph dates from the thirty years before 1914). In fact, grand opera flourished enormously, and even absorbed the *avant garde* for the benefit of the fashionable public, in the form of the Russian ballet. The great names of that period are still legendary: Caruso, Chaliapin, Melba, Nijinsky. The 'light classics' or the popular operettas, songs and short compositions essentially in their idiom, flourished greatly, as in the Habsburg operetta (Lehar, 1870–1948) and 'musical comedy'. The repertoire of Palm Court orchestras, bandstands and even of present-day Muzak bear witness to its appeal.

The 'serious' prose literature of the time has found and kept its place, though not always its contemporary popularity. If the reputation of Thomas Hardy, Thomas Mann or Marcel Proust has (rightly) risen – most of their work was published after 1914, though Hardy's novels appeared mostly between 1871 and 1897 – the fortunes of Arnold Bennett and H. G. Wells, Romain Rolland and Roger Martin du Gard, Theodore Dreiser and Selma Lagerlöf, have been more chequered. Ibsen and Shaw, Chekhov and (in his own country) Hauptmann have survived initial scandal to become part of classic theatre. For that matter, the revolutionaries of the late-nineteenth-century visual arts, Impressionists and Post-Impressionists, came to be accepted in the twentieth century as 'great masters' rather than as indicators of their admirers' modernity.

The real dividing-line runs through the period itself. It is the experimental *avant garde* of the last pre-war years which, outside a small community of the 'advanced' – intellectuals, artists and critics and the fashion-conscious – was never to find a genuine, spontaneous welcome among the broad public. They might console themselves with the thought that the future was theirs, but for Schönberg the future was not to come as it did for Wagner (though it may be argued that it did come for Stravinsky); for the Cubists it was not to come as it did for Van Gogh. To state this fact is not to judge the works, still less to undervalue the talents of their creators, which could be enormously impressive. Yet it is hard to deny that Pablo Picasso (1881–1973), a man of extraordinary genius and vast productivity, is mainly admired as a phenomenon rather than (except for a handful of paintings, mainly from his pre-Cubist period) for the depth of impact, or even our simple enjoyment, of his works. He may well be the first artist of equivalent gifts since the Renaissance of whom this can be said.

It is therefore pointless to survey the arts of this period, as the historian is tempted to do so for the earlier nineteenth century, in terms of their achievement. Yet it must be emphasized that they flourished notably. The sheer increase in the size and wealth of an urban middle class able to devote more of its attention to culture, as well as the great extension of literate and culture-hungry lower-middle classes and sections of the working classes, would have been enough to ensure this. The number of theatres in Germany tripled between 1870 and 1896, from two hundred to six hundred.[4] This was the period when in Britain the Promenade Concerts began (1895), when the new Medici Society (1908) mass-produced cheap reproductions of the great masters of painting for the culturally aspiring, when Havelock Ellis, better known as a sexologist, edited an inexpensive Mermaid Series of Elizabethan and Jacobean dramatists, when such series as the World's Classics and the Everyman Library brought international literature to readers of small means. At the top of the scale of wealth, prices of old masters and other symbols of big money, dominated by the competitive buying of American multi-millionaires advised by dealers and their associated experts like Bernard Berenson, both of whom did extremely well out of this traffic, reached an all-time peak in real terms. The cultured sectors of the rich, and occasionally the very rich, in suitable regions, and the well-financed museums, chiefly of Germany, brought not only the best of the old, but also the best of the new, including the extreme *avant gardes* which survived economically largely on the patronage of a handful of such collectors, such as the Muscovite businessmen Morozov and Shchukin. The less cultured had themselves, or more frequently their wives, painted by John Singer Sargent or Boldini and their houses designed by fashionable architects.

There is thus no doubt that the public for the arts, richer, more cultured and more democratized, was enthusiastic and receptive. This was, after all, a period when cultural activities, long an indicator of status among the wealthier middle classes, found concrete symbols to express the aspirations and modest material achievements of wider strata, as in the upright piano, which, financially accessible through instalment paying, now penetrated the front parlours of clerks, the better-paid workers (at least in Anglo-Saxon countries) and comfortable peasants anxious to demonstrate their modernity. Moreover, culture represented not only individual but collective aspirations, nowhere more so than in the new mass labour movements. The arts also symbolized political aims and achievements in an age of democracy, to the material benefit of architects who designed the gigantic monuments to national self-congratulation and imperial propaganda, which filled the new German Empire and Edwardian Britain and India with masses of masonry, and of sculptors who supplied this golden age of what has been called 'statuomania'[5] with objects ranging from the titanic (as in Germany and the USA) to the modest busts of Marianne and the memorials of local worthies in French rural communes.

The arts are not to be measured by sheer quantity, nor is their achievement a simple function of expenditure and market demand. Yet there is no denying that there were in this period more people trying to earn their living as creative artists (or a higher proportion of such people in the labour force). It has even been suggested that the various breakaways from the official art establishments which controlled the official public exhibitions (the New English Arts Club, the frankly entitled 'Secessions' of Vienna and Berlin, etc., successors to the French

Impressionist Exhibition of the early 1870s) were largely due to the overcrowding of the profession and its official institutes, which naturally tended to be dominated by the older and established artists.[6] It might even be argued that it now became easier than ever before to earn a living as a professional creator, because of the striking growth of the daily and periodical press (including the illustrated press) and the appearance of the advertising industry, as well as of consumer goods designed by artist–craftsmen or other experts with professional standing. Advertising created at least one new form of the visual arts which enjoyed a small golden age in the 1890s: the poster. No doubt this proliferation of professional creators produced a great deal of hackwork, or was resented as such by its literary and musical practitioners, who dreamed of symphonies as they wrote operettas or song-hits, or like George Gissing, of great novels and poems as they churned out reviews and 'essays' or *feuilletons*. But it was paid work, and it could be reasonably paid: aspiring women journalists, probably the largest body of new female professionals, were assured that £150 a year could be earned by supplying the Australian press alone.[7]

Moreover, there is no denying that during this period artistic creation itself flourished remarkably, and over a wider area of western civilization than ever before. Indeed it now became internationalized as never before, if we omit music, which already enjoyed a basically international repertoire, mainly of Austro-German origin. The fertilization of western arts by exotic influences – from Japan since the 1860s, from Africa in the early 1900s – has already been mentioned in connection with imperialism (see above, pp. 80–1). In the popular arts influences from Spain, Russia, Argentina, Brazil and above all North America spread across the western world. But culture in the accepted elite sense was also notably internationalized by the sheer ease of personal movement within a broad cultural zone. One thinks not so much of the actual 'naturalization' of foreigners attracted by the prestige of certain national cultures, which made Greeks (Moreas), Americans (Stuart Merill, Francis Vielé-Griffin) and Englishmen (Oscar Wilde) write symbolist compositions in French; prompted Poles (Joseph Conrad) and Americans (Henry James, Ezra Pound) to establish themselves in England; and ensured that the École de Paris for painters consisted less of Frenchmen than of Spaniards (Picasso, Gris), Italians (Modigliani), Russians (Chagall, Lipchitz, Soutine) Rumanians (Brancusi), Bulgarians (Pascin) and Dutchmen (Van Dongen). In a sense this was merely one aspect of that spray of intellectuals which in this period distributed itself across the cities of the globe, as emigrants, leisured visitors, settlers and political refugees or through universities and laboratories, to fertilize international politics and culture.* One thinks rather of the western readers who discovered Russian and Scandinavian literature (in translation) in the 1880s, the central Europeans who found inspiration in the British arts-and-crafts movement, the Russian ballet which conquered fashionable Europe before 1914. High culture, from the 1880s, rested on a combination of native manufactures and imports.

However, national cultures, at least in their less conservative and conventional manifestations, were clearly in a healthy state – if this is the right word for some arts and creative talents who took pride in the 1880s and 1890s in being considered 'decadent'. Value judgments in this vague territory are notoriously difficult, for national sentiment is apt to exaggerate the merits of cultural achievements in its own language. Moreover, as we have seen, there were now flourishing written literatures in languages understood by few foreigners. For the overwhelming majority of us the greatness of prose and especially poetry in Gaelic, Hungarian or Finnish must remain a matter of faith, as does the greatness of the poetry of Goethe or Pushkin for those who know no German or Russian. Music is luckier in this respect. In any case there were no valid criteria of judgment, except perhaps inclusion in a recognized *avant garde*, for singling out some national figure from his or her contemporaries for international recognition. Was Rubén Darío (1867–1916) a better poet than any of his Latin American contemporaries? He may well have been, but all we can be sure of is that this son of Nicaragua gained international recognition in the Hispanic world as an influential poetic innovator. This difficulty in establishing international criteria of literary judgment has made the choice of the Nobel prize for literature (instituted in 1897) permanently unsatisfactory.

Cultural efflorescence was perhaps less noticeable in countries of recognized prestige and unbroken achievement in the high arts, though even there one notes the liveliness of the cultural scene in the French Third Republic and in the German Empire after the 1880s (compared to the mid-century decades), and the growth of new foliage on branches of the creative arts hitherto fairly bare: drama and musical composition in Britain, literature and painting in Austria. But what is particularly impressive is the unquestionable flowering of the arts in small or marginal countries or regions not hitherto much noted, or long dormant: in Spain, Scandinavia or Bohemia. This is very obvious in an international fashion such as the variously named art nouveau (*Jugendstil, stile liberty*) of the late century. Its epicentres were found not only in some major

* The role of such émigrés from Russia in the politics of other countries is familiar: Luxemburg, Helphand-Parvus and Radek in Germany, Kuliscioff and Balabanoff in Italy, Rappoport in France, Dobrogeanu-Gherea in Rumania, Emma Goldman in the USA.

cultural capitals (Paris, Vienna), but also, and indeed above all, in more or less peripheral ones: Brussels and Barcelona, Glasgow and Helsingfors (Helsinki). Belgium, Catalonia and Ireland are striking examples.

Probably at no time since the seventeenth century did the rest of the world need to take as much cultural notice of the southern Low Countries as in the final decades of the nineteenth century. For that is when Maeterlinck and Verhaeren briefly became major names in European literature (one of them is still familiar as the writer of Debussy's *Pelléas et Mélisande*), James Ensor became a familiar name in painting, while the architect Horta launched art nouveau, Van de Velde brought a British-derived 'modernism' into German architecture, and Constantin Meunier invented the international stereotype of the sculptured proletarian. As for Catalonia, or rather the Barcelona of *modernisme*, among whose architects and painters Gaudi and Picasso are only the most world-famous, it can safely be said that only the most self-confident Catalans would have envisaged such cultural glory in, say, 1860. Nor would an observer of the Irish scene in that year have predicted the extraordinary efflorescence of (mainly Protestant) writers who emerged from that island in the generation after 1880: George Bernard Shaw, Oscar Wilde, the great poet W. B. Yeats, John M. Synge, the young James Joyce, and others of more localized celebrity.

Yet it plainly will not do to write the history of the arts in our period simply as a success story, which it certainly was in terms of economics and the democratization of culture, and, at a level somewhat more modest than the Shakespearean or Beethovenian, in widely distributed creative achievement. For even if we remain in the sphere of 'high culture' (which was already being made technologically obsolescent), neither the creators in the arts nor the public for what was classified as 'good' literature, music, painting, etc., saw it in such terms. There were still, notably in the border-zone where artistic creation and technology overlapped, expressions of confidence and triumph. Those public palaces of the nineteenth century, the great railway stations, were still being built as massive monuments to the fine arts: in New York, St Louis, Antwerp, Moscow (the extraordinary Kazan station), Bombay and Helsinki. The sheer achievement of technology, as demonstrated in the Eiffel Tower and the novel American skyscrapers, dazzled even those who denied it aesthetic appeal. For the aspiring and increasingly literate masses, the mere accessibility of high culture still seen as a continuum of past and present, 'classic' and 'modern', was itself a triumph. The (British) Everyman's Library published its achievements in volumes whose design echoed William Morris, ranging from Homer to Ibsen, from Plato to Darwin.[8] And, of course, public statuary and the celebration of history and culture on the walls of public buildings – as in the Paris Sorbonne and the Vienna Burgtheater, University and Art History Museum – flourished as never before. The incipient struggle between Italian and German nationalism in the Tyrol crystallized round the erection of monuments to Dante and Walther von der Vogelweide (a medieval lyricist) respectively.

II

Nevertheless, the late nineteenth century does not suggest widespread triumphalism and cultural self-confidence, and the familiar implications of the term *fin de siècle* are rather misleadingly those of the 'decadence' in which so many established and aspiring artists – the young Thomas Mann comes to mind – took pride in the 1880s and 1890s. More generally, the 'high' arts were ill at ease in society. Somehow, in the field of culture as elsewhere, the results of bourgeois society and historical progress, long conceived as a co-ordinated forward march of the human mind, were different from what had been expected. The first great liberal historian of German literature, Gervinus, had argued before 1848 that the (liberal and national) ordering of German political affairs was the indispensable precondition for another flowering of German literature.[9] After the new Germany had actually come into being, the textbooks of literary history confidently forecast the imminence of this golden age, but by the end of the century such optimistic prognoses turned into glorification of the classical heritage against contemporary writing seen as disappointing or (in the case of the 'modernists') undesirable. For greater minds than the run-of-the-mill pedagogues it seemed already clear that 'the German spirit of 1888 marks a regression from the German spirit of 1788' (Nietzsche). Culture seemed a struggle of mediocrity consolidating itself against 'the dominance of the mob and the eccentrics (both mainly in alliance)'.[10] In the European battle between ancients and moderns, engaged at the end of the seventeenth century and so evidently won by the moderns in the Age of Revolution, the ancients – now no longer situated in classical antiquity – were once again winning.

The democratization of culture through mass education – even through the numerical growth of culture-hungry middle and lower-middle classes – was itself sufficient to make elites look for more exclusive cultural status–symbols. But the crux of the crisis of the arts lay in the growing divergence between what was contemporary and what was 'modern'.

At first this divergence was not obvious. Indeed, after 1880, when 'modernity' became a slogan and the term '*avant garde*', in its modern sense, first crept into the conversation of French painters and writers, the gap between the public and the more adventurous arts seemed actually to be narrowing. This was partly because, especially in the decades of economic depression and social tension, 'advanced' views on society and culture appeared to combine naturally, and partly because – perhaps through the public recognition of emancipated (middle-class) women and youth as a group and through the more unbuttoned and leisure-oriented phase of bourgeois society (see chapter 7 above) – important sectors of middle-class taste become distinctly more flexible. The fortress of the established bourgeois public, grand opera, which had been shocked by the populism of Bizet's *Carmen* in 1875, had by the early 1900s accepted not only Wagner, but the curious combination of arias and social realism (*verismo*) about the lower orders (Mascagni's *Cavalleria Rusticana*, 1890; Charpentier's *Louise*, 1900). It was prepared to make the fortunes of a composer like Richard Strauss, whose *Salome* (1905) combined everything designed to shock the bourgeoisie of 1880: a symbolist libretto based on a work by a militant and scandalous aesthete (Oscar Wilde) and an uncompromisingly post-Wagnerian musical idiom. At another, and commercially more significant level, anti-conventional minority taste now become marketable, as witness the fortunes of the London firms of Heals (furniture makers) and Liberty (fabrics). In Britain, the epicentre of this stylistic earthquake, as early as 1881 a spokesman of blinkered convention, the Gilbert and Sullivan operetta *Patience*, satirized an Oscar Wilde figure and attacked the novel preference of young ladies (favouring 'aesthetic' robes inspired by art galleries) for symbolist poets with lilies rather than sturdy dragoon officers. Shortly thereafter William Morris and arts-and-crafts provided the model for the villas, rural cottages and interiors of the comfortable and educated bourgeoisie ('my class', as the economist J. M. Keynes was later to call it).

Indeed, the fact that the same words were used to describe social, cultural and aesthetic innovation underlines the convergence. The New English Arts Club (1886), art nouveau and the *Neue Zeit*, the major journal of international Marxism, used the same adjective as was supplied to the 'new woman'. Youth and springtime growth were the metaphors which described the German version of art nouveau (*Jugendstil*), the artistic rebels of Jung-Wien (1890) and the devisers of images of spring and growth for the May Day demonstrations of labour. The future belonged to socialism – but the 'music of the future' (*Zukunftsmusik*) of Wagner had a conscious socio-political dimension, in which even political revolutionaries of the left (Bernard Shaw; Victor Adler, the Austrian socialist leader; Plekhanov, the pioneer Russian

Marxist) thought they discerned socialist elements which escape most of us today. Indeed the anarchist (though perhaps less the socialist) left even discovered ideological merits in the great, but far from politically 'progressive' genius of Nietzsche who, whatever his other characteristics, was undoubtedly 'modern'.[11]

It was no doubt natural that 'advanced' ideas should develop an affinity for artistic styles inspired by 'the people' or which, pushing realism (cf. *The Age of Capital*) forward into 'naturalism', took the oppressed and exploited and even the struggle of labour as their subject-matter. And the other way round. In the socially conscious Depression era there was a considerable amount of such work, a good deal of it – e.g. in painting – by people who did not subscribe to any manifesto of artistic rebellion. It was natural that the 'advanced' should admire writers who shattered bourgeois conventions about what it was 'proper' to write about. They favoured the great Russian novelists, largely discovered and popularized in the west by 'progressives', Ibsen (and in Germany other Scandinavians like the young Hamsun and – a more unexpected choice – Strindberg), and above all 'naturalist' writers accused by the respectable of concentrating on the filthy underside of society, and often, sometimes temporarily, attracted to the democratic left of various kinds, like Émile Zola and the German dramatist Hauptmann.

Nor did it seem strange that artists should express their passionate commitment to suffering humanity in ways which went beyond the 'realism' whose model was a dispassionate scientific recording: Van Gogh, then still quite unknown; the Norwegian Munch, a socialist; the Belgian James Ensor, whose 'Entry of Jesus Christ into Brussels in 1889' included a banner for the Social Revolution; or the German proto-expressionist Käthe Kollwitz, commemorating the revolt of the hand-loom weavers. Yet militant aesthetes and believers in art for art's sake, champions of 'decadence' and schools designed to be difficult of mass access such as 'symbolism', also declared a sympathy for socialism, like Oscar Wilde and Maeterlinck, or at least an interest in anarchism. Huysmans, Leconte de Lisle and Mallarmé were among the subscribers to *La Révolte* (1894).[12] In short, until the new century there was no general rift between political and artistic 'modernity'.

The British-based revolution in architecture and the applied arts illustrates the connection between both, as well as their eventual incompatibility. The British roots of the 'modernism' which led to the Bauhaus were, paradoxically, Gothic. In the smoky workshop of the world, a society of egoism and aesthetic vandals, where the small craftsmen so visible elsewhere in Europe could no longer be seen in the fog generated by the factories, the Middle Ages of peasants and artisans had long seemed a model of a society both socially and artistically more satis-factory. Given the irreversible industrial revolution, it inevitably tended to become a model inspiring a future vision rather than something that could be preserved, let alone restored. William Morris (1834–96) demonstrates the entire trajectory from late–romantic medievalist to a sort of Marxian social revolutionary. What made Morris and the associated arts-and-craft movement so remarkably influential was ideol-ogy, rather than his astonishing and manifold gifts as a designer, decorator and craftsman. For this movement of artistic renovation specifically sought to restore the broken links between art and the worker in production, and to transform the environment of daily living – from interior furnishings to house, and indeed village, city and land-scape – rather than the self-contained sphere of the 'fine arts' for the rich and leisured. The arts-and-crafts movement was disproportionately influential, because its impact automatically stretched beyond small circles of artists and critics, and because it inspired those who wished to change human life, not to mention practical men interested in producing structures and objects of use and in the relevant branches of education. Not least, it attracted a clutch of progressively minded architects, drawn to the new and urgent tasks of 'town-planning' (the term became familiar after 1900) by the vision of utopia so readily associated with their profession and its associated propagandists: the 'garden city' of Ebenezer Howard (1898), or at least the 'garden suburb'.

With the arts-and-crafts movement an artistic ideology thus became more than a fashion among creators and connoisseurs, because its commitment to social change linked it to the world of public institutions and reforming public authorities which could translate it into the public reality of art schools and redesigned or expanded cities and communities. And it linked the men and – to a notably increased extent – the women active in it to productions, because its object was essentially to produce 'applied arts', or arts used in real life. The most lasting memorial to William Morris is a set of marvellous wallpaper and textile designs which were still commercially available in the 1980s.

The culmination of this socio-aesthetic marriage between crafts, architecture and reform was the style which – largely, though not entirely, propelled by British example and its propagandists – swept Europe in the later 1890s under various names of which art nouveau is the most familiar. It was deliberately revolutionary, anti-historicist, anti-academic and, as its champions never ceased to repeat, 'con-temporary'. It combined the indispensable modern technology – its most prominent monuments were the stations of the Paris and Vienna municipal transport systems – with the artisan's union of adornment and fitness for purpose; so much so that today it suggests above all a profusion of interlaced curvilinear decoration based on stylized mainly biological motifs, botanical or female. They were the metaphors of nature, youth, growth and movement so characteristic of the time. And indeed, even outside Britain, artists and architects in this idiom were associated with socialism and labour – like Berlage, who built a trade union headquarters in Amsterdam, and Horta, who built the 'Maison du Peuple' in Brussels. Essentially art nouveau triumphed through furniture, motifs of interior decoration, and innumerable smallish domestic objects ranging from the expensive luxuries of Tiffany, Lalique and the Wiener Werkstätte to the table-lamps and cutlery which mechanical imitation spread through modest suburban homes. It was the first all-conquering 'modern' style.*

Yet there were flaws at the heart of art nouveau, which may be partly responsible for its rapid disappearance, at least from the high cultural scene. They were the contradictions which drove the *avant garde* into isolation. In any case the tensions between the elitism and the populist aspirations of 'advanced' culture, i.e. between the hope of general renewal and the pessimism of educated middle classes faced with 'mass society', had only been temporarily obscured. From the middle 1890s, when it was clear that the great forward surge of socialism led not to revolution but to organized mass movements engaged in hopeful but routine activities, the artists and aesthetes found them less inspiring. In Vienna Karl Kraus, originally attracted to social democracy, moved away from it in the new century. Electoral campaigns did not excite him, and the cultural policy of the movement had to take account of the conventional tastes of its proletarian militants, and had indeed trouble enough fighting off the influence of pulp thrillers, romances and other forms of *Schundliteratur* against which socialists (notably in Scandinavia) waged embittered campaigns.[13] The dream of an art for the people confronted the reality of an essentially upper- and middle-class public for the 'advanced' arts, give or take a few figures whose subject-matter showed them to be politically acceptable to worker militants. Unlike the *avant gardes* of 1880–95, those of the new century, apart from the survivors of the older generation, were not attracted by radical politics. They were a-political or even, in some schools, like the Italian futurists, moving towards the right. Only war, the October Revolution and the apocalyptic mood which both brought with them were to fuse revolution in the arts and in society once again, thus casting a retrospective red glow over Cubism and 'constructivism',

---

* As this is written, the writer stirs his tea with a spoon made in Korea, whose decorative motifs visibly derive from art nouveau.

which had no such associations before 1914. 'The majority of artists today', complained the old Marxist Plekhanov in 1912–13, 'follow bourgeois points of view and are entirely resistant to the great ideals of liberty in our time.'[14] And in France it was noted that the *avant garde* of painters were entirely caught up in their technical debates and kept out of the way of other intellectual and social movements.[15] Who would have expected this in 1890?

III

Yet there were more fundamental contradictions within the *avant garde* arts. They concerned the nature of the two things for which the motto of the Vienna Secession called ('Der Zeit ihre Kunst, der Kunst ihre Freiheit' – 'To our era its art, to art its freedom'), or 'Modernity' and 'reality'. 'Nature' remained the subject-matter of the creative arts. Even in 1911 the painter later regarded as the herald of pure abstraction, Vassily Kandinsky (1866–1944), refused to sever all connection with it, since this would simply produce patterns 'like a necktie or a carpet (to put it bluntly)'.[16] But, as we shall see, the arts merely echoed a new and fundamental uncertainty about what nature was (see chapter 10 below). They faced a triple problem. Granted its objective and describable reality – a tree, a face, an event – how could description catch the reality? The difficulties of making reality 'real' in a 'scientific' or objective sense had already led e.g. Impressionist painters far beyond the visual language of representational convention (see *The Age of Capital*, chapter 15, IV), though, as the event proved, not beyond the comprehension of laymen. It took their followers considerably further, into the pointillism of Seurat (1859–91) and the search for the basic structure as against the appearance of visual reality, which the Cubists, claiming the authority of Cézanne (1839–1906), thought they could discern in some three-dimensional shapes of geometry.

Second, there was the duality between 'nature' and 'imagination', or art as the communication of descriptions and of ideas, emotions and values. The difficulty lay not in choosing between them, since few, even among the ultra-positivist 'realists' or 'naturalists', saw themselves entirely as dispassionate human cameras. It lay in the crisis of nineteenth-century values diagnosed by the powerful vision of Nietzsche, and consequently of the conventional language, representational or symbolic, for translating ideas and values into the creative arts. The flood of official statuary and building in the traditional idiom which inundated the western world between 1880 and 1914, from the Statue of Liberty (1886) to the Victor Emmanuel Monument (1912), represented a dying, and after 1918 clearly a dead, past. Yet the search for other idioms, often exotic, which was pursued from the ancient Egyptians and Japanese to the islands of Oceania and the sculptures of Africa, reflected not only dissatisfaction with the old, but uncertainty about the new. In a sense art nouveau was, for this reason, the invention of a new tradition which happened not to work out.

Third, there was the problem of combining reality and subjectivity. For part of the crisis of 'positivism', which will be more fully discussed in the next chapter, was the insistence that 'reality' was not just *there*, to be discovered, but was something perceived, shaped, even constructed through and by the mind of the observer. In the 'weak' version of this view, reality was objectively there, but apprehended exclusively through the states of mind of the individual who apprehended and reconstructed it, as in Proust's vision of French society as the by-product of one man's long expedition to explore his own memory. In the 'strong' version, nothing remained of it but the creator's ego and its emanations in words, sound or paint. Inevitably such art had enormous difficulties of communication. Inevitably it lent itself to, and unsympathetic critics dismissed it as, pure subjectivism verging on solipsism.

But *avant garde* art did of course want to communicate something other than the artist's state of mind or his technical exercises. However, the 'modernity' it sought to express held a contradiction which proved fatal to Morris and art nouveau. The social renewal of the arts along Ruskin–Morris lines had no real place for the machine, the core of that capitalism which was, to adapt a phrase from Walter Benjamin, the era when technology learned to reproduce works of art. Indeed, the *avant gardes* of the late nineteenth century attempted to create the art of the new era by prolonging the methods of the old, whose forms of discourse they still shared. 'Naturalism' extended the field of literature as representation of 'reality', by enlarging its subject–matter, notably to include the lives of the poor and sexuality. The established language of symbolism and allegory was modified or adapted to express new ideas and aspirations, as in the new Morrisian iconography of the socialist movements, and indeed in the other major *avant garde* school of 'symbolism'. Art nouveau was the culmination of this attempt to say the new in a version of the language of the old.

But how could it express precisely what the arts-and-crafts tradition disliked, namely the society of the machine and modern science? Was not the very mass production of the branches, flowers and female forms, the motifs of artisanal decoration and idealism which the commercial vogue for art nouveau entailed, a *reductio ad absurdum* of the Morris dream of craft revival? As Van de Velde felt – he had initially been a champion of Morris and the art-nouveau trends – must not sentimentalism, lyricism, romanticism be incompatible with modern man who lived in the new rationality of the machine age? Must not art express a new human rationality reflecting that of the technological economy? Was there not a contradiction between the simple, utilitarian functionalism inspired by the old crafts and the craftsman's joy in decoration, out of which art nouveau developed its ornamental jungle? 'Ornament is crime' declared the architect Adolf Loos (1870–1933), equally inspired by Morris and the crafts. Significantly the architects, including persons originally associated with Morris or even art nouveau, like Berlage in Holland, Sullivan in the USA, Wagner in Austria, Mackintosh in Scotland, Auguste Perret in France, Behrens in Germany, even Horta in Belgium, now moved towards the new utopia of functionalism, the return to the purity of line, form and material undisguised by ornament, and adapted to a technology no longer identifiable with masons and carpenters. For, as one of them (Muthesius) – also, typically, an enthusiast for the British 'vernacular style' – argued in 1902: 'The result of the machine can only be the unadorned, factual form.'[17] We are already in the world of the Bauhaus and Le Corbusier.

For the architects, now engaged on buildings to whose structure craft tradition was irrelevant and where decoration was an applied embellishment, the appeal of such rational purity was understandable; even though it sacrificed the splendid aspiration of a total union of structure and decoration, of sculpture, painting and the applied arts, which Morris derived from his admiration of the Gothic cathedrals, a sort of visual equivalent of Wagner's 'total work of art' or *Gesamtkunstwerk*. This unity, the arts culminating in art nouveau had still tried to achieve. But if one can understand the appeal of the new architects' austerity, one should also observe that there is absolutely no convincing reason why the use of a revolutionary technology in building *must* entail a decoratively stripped 'functionalism' (especially when, as so often, it became an anti-functional aesthetic), or why anything except machines should aspire to look like machines.

Thus it would have been quite as possible, and indeed more logical, to hail the triumph of revolutionary technology with the full twenty-one-gun salute of conventional architecture, in the manner of the great nineteenth-century railway stations. There was no compelling logic to the movement of architectural 'modernism'. What it expressed was primarily the emotional conviction that the conventional language of the visual arts, based on historical tradition, was somehow inappropriate or inadequate for the modern world. To be more precise, they felt that such a language could not possibly *express* but could only obscure the new world which the nineteenth century had brought into being. The machine, as it were, grown to giant size, cracked the fine-arts façade behind which it had been hidden. Nor could the old idiom, they felt, express the crisis of human understanding and values which this century of revolution had produced and was now forced to confront.

In a sense the *avant garde* blamed the traditionalists and the *fin de siècle* modernists equally for what Marx had accused the revolutionaries of 1789–1848 of doing, namely 'conjur[ing] up the spirits of the past to their service, and borrow[ing] from them names, battle slogans and costumes in order to present the new scene of world history in this time-honoured disguise and in this borrowed language'.[18] Only they did not have a new language, or they did not know what it would be. For what was the language in which to express the new world, especially as (technology apart) its only recognizable aspect was the disintegration of the old? Such was the dilemma of 'modernism' at the outset of the new century.

What led the *avant garde* artists forward was therefore not a vision of the future, but a reversed vision of the past. Often indeed, as in architecture and music, they were eminent practitioners of the styles derived from tradition which they abandoned only because, like the ultra-Wagnerian Schönberg, they felt them incapable of further modification. Architects abandoned ornament, as art nouveau pushed it to its extremes, composers tonality, as music drowned in post-Wagnerian chromaticism. Painters had long been troubled by the inadequacy of the older conventions for representing external reality and their own feelings, but – except for a very few who pioneered complete 'abstraction' on the eve of the war (notably among the Russian *avant garde*) – they found it difficult to abandon painting *something*. The *avant garde* fanned out in various directions, but, broadly speaking, opted either for what seemed to observers like Max Raphael the supremacy of colour and form over content, or for the single-minded pursuit of a non-representational content in the form of emotion ('expressionism'), or for various ways of dismantling the conventional elements of representational reality and reassembling them in different kinds of order or disorder (Cubism).[19] Only the writers, shackled by their dependency on words with known meanings and sounds, found it difficult as yet to make an equivalent formal revolution, though a few began to try. Experiments in abandoning conventional forms of literary composition (e.g. rhymed verse and metre) were neither new nor ambitious. Writers stretched, twisted and manipulated content, i.e. what could be said in ordinary words. Fortunately the poetry of the early twentieth century was a lineal development of, rather than a revolt against, the symbolism of the late nineteenth century: it therefore produced Rilke (1875–1926), Apollinaire (1880–1918), George (1868–1933), Yeats (1865–1939), Blok (1880–1921) and the great Spaniards.

Contemporaries, ever since Nietzsche, had no doubt that the crisis of the arts reflected the crisis of a society – the liberal bourgeois society of the nineteenth century – which, in one way or another, was in the process of destroying the bases of its existence, the systems of value, convention and intellectual understanding which structured and ordered it. Later historians have traced this crisis in the arts in general and in particular cases, such as '*fin de siècle* Vienna'. Here we need only note two things about it. First, the visible break between the *fin de siècle* and the twentieth-century *avant gardes* occurred some time between 1900 and 1910. Amateurs of dates may choose between several, but the birth of Cubism in 1907 is as convenient as any. In the last few years before 1914 virtually everything that is characteristic of the various kinds of post-1918 'modernism' is already present. Second, the *avant garde* henceforth found itself marching in directions the main army of the public was neither willing nor able to follow. Richard Strauss, who had travelled the road away from tonality as an artist, decided after *Elektra* failed (1909), as a supplier of commercial grand opera, that the public would follow him no further, and returned (with enormous success) to the more accessible idiom of *Rosenkavalier* (1911).

A wide gap therefore opened between the main body of 'cultured' taste and the various small minorities who asserted their status as dissident anti-bourgeois rebels by demonstrating admiration for styles of artistic creation inaccessible and scandalous to the majority. Only three major bridges crossed it. The first was the patronage of a handful of those who were both enlightened and well heeled, like the German industrialist Walter Rathenau, or of dealers like Kahnweiler who appreciated the commercial potential of this small but financially rewarding market. The second was a sector of fashionable high society, more than ever enthusiastic for ever-changing but guaranteed unbourgeois styles, preferably exotic and shocking. The third, paradoxically, was business. Lacking aesthetic preconceptions, industry could recognize the revolutionary technology of building and the economy of a functional style – it had always done so – and business could see that *avant garde* techniques were effective in advertising. 'Modernist' criteria had practical value for industrial design and mechanized mass production. After 1918 business patronage and industrial design were to be the main agencies for assimilating the styles originally associated with the high-cultural *avant garde*. However, before 1914 it remained confined within isolated enclaves.

It is therefore misleading to pay too much attention to the 'modernist' *avant garde* before 1914, except as ancestors. Most people, even among the highly cultured, had probably never heard of, say, Picasso or Schönberg, whereas the innovators of the last quarter of the nineteenth century had already become part of the cultural luggage of the educated middle classes. The new revolutionaries belonged to each other, to argumentative groups of the dissident young in the cafés of suitable city quarters, to the critics and drafters of manifestos for new 'isms' (cubism, futurism, vorticism), to little magazines and to a few impresarios and collectors with flair and a taste for new works and their creators: a Diaghilev, an Alma Schindler who, even before 1914, had progressed from Gustav Mahler to Kokoschka, Gropius and (a less successful cultural investment) the expressionist Franz Werfel. They were taken up by a section of high fashion. That was all.

All the same, the *avant gardes* of the last pre-1914 years marks a fundamental break in the history of the high arts since the Renaissance. But what they did *not* achieve was the actual cultural revolution of the twentieth century they aimed at, which was simultaneously taking place as a by-product of the democratization of society, mediated by the entrepreneurs whose eyes were on an entirely non-bourgeois market. The plebeian arts were about to conquer the world, both in their own version of arts-and-crafts and by means of high technology. This conquest constitutes the most important development in twentieth-century culture.

IV

Its early stages are not always easy to trace. At some point in the later nineteenth century the mass migration into the rapidly growing big cities produced both a lucrative market for popular spectacle and entertainment and those specialized city quarters devoted to it, which bohemians and artists also found attractive: Montmartre, Schwabing. Consequently traditional forms of popular entertainment were modified, transformed and professionalized, producing original versions of popular artistic creation.

The world of high culture, or rather its bohemian fringe, was, of course, well aware of the world of popular theatrical entertainment which developed in such entertainment quarters of the great cities. The adventurous young, the *avant garde* or artistic *bohème*, the sexually unconventional, the raffish elements in the upper class who had always patronized the likes of boxers, jockeys and dancers, found themselves at ease in these unrespectable milieux. In fact, in Paris these demotic elements were shaped into the cabaret and show-culture of Montmartre chiefly for the benefit of a public of socialites, tourists and intellectuals, and immortalized in the posters and lithographs of its greatest denizen, the aristocratic painter Toulouse-Lautrec. A culture of *avant garde* bourgeois low-life also showed signs of developing in central Europe, but in Britain the music hall, which appealed to intellectual aesthetes from the 1880s on, was more genuinely aimed at a popular audience. The admiration was justified. The cinema was shortly to turn one figure from the entertainment world of the British poor into the most universally admired artist of the first half of the twentieth century: Charlie Chaplin (1889–1977).

At a considerably more modest level of popular entertainment, or entertainment provided by the poor – the tavern, dance hall, singing café and brothel – an international range of musical innovations appeared towards the end of the century, which spread across frontiers and oceans partly through tourism and the medium of the musical stage, mainly through the new practice of social dancing in public. Some, like the Neapolitan *canzone*, then in its golden age, remained localized. Others showed greater powers of expansion, like the Andalusian *flamenco*, enthusiastically taken up from the 1880s by populist Spanish intellectuals, or the tango, a product of the brothel quarter of Buenos Aires, which had reached the European *beau monde* before 1914. None of these exotic and plebeian creations was to have a more triumphant and global future than the musical idiom of North American Negroes which – once again via the stage, commercialized popular music and social dancing – had already crossed the ocean by 1914. These fused with the arts of the plebeian *demi-monde* of great cities, occasionally reinforced by declassed bohemians and hailed by high-class *aficionados*. They were an urban equivalent of folk-art, which now formed the base of a commercialized entertainment industry, though their mode of creation owed nothing to their mode of exploitation. But, above all, they were essentially arts which owed nothing of substance to bourgeois culture, either in the form of 'high' art or in the form of middle-class light entertainment. On the contrary, they were about to transform bourgeois culture from below.

The real art of technological revolution, based on the mass market, was meanwhile developing with a rapidity for which there was no parallel in past history. Two of these technological–economic media were as yet of minor significance: the mechanical broadcasting of sound and the press. The impact of the phonograph was limited by the cost of the devices it required, which still confined their ownership largely to the relatively well off. The impact of the press was limited by its reliance on the old-fashioned printed word. Its content was broken up into small and self-contained chunks for the benefit of a class of readers with less education and willingness to concentrate than the solid middle-class elites who read *The Times*, the *Journal des Débats* and the *Neue Freie Presse*, but that was all. Its purely visual innovations – fat headlines, page lay-out, the mixture of text and picture, and especially display advertisements – were plainly revolutionary, as the Cubists recognized by including newspaper fragments in their pictures, but perhaps the only genuinely innovatory forms of communication the press revived were cartoons, and even the early versions of the modern strip-cartoons which they took over from popular pamphlets and broadsheets in forms simplified for technical reasons.[20] The mass press, which began to reach circulations of a million or more in the 1890s, transformed the environment of print, but not its content or associations – perhaps because men who founded newspapers were probably educated and certainly rich, and therefore sensitive to the values of bourgeois culture. Besides, there was nothing in principle new about newspapers and periodicals.

On the other hand, the cinema, which (eventually also via television and video) was to dominate and transform all the twentieth-century arts, was utterly novel, in its technology, its mode of production and its manner of presenting reality. Here, indeed, was the first art which could not have existed except in the industrial society of the twentieth century, and which had no parallel or precedent in the earlier arts – not even in the still photography which could be considered as no more than an alternative to sketching or painting (see *The Age of Capital*, chapter 15, IV). For the first time in history the visual presentation of movement was emancipated from immediate, living performance. And for the first time in history story, drama or spectacle were freed from the constraints imposed by time, space and the physical nature of the observer, not to mention the previous limits on stage illusion. The movement of the camera, the variability of its focus, the unlimited scope of trick photography and, above all, the ability to cut the strip of film which recorded it all into suitable pieces and to assemble or reassemble them at will, were immediately obvious and immediately exploited by film-makers who rarely had any interest in or sympathies for the *avant garde* arts. Yet no art represents the requirements, the unintended triumph, of an utterly untraditional artistic modernism more dramatically than the cinema.

And the triumph of the cinema was quite extraordinary and unparalleled in its speed and scale. The moving photograph did not become technically feasible until about 1890. Though the French were the main pioneers of showing these moving pictures, short films were first shown as fairground or vaudeville novelties in 1895–6, almost simultaneously in Paris, Berlin, London, Brussels and New York.[21] Barely a dozen years later there were 26 million Americans who went to see motion pictures *every week*, most probably in the 8000–10,000 small 'nickelodeons'; that is to say roughly a figure as large as 20 per cent of the entire population of the USA.[22] As for Europe, even in backward Italy there were by then almost five hundred cinemas in the major cities, forty of them in Milan alone.[23] By 1914 the American film audience had risen to almost 50 millions.[24] Films were now big business. The film-star system had been invented (in 1912 by Carl Laemmle for Mary Pickford). And the film industry had begun to settle in what was already on the way to being its global capital, on a hillside in Los Angeles.

This extraordinary achievement was due, in the first place, to the total lack of interest of the film pioneers in anything except profitable entertainment for a mass public. They entered the industry as showmen, sometimes small-time fairground showmen like the first movie mogul, Charles Pathé (1863–1957) of France – though he was not typical of the European entrepreneurs. More often they were, as in the USA, poor but energetic Jewish immigrant hucksters who would as willingly have gone on selling clothes, gloves, furs, hardware or meat, if they had looked equally lucrative. They moved into production in order to fill their shows. They aimed unhesitatingly at the least educated, the least intellectual, the least sophisticated, the least self-improving who filled the nickelodeons in which Carl Laemmle (Universal Films), Louis B. Mayer (Metro-Goldwyn-Mayer), the Warner Brothers and William Fox (Fox Films) got their start around 1905. In *The Nation* (1913), American populist democracy welcomed this triumph of the lower orders by means of 5-cent admissions, while European social democracy, concerned to bring workers the higher things in life, dismissed films as the diversion of the lumpenproletariat in search of escapism.[25] The film therefore developed according to the formulas for sure-fire applause tried and tested since the ancient Romans.

What is more, the film enjoyed one unanticipated but absolutely crucial advantage. Since it could, until the late 1920s, reproduce only images, not words, it was forced into silence, broken only by the sounds of the musical accompaniment, which multiplied the possibilities of employment for second-rate instrumentalists. Freed from the constraints of the Tower of Babel, the movies therefore developed a universal language which, in effect, enabled them to exploit the global market irrespective of language.

There is no doubt that the revolutionary innovations of films as an art, practically all of which had been developed in the USA by 1914, were due to its need to address a potentially universal public exclusively through the – technically manipulable – eye, but also that innovations which left the high-cultural *avant garde* far behind in their daring were readily accepted by the masses, because this was an art which transformed everything except its content. What the public saw and loved in the movies was precisely what had astonished, excited, amused and moved audiences as long as there had been professional enter-tainment. Paradoxically, this is where high culture made its only sig-nificant impact on the American film industry, which by 1914 was on the way to conquer and utterly dominate the global market.

For while American storefront showmen were about to make them-selves millionaires out of the nickels of immigrants and workers, other theatrical and vaudeville entrepreneurs (not to mention some of the nickelodeon hucksters) dreamed of tapping the greater purchasing-power and 'class' of the respectable family public, and especially the cash-flow of America's 'new woman' and her children. (For 75 per cent of the public in the nickelodeon era were adult males.) They required expensive stories and prestige ('screen classics'), which the anarchy of cut-price American movie production was disinclined to risk. But these could be imported from the pioneer French industry, which still domi-nated a third of the world's output, or from other Europeans. For in Europe orthodox theatre, with its established middle-class market, had been the natural source for more ambitious film entertainment, and if dramatic adaptations of biblical stories and secular classics (Zola, Dumas, Daudet, Hugo) were successful, why not film adaptations? Imports of elaborate costume productions with famous actresses like Sarah Bernhardt, or elaborate epic equipment, in which the Italians specialized, proved commercially successful in the last pre-war years. Stimulated by the dramatic turn from documentary films to stories and comedies, which seems to have made itself felt in 1905–9, they encouraged American producers to make their own cinematic novels and epics. These in turn gave otherwise uninteresting minor literary talents of sound American white-collar stock like D. W. Griffith the chance to transform the motion picture into a major and original art-form.

Hollywood was based on the junction between nickelodeon populism and the culturally and morally rewarding drama and sentiment expected by the equally large mass of middle Americans. Its strength and its weakness lay precisely in its single-minded concentration on the mass-market box-office. The strength was in the first instance economic. The European cinema opted, not without some resistance from populist showmen,* for the educated public at the expense of the uneducated. Who would otherwise have made the famous German UFA films of the 1920s? Meanwhile the American industry could exploit to the full a mass market on the basis of a population which, on paper, was not

---

* 'Our industry, which has progressed by means of its popular appeal, needs the support of all social classes. It must not become the favourite of the better-off classes only, who can afford to pay almost as much for cinema tickets as they do to go to the theatre' – *Vita Cinematografica* (1914).[26]

more than a third larger than that provided by the population of Germany. This allowed it to cover costs and earn ample profits at home, and therefore to conquer the rest of the world by undercutting it. The First World War was to reinforce this decisive advantage and make the American position unchallengeable. Boundless resources would also enable Hollywood to buy up talent from all over the world, notably after the war from central Europe. It did not always make adequate use of it.

The weaknesses of Hollywood were equally obvious. It created an extraordinary medium with extraordinary potential, but one with an artistically negligible message, at least until the 1930s. The number of American silent films which are in the living repertoire, or which even the educated can recall, is tiny – except for comedies. Given the enormous rate at which motion pictures were produced, they form an entirely insignificant percentage of the output. Ideologically, indeed, the message was far from ineffective or negligible. If hardly anyone recalls the great mass of B-movies, their values were to be decanted into American high policy in the late twentieth century.

Nevertheless, industrialized mass entertainment revolutionized the twentieth-century arts, and it did so separately and independently from the *avant garde*. For before 1914 the arts *avant garde* had no part in films, and it appears to have taken no interest in them, apart from one Russian-born Cubist in Paris who is said to have thought about an abstract film sequence in 1913.[27] It only took the medium up seriously in the middle of the war, when it was already virtually mature. The typical pre-1914 form of *avant garde* show-business was the Russian ballet, for which the great impresario Serge Diaghilev mobilized the most revolutionary and exotic composers and painters. But the Russian ballet was aimed at an elite of well-heeled or well-born cultural snobs as unhesitatingly as American film producers aimed at the lowest permissible common denominator of humanity.

So the 'modern', the truly 'contemporary' art of this century developed unexpectedly, overlooked by the guardians of cultural values, and with the speed to be expected of a genuine cultural revolution. But it was no longer, and could no longer be, the art of the bourgeois world and the bourgeois century, except in one crucial respect: it was profoundly capitalist. Was it 'culture' in the bourgeois sense at all? Almost certainly most educated persons in 1914 would have thought it was not. And yet this new and revolutionary medium of the masses was stronger by far than the élite culture, whose search for a new way of expressing the world fills most histories of twentieth-century arts.

Few figures represent the old tradition, in its conventional and revolutionary versions, more obviously than two composers of pre-

1914 Vienna: Erich Wolfgang Korngold, an infant prodigy of the middlebrow musical scene already launching himself into symphonies, operas and the rest; and Arnold Schönberg. The first ended his life as a highly successful composer of sound tracks for Hollywood motion pictures and musical director of Warner Brothers. The second, after revolutionizing nineteenth-century classical music, ended his life in the same city, still without a public, but admired and subsidized by more adaptable and vastly more prosperous musicians who earned money in the motion picture industry by not applying the lessons they had learned from him.

The arts of the twentieth century were therefore revolutionized, but not by those who set themselves the task of doing so. In this respect they differed dramatically from the sciences.

CHAPTER 10

CERTAINTIES UNDERMINED: THE SCIENCES

What is the material universe composed of? Ether, Matter and Energy.
S. Laing, 1885[1]

It is generally agreed that during the past fifteen years there has been a great advance in our knowledge of the fundamental laws of heredity. Indeed, it may fairly be said that more has been gained in this regard within this period than in the entire previous history of the field of knowledge.
Raymond Pearl, 1913[2]

Space and time have ceased to be, for relativity physics, part of the bare bones of the world, and are now admitted to be constructions.
Bertrand Russell, 1914[3]

There are times when man's entire way of apprehending and structuring the universe is transformed in a fairly brief period of time, and the decades which preceded the First World War were one of these. This transformation was as yet understood, or even observed, by relatively exiguous numbers of men and women in a handful of countries, and sometimes only by minorities even within the fields of intellectual and creative activity which were being transformed. And by no means all such fields saw a transformation, or were transformed in the same way. A fuller study would have to distinguish between fields in which men were conscious of linear progress rather than transformation (such as the medical sciences) and those which were revolutionized (such as physics); between old sciences revolutionized and sciences which themselves constituted innovations, since they were born in our period (such as genetics); between scientific theories destined to be the base of a new consensus or orthodoxy, and others which were to remain on the margins of their disciplines, such as psychoanalysis. It would also have to distinguish between accepted theories challenged but successfully re-established in a more or less modified form, such as Darwinism, and other parts of the mid-nineteenth century intellectual heritage which disappeared except from the less advanced textbooks, such as the physics of Lord Kelvin. And it would certainly have to distinguish between the natural sciences and social sciences which, like the traditional fields of scholarship in the humanities, increasingly diverged from them – creating a widening gap into which the large body of what the nineteenth century had regarded as 'philosophy' looked like disappearing. Still, however we qualify the global statement, it remains true. The intellectual landscape in which peaks named Planck, Einstein and Freud could now be seen to emerge, not to mention Schönberg and Picasso, was clearly and fundamentally different from that which intelligent observers believed themselves to perceive in, say, 1870.

The transformation was of two kinds. Intellectually it implied the end of an understanding of the universe in the image of the architect or engineer: a building as yet unfinished, but whose completion would not be very long delayed; a building based on 'the facts', held together by the firm framework of causes determining effects and 'the laws of nature' and constructed with the reliable tools of reason and scientific method; a construction of the intellect, but one which also expressed, in an ever more accurate approximation, the objective realities of the cosmos. In the minds of the triumphant bourgeois world the giant static mechanism of the universe inherited from the seventeenth century, but since amplified by extension into new fields, produced not only permanence and predictability but also transformation. It produced evolution (which could be easily identified with secular 'progress', at least in human affairs). It was this model of the universe and the human mind's way of understanding it which now broke down.

But this breakdown had a crucial psychological aspect. The intellectual structuring of the bourgeois world eliminated the ancient forces of religion from the analysis of a universe in which the supernatural and the miraculous could have no part, and left little analytical place for the emotions, except as products of the laws of nature. Nevertheless, with marginal exceptions, the intellectual universe appeared to fit in both with the intuitive human grasp of the material world (with 'sense experience') and with the intuitive, or at least age-old, concepts of the operation of human reasoning. Thus it was still possible to think of physics and chemistry in mechanical models (the 'billiard-ball atom').* But the new structuring of the universe increasingly found itself obliged to jettison intuition and 'common sense'. In a sense 'nature' became less 'natural' and more incomprehensible. Indeed, though all of us

---

* As it happened, the atom, soon to be broken up into lesser particles, returned in this period as the basic building-block of the physical sciences, after a period of relative neglect.

today live by and with a technology which rests on the new scientific revolution, in a world whose visual appearance has been transformed by it, and one in which educated lay discourse may echo its concepts and vocabulary, it is far from clear to what extent this revolution has been absorbed into the common processes of thought of the lay public even today. One might say that it has been existentially rather than intellectually absorbed.

The process of divorcing science and intuition may perhaps be illustrated by the extreme example of mathematics. Some time in the middle of the nineteenth century the progress of mathematical thought began to generate not only (as it had already done earlier – see *The Age of Revolution*) results which conflicted with the real world as apprehended by the senses, such as non-Euclidean geometry, but results which appeared shocking even to mathematicians, who found, like the great Georg Cantor, that 'je vois mais ne le crois pas'.[4] What Bourbaki calls 'the pathology of mathematics' began.[5] In geometry, one of the two dynamic frontiers of nineteenth-century mathematics, all manner of as it were unthinkable phenomena appear, such as curves without tangents. But the most dramatic and 'impossible' development was perhaps the exploration of infinite magnitudes by Cantor, which produced a world in which the intuitive concepts of 'greater' and 'smaller' no longer applied and the rules of arithmetic no longer gave their expected results. It was an exciting advance, a new mathematical 'paradise', to use Hilbert's phrase, from which the *avant garde* of mathematicians refused to be expelled.

One solution – subsequently followed by the majority of mathematicians –was to emancipate mathematics from any correspondence with the real world, and to turn it into the elaboration of postulates, *any* postulates, which required only to be precisely defined and linked by the need not to be contradictory. Mathematics was henceforth based on a rigorous suspension of belief in anything except the rules of a game. In the words of Bertrand Russell – a major contributor to the rethinking of the foundations of mathematics which now moved to the centre of the stage, perhaps for the first time in its history – mathematics was the subject in which no one knew what he was talking about or whether what he said was true.[6] Its foundations were reformulated by rigorously excluding any appeal to intuition.

This imposed enormous psychological difficulties, as well as some intellectual ones. The relation of mathematics to the real world was undeniable, even though, from the point of view of mathematical formalists, it was irrelevant. In the twentieth century the 'purest' mathematics has, time and again, found some correspondence in the real world, and indeed served to explain this world or to dominate it by means of technology. Even G. H. Hardy, a pure mathematician specializing in number theory – and incidentally the author of a brilliant piece of autobiographical introspection – a man who claimed with pride that nothing he had done was of any practical use, contributed a theorem, which is at the base of modern population genetics (the so-called Hardy–Weinberg law). What was the nature of the relationship between the mathematical game and the structure of the real world which corresponded with it? Perhaps this did not matter to mathematicians in their mathematical capacity, but in fact even many of the formalists, such as the great Hilbert (1862–1943), seem to have believed in an objective mathematical truth, i.e. that it was not irrelevant what mathematicians thought about the 'nature' of the mathematical entities they manipulated or the 'truth' of their theorems. An entire school of 'intuitionists', anticipated by Henri Poincaré (1854–1912) and led, from 1907, by the Dutchman L. E. J. Brouwer (1882–1966), bitterly rejected formalism, if necessary at the cost of abandoning even those triumphs of mathematical reasoning whose literally incredible results had led to the reconsideration of the bases of mathematics, and notably Cantor's own work in set theory, propounded, against impassioned opposition by some, in the 1870s. The passions evoked by this battle in the stratosphere of pure thought indicate the profundity of the intellectual and psychological crisis which the collapse of the old links between mathematics and the apprehension of the world produced.

Moreover, the rethinking of the foundations of mathematics itself was far from unproblematic, for the attempt to base it on rigorous definitions and non-contradiction itself (which also stimulated the development of mathematical logic) ran into difficulties which were to turn the period between 1900 and 1930 into the 'great crisis of the foundations' (Bourbaki).[7] The ruthless exclusion of intuition itself was possible only by a certain narrowing of the mathematician's horizon. Beyond that horizon lay the paradoxes which mathematicians and mathematical logicians now discovered – Bertrand Russell formulated several in the early 1900s – and which raised the most profound difficulties.* Eventually (in 1931) the Austrian mathematician Kurt Gödel proved that for certain fundamental purposes contradiction could not be eliminated at all: we cannot prove that the axioms of

* A simple example (Berry and Russell) is the statement that 'the class of integers whose definition can be expressed in less than sixteen words is finite'. It is impossible without contradiction to define an integer as 'the smallest integer not definable in less than sixteen words', since the second definition contains only ten words. The most fundamental of these paradoxes is 'Russell's Paradox', which asks whether the set of all sets that are not members of themselves is a member of itself. This is analogous to the ancient paradox of the Greek philosopher Zeno about whether we can believe the Cretan who says 'All Cretans are liars'.

246

arithmetic are consistent by a finite number of steps which do not lead to contradictions. However, by that time mathematicians had accustomed themselves to live with the uncertainties of their subject. The generations of the 1890s and 1900s were far from reconciled to them as yet.

Except for a handful of people the crisis in mathematics could be overlooked. A much larger body of scientists as well as eventually most educated human beings found themselves involved in the crisis of the Galilean or Newtonian universe of physics, whose beginning can be fairly precisely dated in 1895, and which was to be replaced by the Einsteinian universe of relativity. It met with less resistance in the world of physicists than the mathematical revolution, probably because it had not yet revealed itself as implying a challenge to the traditional beliefs in certainty and the laws of nature. That was to come only in the 1920s. On the other hand it met with enormous resistance from the laity. Indeed, even as late as 1913 a learned and plainly by no means foolish German author of a four-volume history and survey of science (who admittedly mentioned neither Planck – except as an epistemologist – nor Einstein, J. J. Thomson nor a number of others who would now hardly be omitted) denied that anything exceptionally revolutionary was happening in the sciences: 'It is a sign of bias when science is presented as though its foundations had now become unstable, and our era must set about their reconstruction'.[8] As we know, modern physics is still as remote to most laymen, even those who attempt to follow the often brilliant attempts to explain it to them which have multiplied since the First World War, as the higher reaches of scholastic theology were to most believers in Christianity in fourteenth-century Europe. Ideologists on the left were to reject relativity as incompatible with their idea of science, and those on the right condemned it as Jewish. In short science henceforth became not only something which few people could understand, but something of which many disapproved while increasingly recognizing that they depended on it.

The shock to experience, common sense and accepted conceptions of the universe can perhaps best be illustrated by the problem of the 'luminiferous ether', now almost as forgotten as that of the phlogiston by which combustion had been explained in the eighteenth century before the chemical revolution. There was no evidence for the ether, an elastic, rigid, incompressible and frictionless something believed to fill the universe, but it had to exist, in a world picture which was essentially mechanical and excluded any so-called 'action at a distance', chiefly because nineteenth-century physics was full of waves, starting with those of light (whose actual velocity was established for the first time) and multiplied by the progress of researches into electro-magnetism, which, since Maxwell, appeared to include lightwaves. But in a mechanically conceived physical universe waves had to be waves in *something*, just as seawaves were waves in water. As wave motion became ever more central to the physical world picture (to quote a by no means naive contemporary), 'ether was discovered in this century, in the sense that all known evidence of its existence was gathered in this epoch'.[9] In short, it was invented because, as all the 'authoritative physicists' held (with only the rarest dissenters like Heinrich Hertz (1857–94), the discoverer of radio waves, and Ernst Mach (1836–1916), best known as a philosopher of science), 'we should know nothing of light, of radiant heat, of electricity or magnetism; without it there would probably be no such thing as gravitation',[10] since a mechanical world picture also required it to exert its force through some material medium.

Yet, if it existed, it must have mechanical properties, whether or not they were elaborated by means of the new electromagnetic concepts. These raised considerable difficulties, as physics (since Faraday and Maxwell) operated with two conceptual schemes which were not readily combined and in fact tended to move apart: the physics of discrete particles (of 'matter') and those of continuous media of 'fields'. It seemed easiest to assume – the theory was elaborated by H. A. Lorentz (1853–1928), one of the eminent Dutch scientists who made our period into a golden age of Dutch science comparable to the seventeenth century – that the ether was stationary with respect to matter in motion. But this could now be tested, and two Americans, A. A. Michelson (1852–1931) and E. W. Morley (1838–1923), attempted to do so in a celebrated and imaginative experiment in 1887, which produced a result that seemed profoundly inexplicable. So inexplicable, and so incompatible with deep-rooted beliefs, that it was periodically repeated with all possible precautions until the 1920s: always with the same result.

What was the velocity of the movement of the earth through the stationary ether? A beam of light was divided into two parts, which travelled to and fro along two equal paths at right angles to one another, and were then reunited again. If the earth travelled through the ether in the direction of one of the beams, the motion of the apparatus during the passage of light ought to make the paths of the beams unequal. This could be detected. But it could not. It seemed that the ether, whatever it was, moved with the earth, or presumably with anything else that was measured. The ether appeared to have no physical characteristics at all or to be beyond any form of material apprehension. The alternative was to abandon the established scientific image of the universe.

It will not surprise readers familiar with the history of science that

Lorentz preferred theory to fact, and therefore attempted to explain away the Michelson–Morley experiment, and thus to save that ether which was considered 'the fulcrum of modern physics',[11] by an extraordinary piece of theoretical acrobatics which was to turn him into 'the John the Baptist of relativity'.[12] Suppose that time and space could be pulled slightly apart, so that a body might turn out to be shorter when facing in the direction of its motion than it would be if it were at rest, or facing crosswise. Then the contraction of Michelson-Morley's apparatus might have concealed the stationariness of the ether. This supposition, it is argued, was very close indeed to Einstein's special theory of relativity (1905), but the point about Lorentz and his contemporaries was that they broke the egg of traditional physics in a desperate attempt to maintain it intact, whereas Einstein, who had been a child when Michelson and Morley came to their surprising conclusion, was prepared simply to abandon the ancient beliefs. There was no absolute motion. There was no ether, or if there was it was of no interest to physicists. One way or another the old order in physics was doomed.

Two conclusions can be drawn from this instructive episode. The first, which fits in with the rationalist ideal which science and its historians have inherited from the nineteenth century, is that facts are stronger than theories. Given the developments in electromagnetism, the discovery of new kinds of radiation – radio waves (Hertz 1883), X-rays (Röntgen 1895), radioactivity (Becquerel 1896), given the need increasingly to stretch orthodox theory into curious shapes, given the Michelson–Morley experiment, sooner or later theory would have to be fundamentally altered to fit in with fact. It is not surprising that this did not happen immediately, but it happened soon enough: the transformation can be dated with some precision in the decade 1895–1905.

The other conclusion is the exact opposite. The view of the physical universe which fell apart in 1895–1905 had been based not on 'the facts' but on *a priori* assumptions about the universe, based partly on a seventeenth-century mechanical model, partly on even more ancient intuitions of sense experience and logic. There had never been any greater intrinsic difficulty about applying relativity to electrodynamics or anything else than to classical mechanics, where it had been taken for granted since Galileo. All that physics can say about two systems within each of which Newtonian laws hold (e.g. two railway trains) is that they move in relation to each other, but not that one is in any absolute sense 'at rest'. The ether had been invented because the accepted mechanical model of the universe required something like it, and because it seemed intuitively inconceivable that in some sense there was no distinction between absolute motion and absolute rest *somewhere*. Having been invented, it precluded the extension of relativity to electrodynamics or to the laws of physics in general. In short, what made the revolution in physics so revolutionary was not the discovery of new facts, though this certainly look place, but the reluctance of physicists to reconsider their paradigms. As always, it was not the sophisticated intelligences which were prepared to recognize that the emperor wore no clothes: they spent their time inventing theories to explain why these clothes were both splendid and invisible.

Now both conclusions are correct, but the second is much more useful to the historian than the first. For the first does not really explain adequately how the revolution in physics came about. Old paradigms do not usually, and did not then, inhibit the progress of research, or the formation of theories which appeared to be both consistent with the facts and intellectually fertile. They merely produce what can be seen in retrospect (as in the case of the ether) to have been unnecessary and unduly complicated theories. Conversely, the revolutionaries in physics – mainly belonging to that 'theoretical physics' which was hardly yet recognized as a field in its own right situated somewhere between mathematics and the laboratory apparatus – were plainly not fundamentally motivated by any desire to clear up inconsistencies between observation and theory. They went their own way, sometimes moved by purely philosophical or even metaphysical preoccupations like Max Planck's search for 'the Absolute', which took them into physics against the advice of teachers who were convinced that only minor corners still remained to be tidied up in that science, and into parts of physics which others regarded as uninteresting.[13] Nothing is more surprising in the brief autobiographical sketch written in old age by Max Planck, whose quantum theory (announced in 1900) marked the first public breakthrough of the new physics, than the sense of isolation, of being misunderstood, almost of failure, which evidently never left him. After all, few physicists have been more honoured, in their own country and internationally, than he was in his lifetime. Much of it was clearly the result of the twenty-five years, starting with his dissertation in 1875, during which the young Planck vainly tried to get his admired seniors – including men whom he would eventually convert – to understand, to respond to, even to read, the work he submitted to them: work about whose conclusiveness in his opinion, no doubt was possible. We look back and see scientists recognizing crucial unsolved problems in their field and setting about solving them, some pursuing the right path, the majority the wrong one. But in fact, as historians of science have reminded us, at least since Thomas Kuhn (1962), this is not the way scientific revolutions operate.

What, then, explains the transformation of mathematics and physics at this period? For the historian this is the crucial question. Moreover, for the historian who does not focus exclusively on the specialized debates among the theorists, the question is not simply about the change in the scientific image of the universe, but about the relation of this change to the rest of what was happening in the period. The processes of the intellect are not autonomous. Whatever the nature of the relations between science and the society in which it is embedded, and the peculiar historical conjuncture in which it takes place, there is such a relation. The problems which scientists recognize, the methods they use, the types of theories they regard as satisfactory in general or adequate in particular, the ideas and models they use in solving them, are those of men and women whose life, even in the present, is only partly confined within laboratory or study.

Some of these relations are simple to the point of crudity. A substantial part of the impetus for the development of bacteriology and immunology was a function of imperialism, given that empires provided a strong incentive for the conquest of tropical diseases such as malaria and yellow fever which inhibited the activities of white men in colonial areas.[14] A direct line thus links Joseph Chamberlain and (Sir) Ronald Ross, Nobel laureate in medicine in 1902. Nationalism played a part which is far from negligible. Wassermann, whose syphilis test provided the incentive to the development of serology, was urged on in 1906 by the German authorities, who were anxious to catch up with what they regarded as the undue advance of French research into syphilis.[15] While it would be unwise to neglect such direct links between science and society, whether in the form of government or business patronage and pressure, or in the less trivial form of scientific work stimulated by or arising out of the practical progress of industry or its technical requirements, these relations cannot be satisfactorily analysed in such terms, least of all in the period 1873–1914. On the one hand the relations between science and its practical uses were far from close, if we except chemistry and medicine. Thus in the Germany of the 1880s and 1890s – a few countries took the practical implications of science more seriously – the technical academies (Technische Hochschulen) complained that their mathematicians did not confine themselves purely to the teaching of the mathematics required by engineers, and the professors of engineering confronted those of mathematics in open battle in 1897. Indeed the bulk of German engineers, though inspired by American progress to install technological laboratories in the 1890s, were not in close touch with current science. Industry, conversely, complained that the universities were not interested in its problems and did their own research – though slow to do even this. Krupp (who did not allow his son to attend a technical academy until 1882) did not take an interest in physics, as distinct from chemistry, until the mid-1890s.[16] In short, universities, technical academies, industry and the government were far from co-ordinating their interests and efforts. Government-sponsored research institutions were indeed coming into being, but they were hardly yet advanced: the Kaiser-Wilhelm-Gesellschaft (today the Max-Planck-Gesellschaft), which funded and co-ordinated basic research, was not founded until 1911, though it had privately financed predecessors. Moreover, while governments were undoubtedly beginning to commission and even press forward researches they considered of significance, we can hardly as yet speak of government as a major force commissioning fundamental research, any more than we can of industry, with the possible exception of the Bell laboratories. Moreover, the one science other than medicine in which pure research and its practical applications were adequately integrated at this time was chemistry, which was certainly undergoing no fundamental or revolutionary transformations during our period.

These scientific transformations would not have been possible but for technical developments in the industrial economy, such as those which made electricity freely available, provided adequate vacuum pumps and accurate measuring instruments. But a necessary element in any explanation is not in itself a sufficient explanation. We must look further. Can we understand the crisis of traditional science by analysing the social and political preoccupations of scientists?

These were obviously dominant in the social sciences; and, even in those natural sciences which appeared to be directly relevant to society and its concerns, the social and political element was often crucial. In our period this was plainly the case in those fields of biology which touched directly on social man, and all those which could be linked with the concept of 'evolution' and the increasingly politicized name of Charles Darwin. Both carried a high ideological charge. In the form of racism, whose central role in the nineteenth century cannot be overemphasized, biology was essential to a theoretically egalitarian bourgeois ideology, since it passed the blame for visible human inequalities from society to 'nature' (see *The Age of Capital*, chapter 14, II). The poor were poor because born inferior. Hence biology was not only potentially the science of the political right, but the science of those who suspected science, reason and progress. Few thinkers were more sceptical of the mid-nineteenth-century verities, including science, than the philosopher Nietzsche. Yet his own writings, and notably his most ambitious work, *The Will to Power*,[17] can be read as a variant of Social Darwinism, a discourse conducted in the language of 'natural selection', in this instance selection destined to produce a new race of 'superman' who will dominate human inferiors as man in nature dominates and exploits brute creation. And the links between biology and ideology are indeed particularly evident in the interplay between 'eugenics' and the new science of 'genetics', which virtually came into existence around 1900, receiving its name from William Bateson shortly thereafter (1905).

Eugenics, which was a programme for applying the selective breeding techniques familiar in agriculture and livestock-raising to people, long preceded genetics. The name dates from 1883. It was essentially a political movement, overwhelmingly confined to members of the bourgeoisie or middle classes, urging upon governments a programme of positive or negative actions to improve the genetic condition of the human race. Extreme eugenists believed that the condition of man and society could be ameliorated *only* by the genetic improvement of the human race – by concentrating on encouraging valuable human strains (usually identified with the bourgeoisie or with suitably tinted races such as the 'Nordic'), and eliminating undesirable strains (usually identified with the poor, the colonized or unpopular strangers). Less extreme eugenists left some scope for social reforms, education and environmental change in general. While eugenics could become a fascist and racist pseudo-science which turned to deliberate genocide under Hitler, before 1914 it was by no means exclusively identified with any one branch of middle-class politics any more than the widely popular theories of race in which it was implicit. Eugenic themes occur in the ideological music of liberals, social reformers, Fabian socialists and some other sections of the left, in those countries in which the movement was fashionable,* though in the battle between heredity and environment, or, in Karl Pearson's phrase 'nature' and 'nurture', the left could hardly opt *exclusively* for heredity. Hence, incidentally, the marked lack of enthusiasm for genetics among the medical profession at this period. For the great triumphs of medicine at this time were environmental, both by means of the new treatment for microbial diseases (which, since Pasteur and Koch, had given rise to the new science of bacteriology) and through public hygiene. Doctors were as reluctant as social reformers to believe with Pearson that '£1,500,000 spent in encouraging healthy parentage would do more than the establishment of a sanatorium in every township' to eliminate tuberculosis.[18] They were right.

What made eugenics 'scientific' was precisely the rise of the science of genetics after 1900, which appeared to suggest that environmental influences on heredity could be absolutely excluded, and that most or all traits were determined by a single gene, i.e. that the selective

---

* The movement for birth control was closely linked with eugenic arguments.

breeding of human beings along Mendelian lines was possible. It would be impermissible to argue that genetics grew out of eugenical pre-occupations, even though there are cases of scientists who were drawn into research on heredity 'as a *consequence* of a prior commitment to race-culture', notably Sir Francis Galton and Karl Pearson.[19] On the other hand the links between genetics and eugenics between 1900 and 1914 were demonstrably close, and in both Britain and the USA leading figures in the science were associated with the movement, though even before 1914, at least in both Germany and the USA, the line between science and racist pseudo-science was far from clear.[20] Between the wars this led serious geneticists to move out of the organizations of committed eugenists. At all events the 'political' element in genetics is evident. The future Nobel laureate H.J. Muller was to declare in 1918: 'I've never been interested in genetics purely as an abstraction, but always because of its fundamental relation to man – his characteristics and means of self-betterment.'[21]

If the development of genetics must be seen in the context of the urgent preoccupation with social problems for which eugenics claimed to provide biological solutions (sometimes as alternatives to socialist ones), the development of evolutionary theory, into which it fitted, also had a political dimension. The development of 'sociobiology' in recent years has once again drawn attention to this. This had been evident from the inception of the theory of 'natural selection', whose key model, the 'struggle for existence', had been primarily derived from the social sciences (Malthus). Observers at the turn of the century noted a 'crisis in Darwinism' which produced various alternative speculations – the so-called 'vitalism', 'neo-Lamarckism' (as it was called in 1901), and others. It was due not only to scientific doubts about the formulations of Darwinism, which had become something like a biological orthodoxy by the 1880s, but also to doubts about its wider implications. The marked enthusiasm of social democrats for Darwinism was enough to ensure that it would not be discussed in exclusively scientific terms. On the other hand, while the dominant politico-Darwinist trend in Europe saw it as reinforcing Marx's view that evolutionary processes in nature and society take place regardless of men's will and consciousness – and every socialist knew where they would inevitably lead – in America 'Social Darwinism' stressed free competition as nature's fundamental law, and the triumph of the fittest (i.e. successful businessmen) over the unfit (i.e. the poor). The survival of the fittest could also be indicated, and indeed ensured, by the conquest of inferior races and people or war against rival states (as the German general Bernhardi suggested in 1913 in his book on *Germany and the Next War*).[22]

Such social themes entered the debates of scientists themselves. Thus the early years of genetics were bedevilled by a persistent and embittered quarrel between the Mendelians (most influential in the USA and among experimentalists) and the so-called biometricians (relatively stronger in Britain and among mathematically advanced statisticians). In 1900 Mendel's long-neglected researches into the laws of heredity were simultaneously and separately rediscovered in three countries, and were – against biometrical opposition – to provide the foundation of modern genetics, though it has been suggested that the biologists of 1900 read into the old reports on growing sweet-peas a theory of genetic determinants which was not in Mendel's mind in his monastery garden in 1865. A number of reasons for this debate have been suggested by historians of science, and one set of such reasons has a clear political dimension.

The major innovation which, together with Mendelian genetics, restored a markedly modified 'Darwinism' to its position as the scientifically orthodox theory of biological evolution was the introduction into it of unpredictable and discontinuous genetic 'leaps', sports or freaks, mostly unviable but occasionally of potential evolutionary advantage, upon which natural selection would operate. They were called 'mutations' by Hugo De Vries, one of the several contemporaneous rediscoverers of Mendel's forgotten researches. De Vries himself had been influenced by the chief British Mendelian, and inventor of the word 'genetics', William Bateson, whose studies in variation (1894) had been conducted 'with special regard to discontinuity in the origin of species'. Yet continuity and discontinuity were not a matter of plant-breeding alone. The chief of the biometricians, Karl Pearson, rejected discontinuity even before he became interested in biology, because 'no great social reconstruction, which will permanently benefit any class of the community, is ever brought about by a revolution. . . . human progress, like Nature, never leaps'.[23]

Bateson, his great antagonist, was far from a revolutionary. Yet if one thing is clear about the views of this curious figure, it is his distaste for existing society (outside the University of Cambridge, which he wished to preserve from all reform except the admission of women), his hatred of industrial capitalism and 'sordid shopkeeper utility' and his nostalgia for an organic feudal past. In short, for both Pearson and Bateson the variability of species was a question of ideology as well as of science. It is pointless, and indeed usually impossible, to equate specific scientific theories and specific political attitudes, least of all in such fields as 'evolution' which lend themselves to a variety of different ideological metaphors. It is almost as pointless to analyse them in terms of the social class of their practitioners virtually all of whom, in this period, belonged almost by definition to the professional middle classes.

Nevertheless, in such fields as biology, politics, ideology and science cannot be kept apart, for their links are too obvious.

In spite of the fact that theoretical physicists and even mathematicians are also human beings, these links are not obvious in their case. Conscious or unconscious political influences may be read into their debates, but not with much profit. Imperialism and the rise of mass labour movements may help to elucidate developments in biology, but hardly in symbolic logic or quantum theory. Events in the world outside their studies in the years from 1875 and 1914 were not so cataclysmic as to intervene directly in their labours – as they were to do after 1914, and as they may have done in the late eighteenth and early nineteenth centuries. Revolutions in the world of the intellect in this period can hardly be derived by analogy from revolutions in the outside world. And yet every historian is struck by the fact that the revolutionary transformation of the scientific world view in these years forms part of a more general, and dramatic, abandonment of established and often long-accepted values, truths and ways of looking at the world and structuring it conceptually. It may be pure accident or arbitrary selection that Planck's quantum theory, the rediscovery of Mendel, Husserl's *Logische Untersuchungen*, Freud's *Interpretation of Dreams* and Cézanne's *Still Life with Onions* can all be dated 1900 – it would be equally possible to open the new century with Ostwald's *Inorganic Chemistry*, Puccini's *Tosca*, Colette's first 'Claudine' novel and Rostand's *L'Aiglon* – but the coincidence of dramatic innovation in several fields remains striking.

One clue to the transformation has already been suggested. It was negative rather than positive, insofar as it replaced what had been regarded, rightly or wrongly, as a coherent, potentially comprehensive scientific view of the world in which reason was not at odds with intuition, with no equivalent alternative. As we have seen, the theorists themselves were puzzled and disoriented. Neither Planck nor Einstein was prepared to give up the rational, causal, determinist universe which their work did so much to destroy. Planck was as hostile as Lenin to Ernst Mach's neo-positivism. Mach, in turn, though one of the rare early sceptics about the physical universe of late-nineteenth-century scientists, was to be equally sceptical of the theory of relativity.[24] The small world of mathematics, as we have seen, was split by battles about whether mathematical truth could be more than formal. At least the natural numbers and time were 'real', thought Brouwer. The truth is that theorists found themselves faced with contradictions which they could not resolve, for even the 'paradoxes' (a euphemism for contradictions) which the symbolic logicians tried so hard to overcome were not satisfactorily eliminated – not even, as Russell was to admit, by the monumental labours of his and Whitehead's *Principia Mathematica* (1910–13). The least troublesome solution was a retreat into that neo-positivism which was to become the nearest thing to an accepted philosophy of science in the twentieth century. The neo-positivist current which emerged towards the end of the nineteenth century, with writers like Duhem, Mach, Pearson and the chemist Ostwald, is not to be confused with the positivism which dominated the natural and social sciences before the new scientific revolution. That positivism believed that it could found the coherent view of the world which was about to be challenged on true theories based on the tested and systematized experience of the (ideally experimental) sciences, i.e. on 'the facts' of nature as discovered by scientific method. In turn these 'positive' sciences, as distinct from the undisciplined speculation of theology and metaphysics, would provide the firm foundation for law, politics, morality and religion – in short, for the ways in which human beings lived together in society and articulated their hopes for the future.

Non-scientific critics like Husserl pointed out that 'the exclusiveness with which the total world view of modern man, in the second half of the nineteenth century, let itself be determined by the positive sciences and be blinded by the "prosperity" which they produced, meant an indifferent turning away from the questions which were decisive for a genuine humanity.'[25] Neo-positivists concentrated on the conceptual defects of the positive sciences themselves. Faced with scientific theories which, now seen to be inadequate, could also be seen to be 'a forcing of language and a straining of definitions',[26] and with pictorial models (like the 'billiard-ball atom') which were unsatisfactory, they chose two linked ways out of the difficulty. On the one hand they proposed a reconstruction of science on a ruthlessly empiricist and even phenomenalist basis, on the other a rigorous formalization and axiomatization of the bases of science. This eliminated speculations about the relations between the 'real world' and our interpretations of it, i.e. about the 'truth' as distinct from the internal consistency and usefulness of propositions, without interfering with the actual practice of science. Scientific theories, as Henri Poincaré said flatly, were 'neither true nor false' but merely useful.

It has been suggested that the rise of neo-positivism at the end of the century made possible the scientific revolution by allowing physical ideas to be transformed without bothering about prior preconceptions about the universe, causality and natural laws. This, in spite of Einstein's admiration for Mach, is both to give too much credit to philosophers of science – even those who tell scientists not to bother about philosophy – and to underestimate the very general crisis of accepted nineteenth-century ideas in this period, of which neo-positivist agnosticism and the rethinking of mathematics and physics were only some aspects. For if we are to see this transformation in its historical context at all, it must be as part of this general crisis. And if we are to find a common denominator for the multiple aspects of this crisis, which affected virtually all branches of intellectual activity in varying degrees, it must be that all were confronted after the 1870s with the unexpected, unpredicted and often incomprehensible results of Progress. Or, to be more precise, with the contradictions it generated.

To use a metaphor suited to the confident Age of Capital, the railway lines constructed by humanity were expected to lead to destinations which the travellers might not know, having not yet arrived there, but about whose existence and general nature they had no real doubt. Just so Jules Verne's travellers to the moon had no doubt about the existence of that satellite, or about what, having got there, they would already know and what remained to be discovered by closer inspection on the ground. The twentieth century could be predicted, by extrapolation, as an improved and more splendid version of the mid-nineteenth.* And yet, as the travellers looked out of the window of humanity's train while it moved steadily forward into the future, could the landscape they saw, unanticipated, enigmatic and troubling, really be on the way to the destination indicated on their tickets? Had they entered the wrong train? Worse: had they entered the right train which was somehow taking them in a direction they neither wanted nor liked? If so, how had this nightmare situation arisen?

The intellectual history of the decades after 1875 is full of the sense of expectations not only disappointed – 'how beautiful the Republic was when we still had the Emperor', as a disenchanted Frenchman joked – but somehow turning into their opposite. We have seen this sense of reversal troubling both the ideologists and the practitioners of politics at this time (see chapter 4 above). We have already observed it in the field of culture, where it produced a small but flourishing genre of bourgeois writing on the decline and fall of modern civilization from the 1880s. *Degeneration* by the future Zionist Max Nordau (1893) is a good, and suitably hysterical, example. Nietzsche, the eloquent and menacing prophet of an impending catastrophe whose exact nature he did not quite define, expressed this crisis of expectations better than anyone else. His very mode of literary exposition, by means of a succession of poetic and prophetic aphorisms containing visionary intuitions or unargued truths, seemed a contradiction of the rationalist system-building discourse of philosophy which he claimed to practise.

* Except insofar as the Second Law of Thermodynamics predicted an eventual frozen death of the universe, thus providing a properly Victorian basis for pessimism.

His enthusiastic admirers multiplied among middle-class (male) youth from 1890.

For Nietzsche, the *avant garde* decadence, pessimism and nihilism of the 1880s was more than a fashion. They were 'the logical end-product of our great values and ideals'.[27] Natural science, he argued, produced its own internal disintegration, its own enemies, an anti-science. The consequences of the modes of thought accepted by nineteenth-century politics and economics were nihilist.[28] The culture of the age was threatened by its own cultural products. Democracy produced social-ism, the fatal swamping of genius by mediocrity, strength by weakness – a note also struck, in a more pedestrian and positivistic key, by the eugenists. In that case was it not essential to reconsider all these values and ideals and the system of ideas of which they formed a part, for in any case the 'revaluation of all values' was taking place? Such reflections multiplied as the old century drew to its end. The only ideology of serious calibre which remained firmly committed to the nineteenth-century belief in science, reason and progress was Marxism, which was unaffected by disillusion about the present because it looked forward to the future triumph of precisely those 'masses' whose rise created so much uneasiness among middle-class thinkers.

The developments in science which broke the mould of established explanation were themselves part of this general process of expectations transformed and reversed which is found at this time wherever men and women, in public or private capacities, confronted the present and compared it with their own or their parents' expectations. Could one suppose that in such an atmosphere thinkers might be readier than at other times to question the established ways of the intellect, to think, or at least to consider, the hitherto unthinkable? Unlike the early nineteenth century, the revolutions echoed, in some sense, in the prod-ucts of the mind were not actually taking place, but were rather to be expected. They were implicit in the crisis of a bourgeois world which simply could no longer be understood in its own old terms. To look at the world anew, to change one's perspective, was not merely easier. It was what, in one way or another, most people actually had to do in their lives.

However, this sense of intellectual crisis was strictly a minority phenomenon. Among the scientifically educated, one would guess, it was confined to the few people directly involved in the collapse of the nineteenth-century way of looking at the world, and by no means all of these felt it acutely. The numbers concerned were tiny, for even where scientific education had expanded dramatically – as in Germany, where the number of science students multiplied eightfold between 1880 and 1910 – they could still be counted in thousands rather than tens of thousands.[29] And most of them went into industry or fairly routine teaching where they were unlikely to worry much about the collapse of the established image of the universe. (One-third of Britain's science graduates in 1907–10 were primary school teachers.)[30] The chemists, by far the largest body of professional scientists of the time, were still only on the fringes of the new scientific revolution. Those who felt the intellectual earthquake directly were the mathematicians and physicists, whose numbers were not even growing very fast as yet. In 1910 the German and British Physical Societies together had only about 700 members, compared to more than ten times that number in the combined British and German learned societies for chemistry.[31]

Moreover, even in its most extended definition, modern science remained a geographically concentrated community. The distribution of the new Nobel prizes shows that its major achievements still clustered in the traditional area of scientific advance, central and north-western Europe. Out of the first seventy-six Nobel laureates[32] all but ten came from Germany, Britain, France, Scandinavia, the Low Countries, Austria–Hungary and Switzerland. Only three came from the Mediterranean, two from Russia and three from the rapidly rising, but still secondary, scientific community of the USA. The rest of non-European science and mathematics were making their mark – sometimes an extremely distinguished mark, as with the New Zealand physicist Ernest Rutherford – chiefly through their work in Britain. In fact, the scientific community was more concentrated than even these figures imply. More than 60 per cent of all Nobel laureates came from the German, British and French scientific centres.

Again, the western intellectuals who tried to elaborate alternatives to nineteenth-century liberalism, the educated bourgeois youth which welcomed Nietzsche and irrationalism, were small minorities. Their spokesmen numbered a few dozens, their public essentially belonged to new generations of the university-trained, who were, outside the USA, an exiguous educational elite. There were in 1913 14,000 students in Belgium and the Netherlands out of a total population of 13–14 millions, 11,400 in Scandinavia (minus Finland) out of almost 11 millions, and even in studious Germany only 77,000 out of 65 millions.[33] When journalists talked about 'the generation of 1914', what they meant was usually a café-table full of young men speaking for the network of friends they had made when they entered the École Normale Supérieure in Paris or some self-selected leaders of intellectual fashion in the universities of Cambridge or Heidelberg.

This should not lead us to underestimate the impact of the new ideas, for numbers are no guide to intellectual influence. The total number of men elected to the small Cambridge discussion society usually known as the 'Apostles' between 1890 and the war was only thirty-seven; but they included the philosophers Bertrand Russell, G. E. Moore and Ludwig Wittgenstein, the future economist J. M. Keynes, the mathematician G. H. Hardy and a number of persons reasonably famous in English literature.[34] In Russian intellectual circles the impact of the revolution in physics and philosophy was already such in 1908 that Lenin felt impelled to write a large book against Ernst Mach, whose political impact on the Bolsheviks he regarded as both serious and deleterious: *Materialism and Empiriocriticism.* Whatever we think of Lenin's judgments on science, his assessment of political realities was highly realistic. Moreover, it would not take long, in a world which was already formed (as Karl Kraus, satirist and enemy of the press, argued) by the modern media, for distorted and vulgarized notions of major intellectual changes to penetrate a wider public. In 1914 the name of Einstein was hardly a household word outside the great physicist's own household, but by the end of the world war 'relativity' was already the subject of uneasy jokes in central European cabarets. Within a few years of the First World War Einstein, in spite of the total impenetrability of his theory for most laymen, had become perhaps the only scientist since Darwin whose name and image were generally recognized among the educated lay public all over the world.

CHAPTER 11

REASON AND SOCIETY

They believed in Reason as the Catholics believed in the Blessed Virgin.
Romain Rolland, 1915[1]

In the neurotic, we see the instinct of aggression inhibited, while class consciousness liberates it; Marx shows how it can be gratified in keeping with the meaning of civilization; by grasping the true causes of oppression, and by suitable organization.
Alfred Adler, 1909[2]

We do not share the obsolete belief that the totality of cultural phenomena can be deduced as the product or function of constellations of 'material' interests. Nevertheless we do believe that it was scientifically creative and fertile to analyse social phenomena and cultural events in the special light of the extent to which they are economically conditioned. It will remain so for the foreseeable future, so long as this principle is applied with care and not shackled by dogmatic partiality.
Max Weber, 1904[3]

Perhaps another form of confronting the intellectual crisis should be mentioned here. For one way of thinking the then unthinkable was to reject reason and science altogether. It is difficult to measure the strength of this reaction against the intellect in the last years of the old century, or even, in retrospect, to appreciate its strength. Many of its more vocal champions belonged to the underworld or *demi-monde* of the intelligence, and are today forgotten. We are apt to overlook the vogue for occultism, necromancy, magic, parapsychology (which preoccupied some leading British intellectuals) and various versions of eastern mysticism and religiosity, which swept along the fringes of western culture. The unknown and incomprehensible became more popular than they had been since the early romantic era (see *The Age of Revolution*, chapter 14, 11). We may note in passing that the fashion for such matters, which had once been located largely on the self-educated left, now tended to move sharply to the political right. For the heterodox disciplines were no longer, as they had once been, would-be sciences like phrenology, homeopathy, spiritualism and other forms of parapsychology, favoured by those who were sceptical of the conventional learning of the establishment, but *rejections* of science and all its methods. However, while these forms of obscurantism made some contributions of substance to the *avant garde* arts (as, for instance, via the painter Kandinsky and the poet W. B. Yeats), their impact on the natural sciences was negligible.

Nor, indeed, did they make much impact among the general public. For the great mass of the educated, and especially the newly educated, the old intellectual verities were not in question. On the contrary, they were triumphantly reaffirmed by men and women for whom 'progress' had far from exhausted its promise. The major intellectual development of the years from 1875 to 1914 was the massive advance of popular education and self-education and of a popular reading public. In fact, self-education and self-improvement was one of the major functions of the new working-class movements and one of the major attractions for its militants. And what the masses of newly educated lay persons absorbed, and welcomed if they were politically on the democratic or socialist left, was the rational certainties of nineteenth-century science, enemy of superstition and privilege, presiding spirit of education and enlightenment, proof and guarantee of progress and the emancipation of the lowly. One of the crucial attractions of Marxism over other brands of socialism was precisely that it was 'scientific socialism'. Darwin and Gutenberg, inventor of the printing press, were as honoured among radicals and social democrats as Tom Paine and Marx. Galileo's 'And still it moves' was persistently quoted in socialist rhetoric to indicate the inevitable triumph of the workers' cause.

The masses were both on the move and being educated. Between the mid-1870s and the war the number of primary school teachers grew by anything between about one-third in well-schooled countries like France, to seven or even thirteen times its 1875 figure in formerly ill-schooled ones like England and Finland; the number of secondary school teachers might multiply up to four or five times (Norway, Italy). The very fact that they were both on the move and educated, pushed the front of the old science forward even as its supply base in the rear was getting ready for reorganization. For school teachers, at least in Latin countries, lessons in science meant inculcating the spirit of the Encyclopaedists, of progress and rationalism, of what a French manual (1898) called 'the freeing of the spirit',[4] easily identified with 'free thought' or liberation from Church and God. If there was any crisis for such men and women, it was not that of science or philosophy, but of the world of those who lived by privilege, exploitation and superstition. And in the world beyond western democracy and socialism, science meant power and progress in an even less metaphorical sense. It meant the ideology of modernization, forced upon backward and superstitious rural masses by the *científicos*, enlightened political elites of oligarchs inspired by positivism – as in the Brazil of the Old Republic and the Mexico of Porfirio Díaz. It meant the secret of western technology. It meant the Social Darwinism that legitimated American multi-millionaires.

The most striking proof of this advance of the simple gospel of science and reason was the dramatic retreat of traditional religion, at least in the European heartlands of bourgeois society. This is not to say that a majority of the human race were about to become 'free thinkers' (to use the contemporary phrase). The great majority of human beings, including the virtual totality of its female members, remained committed to a belief in the divinities or spirits of whatever was the religion or their locality and community, and to its rites. As we have seen (see p. 210 above), Christian Churches were markedly feminized in consequence. Considering that all major religions distrusted women and insisted firmly on their inferiority, and some, like the Jews, virtually excluded them from formal religious worship, the female loyalty to the gods seemed incomprehensible, and surprising to rationalist men, and was often considered yet another proof of the inferiority of their gender. Thus gods and anti-gods conspired against them, though the supporters of free thought, theoretically committed to the equality of the sexes, did so shamefacedly.

Again, over most of the non-white world, religion still remained the only language for talking about the cosmos, nature, society and politics, and both formulated and sanctioned what people thought and did. Religion was what mobilized men and women for purposes which westerners expressed in secular terms, but which in fact could not be entirely translated into the secular idiom. British politicians might wish to reduce Mahatma Gandhi to a mere anti-imperialist agitator using religion to rouse superstitious masses, but for the Mahatma a saintly and spiritual life was more than a political instrument for winning independence. Whatever its meaning, religion was ideologically omnipresent. The young Bengali terrorists of the 1900s, the nursery of what later came to be Indian Marxism, were initially inspired by a Bengali ascetic and his successor Swami Vivekananda (whose Vedanta doctrine is probably best known through a more anodyne Californian version), which they interpreted, not implausibly, as calling for a rising of the country now subject to a foreign power, but destined to give a universal faith to mankind.* It has been said that 'not through secular politics

* 'Oh India ... wouldst thou attain, by means of thy graceful cowardice, that freedom deserved only by the brave and the heroic? ... Oh Thou Mother of strength, take away my weakness, take away my unmanliness, and make me a man' – Vivekananda.[5]

but through quasi-religious societies educated Indians first fell into the habit of thinking and organising on a national scale'.[6] Both the absorption of the west (through groups like the Brahmo Samaj – see *The Age of Revolution*, chapter 12, II) and the rejection of the west by nativist middle classes (through the Arya Samaj, founded 1875) took this form; not to mention the Theosophical Society, whose connections with the Indian national movement will be noted below.

And if in countries like India the emancipated, the educated strata which welcomed modernity, thus found their ideologies inseparable from religion (or, if they did find them separable, had to be careful to conceal the fact), then it is obvious that the appeal of purely secular ideological language to the masses was negligible, and a purely secular ideology incomprehensible. Where they rebelled, it was quite likely to be under the banners of their gods, as they still did after the First World War against the British because of the fall of the Turkish sultan, who had been *ex officio* khalif, or head of all the Muslim faithful, or against the Mexican revolution for Christ the King. In short, on a global scale, it would be absurd to think of religion as significantly weaker in 1914 than in 1870, or in 1780.

Yet in the bourgeois heartlands, though perhaps not in the USA, traditional religion was receding with unprecedented rapidity, both as an intellectual force and among the masses. This was to some extent an almost automatic consequence of urbanization, since it was practically certain that, other things being equal, city was likely to discourage piety more than country, big city more than small town. But even the cities became less religious as the immigrants from the pious countryside assimilated to the a-religious or sceptical native townees. In Marseilles half the population had still attended Sunday worship in 1840, but by 1901 only 16 per cent did so.[7] Moreover, in the Roman Catholic countries, which comprised 45 per cent of the European population, faith retreated particularly fast in our period, before the joint offensive of (to quote a French clerical complaint) middle-class rationalism and the socialism of school teachers,[8] but especially of the combination of emancipatory ideals and political calculation which made the fight against the Church the key issue in politics. The word 'anti-clerical' first occurs in France in the 1850s, and anti-clericalism became central to the politics of the French centre and left from the middle of the century, when freemasonry passed under anti-clerical control.[9]

Anti-clericalism became central to politics in the Catholic countries for two main reasons: because the Roman Church had opted for a total rejection of the ideology of reason and progress, and thus could not but be identified with the political right, and because the struggle against superstition and obscurantism united liberal bourgeoisie and working class, rather than dividing capitalist from proletarian. Shrewd politicians did not fail to bear this in mind in appeals for the unity of all good men: France surmounted the Dreyfus affair by such a united front and immediately disestablished the Catholic Church.

One of the by-products of this struggle, which thus lead to the separation of Church and state in France in 1905, was a sharp acceleration of militant de-Christianization. In 1899 only 2.5 per cent of children in the diocese of Limoges had not been baptized; in 1904 – the peak of the movement – the percentage was 34 per cent. But even where the struggle of Church and state was not at the centre of politics, the organization of mass labour movements, or the entry of the common man (for women were much more loyal to the faith) into political life, had the same effect. In the pious Po valley of north Italy the complaints about the decline of religion multiply at the end of the century. (In the city of Mantua two-thirds already abstained from Easter communion in 1885.) The Italian labourers who migrated into the Lorraine steelworks before 1914 were already godless. In the Spanish (or rather Catalan) diocese of Barcelona and Vich the proportion of children baptized in their first week of life halved between 1900 and 1910.[11] In short, for most of Europe progress and secularization went together. And both advanced all the more rapidly inasmuch as Churches were increasingly deprived of that official status which gave them the advantages of the monopolist. The universities of Oxford and Cambridge, which excluded or discriminated against non-Anglicans until 1871, rapidly ceased to be refuges for Anglican clergymen. If in Oxford (1891) most heads of colleges were still in holy orders, none of the professors were so any longer.[12]

There were indeed little eddies in the contrary direction: upper-class Anglicans who converted to the more full-blooded faith of Roman Catholicism, *fin de siècle* aesthetes attracted by colourful ritual, and perhaps especially irrationalists for whom the very intellectual absurdity of traditional faith proved its superiority to mere reason, and reactionaries who backed the great bulwark of ancient tradition and hierarchy even when they did not believe in it, as was the case of Charles Maurras, in France the intellectual leader of the royalist and ultra-Catholic *Action Française*. There were indeed many who practised their religion, and even some fervent believers among scholars, scientists and philosophers, but the religious faith of few of them could have been inferred from their writings.

In short, intellectually western religion was never more hard-pressed than in the early 1900s, and politically it was in full retreat, at least into confessional enclosures barricaded against assault from outside.

The natural beneficiary of this combination of democratization and secularization was the political and ideological left, and it was in these quarters that the old bourgeois belief in science, reason and progress bloomed.

The most impressive heir to the (politically and ideologically transformed) old certainties was Marxism, the corpus of theory and doctrine elaborated after the death of Karl Marx out of his and Friedrich Engels' writings, mainly within the German Social Democratic Party. In many ways Marxism, in the version of Karl Kautsky (1854–1938), definer of its orthodoxy, was the last triumph of nineteenth-century positivist scientific confidence. It was materialist, determinist, inevitabilist, evolutionist, and firmly identified the 'laws of history' with the 'laws of science'. Kautsky himself began by seeing Marx's theory of history as 'nothing but the application of Darwinism to social development', and held in 1880 that Darwinism in social science taught that 'the transition from an old to a new conception of the world occurs irresistibly'.[13] Paradoxically, for a theory so firmly attached to science, Marxism was generally rather suspicious of the dramatic contemporary innovations in science and philosophy, perhaps because they appeared to be attached to a weakening of the materialist (i.e. free-thinking and deterministic) certainties which were so attractive. Only in the Austro-Marxist circles of intellectual Vienna, where so many innovations met, did Marxism keep in touch with these developments, though it might have done so more among the revolutionary Russian intellectuals but for the even more militant attachment to materialism of its Marxist gurus.* Natural scientists of the period therefore had little professional reason to take an interest in Marx and Engels, and, though some were on the political left, as in the France of the Dreyfus affair, few took an interest in them. Kautsky did not even publish Engels' *Dialectics of Nature*, on the advice of the only professional physicist in the party, for whose sake the German Empire passed the so-called Lex Arons (1898) which banned Social Democratic scholars from university appointments.[15]

However, Karl Marx, whatever his personal interest in the progress of mid-nineteenth-century natural sciences, had devoted his time and intellectual energy overwhelmingly to the social sciences. And on these, as well as on history, the impact of Marxian ideas was substantial.

Their influence was both direct and indirect.[16] In Italy, east-central Europe and above all in the Tsarist Empire, regions which seemed on

---

* For instance, Sigmund Freud took over the apartment of the Austrian Social Democratic leader Victor Adler in the Berggasse, where Alfred Adler (no relation), a committed Social Democrat among the psychoanalysts, read a paper in 1909 on 'The Psychology of Marxism'. Victor Adler's son Friedrich, meanwhile, was a scientist and admirer or Ernst Mach.[14]

the verge of social revolution or disintegration, Marx immediately attracted a large, extremely brilliant, but sometimes temporary, body of intellectual support. In such countries or regions there were times, for instance during the 1890s, when virtually all younger academic intellectuals were some kind of revolutionary or socialist, and most thought of themselves as Marxist, as has often happened in the history of Third World countries since. In western Europe few intellectuals were strongly Marxist, in spite of the size of the mass labour movements dedicated to a Marxian social democracy – except, oddly, in the Netherlands, then entering upon her early industrial revolution. The German Social Democratic Party imported its Marxist theorists from the Habsburg Empire (Kautsky, Hilferding), and from the Tsarist Empire (Rosa Luxemburg, Parvus). Here Marxism was chiefly influential through people who were sufficiently impressed by its intellectual as well as its political challenge to criticize its theory or to seek alternative non-socialist responses to the intellectual questions it raised. In the case both of its champions and of its critics, not to mention the ex-Marxists or post-Marxists who began to appear from the late 1890s, such as the eminent Italian philosopher Benedetto Croce (1866–1952), the political element was clearly dominant; in countries like Britain, which did not have to worry about a strong Marxist labour movement, nobody bothered much about Marx. In countries which had strong movements of this kind, very eminent professors like Eugen von Böhm-Bawerk (1851–1914) in Austria took time off their duties as teachers and cabinet ministers to rebut Marxist theory.[17] But of course Marxism would hardly have stimulated so substantial and heavyweight a literature, for and against, if its ideas had not been of considerable intellectual interest.

The impact of Marx on the social sciences illustrates the difficulty of comparing their development with that of the natural sciences in this period. For they dealt essentially with the behaviour and problems of human beings, who are very far from neutral and dispassionate observers of their own affairs. As we have seen, even in the natural sciences ideology becomes more prominent as we move from the inanimate world to life, and especially to problems of biology which directly involve and concern human beings. The social and human sciences operate entirely, and by definition, in the explosive zone where all theories have direct political implications, and where the impact of ideology, politics and the situation in which thinkers find themselves is paramount. It was quite possible in our (or any) period to be both a distinguished astronomer and a revolutionary Marxist, like A. Pannekoek (1873–1960), whose professional colleagues doubtless thought his politics as irrelevant to his astronomy as his comrades felt his astronomy to be to the class struggle. Had he been a sociologist nobody would have regarded his politics as irrelevant to his theories. The social sciences have zigzagged, crossed and recrossed the same territory or turned in a circle often enough for this reason. Unlike the natural sciences, they lacked a generally accepted central body of cumulative knowledge and theory, a structured field of research in which progress could be claimed to result from an adjustment of theory to new discoveries. And in the course of our period the divergence between the two branches of 'science' became accentuated.

In a way this was new. During the heyday of the liberal belief in progress, it looked as though most of the social sciences – ethnography/anthropology, philology/linguistics, sociology and several important schools of economics – shared a basic framework of research and theory with the natural sciences in the form of evolutionism (see *The Age of Capital*, chapter 14, II). The core of social science was the study of the ascent of man from a primitive state to the present, and the rational understanding of that present. This process was usually conceived of as a progress by humanity through various 'stages', though leaving behind on its margins survivals from earlier stages, rather similar to living fossils. The study of human society was a positive science like any other evolutionary discipline from geology to biology. It seemed perfectly natural for an author to write a study of the conditions of progress under the title *Physics and Politics, Or thoughts on the application of the principles of 'natural selection' and 'inheritance' to political society*, and for such a book to be published in the 1880s in a London publisher's International Scientific Series, cheek by jowl with volumes on *The Conservation of Energy, Studies in Spectrum Analysis, The Study of Sociology, General Physiology of Muscles and Nerves* and *Money and the Mechanism of Exchange*.[18]

However, this evolutionism was congenial neither to the new fashions in philosophy and neo-positivism, nor to those who began to have their doubts about a progress which looked like leading in the wrong direction, and hence about 'historical laws' which made it apparently inevitable. History and science, so triumphantly combined in the theory of evolution, now found themselves being separated. The German academic historians rejected 'historical laws' as part of generalizing science, which had no place in human disciplines devoted specifically to the unique and unrepeatable, even to 'the subjective–psychological way of looking at things' which was separated by so 'vast a chasm from the crude objectivism of the Marxists'.[19] For the heavy artillery of theory mobilized in the senior European historical periodical in the 1890s, the *Historische Zeitschrift* – though originally directed against other historians too inclined towards social or any other science – could soon be seen to be firing primarily against the Social Democrats.[20]

On the other hand such social and human sciences as could aspire to rigorous or mathematical argument, or to the experimental methods of natural sciences, also abandoned historical evolution, sometimes with relief. Even some who could aspire to neither, did so, like psychoanalysis, which has been described by one perceptive historian as 'an a-historical theory of man and society that could make bearable (to Freud's fellow-liberals in Vienna) a political world spun out of orbit and beyond control'.[21] Certainly in economics a bitterly fought 'battle of methods' in the 1880s turned on history. The winning side (led by Carl Menger, another Viennese liberal) represented not only a view of scientific method – deductive as against inductive argument – but a deliberate narrowing of the hitherto wide perspectives of the economists' science. Historically minded economists were either, like Marx, expelled into the limbo of cranks and agitators, or like the 'historical school', which was then dominant in German economics, asked to reclassify themselves as something else, for instance, economic historians or sociologists, leaving real theory to the analysts of neo-classical equilibria. This meant that questions of historical dynamics, of economic development and indeed of economic fluctuations and crises were largely extruded from the fields of the new academic orthodoxy. Economics thus became the only social science in our period undisturbed by the problem of non-rational behaviour, since it was so defined as to exclude all transactions which could not be described as being in some sense rational.

Similarly linguistics, which had been (with economics) the first and most confident of the social sciences, now seemed to lose interest in the model of linguistic evolution which had been its greatest achievement. Fernand de Saussure (1857–1913), who posthumously inspired all the structuralist fashions after the Second World War, concentrated instead on the abstract and static structure of communication, of which words happened to be one possible medium. Where the practitioners of social or human sciences could, they assimilated themselves to experimental scientists, as notably in one part of psychology, which rushed into the laboratory to pursue its studies in perception, learning and the experimental modification of behaviour. This produced a Russo-American theory of 'behaviourism' (I. Pavlov, 1849–1936; J. B. Watson, 1878–1958), which is hardly an adequate guide to the human mind. For the complexities of human societies, or even ordinary human lives and relations, did not lend themselves to the reductionism of laboratory positivists, however eminent, nor could the study of transformations over time be conducted experimentally. The most far-reaching practical consequence of experimental psychology, intelligence testing (pioneered by Binet in France from 1905), found it easier for this reason to determine the limits of a person's intellectual development by means of an apparently permanent 'IQ' than the nature of that development, or how it took place, or where it might lead.

Such positivist or 'rigorous' social sciences grew, generating university departments and professions, but without anything much that can be compared to the capacity to surprise and shock which we find in the revolutionary natural sciences of the period. Indeed, where they were being transformed, the pioneers of the transformation had already done their work in an earlier period. The new economics of marginal utility and equilibrium looked back to W. S. Jevons (1835–82), Léon Walras (1834–1910) and Carl Menger (1840–1921), whose original work was done in the 1860s and 1870s; the experimental psychologists, even though their first journal under that title was that of the Russian Bekhterev in 1904, looked back to the German school of Wilhelm Wundt, established in the 1860s. Among the linguists the revolutionary Saussure was still barely known, outside Lausanne, since his reputation rests on lecture notes published after his death.

The more dramatic and controversial developments in the social and human sciences were closely connected with the intellectual *fin de siècle* crisis of the bourgeois world. As we have seen, this took two forms. Society and politics themselves appeared to require rethinking in the era of the masses, and in particular the problems of social structure and cohesion, or (in political terms) citizen loyalty and government legitimacy. It was, perhaps, the fact that the capitalist economy in the west appeared to face no equally grave problems – or at least only temporary ones – which preserved economics from greater intellectual convulsions. More generally there were the new doubts about nineteenth-century assumptions with regard to human rationality and the natural order of things.

The crisis of reason is most obvious in psychology, at least insofar as it tried to come to terms not with experimental situations, but with the human mind as a whole. What remained of the solid citizen pursuing rational aims by maximizing personal utilities, if this pursuit was based on a bundle of 'instincts' like those of animals (MacDougall),[22] if the rational mind was only a boat tossed on the waves and currents of the unconscious (Freud), or even if rational consciousness was only a special kind of consciousness 'whilst all about it, parted from it by the flimsiest of screens, there lie potential forms of consciousness entirely different' (William James, 1902)?[23] Such observations were of course familiar to any reader of great literature, any lover of art, or to most introspective mature adults. Yet it was now and not before that they became part of what claimed to be the scientific study of the human psyche. They did not fit into the psychology of the laboratory or the test-score, and the two branches of the investigation into the human psyche coexisted uneasily. Indeed, the most dramatic innovator in this field, Sigmund Freud, created a discipline, psychoanalysis, which separated itself from the rest of psychology and whose claims to scientific status and therapeutic value have been treated with suspicion ever since in conventional scientific circles. On the other hand its impact on a minority of emancipated intellectual laymen and laywomen was rapid and considerable, including some in the humanities and social sciences (Weber, Sombart). Vaguely Freudian terminology was to penetrate the common discourse of educated lay persons after 1918, at least in the zones of German and Anglo-Saxon culture. With Einstein, Freud is probably the only scientist of the period (for he saw himself as such) whose name is generally familiar to the man in the street. No doubt this was due to the convenience of a theory which allowed men and women to throw the blame for their actions on something they could not help, such as their unconscious, but even more to the fact that Freud could be seen, correctly, as a breaker of sexual taboos and, incorrectly, as a champion of freedom from sexual repression. For sexuality, a subject which became opened to public discussion and investigation in our period and to a fairly undisguised treatment in literature (one has only to think of Proust in France, Arthur Schnitzler in Austria and Frank Wedekind in Germany)* was central to Freud's theory. Of course Freud was not the only or even the first writer to investigate it in depth. He does not really belong to the growing body of sexologists, who appeared after the publication of Richard von Krafft-Ebing's *Psychopathia Sexualis* (1886), which invented the term 'masochism'. Unlike Krafft-Ebing, most of them were reformers, seeking to win public toleration for various forms of unconventional ('abnormal') sexual inclinations, to provide information and to free from guilt those who belonged to such sexual minorities (Havelock Ellis 1859–1939, Magnus Hirschfeld 1868–1935†). Unlike the new sexologists, Freud appealed not so much to a public specifically concerned with sexual problems, as to all reading men and women sufficiently emancipated from traditional Judaeo-Christian taboos to accept what they had long suspected, namely the enormous power, ubiquity and multiformity of the sexual impulse.

Freudian or non-Freudian, individual or social, what concerned

---

* Proust for both male and female homosexuality, Schnitzler – a medical man – for a frank treatment of casual promiscuity (*Reigen*, 1903, originally written 1896–7); Wedekind (*Frühlings Erwachen*, 1891) for teenage sexuality.

† Ellis began to publish his *Studies in the Psychology of Sex* in 1897; Dr Magnus Hirschfeld began to publish his *Jahrbuch für sexuelle Zwischenstufen* (Yearbook for Sexual Borderline Cases) in the same year.

psychology was not how human beings reasoned, but how little their capacity to reason affected their behaviour. In doing so it was apt to reflect the era of the politics and economy of the masses in two ways, both of them critical, by means of the consciously anti-democratic 'crowd psychology' of Le Bon (1841–1931), Tarde (1843–1904) and Trotter (1872–1939), who held that all men in a mob abdicated from rational behaviour, and through the advertising industry, whose enthusiasm for psychology was notorious, and which had long since discovered that soap was not sold by argument. Works on the psychology of advertising appeared from before 1909. However, psychology, most of which dealt with the individual, did not have to come to terms with the problems of a changing society. The transformed discipline of sociology did.

Sociology was probably the most original product of the social sciences in our period; or, more precisely, the most significant attempt to come to intellectual grips with the historical transformations which are the main subject of this book. For the fundamental problems which preoccupied its most notable exponents were political. How did societies cohere, when no longer held together by custom and the traditional acceptance of cosmic order, generally sanctioned by some religion, which once justified social subordination and rule? How did societies function as political systems under such conditions? In short, how could a society cope with the unpredicted and troubling consequences of democratization and mass culture; or, more generally, of an evolution of bourgeois society which looked like leading to some other kind of society? This set of problems is what distinguishes the men now regarded as the founding fathers of sociology from the bulk of now forgotten positivistic evolutionists inspired by Comte and Spencer (see *The Age of Capital*, chapter 14, ii) who had hitherto represented the subject.

The new sociology was not an established, or even a well-defined, academic subject, or one which has ever since succeeded in establishing an international consensus about its exact content. At most, something like an academic 'field' emerged in this period in some European countries, around a few men, periodicals, societies and even one or two university chairs; most notably in France around Emile Durkheim (1858–1917) and in Germany around Max Weber (1864–1920). Only in the Americas, and especially in the USA, did sociologists exist under that name in significant numbers. In fact, a good deal of what would now be classified as sociology was the work of men who still continued to regard themselves as something else – Thorstein Veblen (1857–1929) as an economist, Ernst Troeltsch (1865–1923) as a theologian, Vilfredo Pareto (1848–1923) as an economist, Gaetano Mosca (1858–1941) as a political scientist, even Benedetto Croce as a philosopher. What gave

273

the field some kind of unity was the attempt to understand a society which the theories of political and economic liberalism could not, or could no longer, comprehend. However, unlike the vogue for sociology in some of its later phases, its major concern in this period was how to contain change rather than how to transform, let alone revolutionize society. Hence its ambiguous relation to Karl Marx, who is now often bracketed with Durkheim and Weber as a founding father of twentieth-century sociology, but whose disciples did not always take kindly to this label. As a contemporary German scholar put it: 'Quite apart from the practical consequences of his doctrines, and the organisation of his followers, who are committed to them, Marx has, even from a scientific point of view, tied the knots which we must make an effort to dis-entangle.'[24]

Some of the practitioners of the new sociology concentrated on how societies actually worked, as distinct from how liberal theory supposed them to operate. Hence a profusion of publications in what would today be called 'political sociology', largely based on the experience of the new electoral–democratic politics, of mass movements or both (Mosca, Pareto, Michels, S. and B. Webb). Some concentrated on what they thought held societies together against the forces of disruption by the conflict of classes and groups within them, and the tendency of liberal society to reduce humanity to a scattering of disoriented and rootless individuals ('anomie'). Hence the preoccupation of leading and almost invariably agnostic or atheist thinkers like Weber and Durkheim with the phenomenon of religion, and hence the beliefs that all societies needed either religion or its functional equivalent to maintain their fabric, and that the elements of all religion were to be found in the rites of the Australian aborigines, then usually regarded as survivals from the infancy of the human race (see *The Age of Capital*, chapter 14, II). Conversely, the primitive and barbarous tribes which imperialism now allowed, and sometimes required, anthropologists to study at close quarters – 'field-work' became a regular part of social anthropology in the early twentieth century – were now seen not primarily as exhibits of past evolutionary stages, but as effectively functioning social systems.

But whatever the nature of the structure and cohesion of societies, the new sociology could not avoid the problem of the historical evolution of humanity. Indeed, social evolution still remained the core of anthro-pology, and for men such as Max Weber the problem of where bourgeois society had come from and whither it was evolving remained as crucial as it did for the Marxists, and for analogous reasons. For Weber, Durkheim and Pareto – all three liberals of varying degrees of scep-ticism – were preoccupied with the new socialist movement, and made it their business to refute Marx, or rather his 'materialist conception of history', by elaborating a more general perspective of social evolution. They set out, as it were, to give non-Marxian answers to Marxian questions. This is least obvious in Durkheim, for in France Marx was not influential, except as someone providing a slightly redder tinge for the old jacobin–communard revolutionism. In Italy Pareto (best remembered as a brilliant mathematical economist) accepted the reality of the class struggle, but argued that it would lead not to the overthrow of all ruling classes but to the replacement of one ruling elite by another. In Germany Weber has been called 'the bourgeois Marx' because he accepted so many of Marx's questions, while standing his method of answering them ('historical materialism') on its head.

What motivated and determined the development of sociology in our period was thus the sense of crisis in the affairs of bourgeois society, the consciousness of the need to do something to prevent its disintegration or transformation into different, and no doubt less desirable, kinds of society. Did it revolutionize the social sciences, or even create an adequate foundation for the general science of society its pioneers set out to construct? Opinions differ, but most of them are probably sceptical. However, another question about them can be answered with more confidence. Did they provide a means of avoiding the revolution and disintegration which they hoped to hold at bay or reverse?

They did not. For every year brought the combination of revolution and war nearer. We must now trace it.

CHAPTER 12

TOWARDS REVOLUTION

Have you heard of Sinn Fein in Ireland? . . . It is a most interesting movement and resembles very closely the so-called Extremist movement in India. Their policy is not to beg for favours but to wrest them.

Jawaharlal Nehru (aged eighteen) to his father, 12 September 1907[1]

In Russia the sovereign and the people are both of the Slav race, but simply because the people cannot bear the poison of autocracy, they are willing to sacrifice millions of lives to buy freedom. . . . But when I look at my country I cannot control my feelings. For not only has it the same autocracy as Russia but for 200 years we have been trampled upon by foreign barbarians.

A Chinese revolutionary, *c*. 1903–4[2]

You are not alone, workers and peasants of Russia! If you succeed in overthrowing, crushing and destroying the tyrants of feudal, police-ridden landlord and tsarist Russia your victory will serve as a signal for a world struggle against the tyranny of·capital.

V. I. Lenin, 1905[3]

I

We have so far considered the Indian summer of nineteenth-century capitalism as a period of social and political stability: of regimes not only surviving but flourishing. And indeed, if we were to concentrate only on the countries of 'developed' capitalism, this would be reasonably plausible. Economically, the shadows of the years of the Great Depression lifted, to give way to the brilliantly sunny expansion and prosperity of the 1900s. Political systems which did not quite know how to deal with the social agitations of the 1880s, with the sudden emergence of mass working-class parties dedicated to revolution, or with the mass mobilizations of citizens against the state on other grounds, appeared to discover flexible ways of containing and integrating some and isolating others. The fifteen years or so from 1899 to 1914 were a *belle époque* not only because they were prosperous and life was exceedingly attractive for those who had money and golden for those who were rich, but also because the rulers of most western countries were perhaps worried about the future, but not really frightened about the present. Their societies and regimes, by and large, seemed manageable.

Yet there were considerable areas of the world in which this clearly was not the case. In these areas the years from 1880 to 1914 were an era of constantly possible, of impending or even of actual revolution. Though some of these countries were to be plunged into world war, even in these 1914 is not the apparently sudden break which separates tranquillity, stability and order from an era of disruption. In some – e.g. the Ottoman Empire – the world war itself was merely one episode in a series of military conflicts which had already begun some years earlier. In others – possibly Russia and certainly the Habsburg Empire – the world war was itself largely the product of the insolubility of the problems of domestic politics. In yet another group of countries – China, Iran, Mexico – the war of 1914 played no significant part at all. In short, for the vast area of the globe which thus constituted what Lenin in 1908 acutely called 'combustible material in world politics',[4] the idea that somehow or other, but for the unforeseen and avoidable intervention of catastrophe in 1914, stability, prosperity and liberal progress would have continued, has not even the most superficial plausibility. On the contrary. After 1917 it became clear that the stable and prosperous countries of western bourgeois society themselves would be, in one way or another, drawn into the global revolutionary upheavals which began on the periphery of the single, interdependent world system this society had created.

The bourgeois century destabilized its periphery in two main ways: by undermining the old structures of its economies and the balance of its societies, and by destroying the viability of its established political regimes and institutions. The first of these effects was the more profound and explosive. It accounts for the difference in historical impact between the Russian and Chinese revolutions and the Persian and Turkish. But the second was more readily visible. For, with the exception of Mexico, the global political earthquake zone of 1900–14 consisted mainly of the great geographical belt of ancient empires, some reaching back into the mists of antiquity, which stretched from China in the east to the Habsburgs and perhaps Morocco in the west.

By the standards of the western bourgeois nation-states and empires these archaic political structures were rickety, obsolete and, as the many contemporary believers in Social Darwinism would have argued, doomed to disappear. It was their breakdown and break-up which provided the setting for the revolutions of 1910–14, and indeed, in Europe, the immediate setting for both the coming world war and the Russian Revolution. The empires which fell in these years were among the most ancient political forces in history. China, though sometimes disrupted and occasionally conquered, had been a great empire and the centre of civilization for at least two millennia. The great imperial civil service examinations, which selected the scholar–gentry that ruled it, had been held annually with occasional interruptions for over two thousand years. When they were abandoned in 1905, the end of the empire could not but be close. (In fact it was six years away.) Persia had been a great empire and centre of culture for a similar period, though her fortunes fluctuated more dramatically. She had survived her great antagonists, the Roman and Byzantine empires, resurfaced again after conquests by Alexander the Great, Islam, Mongols and Turks. The Ottoman Empire, though very much younger, was the last of that succession of nomadic conquerors who had ridden out of Central Asia since the days of Attila the Hun to overthrow and take over the eastern and western realms: Avars, Mongols, various brands of Turks. With its capital in Constantinople, the former Byzantium, the city of Caesars (Tsarigrad), it was the lineal heir of the Roman Empire, whose western half had collapsed in the fifth century AD but whose eastern half had survived – until conquered by the Turks – for another thousand years. Though the Ottoman Empire had been pushed back since the end of the seventeenth century, it still remained a formidable tri-continental territory. Moreover the sultan, its absolute ruler, was regarded by the majority of the world's Moslems as their khalif, the head of their religion, and as such the successor of the prophet Mohammed and his seventh-century conquering disciples. The six years which saw the transformation of all three of these empires into constitutional monarchies or republics on the western bourgeois model patently mark the end of a major phase of the world's history.

Russia and the Habsburgs, the two great and shaky multinational European empires which were also about to collapse, were not quite comparable, except insofar as both represented a type of political structure – countries run, as it were, like family properties – which increasingly looked like some prehistoric survival into the nineteenth century. Moreover both claimed the title of Caesar (tsar, Kaiser), the former through medieval barbarian ancestors looking to the Roman Empire of the east, the latter to similar ancestors reviving the memories of the Roman Empire of the west. In fact, as empires and European powers both were comparatively recent. Moreover, unlike the ancient empires, they were situated in Europe, on the borders between the zones of economic development and backwardness, and thus partly integrated from the start into the economically 'advanced' world, and as 'great powers' totally integrated into the political system of Europe, a continent whose very definition has always been political.* Hence, incidentally, the enormous repercussions of the Russian Revolution and, in a different way, of the collapse of the Habsburg Empire on the European and global political scene, compared with the relatively modest or purely regional repercussions of, say, the Chinese, Mexican or Iranian revolutions.

The problem of the obsolete empires of Europe was that they were simultaneously in both camps: advanced and backward, strong and weak, wolves and sheep. The ancient empires were merely among the victims. They seemed destined for collapse, conquest or dependency, unless they could somehow acquire from the western imperialists what made them so formidable. By the end of the nineteenth century this was perfectly clear, and most of the larger states and rulers of the ancient world of empires tried, in varying degree, to learn what they understood to be the lessons of the west, but only Japan succeeded in this difficult task and had by 1900 become a wolf among the wolves.

II

Without the pressure of imperialist expansion, it is not likely that there would have been revolution in the ancient, but by the nineteenth century rather decrepit, empire of Persia, any more than in the most westerly of the islamic kingdoms, Morocco, where the sultan's government (the Maghzen) tried, with indifferent success, to extend its area of administration and to establish some sort of effective control over the anarchic and formidable world of Berber fighting clans. (It is indeed not certain whether the events of 1907–8 in Morocco deserve even the courtesy title of a revolution.) Persia was under the double pressure of Russia and Britain, from which she desperately tried to escape by calling in advisers and helpers from other western states – Belgium (on which the Persian constitution was to be modelled), the USA and, after 1914, Germany – who were in no position to provide a real counterweight. Iranian politics already contained the three forces whose conjunction was to make an even greater revolution in 1979: the emancipated and westernized intellectuals, keenly aware of the coun-

* Since there is no geographical feature which clearly demarcates the western prolongation of the Asian land-mass which we call Europe from the rest of Asia.

try's weakness and social injustice, the bazaar merchants, keenly aware of foreign economic competition, and the collectivity of the Moslem clergy, who represented the Shia branch of Islam, which functioned as a sort of national Persian religion, capable of mobilizing the traditional masses. They in turn were keenly aware of the incompatibility of western influence and the Koran. The alliance between radicals, *bazaris* and clergy had already shown its force in 1890–2, when an imperial grant of the tobacco monopoly to a British businessman had to be cancelled following riot, insurrection and a remarkably successful nationwide boycott on the sale and use of tobacco, joined even by the shah's wives. The Russo-Japanese war of 1904–5, and the first Russian Revolution, temporarily eliminated one of Persia's tormentors, and gave Persian revolutionaries both encouragement and a programme. For the power which had defeated a European emperor was not only Asian but also a constitutional monarchy. A constitution could thus be seen not only (by emancipated radicals) as the obvious demand of a western revolution but also (by wider sections of public opinion) as some sort of 'secret of strength'. In fact, a mass departure of ayatollahs to the holy city of Qom, and a mass flight of bazaar merchants into the British legation, which incidentally brought Teheran business to a standstill, secured an elected assembly and a constitution in 1906. In practice the 1907 agreement between Britain and Russia to divide Persia peacefully among them gave Persian politics little chance. *De facto* the first revolutionary period ended in 1911, though Persia remained, nominally, under something like the constitution of 1906–7 until the revolution of 1979.[5] On the other hand, the fact that no other imperialist power was in a real position to challenge Britain and Russia probably saved the existence of Persia as a state and of her monarchy, which had little enough power of its own, except a Cossack brigade, whose commander after the first war made himself into the founder of the last imperial dynasty, the Pahlavis (1921–79).

In this respect Morocco was unluckier. Situated at a particularly strategic spot on the global map, the north-western corner of Africa, she looked like a suitable prey to France, Britain, Germany, Spain and anyone else within naval distance. The monarchy's internal weakness made her particularly vulnerable to foreign ambitions, and the international crises which arose out of the quarrels between the various predators – notably in 1906 and 1911 – played a major role in the genesis of the First World War. France and Spain partitioned her, with international (i.e. British) interests being taken care of by a free port at Tangier. On the other hand, while Morocco lost her independence, the absence of her sultan's control over the Berber fighting clans was to make the actual French, and even more the Spanish, military conquest of the territory difficult and prolonged.

III

The internal crises of the great Chinese and Ottoman empires were both more ancient and more profound. The Chinese Empire had been shaken by major social crisis from the middle of the nineteenth century (see *The Age of Capital*). It had only overcome the revolutionary threat of the Taiping at the cost of virtually liquidating the empire's central administrative power and throwing it on the mercy of the foreigners, who had established extra-territorial enclaves and virtually taken over the main source of imperial finance, the Chinese customs administration. The enfeebled empire, under the empress–dowager Tzu-hsi (1835–1908), who was more feared within the empire than outside it, seemed destined to disappear under the combined onslaughts of imperialism. Russia advanced into Manchuria, whence it was to be expelled by its rival Japan, which detached Taiwan and Korea from China after a victorious war in 1894–5 and prepared to take over more. Meanwhile the British had enlarged their Hong Kong colony and had practically detached Tibet, which they saw as a dependency of their Indian empire; Germany carved out bases for herself in north China; the French exerted some influence in the neighbourhood of their Indochinese empire (itself detached from China) and extended their positions in the south; and even the feeble Portuguese achieved the cession of Macão (1887). While the wolves were ready to form a pack against the prey, as they did when Britain, France, Russia, Italy, Germany, the USA and Japan joined to occupy and loot Peking in 1900 on the pretext of putting down the so-called Boxer Rising, they could not agree on the division of the immense carcass. All the more so since one of the more recent imperial powers, the United States, now increasingly prominent in the Western Pacific, which had long been an area of US interest, insisted on 'the open door' to China, i.e. that it had as much right to booty as earlier imperialists. As in Morocco, these Pacific rivalries over the decaying body of the Chinese Empire contributed to the coming of the First World War. More immediately, they both saved China's nominal independence and caused the final collapse of the world's most ancient surviving political entity.

Three major forces of resistance existed in China. The first, the imperial establishment of court and Confucian senior civil servants, recognized clearly enough that only modernization on the western (or perhaps more precisely, the western-inspired Japanese) model could save China. But this would have meant the destruction of precisely that moral and political system they represented. Conservative-led reform was bound to fail, even if it had not been hampered by court intrigues and divisions, weakened by technical ignorance and wrecked, every few years, by yet another bout of foreign aggression. The second, the ancient and powerful tradition of popular rebellion and secret societies imbued with ideologies of opposition, remained as powerful as ever. In fact, in spite of the defeat of the Taiping, everything combined to reinforce it, as 9–13 millions died of starvation in the north China famine of the late 1870s and the dykes of the Yellow River broke, signifying the failure of an empire whose duty it was to protect them. The so-called Boxer Rising of 1900 was indeed a mass movement, whose vanguard was formed by the organization Fist-fighters for Justice and Unity which was a sprig of the large and ancient Buddhist secret society known as the White Lotus. Yet, for obvious reasons, the cutting edge of these rebellions was militantly xenophobic and anti-modern. It was directed against foreigners, Christianity and machines. While it provided some of the force for a Chinese revolution it could provide neither programme nor perspective for it.

Only in southern China, where business and trade had always been important and foreign imperialism laid the basis for some indigenous bourgeois development, was there a foundation, as yet narrow and unstable, for such a transformation. The local ruling groups were already quietly drawing away from the Manchu dynasty, and here alone the ancient secret societies of opposition allied with, or even developed an interest in, something like a modern and concrete programme for Chinese renewal. The relations between the secret societies and the young southern movement of republican revolutionaries, among whom Sun Yat-sen (1866–1925) was to emerge as the chief inspirer of the first phase of the revolution, have been the subject of much debate and some uncertainty, but there can be no doubt that they were close and essential. (Chinese republicans in Japan, which was a base for their agitation, even formed a special lodge of the Triads in Yokohama for their own use.)[6] Both shared a rooted opposition to the Manchu dynasty – the Triads were still dedicated to the restoration of the old Ming dynasty (1368–1644) – a hatred of imperialism, which could be formulated in the phraseology of traditional xenophobia or the modern nationalism borrowed from western revolutionary ideology, and a concept of social revolution, which the republicans transposed from the key of the ancient anti-dynastic uprising to that of the modern western revolution. Sun's famous 'three principles' of nationalism, republicanism and socialism (or more precisely, agrarian reform) may have been formulated in terms derived from the west, notably from John Stuart Mill, but in fact even Chinese who lacked his western

background (as a mission-educated and widely travelled medical prac-
titioner) could see them as logical extensions of familiar anti-Manchu
reflections. And for the handful of republican city intellectuals the secret
societies were essential to reach the urban and especially the rural
masses. They probably also helped to organize support among the
overseas communities of Chinese emigrants which Sun Yat-sen's movement was the first to mobilize politically for national purposes.

Nevertheless, the secret societies (as the communists would also later
discover) were hardly the best foundation for a new China, and the
westernized or semi-westernized radical intellectuals from the southern
seaboard were as yet not sufficiently numerous, influential or organized
to take power. Nor did the western liberal models inspiring them
provide a recipe for governing the empire. The empire fell in 1911 to
a (southern and central) revolt in which elements of military rebellion,
republican insurrection, withdrawal of loyalty by the gentry, and
popular or secret society revolt were combined. However, in practice
it was replaced for the time being not by a new regime, but by a
congeries of unstable and shifting regional power-structures, mainly
under military control ('war lords'). No stable new national regime
was to emerge in China for almost forty years – until the triumph of
the Communist Party in 1949.

IV

The Ottoman Empire had long been crumbling, though, unlike all
other ancient empires, it remained a military force strong enough to
give even the armies of great powers a distinctly hard time. Since the
end of the seventeenth century its northern frontiers had been pushed
back into the Balkan peninsula and Transcaucasia by the advance of
the Russian and Habsburg empires. The Christian subject peoples of
the Balkans were increasingly restless and, with the encouragement and
assistance of rival great powers, had already transformed much of the
Balkans into a collection of more or less independent states which
gnawed and nibbled at what remained of Ottoman territory. Most of
the remoter regions of the empire, in North Africa and the Middle East,
had not been under regular effective Ottoman rule for a long time.
They now increasingly, if not quite officially, passed into the hands of
the British and French imperialists. By 1900 it was clear that everything
from the western borders of Egypt and the Sudan to the Persian Gulf
was likely to come under British rule or influence, except Syria from
the Lebanon northwards, where the French maintained claims, and
most of the Arab peninsula, which, since no oil or anything else of

commercial value had yet been discovered there, could be left to the disputes of the local tribal chieftains and the Islamic revivalist movements of Beduin preachers. In fact, by 1914 Turkey had almost entirely disappeared from Europe, had been totally eliminated from Africa, and maintained a feeble empire only in the Middle East, where she did not outlast the world war. Yet, unlike Persia and China, Turkey had available an immediate potential alternative to the collapsing empire: a large bloc of an ethnically and linguistically Turkish Moslem population in Asia Minor, which could form the basis of something like a 'nation-state' on the approved occidental nineteenth-century model.

This was almost certainly not initially in the mind of the westernized officers and civil servants, supplemented by members of the new secular professions such as law and journalism,* who set out to revive the empire by means of revolution, since the empire's own half-hearted attempts to modernize itself – most recently in the 1870s – had run into the sand. The Committee for Union and Progress, better known as the Young Turks (founded in the 1890s), which seized power in 1908 in the aftermath of the Russian Revolution, aimed to establish an all-Ottoman patriotism which cut across ethnic, linguistic and religious divisions, on the basis of the secular verities of the (French) eighteenth-century Enlightenment. The version of the Enlightenment which they chiefly cherished was inspired by the positivism of August Comte, which combined a passionate belief in science and inevitable modernization with the secular equivalent of a religion, non-democratic progress ('order and progress', to quote the positivist motto) and planned social engineering undertaken from above. For obvious reasons this ideology appealed to smallish modernizing elites in power in backward, traditionalist countries which they tried by main force to wrench into the twentieth century. It was probably never as influential as in the last part of the nineteenth century in non-European countries.

In this respect as in others the Turkish revolution of 1908 failed. Indeed, it accelerated the collapse of what remained of the Turkish Empire, while saddling the state with the classic liberal constitution, multi-party parliamentary system and the rest, designed for bourgeois countries in which governments were not actually supposed to govern very much, since the affairs of society were in the hidden hands of a dynamic and self-regulating capitalist economy. That the Young Turk regime also continued the empire's economic and military commitment to Germany, which brought Turkey on to the losing side in the First World War, was to be fatal to them.

* Islamic law did not require a special legal profession. Literacy trebled in the years 1875–1900, thus providing a market for more periodicals.

Turkish modernization therefore shifted from a liberal–parliamentary to a military–dictatorial frame and from the hope in a
secular–imperial political loyalty to the reality of a purely Turkish
nationalism. Unable any longer to overlook group loyalties or to dominate non-Turkish communities, Turkey after 1915 was to opt for an
ethnically homogeneous nation, which implied the forcible assimilation
of such Greeks, Armenians, Kurds and others as were not either expelled
en bloc or massacred. An ethno-linguistic Turkish nationalism even
permitted imperial dreams on a secular nationalist basis, for large parts
of Western and Central Asia, mainly in Russia, were inhabited by
people speaking varieties of Turkish languages, whom it was surely
the destiny of Turkey to gather into a greater 'Pan-Turanian' union.
Within the Young Turks the balance thus tilted from westernizing and
transnational modernizers to westernizing but strongly ethnic or even
racialist modernizers like the national poet and ideologist Zia Gökalp
(1876–1924). The real Turkish revolution, starting with the actual
abolition of the empire itself, took place under such auspices after 1918.
But its content was already implicit in the aims of the Young Turks.

Unlike Persia and China, Turkey thus did not only liquidate an old
regime but proceeded fairly soon to construct a new one. The Turkish
Revolution inaugurated perhaps the first of the contemporary Third
World modernizing regimes: passionately committed to progress and
enlightenment against tradition, 'development' and a sort of populism
untroubled by liberal debating. In the absence of a revolutionary
middle class, or indeed any other revolutionary class, intellectuals and
especially, after the war, soldiers were to take over. Their leader, Kemal
Atatürk, a tough and successful general, was to carry out the Young
Turk modernizing programme ruthlessly: a republic was proclaimed,
Islam abolished as a state religion, the Roman alphabet substituted for
the Arabic, the women were unveiled and sent to school, and Turkish
men, if necessary by military force, were put under bowler hats or other
western headgear instead of turbans. The weakness of the Turkish
Revolution, notable in its economy, lay in its inability to impose itself
on the great mass of rural Turks or to change the structure of agrarian
society. Nevertheless, the historical implications of this revolution were
great, even though they have been insufficiently recognized by historians whose eyes tend to be fixed before 1914 on the immediate
international consequences of the Turkish Revolution – the collapse of
the empire and its contribution to the origin of the First World War –
and after 1917 on the much greater Russian Revolution. For obvious
reason, these events overshadowed contemporary Turkish developments.

V

An even more overlooked revolution of the time began in Mexico in 1910. It attracted little foreign attention outside the United States, partly because diplomatically Central America was Washington's exclusive backyard ('Poor Mexico,' its overthrown dictator had exclaimed, 'so far from God, so near to the USA'), and because initially the implications of the revolution were entirely unclear. There seemed no immediately evident distinction between this and the 114 other violent changes of government in nineteenth-century Latin America which still form the largest class of events commonly known as 'revolutions'.[7] Moreover, by the time the Mexican Revolution had emerged as a major social upheaval, the first of its kind in a Third World peasant country, it was to be, once again, overshadowed by events in Russia.

And yet the Mexican revolution is significant, because it was directly born of the contradictions within the world of empire, and because it was the first of the great revolutions in the colonial and dependent world in which the labouring masses played a major part. For while anti-imperialist and what would later be called colonial liberation movements were indeed developing within the old and new colonial empires of the metropoles, as yet they did not seem seriously to threaten imperial rule.

By and large, colonial empires were still controlled as easily as they had been acquired – apart from those mountainous warrior zones such as Afghanistan, Morocco and Ethiopia, which still held off foreign conquest. 'Native risings' were repressed without much trouble, though sometimes – as in the case of the Herero in German South-west Africa (the present Namibia) – with notable brutality. Anti-colonial or autonomist movements were indeed beginning to develop in the socially and politically more complex of the colonized countries, but did not usually achieve that alliance between the educated and westernizing minority and the xenophobic defenders of ancient tradition which (as in Persia) made them into a serious political force. Both distrusted one another for obvious reasons, to the benefit of the colonial power. In French Algeria resistance was centred in the Moslem clergy (*oulema*) who were already organizing, while the secular *évolués* tried to become Frenchmen of the republican left. In the protectorate of Tunisia it was centred in the educated westernizers, who were already forming a party demanding a constitution (the Destour) and which was the lineal ancestor of the Neo-Destour Party, whose leader, Habib Bourguiba, became the head of independent Tunisia in 1954.

Of the great colonial powers only the oldest and greatest, Britain, had serious premonitions of impermanence (see p. 82 above). She

acquiesced in the virtual independence of the colonies of white settlement (called 'dominions' from 1907). Since this was not to be resisted,
it was not expected to create problems; not even in South Africa, where
the Boers, recently annexed after defeat in a difficult war, seemed
reconciled by a generous Liberal settlement, and by the common front
of British and Boer whites against the non-white majority. In fact,
South Africa caused no serious trouble in either of the two world wars,
after which the Boers took that subcontinent over once again. Britain's
other 'white' colony, Ireland, was – and has remained – endlessly
troublesome, though, as it happened, after 1890 the explosive unrest of
the years of the Land League and Parnell seemed to have been defused
by Irish political quarrels and by a powerful combination of repression
and far-reaching agrarian reform. The problems of British parliamentary politics revived the Irish issue again after 1910, but the base
of support for the Irish insurrectionaries remained so narrow and shaky
that their strategy for broadening it was essentially to court martyrdom
by a foredoomed rebellion, whose suppression would win the people to
their cause. This is indeed what happened after the Easter Rising of
1916, a small putsch by a handful of totally isolated armed militants.
The war, as so often, revealed the fragility of political buildings which
had seemed stable.

There appeared to be no immediate threat to British rule anywhere
else. And yet a genuine colonial liberation movement was visibly developing both in the oldest and in one of the youngest of Britain's dependencies. Egypt, even after the suppression of the young soldiers'
insurrection of Arabi Pasha in 1882, had never been reconciled to
British occupation. Its ruler, the khedive, and the local ruling class of
large landowners, whose economy had long since been integrated into
the world market, accepted the administration of the British 'proconsul'
Lord Cromer with a marked lack of enthusiasm. The autonomist
movement/organization/party later known as the Wafd was already
taking shape. British control remained quite firm – indeed it was to last
until 1952 – but the unpopularity of direct colonial rule was such that
it was to be abandoned after the war (1922) for a less direct form of
management, which implied a certain Egyptianization of the administration. Irish semi-independence and Egyptian semi-autonomy, both
won in 1921–2, were to mark the first partial retreat of empires.

The liberation movement in India was far more serious. In this
subcontinent of almost 300 million inhabitants, an influential bourgeoisie – both commercial, financial, industrial and professional – and
an important cadre of educated officials who administered it for
Britain were increasingly resentful of economic exploitation, political
impotence and social inferiority. One has only to read E. M. Forster's

A Passage to India to understand why. An autonomist movement had already emerged. Its chief organization, the Indian National Congress (founded 1885), which was to become the party of national liberation, initially reflected both this middle-class discontent and the attempt by intelligent British administrators like Allan Octavian Hume (who actually founded the organization) to disarm agitation by giving recognition to respectable protest. However, by the early twentieth century Congress had begun to escape from British tutelage, thanks in part to the influence of the apparently non-political ideology of theosophy. As admirers of eastern mysticism, western adepts of this philosophy were apt to sympathize with India, and some, like the ex-secularist and ex-socialist militant Annie Besant, had no difficulty in converting themselves into champions of Indian nationalism. Educated Indians, and indeed Ceylonese, naturally found western recognition of their own cultural values congenial. However, Congress, though a growing force – and incidentally strictly secular and western-minded – remained an elite organization. Nevertheless, an agitation which set out to mobilize the uneducated masses by the appeal to traditional religion was already on the scene in the west of India. Bal Ganghadar Tilak (1856–1920) defended the holy cows of Hinduism against the foreign menace with some popular success.

Moreover, there were by the early twentieth century two other even more formidable nurseries of Indian popular agitation. The Indian emigration to South Africa had begun to organize collectively against the racism of that region, and the chief spokesman of its successful movement of passive or non-violent mass resistance, as we have seen, was the young Gujerati lawyer who, on his return to India in 1915, was to become the major force for mobilizing the Indian masses in the cause of national independence: Gandhi (see pp. 77–8 above). Gandhi invented the enormously powerful role in Third World politics of the modern politician as a saint. At the same time a more radical version of the politics of liberation was emerging in Bengal, with its sophisticated vernacular culture, its large Hindu middle class, its vast mass of educated and modestly employed lower-middle class, and its intellectuals. The British plan to partition this large province into a predominantly Moslem region allowed the anti-British agitation to develop on a massive scale in 1906–9. (The scheme was abandoned.) The Bengali nationalist movement, which stood to the left of Congress from the start and was never quite integrated into it, combined – at this stage – a religio-ideological appeal to Hinduism with a deliberate imitation of congenial western revolutionary movements such as the Irish and the Russian Narodniks. It produced the first serious terrorist movement in India – just before the war there were to be others in north India, based on returned Punjabi emigrants from America (the 'Ghadr party') – and by 1905 it already constituted a serious problem for the police. Moreover, the first Indian communists (e.g. M. N. Roy [1887–1954]) were to emerge from the Bengali terrorist movement during the war.[8] While British control of India remained firm enough, it was already evident to intelligent administrators that some sort of devolution leading, however slowly, to some preferably modest degree of autonomy would become unavoidable. Indeed, the first of such proposals was to be made by London during the war.

Where global imperialism was at its most immediately vulnerable was in the grey zone of informal rather than formal empire, or what would after the Second World War be called 'neo-colonialism'. Mexico was certainly a country both economically and politically dependent on its great neighbour, but technically it was an independent sovereign state with its own institutions and political decisions. It was a state like Persia rather than a colony like India. Moreover, economic imperialism was not unacceptable to its native ruling classes, inasmuch as it was a potential modernizing force. For throughout Latin America the landowners, merchants, entrepreneurs and intellectuals who constituted the local ruling classes and elites dreamed only of achieving that progress which would give their countries, which they knew to be backward, feeble, unrespected and on the margins of the western civilization of which they saw themselves as an integral part, the chance to fulfil their historic destiny. Progress meant Britain, France and, increasingly clearly, the USA. The ruling classes of Mexico, especially in the north where the influence of the neighbouring US economy was strong, had no objection to integrating themselves into the world market and therefore into the world of progress and science, even when despising the ungentlemanly boorishness of gringo businessmen and politicians. In fact, after the revolution it was to be the 'Sonora gang', chieftains of the economically most advanced agrarian middle class of that most northern of Mexico's states, who emerged as the decisive political group in the country. Contrariwise, the great obstacle to modernization was the vast mass of the rural population, immobile and immovable, wholly or partly Indian or black, plunged into ignorance, tradition and superstition. There were moments when the rulers and intellectuals of Latin America, like those of Japan, despaired of their peoples. Under the influence of the universal racism of the bourgeois world (see *The Age of Capital*, chapter 14, II) they dreamed of a biological transformation of their populations which would make them amenable to progress: by the mass immigration of people of European stock in Brazil and in the southern cone of South America, by mass interbreeding with whites in Japan.

The Mexican rulers were not particularly attracted by the mass immigration of whites, who were only too likely to be North Americans, and their fight for independence against Spain had already sought legitimation in an appeal to an independent and largely fictitious pre-Hispanic past identified with the Aztecs. Mexican modernization therefore left biological dreaming to others and concentrated directly on profit, science and progress as mediated by foreign investment and the philosophy of Auguste Comte. The group of so-called *científicos* devoted itself single-mindedly to these objects. Its uncontested chief, and the political boss of the country since the 1870s, i.e. for the entire period since the great forward surge of the world imperialist economy, was President Porfirio Díaz (1830–1915). And, indeed, the economic development of Mexico under his presidency had been impressive, not to mention the wealth which some Mexicans derived from it, especially those who were in a position to play off rival groups of European entrepreneurs (such as the British oil and constructional tycoon Weetman Pearson) against each other and against the steadily more dominant North Americans.

Then, as now, the stability of regimes between the Rio Grande and Panama was jeopardized by the loss of goodwill in Washington, which was militantly imperialist and took the view 'that Mexico is no longer anything but a dependency of the American economy'.[9] Díaz's attempts to keep his country independent by playing off European against North American capital made him extremely unpopular north of the border. The country was rather too big for military intervention, which the USA practised with enthusiasm at this time in smaller states of Central America, but by 1910 Washington was not in a mood to discourage well-wishers (like Standard Oil, irritated by British influence in what was already one of the major oil-producing countries) who might wish to assist Díaz's overthrow. There is no doubt that Mexican revolutionaries benefited greatly from a friendly northern border; and Díaz was all the more vulnerable because, after winning power as a military leader, he had allowed the army to atrophy, since he understandably supposed that army coups were a greater danger than popular insurrections. It was his bad luck that he found himself faced by a major armed popular revolution which his army, unlike most Latin American forces, was quite unable to crush.

That he found himself faced with it was due precisely to the striking economic developments over which he had presided so successfully. The regime had favoured business-minded estate owners (*hacendados*), all the more so since the global boom and substantial railway development turned formerly inaccessible stretches of land into potential treasure-chests. The free village communities mainly in the centre and south of the country which had been preserved under Spanish royal law, and probably reinforced in the first generations of independence, were systematically stripped of their lands for a generation. They were to be the core of the agrarian revolution which found a leader and spokesman in Emiliano Zapata (1879–1919). As it happened, two of the areas where agrarian unrest was most intense and readily mobilized, the states of Morelos and Guerrero, were within easy riding-distance of the capital, and therefore in a position to influence national affairs.

The second area of unrest was in the north, rapidly transformed (especially after the defeat of the Apache Indians in 1885) from an Indian frontier into an economically dynamic border region living in a sort of dependent symbiosis with the neighbouring areas of the USA. It contained plenty of potential malcontents, from former communities of Indian-fighting frontiersmen, now deprived of their land, Yaqui Indians resentful of their defeat, the new and growing middle class, and the considerable number of footloose and self-confident men often owning their guns and horses, who could be found in empty ranching and mining country. Pancho Villa, bandit, rustler and eventually revolutionary general, was typical of these. There were also groups of powerful and wealthy estate-owners such as the Maderos – perhaps the richest family in Mexico – who competed for control of their states with the central government or its allies among the local *hacendados*.

Many of these potentially dissident groups were in fact beneficiaries of the Porfirian era of massive foreign investments and economic growth. What turned them into dissidents, or rather what turned a commonplace political struggle over the re-election or possible retirement of President Díaz into a revolution, was probably the growing integration of the Mexican economy into the world (or rather the US) economy. As it happened the American economic slump of 1907–8 had disastrous effects on Mexico: directly in the collapse of Mexico's own markets and the financial squeeze on Mexican enterprise, indirectly in the flood of penniless Mexican labourers returning home after losing their jobs in the USA. Modern and ancient crisis coincided: cyclical slump and ruined harvests with food prices soaring beyond the range of the poor.

It was in these circumstances than an electoral campaign turned into an earthquake. Díaz, having mistakenly allowed public campaigning by the opposition, easily 'won' the elections against the chief challenger, Francisco Madero, but the defeated candidate's routine insurrection turned, to everyone's surprise, in a social and political upheaval in the northern borderlands and the rebellious peasant centre which could no longer be controlled. Díaz fell. Madero took over, soon to be assassinated. The USA looked for but failed to find among the rival generals and politicians someone who was both sufficiently pliable or corrupt and able to establish a stable regime. Zapata redistributed land to his peasant followers in the south, Villa expropriated haciendas in the north when it suited him to pay his revolutionary army, and claimed, as a man sprung from the poor, to be looking after his own. By 1914 nobody had the faintest idea what was going to happen in Mexico, but there could be no doubt whatever that the country was convulsed by a social revolution. The shape of post-revolutionary Mexico was not to become clear until the end of the 1930s.

VI

There is a view among some historians that Russia, perhaps the most rapidly developing economy of the late nineteenth century, would have continued to advance and evolve into a flourishing liberal society had her progress not been interrupted by a revolution which could have been avoided but for the First World War. No prospect would have surprised contemporaries more than this one. If there was one state where revolution was believed to be not only desirable but inevitable, it was the empire of the tsars. Gigantic, lumbering and inefficient, economically and technologically backward, inhabited by 126 million people (1897), of whom 80 per cent were peasants and 1 per cent hereditary nobles, it was organized in a way which to all educated Europeans appeared positively prehistoric by the later nineteenth century, namely as a bureaucratized autocracy. This very fact made revolution the *only* method of changing state policy other than catching the tsar's ear and moving the machinery of state into action from above: the first was hardly available to many, and did not necessarily imply the second. Since change of one sort or another was almost universally felt to be needed, virtually everybody from what in the west would have been moderate conservatives to the extreme left was obliged to be a revolutionary. The only question was, of what kind.

The tsar's governments had been aware since the Crimean War (1854–6) that Russia's status as a major great power could no longer rest safely on the country's mere size, massive population and consequently vast but primitive military forces. It needed to modernize. The abolition of serfdom in 1861 – Russia was, with Rumania, the last stronghold of serf farming in Europe – had been intended to drag Russian agriculture into the nineteenth century, but it produced neither a satisfied peasantry (cf. *The Age of Capital*, chapter 10, II) nor a modernized agriculture. The average yield of grain in European Russia (1898–1902) was just under 9 bushels per acre compared to about 14 in the USA and 35.4 in Britain.[10] Still, the opening of vast areas of the country to grain production for export turned Russia into one of the main cereal-suppliers in the world. The net harvest of all grains increased by 160 per cent between the early 1860s and the early 1900s, exports multiplied between five- and sixfold but at the cost of making Russian peasants more dependent on a world market price, which (for wheat) fell by almost half during the world agricultural depression.[11]

Since peasants were collectively neither seen nor heard outside their villages, the discontent of almost 100 millions of them was easy to overlook, although the famine of 1891 drew some attention to it. And yet this discontent was not merely sharpened by poverty, land-hunger, high taxes and low grain-prices, but possessed significant forms of potential organization through the collective village communities, whose position as officially recognized institutions had been, paradoxically, reinforced by the liberation of the serfs, and was further reinforced in the 1880s when some bureaucrats regarded it as an invaluable bastion of traditionalist loyalty against social revolutionaries. Others, on the opposite ideological grounds of economic liberalism, pressed for its rapid liquidation by transforming its land into private property. An analagous debate divided the revolutionaries. The Narodniks (see *The Age of Capital*, chapter 9) or Populists – with, it must be said, some uncertain and hesitant support from Marx himself – thought a revolutionized peasant commune could be the base of a direct socialist transformation of Russia, by-passing the horrors of capitalist development; the Russian Marxists believed this was no longer possible because the commune was already splitting into a mutually hostile rural bourgeoisie and proletariat. They would have preferred it to, since they put their faith in the workers. Both sides in both debates testify to the importance of the peasant communes, which held 80 per cent of the land in fifty provinces of European Russia in communal tenure, to be periodically redistributed by communal decision. The commune was indeed disintegrating in the more commercialized regions of the south, but more slowly than the Marxists believed: it remained almost universally firm in the north and centre. Where it remained strong, it was a body articulating village consensus for revolution as well as, in other circumstances, for the tsar and Holy Russia. Where it was being eroded, it drew most villagers together in its militant defence. In fact, luckily for the revolution, the 'class struggle in the village' predicted by the Marxists had not yet developed far enough to jeopardize the appearance of a massive movement of *all* peasants, richer and poorer, against gentry and state.

Whatever their views, almost everybody in Russian public life, legal or illegal, agreed that the tsar's government had mismanaged the agrarian reform and neglected the peasants. In fact, it aggravated their discontents at a time when they were already acute, by diverting resources from the agrarian population for a massive bout of state-sponsored industrialization in the 1890s. For the countryside represented the bulk of the Russian tax revenue, and high taxes were, with high protective tariffs and vast capital imports, essential to the project of increasing the power of tsarist Russia by economic modernization. The results, achieved by a mixture of private and state capitalism, were spectacular. Between 1890 and 1904 the railway mileage was doubled (partly by the construction of the Trans-Siberian railway), while the output of coal, iron and steel all doubled in the last five years of the century.[12] But the other side of the coin was that tsarist Russia now also found herself with a rapidly growing industrial proletariat, concentrated in unusually large complexes of plants in a few major centres, and consequently with the beginnings of a labour movement which was, of course, committed to social revolution.

A third consequence of rapid industrialization was its disproportionate development in regions on the non-Great Russian western and southern fringe of the empire – as in Poland, the Ukraine and (the oil industry) Azerbaijan. Both social and national tensions were intensified, especially as the tsarist government attempted to strengthen its political hold by a systematic policy of educational Russification from the 1880s. As we have seen, the combination of social with national discontents is indicated by the fact that among several, perhaps most, of the politically mobilized minority peoples in the Tsarist Empire, variants of the new social democratic (Marxist) movement became the de facto 'national' party (see page 162 above). That a Georgian (Stalin) should become the ruler of a revolutionized Russia was less of a historical accident than that a Corsican (Napoleon) should have become the ruler of a revolutionized France.

All European liberals since 1830 were familiar with, and sympathized with, the gentry-based national liberation movement of Poland against the tsarist government, which occupied much the largest part of that partitioned country, although since the defeated insurrection of 1863 revolutionary nationalism was not very visible there.* From about 1870 they also got used to, and supported, the novel idea of an impending revolution in the very heart of the empire ruled by the 'autocrat of all the Russias', both because tsarism itself showed signs of internal and external weakness, and because of the emergence of a highly visible

---

* The parts annexed by Russia formed the core of Poland. Polish nationalists also resisted, from the weaker position of a minority, in the part annexed by Germany, but came to a fairly comfortable compromise in the Austrian sector with the Habsburg monarchy, which needed Polish support to establish a political balance among its contending nationalities.

revolutionary movement, initially recruited almost entirely from the so-called 'intelligentsia': sons, and to an unprecedented and high degree daughters, of the nobility and gentry, the middle and other educated strata, including – for the first time – a substantial proportion of Jews. The first generation of these were chiefly Narodniks (Populists) (cf. *The Age of Capital*, chapter 9) looking to the peasantry, which took no notice of them. They were rather more successful at small-group terrorism – dramatically so in 1881 when they succeeded in assassinating the tsar, Alexander II. While terrorism did not significantly weaken tsarism, it gave the Russian revolutionary movement its high international profile, and helped to crystallize a virtually universal consensus, except on the extreme right, that a Russian revolution was both necessary and inevitable.

The Narodniks were destroyed and scattered after 1881, though they revived, in the form of a 'Social Revolutionary' party in the early 1900s, but by this time the villages were prepared to listen to them. They were to become the major rural party of the left, though they also revived their terrorist wing, which was by this time infiltrated by the secret police.* Like all who looked to any sort of Russian revolution, they had been assiduous students of suitable theories from the west, and hence of the most powerful and, thanks to the First International, prominent theorist of social revolution, Karl Marx. In Russia even people who would elsewhere have been liberals were Marxists before 1900, given the social and political implausibility of western liberal solutions, for Marxism at least predicted a phase of capitalist development on the way to its overthrow by the proletariat.

Not surprisingly, the revolutionary movements which grew on the ruins of the Populism of the 1870s were Marxist, although they were not organized into a Russian social democratic party – or rather a complex of rival, though occasionally co-operating social democratic organizations under the general wing of the International – until the late 1890s. By then the idea of a party based on the industrial proletariat had some realistic basis, even though the strongest mass support for social democracy at this time was probably still to be found among the poverty-stricken and proletarianized handicraftsmen and outworkers in the northern part of the Pale, stronghold of the Jewish Bund (1897). We have been used to tracing the progress of the specific group among the Marxist revolutionaries which eventually prevailed, namely that led by Lenin (V. I. Ulyanov, 1870–1924), whose brother had been executed for his part in the assassination of the tsar. Important though

---

* Its head, the police agent Azev (1869–1918), faced the complex task of assassinating enough prominent persons to satisfy his comrades, and to deliver up enough of them to satisfy the police, without losing the confidence of either.

this is, not least because of Lenin's extraordinary genius for combining revolutionary theory and practice, three things should be remembered. The Bolsheviks* were merely one among several tendencies in and around Russian social democracy (which was in turn distinct from other nationally based socialist parties of the empire). They did not, in effect, become a separate party until 1912, about the time when they almost certainly became the majority force among the organized working class. Thirdly, from the point of view of foreign socialists, and probably of ordinary Russian workers, the distinctions between different kinds of socialists were incomprehensible or seemed secondary, all being equally deserving of support and sympathy as enemies of tsarism. The main difference between the Bolsheviks and others was that Lenin's comrades were better organized, more efficient and more reliable.[13]

That social and political unrest was rising and dangerous became obvious to the tsar's governments, even though peasant unrest subsided for some decades after emancipation. Tsarism did not discourage, and sometimes encouraged, the mass anti-Semitism for which there was an enormous amount of popular support, as the wave of pogroms after 1881 revealed, though there was less support among Great Russians than in Ukraine and the Baltic regions, where the bulk of the Jewish population was concentrated. The Jews, increasingly mistreated and discriminated against, were more and more attracted to revolutionary movements. On the other hand the regime, aware of the potential danger of socialism, played with labour legislation and even, briefly, organized counter-trade unions under police auspices in the early 1900s, which effectively became real unions. It was the massacre of a demonstration led from such quarters which actually precipitated the 1905 revolution. However, it became increasingly evident, from 1900 on, that social unrest was rising rapidly. Peasant rioting, long semi-dormant, clearly began to revive from about 1902, at the same time as workers organized what amounted to general strikes in Rostov-on-Don, Odessa and Baku (1902–3).

Insecure regimes are well advised to avoid adventurous foreign policies. Tsarist Russia plunged into them, as a great power (however clay-footed) which insisted on playing what it felt to be its due part in imperialist conquest. Its chosen territory was the Far East – the Trans-Siberian railway was constructed largely to penetrate it. There Russian expansion encountered Japanese expansion, both at the expense of China. As usual in these imperialist episodes, obscure and hopefully

---

* So named after a temporary majority at the first effective congress of the RSDLP (1903). Russian *bolshe* = more; *menshe* = less.

lucrative deals by shady entrepreneurs complicated the picture. Since only the hapless hulk of China had fought a war against Japan, the Russian Empire was the first in the twentieth century to underestimate that formidable state. The Russo-Japanese war of 1904–5, though it killed 84,000 Japanese and wounded 143,000,[14] was a rapid and humiliating disaster for Russia, which underlined the weakness of tsarism. Even the middle-class liberals, who had begun to organize as a political opposition since 1900, ventured into public demonstrations. The tsar, conscious of the rising waves of revolution, speeded up negotiations for peace. The revolution broke out in January of 1905 before they had been concluded.

The 1905 revolution was, as Lenin said, a 'bourgeois revolution achieved by proletarian means'. 'Proletarian means' is perhaps an oversimplification, though it was mass workers' strikes in the capital and sympathetic strikes in most industrial cities of the empire which initiated the government's retreat and later, once again, exerted the pressure which led to the grant of something like a constitution on 17 October. Moreover, it was the workers who, doubtless with village experience behind them, spontaneously formed themselves into 'councils' (Russian: *soviets*), among which the St Petersburg Soviet of Workers' Deputies, established 13 October, functioned not merely as a sort of workers' parliament but probably for a brief period as the most effective actual authority in the national capital. The socialist parties quickly recognized the significance of such assemblies and some took a prominent part in them – like the young L. B. Trotsky (1879–1940) in St Petersburg.* For, crucial as the intervention of the workers was, concentrated as they were in the capital and other politically sensitive centres, it was – as in 1917 – the outbreak of peasant revolts on a massive scale in the Black Earth region, the Volga valley and parts of Ukraine, and the crumbling of the armed forces, dramatized by the mutiny of the battleship *Potemkin*, which broke the back of tsarist resistance. The simultaneous mobilization of revolutionary resistance among the minor nationalities was equally significant.

The 'bourgeois' character of the revolution could be, and was, taken for granted. Not only were the middle classes overwhelmingly in favour of the revolution, and the students (unlike in October 1917) overwhelmingly mobilized to fight for it, but it was accepted, almost without dissent, by both liberals and Marxists, that the revolution, if successful, could *only* lead to the establishment of a western bourgeois parliamentary system with its characteristic civil and political liberties,

* Most other well-known socialists were in exile and unable to return to Russia in time to act effectively.

within which the later stages of the Marxian class struggle would have to be fought out. In short, there was a consensus that the construction of socialism was not on the immediate revolutionary agenda, if only because Russia was too backward. It was neither economically nor socially ready for socialism.

On this point everyone agreed, except the Social Revolutionaries, who still dreamed of an increasingly implausible prospect of peasant communes transformed into socialist units – a prospect, paradoxically, realized only among the Palestinian kibbutzim, products of about the least typical muzhiks in the world, socialist–nationalist urban Jews emigrating to the Holy Land from Russia after the failure of the 1905 revolution.

And yet Lenin saw as clearly as the tsarist authorities that the liberal – or any – bourgeoisie in Russia was numerically and politically much too feeble to take over from tsarism, just as Russian private capitalist enterprise was too feeble to modernize the country without foreign enterprise and state initiative. Even at the peak of the revolution the authorities made only modest political concessions far short of a bourgeois–liberal constitution – little more than an indirectly elected parliament (Duma) with limited powers over finance and none over the government and 'fundamental laws'; and in 1907 when revolutionary unrest had subsided and the gerrymandered franchise would still not produce a sufficiently harmless Duma, most of the constitution was abrogated. There was indeed no return to autocracy, but in practice tsarism had re-established itself.

But it could, as 1905 had proved, be overthrown. The novelty of Lenin's position as against his chief rivals the Mensheviks was that he recognized that, given the weakness or absence of the bourgeoisie, the bourgeois revolution had, as it were, to be made without the bourgeoisie. It would be made by the working class, organized and led by the disciplined vanguard party of professional revolutionaries which was Lenin's formidable contribution to twentieth-century politics, and relying on the support of the land-hungry peasantry, whose political weight in Russia was decisive and whose revolutionary potential had now been demonstrated. This, broadly speaking, remained the Leninist position until 1917. The idea that the workers might, given the absence of a bourgeoisie, take power themselves and proceed directly to the next stage of the social revolution ('permanent revolution') had indeed been floated briefly during the revolution – if only in order to stimulate a proletarian revolution in the west, without which the long-term chances of a Russian socialist regime were believed to be negligible. Lenin considered this prospect, but still rejected it as impracticable.

The Leninist perspective rested on a growth of the working class, on the peasantry remaining a revolutionary force – and of course also on mobilizing, allying with, or at least neutralizing the forces of national liberation which were plainly revolutionary assets, inasmuch as they were enemies of tsarism. (Hence Lenin's insistence on the right to self-determination, even of secession from Russia, although the Bolsheviks were organized as a single all-Russian and, as it were, a-national party.) The proletariat was indeed growing, as Russia launched herself into another massive bout of industrialization in the last years before 1914; and the young rural immigrants streaming into the factories in Moscow and St Petersburg were more likely to follow the radical Bolsheviks than the more moderate Mensheviks, not to mention the miserable provincial encampments of smoke, coal, iron, textiles and mud – the Donets, the Urals, Ivanovo – which had always inclined to Bolshevism. After a few years of demoralization following the defeat of the 1905 revolution, an enormous new wave of proletarian unrest once again rose from 1912, its rise dramatized by the massacre of 200 striking workers in the remote (British-owned) Siberian goldfields on the River Lena.

But would the peasants remain revolutionary? The reaction of the tsar's government to 1905, under the able and determined minister Stolypin, was to create a substantial and conservative body of peasants, while simultaneously improving agricultural productivity, by a whole-hearted plunge into the Russian equivalent of the British 'enclosure movement'. The peasant commune was to be systematically broken up into private plots, for the benefit of a class of commercially minded entrepreneurial large peasants, the 'kulaks'. If Stolypin won his bet on 'the strong and sober', the social polarization between village rich and land-poor, the rural class differentiation announced by Lenin would indeed take place; but, faced with the actual prospect, he recognized with his habitual and ruthless eye for political realities that it would not help the revolution. Whether the Stolypin legislation could have achieved the expected political result in the longer run, we cannot know. It was quite widely taken up in the more commercialized southern provinces, notably Ukraine, much less so elsewhere.[15] However, as Stolypin himself was eliminated from the tsar's government in 1911 and assassinated shortly thereafter, and as the empire itself had only eight more years of peace in 1906, the question is academic.

What is clear is that the defeat of the 1905 revolution had produced neither a potential 'bourgeois' alternative to tsarism, nor given tsarism more than a half-dozen years of respite. By 1912–14 the country was clearly once again seething with social unrest. A revolutionary situation, Lenin was convinced, was once again approaching. By the summer of 1914 all that stood in its way was the strength and solid loyalty of the tsar's bureaucracy, police and armed forces which – unlike 1904–5 – were neither demoralized nor otherwise engaged;[16] and perhaps the passivity of the Russian middle-class intellectuals who, demoralized by the defeat of 1905, had largely abandoned political radicalism for irrationalism and the cultural *avant garde.*

As in so many other European states, the outbreak of war relaxed accumulating social and political fervour. When this had passed, it become increasingly evident that tsarism was doomed. In 1917 it fell.

By 1914 revolution had shaken all the ancient empires of the globe from the borders of Germany to the China seas. As the Mexican Revolution, the Egyptian agitations and the Indian national movement showed, it was beginning to erode the new ones of imperialism, formal and informal. However, nowhere was its outcome clear as yet, and the significance of the fires flickering among Lenin's 'inflammable material in world politics' was easy to underestimate. It was not yet clear that the Russian Revolution would produce a communist regime – the first in history – and would become the central event in twentieth-century world politics, as the French Revolution had been the central event of nineteenth-century politics.

And yet it was already obvious that, of all the eruptions in the vast social earthquake zone of the globe, a Russian revolution would have much the greatest international repercussion, for even the incomplete and temporary convulsion of 1905–6 had dramatic and immediate results. It almost certainly precipitated the Persian and Turkish revolutions, it probably accelerated the Chinese, and, by stimulating the Austrian emperor to introduce universal suffrage, it transformed, and made even more unstable, the troubled politics of the Habsburg Empire. For Russia was a 'great power', one of the five keystones of the Euro-centred international system and, taking only home territories into account, much the largest, most populous and best endowed with resources. A social revolution in such a state was bound to have far-reaching global effects, for exactly the same reason that had, among the numerous revolutions of the late eighteenth century, made the French one by far the most internationally significant.

But the potential repercussions of a Russian revolution would be even wider than those of 1789. The sheer physical extent and multi-nationality of an empire which stretched from the Pacific to the borders of Germany meant that its collapse affected a far greater range of countries in two continents than a more marginal or isolated state in Europe or Asia. And the crucial fact that Russia straddled the worlds of the conquerors and the victims, the advanced and the backward, gave its revolution a vast potential resonance in both. It was both a major industrial country and a technologically medieval peasant economy; an imperial power and a semi-colony; a society whose intellectual and cultural achievements were more than a match for the most advanced culture and intellect of the western world, and one whose peasant soldiers in 1904–5 gaped at the modernity of their Japanese captors. In short, a Russian revolution could appear to be simultaneously relevant to western labour organizers and to eastern revolutionaries, in Germany and in China.

Tsarist Russia exemplified all the contradictions of the globe in the Age of Empire. All it would take to make them burst into simultaneous eruption was that world war which Europe increasingly expected, and found itself unable to prevent.

CHAPTER 13

FROM PEACE TO WAR

In the course of the debate [of 27 March 1900] I explained ... that I understood by a world policy merely the support and advancement of the tasks that have grown out of the expansion of our industry, our trade, the labour power, activity and intelligence of our people. We had no intention of conducting an aggressive policy of expansion. We wanted only to protect the vital interests that we had acquired, in the natural course of events, throughout the world.

The German chancellor, von Bülow, 1900[1]

There is no certainty that a woman will lose her son if he goes to the front; in fact, the coal-mine and the shunting-yard are more dangerous places than the camp.

Bernard Shaw, 1902[2]

We will glorify war – the world's only hygiene – militarism, patriotism, the destructive gesture of freedom-bringers, beautiful ideas worth dying for, and scorn for woman.

F. T. Marinetti, 1909[3]

I

The lives of Europeans since August 1914 have been surrounded, impregnated and haunted by world war. At the time of writing most people on this continent over the age of seventy have passed through at least part of two wars in the course of their lives; all over the age of fifty, with the exception of Swedes, Swiss, Southern Irish and Portuguese, have experienced part of at least one. Even those born since 1945, since the guns ceased to fire across frontiers in Europe, have known scarcely a year when war was not abroad somewhere in the world, and have lived all their lives in the dark shadow of a third, nuclear, world conflict which, as virtually all their governments told them, was held at bay only by the endless competition to ensure mutual annihilation. How can we call such an epoch a time of peace, even if global catastrophe has been avoided for almost as long as major war between European powers was between 1871 and 1914? For, as the great philosopher Thomas Hobbes observed:

> War consisteth not in battle only, or in the act of fighting; but in a tract of time, wherein the will to contend by battle is sufficiently known.[4]

Who can deny that this has been the situation of the world since 1945?

This was not so before 1914: peace was the normal and expected framework of European lives. Since 1815 there had been no war involving all the European powers. Since 1871 no European power had ordered its armed men to fire on those of any other such power. The great powers chose their victims from among the weak, and in the non-European world, though they might miscalculate the resistance of their adversaries: the Boers gave the British far more trouble than expected, and the Japanese established their status as a great power by actually defeating Russia in 1904–5 with surprisingly little trouble. On the territory of the nearest and largest of the potential victims, the long-disintegrating Ottoman Empire, war was indeed a permanent possibility as its subject peoples sought to establish or enlarge themselves as independent states and subsequently fought each other, drawing the great powers into their conflicts. The Balkans were known as the powder-keg of Europe, and indeed that is where the global explosion of 1914 began. But the 'Eastern Question' was a familiar item on the agenda of international diplomacy, and while it had produced a steady succession of international crises for a century, and even one quite substantial international war (the Crimean War), it had never entirely escaped from control. Unlike the Middle East since 1945, the Balkans, for most Europeans who did not live there, belonged to the realm of adventure stories, such as those of the German boys' author Karl May, or of operetta. The image of Balkan wars at the end of the nineteenth century was that of Bernard Shaw's *Arms and the Man*, which was, characteristically, turned into a musical (*The Chocolate Soldier*, by a Viennese composer in 1908).

Of course the possibility of a general European war was foreseen, and preoccupied not only governments and their general staffs, but a wider public. From the early 1870s on, fiction and futurology, mainly in Britain and France, produced generally unrealistic sketches of a future war. In the 1880s Friedrich Engels already analysed the chances of a world war, while the philosopher Nietzsche crazily, but prophetically, hailed the growing militarization of Europe and predicted a war which would 'say yes to the barbarian, even to the wild animal within us'.[5] In the 1890s the concern about war was sufficient to produce the

World (Universal) Peace Congresses – the twenty-first was due in Vienna in September 1914 – the Nobel Peace prizes (1897) and the first of the Hague Peace Conferences (1899), international meetings by mostly sceptical representatives of governments, and the first of many gatherings since in which governments have declared their unwavering but theoretical commitment to the ideal of peace. In the 1900s war drew visibly nearer, in the 1910s its imminence could and was in some ways taken for granted.

And yet its outbreak was not really *expected*. Even during the last desperate days of the international crisis in July 1914 statesmen, taking fatal steps, did not really believe they were starting a world war. Surely a formula would be found, as so often in the past. The opponents of war could not believe either that the catastrophe they had so long foretold was now upon them. At the very end of July, *after* Austria had already declared war on Serbia, the leaders of international socialism met, deeply troubled but still convinced that a general war was impossible, that a peaceful solution to the crisis would be found. 'I personally do not believe that there will be a general war,' said Victor Adler, chief of Habsburg social democracy, on 29 July.[6] Even those who found themselves pressing the button of destruction did so, not because they wanted to but because they could not help it, like Emperor William, asking his generals at the very last moment whether the war could not after all be localized in eastern Europe by refraining from attacking France as well as Russia – and being told that unfortunately this was quite impracticable. Those who had constructed the mills of war and turned the switches found themselves watching their wheels beginning to grind in a sort of stunned disbelief. It is difficult for anyone born after 1914 to imagine how deeply the belief that a world war could not 'really' come was engrained in the fabric of life before the deluge.

For most western states, and for most of the time between 1871 and 1914, a European war was thus a historical memory or a theoretical exercise for some undefined future. The major function of armies in their societies during this period was civilian. Compulsory military service – conscription – was by now the rule in all serious powers, with the exception of Britain and the USA, though in fact by no means all young men were conscripted; and with the rise of socialist mass movements generals and politicians were – mistakenly, as it turned out – sometimes nervous about putting arms into the hands of potentially revolutionary proletarians. For the ordinary conscripts, better acquainted with the servitude than the glories of the military life, joining the army became a rite of passage marking a boy's arrival at manhood, followed by two or three years of drill and hard labour, made more tolerable by the notorious attraction of girls to uniforms. For the professional noncommissioned officers the army was a job. For the officers it was a children's game played by adults, the symbol of their superiority to civilians, of virile splendour and of social status. For the generals it was, as always, the field for those political intrigues and career jealousies which are so amply documented in the memoirs of military chieftains.

For governments and ruling classes, armies were not only forces against internal and external enemies, but also a means of securing the loyalty, even the active enthusiasm, of citizens with troubling sympathies for mass movements which undermined the social and political order. Together with the primary school, military service was perhaps the most powerful mechanism at the disposal of the state for inculcating proper civic behaviour and, not least, for turning the inhabitant of a village into the (patriotic) citizen of a nation. School and military service taught Italians to understand, if not to speak, the official 'national' language, and the army turned spaghetti, formerly a regional dish of the impoverished south, into an all-Italian institution. As for the civilian citizenry, the colourful street theatre of military display was multiplied for their enjoyment, inspiration and patriotic identification: parades, ceremonials, flags and music. For the non-military inhabitants of Europe between 1871 and 1914 the most familiar aspect of armies was probably the ubiquitous military band, without which public parks and public occasions were difficult to imagine.

Naturally soldiers, and rather more rarely sailors, also from time to time carried out their primary functions. They might be mobilized against disorder and protest at moments of disturbance and social crisis. Governments, especially those which had to worry about public opinion and their electors, were usually careful about facing troops with the risk of shooting down their fellow citizens: the political consequences of soldiers firing on civilians were apt to be bad, and those of their refusal to do so were apt to be even worse, as demonstrated in Petrograd in 1917. Nevertheless troops were mobilized often enough, and the number of domestic victims of military repression was by no means negligible during this period, even in central and west European states not believed to be on the verge of revolution, like Belgium and the Netherlands. In countries like Italy they could be very substantial indeed.

For the troops, domestic repression was a harmless pursuit, but the occasional wars, especially in the colonies, were more risky. The risk was, admittedly, medical rather than military. Of the 274,000 US troops mobilized for the Spanish–American War of 1898 only 379 were killed and 1600 wounded, but more than 5000 died of tropical diseases. It is not surprising that governments were keen to support the medical researches which, in our period, achieved some control over yellow fever, malaria and other scourges of the territories still known as 'the white man's grave'. France lost in colonial operations between 1871 and 1908 an average of eight officers per year, including the only zone of serious casualties, Tonkin, where almost half the 300 officers killed in those thirty-seven years fell.[7] One would not wish to underestimate the seriousness of such campaigns, all the more so since the losses among the victims were disproportionately heavy. Even for the aggressor countries, such wars could be anything but sporting trips. Britain sent 450,000 men to South Africa in 1899–1902, losing 29,000 killed and died of their wounds and 16,000 by disease, at the cost of £220 million. Such costs were far from negligible. Nevertheless, the soldier's work in western countries was, by and large, considerably less dangerous than that of certain groups of civilian workers such as those in transport (especially by sea) and the mines. In the last three years of the long decades of peace, every year an average of 1430 British coal-miners were killed, an average of 165,000 (or more than 10 per cent of the labour force) injured. And the casualty rate in British coal-mines, though higher than the Belgian or Austrian, was somewhat lower than the French, about 30 per cent below the German, and not much more than one-third of that in the USA.[8] The greatest risks to life and limb were not run in uniform.

Thus, if we omit Britain's South African War, the life of the soldier and sailor of a great power was peaceful enough, though this was not the case for the armies of tsarist Russia, engaged in serious wars against the Turks in the 1870s, and a disastrous one against the Japanese in 1904–5; nor of the Japanese, who fought both China and Russia successfully. It is still recognizable in the entirely non-fighting memories and adventures of that immortal ex-member of the famous 91st Regiment of the imperial and royal Austrian army, the good soldier Schwejk (invented by its author in 1911). Naturally general staffs prepared for war, as was their duty. As usual most of them prepared for an improved version of the last major war within the experience or memory of the commandants of staff colleges. The British, as was natural for the greatest naval power, prepared for only a modest participation in terrestrial warfare, though it increasingly became evident to the generals arranging for co-operation with the French allies in the years before 1914 that much more would be required of them. But on the whole it was the civilians rather than the men who predicted the terrible transformations of warfare, thanks to the advances of that military technology which the generals – and even some of the technically more open-minded admirals – were slow to understand. Friedrich Engels, that old military amateur, frequently drew attention to their obtuseness, but it was a Jewish financier, Ivan Bloch, who in 1898 published in St

Petersburg the six volumes of his *Technical, Economic and Political Aspects of the Coming War*, a prophetic work which predicted the military stalemate of trench warfare which would lead to a prolonged conflict whose intolerable economic and human costs would exhaust the belligerents or plunge them into social revolution. The book was rapidly translated into numerous languages, without making any mark on military planning.

While only some civilian observers understood the catastrophic character of future warfare, uncomprehending governments plunged enthusiastically into the race to equip themselves with the armaments whose technological novelty would ensure it. The technology of killing, already in the process of industrialization in the middle of the century (see *The Age of Capital*, chapter 4, II), advanced dramatically in the 1880s, not only by virtual revolution in the speed and fire-power of small arms and artillery, but also by the transformation of warships by means of far more efficient turbine-engines, more effective protective armour and the capacity to carry far more guns. Incidentally even the technology of civilian killing was transformed by the invention of the 'electric chair' (1890), though executioners outside the USA remained faithful to old and tried methods such as hanging and beheading.

An obvious consequence was that preparations for war became vastly more expensive, especially as states competed to keep ahead of, or at least to avoid falling behind, each other. This arms race began in a modest way in the later 1880s, and accelerated in the new century, particularly in the last years before the war. British military expenses remained stable in the 1870s and 1880s, both as a percentage of the total budget and per head of the population. But it rose from £32 million in 1887 to £44.1 million in 1898/9 and over £77 million in 1913/14. And, not surprisingly, it was the navy, the high-technology wing of warfare which corresponded to the missile sector of modern armaments expenditure, which grew most spectacularly. In 1885 it had cost the state £11 million – about the same order of magnitude as in 1860. In 1913/14 it cost more than four times as much. Meanwhile German naval expenditure grew even more strikingly: from 90 million Marks per annum in the mid-1890s to almost 400 millions.[9]

One consequence of such vast expenditures was that they required either higher taxes, or inflationary borrowing, or both. But an equally obvious, though often overlooked consequence was that they increasingly made death for various fatherlands a by-product of large-scale industry. Alfred Nobel and Andrew Carnegie, two capitalists who knew what had made them millionaires in explosives and steel respectively, tried to compensate by devoting part of their wealth to the cause of peace. In this they were untypical. The symbiosis of war and war production inevitably transformed the relations between government and industry, for, as Friedrich Engels observed in 1892, 'as warfare became a branch of the *grande industrie* ... *la grande industrie* ... became a political necessity'.[10] And conversely, the state became essential to certain branches of industry, for who but the government provided the customers for armaments? The goods it produced were determined not by the market, but by the never-ending competition of governments to secure for themselves a satisfactory supply of the most advanced, and hence the most effective, arms. What is more, governments needed not so much the actual output of weapons, but the capacity to produce them on a wartime scale, if the occasion arose; that is to say they had to see that their industry maintained a capacity far in excess of any peacetime requirements.

In one way or another states were thus obliged to guarantee the existence of powerful national armaments industries, to carry much of their technical development costs, and to see that they remained profitable. In other words, they had to shelter these industries from the gales which threatened the ships of capitalist enterprise sailing the unpredictable seas of the free market and free competition. They might of course have engaged in armaments manufacture themselves, and indeed had long done so. But this was the very moment when they – or at least the liberal British state – preferred to come to an arrangement with private enterprise. In the 1880s private armament producers took on more than a third of supply contracts for the armed forces, in the 1890s 46 per cent, in the 1900s 60 per cent: the government, incidentally, was ready to guarantee them two-thirds.[11] It is hardly surprising that armaments firms were among, or joined, the giants of industry: war and capitalist concentration went together. In Germany Krupp, the king of cannons, employed 16,000 in 1873, 24,000 around 1890, 45,000 around 1900, and almost 70,000 in 1912 when the fifty-thousandth of Krupp's famous guns left the works. In Britain Armstrong, Whitworth employed 12,000 men at their main works in Newcastle, who had increased to 20,000 – or over 40 per cent of all metalworkers on Tyneside – by 1914, not counting those in the 1500 smaller firms who lived by Armstrong's sub-contracts. They were also very profitable.

Like the modern 'military–industrial complex' of the USA, these giant industrial concentrations would have been nothing without the armaments race of governments. It is therefore tempting to make such 'merchants of death' (the phrase became popular among peace campaigners) responsible for the 'war of steel and gold', as a British journalist was to call it. Was it not logical for the armaments industry to encourage the acceleration of the arms race, if necessary by inventing national inferiorities or 'windows of vulnerability', which could be removed by lucrative contracts? A German firm, specializing in the manufacture of machine-guns, managed to get a notice inserted in *Le Figaro* to the effect that the French government planned to double the number of its machine-guns. The German government consequently ordered 40 million Marks' worth of these weapons in 1908–10, thus raising the firm's dividends from 20 to 32 per cent.[12] A British firm, arguing that its government had gravely underestimated the German naval rearmament programme, benefited by £250,000 for each new 'dreadnought' built by the British government, which doubled its naval construction. Elegant and shady persons like the Greek Basil Zaharoff, who acted for Vickers (and was later knighted for his services to the Allies in the First World War), saw to it that the arms industry of the great powers sold its less vital or obsolescent products to states in the Near East and Latin America, who were always ready to buy such hardware. In short, the modern international trade in death was well under way.

And yet we cannot explain the world war by a conspiracy of armourers, even though the technicians certainly did their best to convince generals and admirals more familiar with military parades than with science that all would be lost if they did not order the latest gun or battleship. Certainly the accumulation of armaments which reached fearful proportions in the last five years before 1914 made the situation more explosive. Certainly the moment came, at least in the summer of 1914, when the inflexible machine for mobilizing the forces of death could no longer be put into reserve. But what drove Europe into the war was not competitive armament as such, but the international situation which launched powers into it.

II

The argument about the origins of the First World War has never stopped since August 1914. Probably more ink has flowed, more trees have been sacrificed to make paper, more typewriters have been busy, to answer this question than any other in history – perhaps not even excluding the debate on the French Revolution. As generations have changed, as national and international politics have been transformed, the debate has been revived time and again. Hardly had Europe plunged into catastrophe, before the belligerents began to ask themselves why international diplomacy had failed to prevent it, and to accuse one another of responsibility for the war. Opponents of the war immediately began their own analyses. The Russian Revolution of 1917, which published the secret documents of tsarism, accused imperialism as a whole. The victorious Allies made the thesis of exclusive German 'war guilt' the cornerstone of the Versailles peace settlement of 1919, and precipitated a huge flood of documentation and historical propagandist writings for, but mainly against, this thesis. The Second World War naturally revived the debate, which took on yet another lease of life some years later as a historiography of the left reappeared in the German Federal Republic, anxious to break with conservative and Nazi German patriotic orthodoxies, by stressing their own version of Germany's responsibility. Arguments about the dangers to world peace, which have, for obvious reasons, never ceased since Hiroshima and Nagasaki, inevitably seek for possible parallels between the origins of past world wars and current international prospects. While propagandists preferred comparison with the years before the Second World War ('Munich'), historians increasingly found the similarities between the 1980s and the 1910s troubling. The origins of the First World War were thus, once again, a question of burning, immediate relevance. In these circumstances any historian who tries to explain, as a historian of our period must, why the First World War occurred plunges into deep and turbulent waters.

Still, we can at least simplify his task by eliminating questions he does not have to answer. Chief among these is that of 'war guilt', which is one of moral and political judgment, but concerns historians only peripherally. If we are interested in why a century of European peace gave way to an epoch of world wars, the question whose fault it was is as trivial as the question whether William the Conqueror had a good legal case for invading England is for the study of why warriors from Scandinavia found themselves conquering numerous areas of Europe in the tenth and eleventh centuries.

Of course responsibilities can often be assigned in wars. Few would deny that in the 1930s the posture of Germany was essentially aggressive and expansionist, the posture of her adversaries essentially defensive. None would deny that the wars of imperial expansion in our period, such as the Spanish–American War of 1898 and the South African War of 1899–1902, were provoked by the USA and Britain, and not by their victims. In any case everyone knows that all state governments in the nineteenth century, however concerned about their public relations, regarded wars as normal contingencies of international politics, and were honest enough to admit that they might well take the military initiative. Ministries of War had not yet been universally euphemized into Ministries of Defence.

Yet it is absolutely certain that no government of a great power before 1914 wanted either a general European war or even – unlike the 1850s and 1860s – a limited military conflict with another European great power. This is conclusively demonstrated by the fact that where the political ambitions of the great powers were in direct opposition, namely in the overseas zone of colonial conquests and partitions, their numerous confrontations were always settled by some peaceable arrangement. Even the most serious of these crises, those on Morocco in 1906 and 1911, were defused. On the eve of 1914 colonial conflicts no longer appeared to raise insoluble problems for the various competing powers – a fact which has, quite illegitimately, been used to argue that imperialist rivalries were irrelevant to the outbreak of the First World War.

Of course the powers were far from pacific, let alone pacifist. They prepared for a European war – sometimes wrongly* – even as their foreign ministries did their best to avoid what they unanimously considered a catastrophe. No government in the 1900s pursued aims which, like Hitler's in the 1930s, only war or the constant menace of war could have achieved. Even Germany, whose chief of staff vainly pleaded for a pre-emptive attack against France while her ally Russia was immobilized by war, and later by defeat and revolution, in 1904–5, used the golden opportunity of temporary French weakness and isolation merely to push her imperialist claims on Morocco, a manageable issue over which nobody intended to start a major war, or indeed did so. No government of a major power, even the most ambitious, frivolous and irresponsible, wanted a major one. The old emperor Francis Joseph, announcing the eruption of such a war to his doomed subjects in 1914, was perfectly sincere in saying, 'I did not want this to happen' ('Ich hab es nicht gewollt'), even though it was his government which, in effect, provoked it.

The most that can be claimed is that at a certain point in the slow slide towards the abyss, war seemed henceforth so inevitable that some governments decided that it might be best to choose the most favourable, or least unpropitious, moment for launching hostilities. It has been claimed that Germany looked for such a moment from 1912, but it could hardly have been earlier. Certainly during the final crisis of 1914, precipitated by the irrelevant assassination of an Austrian archduke by a student terrorist in a provincial city deep in the Balkans, Austria knew she risked world war by bullying Serbia, and Germany, deciding to give full backing to her ally, made it virtually certain. 'The balance is tilting against us,' said the Austrian Minister of War on 7 July. Was it not best to fight before it tilted further? Germany followed the same line of argument. Only in this restricted sense has the question

---

* Admiral Raeder even claimed that in 1914 the German naval staff had no plan for war against Britain.[13]

of 'war guilt' any meaning. But, as the event showed, in the summer of 1914, unlike earlier crises, peace had been written off by all the powers – even by the British, whom the Germans half-expected to stay neutral, thus increasing their chances of defeating both France and Russia.* None of the great powers would have given peace the *coup de grâce* even in 1914, unless they had been convinced that its wounds were already fatal.

The problem of discovering the origins of the First World War is therefore not one of discovering 'the aggressor'. It lies in the nature of a progressively deteriorating international situation which increasingly escaped from the control of governments. Gradually Europe found itself dividing into two opposed blocs of great powers. Such blocs, outside war, were in themselves new, and were essentially due to the appearance on the European scene of a unified German Empire, established by diplomacy and war at others' expense (cf. *The Age of Capital*, chapter 4) between 1864 and 1871, and seeking to protect itself against the main loser, France, by peacetime alliances, which in time produced counter-alliance. Alliances in themselves, though they imply the possibility of war, neither ensure it nor even make it probable. Indeed the German chancellor Bismarck, who remained undisputed world champion at the game of multilateral diplomatic chess for almost twenty years after 1871, devoted himself exclusively, and successfully, to maintaining peace between the powers. A system of power-blocs only became a danger to peace when the opposed alliances were welded into permanence, but especially when the disputes between them turned into unmanageable confrontations. This was to happen in the new century. The crucial question is, why?

However, there was one major difference between the international tensions which led up to the First World War and those which underlay the danger of a third, which people in the 1980s still hoped to avoid. Since 1945 there has never been the slightest doubt about the principal adversaries in a third world war: the USA and the USSR. But in 1880 the line-up of 1914 was quite unpredicted. Naturally some potential allies and enemies were easy to discern. Germany and France would be on opposite sides, if only because Germany had annexed large parts of France (Alsace–Lorraine) after her victory in 1871. Nor was it difficult to predict the permanence of the alliance between Germany and Austria–Hungary, which Bismarck had forged after 1866, for the internal political equilibrium of the new German Empire made it

---

* The German strategy (the 'Schlieffen Plan' of 1905) envisaged a rapid knock-out blow against France followed by a rapid knock-out blow against Russia. The former meant the invasion of Belgium, thus providing Britain with an excuse for entering the war, to which she had long been effectively committed.

essential to maintain the multinational Habsburg Empire in being. Its disintegration into national fragments would, as Bismarck well knew, not only lead to the collapse of the state system of central and eastern Europe, but would also destroy the basis of a 'little Germany' dominated by Prussia. In fact, both of these things happened after the First World War. The most permanent diplomatic feature of the period 1871–1914 was the 'Triple Alliance' of 1882, which was in effect a German–Austrian alliance, since the third partner, Italy, soon drifted away and eventually joined the anti-German camp in 1915.

Again, it was obvious that Austria, embroiled in turbulent affairs of the Balkans by virtue of her multinational problems, and more deeply than ever since she took over Bosnia–Hercegovina in 1878, found herself opposed to Russia in that region.* Though Bismarck did his best to maintain close relations with Russia, it was possible to foresee that sooner or later Germany would be forced to choose between Vienna and St Petersburg, and could not but opt for Vienna. Moreover, once Germany gave up the Russian option, as happened in the late 1880s, it was logical that Russia and France would come together – as indeed they did in 1891. Even in the 1880s Friedrich Engels had envisaged such an alliance, naturally directed against Germany. By the early 1890s two power-groups therefore faced each other across Europe.

Though this made international relations more tense, it did not make a general European war inevitable, if only because the issues which divided France and Germany (namely Alsace–Lorraine) were of no interest to Austria, and those which risked conflict between Austria and Russia (namely the degree of Russian influence in the Balkans) were insignificant for Germany. The Balkans, Bismarck had observed, were not worth the bones of a single Pomeranian grenadier. France had no real quarrels with Austria, nor Russia with Germany. For that matter the issues which divided France and Germany, though permanent, were hardly considered worth a war by most French, and those dividing Austria and Russia, though – as 1914 showed – potentially more serious, only arose intermittently. Three developments turned the alliance system into a time-bomb: a situation of international flux, destabilized by new problems for and ambitions within the powers, the logic of joint military planning which froze confronting blocs into permanence, and the integration of the fifth great power, Britain, into one of the blocs. (Nobody worried much about the tergiversations of Italy, which was

---

* The southern Slav peoples were partly under the Austrian half of the Habsburg Empire (Slovenes, Dalmatian Croats), partly under the Hungarian half (Croats, some Serbs), partly under common imperial administration (Bosnia–Hercegovina), the rest in small independent kingdoms (Serbia, Bulgaria and the mini-principality of Montenegro) and under the Turks (Macedonia).

only a 'great power' by international courtesy.) Between 1903 and 1907, to everyone's surprise including her own, Britain joined the anti-German camp. The origin of the First World War can best be understood by tracing the emergence of this Anglo-German antagonism.

The 'Triple Entente' was astonishing both for Britain's enemy and for her allies. In the past Britain had neither tradition of nor any permanent reasons for friction with Prussia – and the same seemed to be true of the super-Prussia now known as the German Empire. On the other hand Britain had been the almost automatic antagonist of France in almost any European war going since 1688. While this was no longer so, if only because France had ceased to be capable of dominating the continent, friction between the two countries was visibly increasing, if only because both competed for the same territory and influence as imperialist powers. Thus relations were unfriendly over Egypt, which was coveted by both but taken over (together with the French-financed Suez Canal) by the British. During the Fashoda crisis of 1898 it looked as though blood might flow, as rival British and French colonial troops confronted each other in the hinterland of the Sudan. In the partition of Africa, more often than not the gains of one were at the expense of the other. As for Russia, the British and Tsarist empires had been permanent antagonists in the Balkan and Mediterranean zone of the so-called 'Eastern Question', and in the ill-defined but bitterly disputed areas of Central and Western Asia which lay between India and the tsar's lands: Afghanistan, Iran and the regions opening on the Persian Gulf. The prospect of Russians in Constantinople – and therefore in the Mediterranean – and of Russian expansion towards India was a standing nightmare for British foreign secretaries. The two countries had even fought in the only nineteenth-century European war in which Britain took part (the Crimean War), and as recently as the 1870s a Russo-British war was seriously on the cards.

Given the established pattern of British diplomacy, a war against Germany was a possibility so remote as to be negligible. A *permanent* alliance with any continental power seemed incompatible with the maintenance of that balance of power which was the chief objective of British foreign policy. An alliance with France could be regarded as improbable, one with Russia almost unthinkable. Yet the implausible became reality: Britain linked up permanently with France and Russia against Germany, settling all differences with Russia to the point of actually agreeing to the Russian occupation of Constantinople – an offer which disappeared from sight with the Russian Revolution of 1917. How and why did this astonishing transformation come about?

It happened because both the players and the rules of the traditional game of international diplomacy changed. In the first instance, the board on which it was played became much larger. Power rivalry, formerly (except for the British) largely confined to Europe and adjoining areas, was now global and imperial – outside most of the Americas, destined for exclusive US imperial expansion by Washington's Monroe Doctrine. The international disputes which had to be settled, if they were not to degenerate into wars, were now as likely to occur over West Africa and the Congo in the 1880s, China in the late 1890s and the Maghreb (1906, 1911) as over the disintegrating body of the Ottoman Empire, and much more likely than over any issues in non-Balkan Europe. Moreover, there were now new players: the USA which, while still avoiding European entanglements, was actively expansionist in the Pacific, and Japan. In fact Britain's alliance with Japan (1902) was the first step towards the Triple Alliance, since the existence of that new power, which was soon to show that it could actually defeat the Tsarist Empire in war, diminished the Russian threat to Britain and thus strengthened Britain's position. It therefore made the defusion of various ancient Russo-British disputes possible.

This globalization of the international power-game automatically transformed the situation of the country which had, until then, been the only great power with genuinely worldwide political objectives. It is hardly an exaggeration to say that for most of the nineteenth century the function of Europe in British diplomatic calculations was to keep quiet so that Britain could get on with its, mainly economic, activities in the rest of the globe. This was the essence of the characteristic combination of a European balance of power with the global Pax Britannica guaranteed by the only navy of global size, which controlled all the world's oceans and sea-lanes. In the mid-nineteenth century all other navies of the world put together were hardly larger than the British navy alone. By the end of the century this was no longer so.

In the second place, with the rise of a worldwide industrial capitalist economy, the international game was now played for quite different stakes. This does not mean that, to adapt Clausewitz's famous phrase, war was henceforth only the continuation of economic competition by other means. This was a view which tempted the historical determinists at the time, if only because they observed plenty of examples of economic expansion by means of machine-guns and gunboats. Nevertheless, it was a gross oversimplification. If capitalist development and imperialism must bear responsibility for the uncontrolled slide into world conflict, it is impossible to argue that many capitalists themselves were conscious warmongers. Any impartial study of the business press, of the private and commercial correspondence of businessmen, of their public declarations as spokesmen for banking, commerce and industry, shows

315

quite conclusively that the majority of businessmen found international peace to their advantage. Indeed, war itself was acceptably only insofar as it did not interfere with 'business as usual', and the major objection to war of the young economist Keynes (not yet a radical reformer of his subject) was not only that it killed his friends, but that it inevitably made an economic policy based on 'business as usual' impossible. Naturally there were bellicose economic expansionists, but the Liberal journalist Norman Angell almost certainly expressed business consensus: the belief that war benefited capital was 'The Great Illusion' which gave his book of 1912 its title.

Why indeed should capitalists – even industrialists, with the possible exception of the arms manufacturers – have wished to disturb international peace, the essential framework of their prosperity and expansion, since the fabric of free international business and financial transactions depended on it? Evidently those who did well out of international competition had no cause for complaint. Just as the freedom to penetrate the world's markets has no disadvantages for Japan today, so German industry could well be content with it before 1914. Those who lost out were naturally apt to demand economic protection from their governments, though this is far from the same as demanding war. Moreover, the greatest of the potential losers, Britain, resisted even these demands, and her business interests remained overwhelmingly committed to peace, in spite of the constant fears of German competition which was stridently expressed in the 1890s, and the actual penetration of the British domestic market by German and American capital. As regards Anglo-American relations, we can go even further. If economic competition alone makes for war, Anglo-American rivalry should logically have prepared the ground for military conflict – as some inter-war Marxists still felt it would. Yet it was precisely in the 1900s that the British Imperial General Staff abandoned even the most remote contingency plans for an Anglo-American war. Henceforth this possibility was totally excluded.

And yet the development of capitalism inevitably pushed the world in the direction of state rivalry, imperialist expansion, conflict and war. After 1870, as historians have pointed out:

> the shift from monopoly to competition was probably the most important single factor in setting the mood for European industrial and commercial enterprise. Economic growth was also economic struggle – struggle that served to separate the strong from the weak, to discourage some and toughen others, to favour the new, hungry nations at the expense of the old. Optimism about a future of indefinite progress gave way to uncertainty and a sense of agony, in

the classical meaning of the word. All of which strengthened and was in turn strengthened by sharpening political rivalries, the two forms of competition merging.[14]

Plainly the economic world was no longer, as it had been in the mid-century, a solar system revolving around a single star, Great Britain. If the financial and commercial transactions of the globe still, and in fact increasingly, ran through London, Britain was evidently no longer the 'workshop of the world', nor indeed its major import market. On the contrary, her relative decline was patent. A number of competing national industrial economies now confronted each other. Under these circumstances economic competition became inextricably woven into the political, even the military, actions of states. The renaissance of protectionism during the Great Depression was the first consequence of this merger. From the point of view of capital, political support might henceforth be essential to keep out foreign competition, and perhaps essential too in parts of the world where the enterprises of national industrial economies competed against one another. From the point of view of states, the economy was henceforth both the very base of international power and its criterion. It was impossible now to conceive of a 'great power' which was not at the same time a 'great economy' – a transformation illustrated by the rise of the USA and the relative weakening of the Tsarist Empire.

Conversely, would not the shifts in economic power, which auto-matically changed the balance of political and military force, logically entail a redistribution of parts on the international stage? Plainly this was a popular view in Germany, whose staggering industrial growth gave her an incomparably greater international weight than Prussia had had. It is hardly an accident that among German nationalists in the 1890s the old patriotic chant of 'The Watch on the Rhine', directed exclusively against the French, lost ground rapidly to the global ambitions of 'Deutschland Über Alles', which in effect became the German national anthem, though not yet officially.

What made this identification of economic and politico-military power so dangerous was not only national rivalry for world markets and material resources, and for the control of regions such as the Near and Middle East where economic and strategic interests often overlapped. Well before 1914 petro-diplomacy was already a crucial factor in the Middle East, victory going to Britain and France, the western (but not yet American) oil companies and an Armenian middle-man, Calouste Gulbenkian, who secured 5 per cent for himself. Con-versely, the German economic and strategic penetration of the Ottoman Empire already worried the British and helped to bring Turkey into the war on the German side. But the novelty of the situation was that, given the fusion between economics and politics, even the peaceful division of disputed areas into 'zones of influence' could not keep international rivalry under control. The key to its controllability – as Bismarck, who managed it with unparalleled mastery between 1871 and 1889, knew – was the deliberate restriction of objectives. So long as states were in a position to define their diplomatic aims precisely – a given shift in frontiers, a dynastic marriage, a definable 'compensation' for the advances made by other states – both calculation and settlement were possible. Neither, of course – as Bismarck himself had proved between 1862 and 1871 – excluded controllable military conflict.

But the characteristic feature of capitalist accumulation was precisely that it had no limit. The 'natural frontiers' of Standard Oil, the Deutsche Bank, the De Beers Diamond Corporation were at the end of the universe, or rather at the limits of their capacity to expand. It was this aspect of the new patterns of world politics which destabilized the structures of traditional world politics. While balance and stability remained the fundamental condition of the European powers in their relations with each other, elsewhere even the most pacific among them did not hesitate to wage war against the weak. Certainly, as we have seen, they were careful to keep their colonial conflicts under control. They never looked like providing the *casus belli* for a major war but undoubtedly precipitated the formation of the international and eventually belligerent blocs: what became the Anglo-Franco-Russian bloc began with the Anglo-French 'cordial understanding' ('Entente Cordiale') of 1904, essentially an imperialist deal by which the French gave up their claims to Egypt in return for British backing for their claims in Morocco – a victim on which Germany also happened to have her eye. Nevertheless, all powers without exception were in an expansionist and conquering mood. Even Britain, whose posture was fundamentally defensive, since her problem was how to protect hitherto uncontested global dominance against the new intruders, attacked the South African republics; nor did she hesitate to consider partitioning the colonies of a European state, Portugal, with Germany. In the global ocean all states were sharks, and all statesmen knew it.

But what made the world an even more dangerous place was the tacit equation of unlimited economic growth and political power, which came to be unconsciously accepted. Thus the German emperor in the 1890s demanded 'a place in the sun' for his state. Bismarck could have claimed as much – and had indeed achieved a vastly more powerful place in the world for the new Germany than Prussia had ever enjoyed. Yet while Bismarck could define the dimensions of his ambitions, carefully avoiding encroachment into the zone of uncontrollability, for William II the phrase became merely a slogan without concrete content. It simply formulated a principle of proportionality: the more powerful a country's economy, the larger its population, the greater the international position of its nation-state. There were no theoretical limits to the position it might thus feel to be its due. As the nationalist phrase went: 'Heute Deutschland, morgen die ganze Welt' (Today Germany, tomorrow the whole world). Such unlimited dynamism might find expression in political, cultural or nationalist–racist rhetoric: but the effective common denominator of all three was the imperative to expand of a massive capitalist economy watching its statistical curves soaring upwards. Without this it would have had as little significance as the conviction of, say, nineteenth-century Polish intellectuals that their (at the time non-existent) country has a messianic mission in the world.

In practical terms, the danger was not that Germany concretely proposed to take Britain's place as a global power, though the rhetoric of German nationalist agitation readily struck the anti-British note. It was rather that a global power required a global navy, and Germany therefore set out (1897) to construct a great battle-fleet, which had the incidental advantage of representing not the old German states but exclusively the new united Germany, with an officer-corps which represented not Prussian *junkers* or other aristocratic warrior traditions, but the new middle classes, that is to say the new nation. Admiral Tirpitz himself, the champion of naval expansion, denied that he planned a navy capable of defeating the British, claiming that he only wanted one threatening enough to force them into supporting German global, and especially colonial, claims. Besides, could a country of Germany's importance not be expected to have a navy corresponding to her importance?

But from the British point of view the construction of a German fleet was more even than yet another strain on the already globally overcommitted British navy, already much outnumbered by the united fleets of rival powers, old and new (though such a union was utterly implausible), and hard put to it to maintain even its more modest aim of being stronger than the next two largest navies combined (the 'two-power standard'). Unlike all other navies, the German fleet's bases were entirely in the North Sea, opposite Britain. Its objective could not be anything except conflict with the British navy. As Britain saw it, Germany was essentially a continental power, and, as influential geopoliticians like Sir Halford Mackinder pointed out (1904), large powers of this sort already enjoyed substantial advantages over a medium-sized island. Germany's legitimate maritime interests were visibly marginal, whereas the British Empire depended utterly on its sea-routes, and had indeed left the continents (except for India) to the armies of states whose element was the land. Even if the German battle-fleet did absolutely nothing, it must inevitably tie down British ships and thus make difficult, or even impossible, British naval control over waters believed to be vital – such as the Mediterranean, the Indian Ocean and the Atlantic sea-lanes. What was for Germany a symbol of her international status, and of undefined global ambitions, was a matter of life or death for the British Empire. American waters could be – and in 1901 were – abandoned to a friendly USA, Far Eastern waters to the USA and Japan, because these were both powers with, at the time, purely regional interests, which in any case did not seem incompatible with Britain's. Germany's navy, even as a regional navy, which it did not intend to remain, was a threat both to the British Isles and to the global position of the British Empire. Britain stood for as much of the status quo as could be preserved, Germany for its change – inevitably, even if not intentionally, at Britain's expense. Under the circumstances, and given the economic rivalry between the two countries' industries, it was not surprising that Great Britain found herself considering Germany as the most probable and dangerous of potential adversaries. It was logical that she should find herself drawing closer to France and, once the Russian danger had been minimized by Japan, to Russia, all the more so since the Russian defeat had, for the first time in living memory, destroyed that equilibrium of the powers on the European continent which British foreign secretaries had so long taken for granted. It revealed Germany as by far the dominant military force in Europe, as she was aready industrially by far the most formidable. This was the background for the surprising Anglo-Franco-Russian Triple Entente.

The division of Europe into the two hostile blocs took almost a quarter of a century, from the formation of the Triple Alliance (1882) to the completion of the Triple Entente (1907). We need not follow it, or the subsequent developments, through all their labyrinthine details. They merely demonstrate that international friction in the period of imperialism was global and endemic, that nobody – least of all the British – knew quite in what direction the cross-currents of their and other powers' interests, fears and ambitions were taking them, and, though it was widely felt that they took Europe towards a major war, none of the governments knew quite what to do about it. Time and again attempts failed to break up the bloc system, or at least to offset it by rapprochements across the blocs: between Britain and Germany, Germany and Russia, Germany and France, Russia and Austria. The blocs, reinforced by inflexible plans for strategy and mobilization, grew more rigid, the continent drifted uncontrollably towards battle, through a series of international crises which, after 1905, were increasingly settled by 'brinkmanship' – i.e. by the threat of war.

For from 1905 on the destabilization of the international situation in consequence of the new wave of revolutions on the margins of the fully 'bourgeois' societies added new combustible material to a world already preparing to go up in flames. There was the Russian Revolution of 1905, which temporarily incapacitated the Tsarist Empire, encouraging Germany to assert her claims in Morocco, browbeating France. Berlin was forced to retreat at the Algeciras conference (January 1906) by British support for France, partly because a major war on a purely colonial issue was politically unattractive, partly because the German navy felt far too weak as yet to face a war against the British navy. Two years later the Turkish Revolution destroyed the carefully constructed arrangements for international balance in the always explosive Near East. Austria used the opportunity formally to annex Bosnia–Hercegovina (which she had previously just administered), thus precipitating a crisis with Russia, settled only by threat of military support for Austria by Germany. The third great international crisis, over Morocco in 1911, admittedly had little to do with revolution, and everything to do with imperialism – and the shady operations of freebooting businessmen who recognized its multiple possibilities. Germany sent a gunboat ready to seize the south Moroccan port of Agadir, in order to gain some 'compensation' from the French for their imminent 'protectorate' over Morocco, but was forced into retreat by what appeared to be a British threat to go to war on the side of the French. Whether this was actually intended is irrelevant.

The Agadir crisis demonstrated that almost any confrontation between two major powers now brought them to the brink of war. When the collapse of the Turkish Empire continued, with Italy attacking and occupying Libya in 1911, and Serbia, Bulgaria and Greece setting about expelling Turkey from the Balkan peninsula in 1912, all the powers were immobilized, either by unwillingness to antagonize a potential ally in Italy, which was by now uncommitted to either side, or by fear of being dragged into uncontrollable problems by the Balkan states. Nineteen-fourteen proved how right they were. Frozen into immobility they watched Turkey being almost driven out of Europe, and a second war between the victorious Balkan pygmy states redrawing the Balkan map in 1913. The most they could achieve was to establish an independent state in Albania (1913) – under the usual German prince, though such Albanians as cared about the matter would have preferred a maverick English aristocrat who later inspired the adventure novels of John Buchan. The next Balkan crisis was precipitated on 28 June 1914 when the Austrian heir to the throne, the Archduke Franz Ferdinand, visited the capital of Bosnia, Sarajevo.

What made the situation even more explosive was that, precisely in this period, domestic politics in the major powers pushed their foreign policies into the danger-zone. As we have seen (see pp. 109, 300 above), after 1905 the political mechanisms for the stable management of regimes began to creak audibly. It became increasingly difficult to control, still more to absorb and integrate, the mobilizations and counter-mobilizations of subjects in the process of turning into democratic citizens. Democratic politics itself had a high-risk element, even in a state like Britain, careful to keep actual foreign policy secret not only from Parliament but from part of the Liberal cabinet. What turned the Agadir crisis from an occasion for potential horse-trading into a zero-sum confrontation was a public speech by Lloyd George, which seemed to leave Germany with no option except war or retreat. Non-democratic politics were even worse. Could one not argue: 'that the principal cause of the tragic Europe breakdown in July 1914 was the inability of the democratic forces in central and eastern Europe to establish control over the militarist elements in their society and the abdication of the autocrats not to their loyal democratic subjects but to their irresponsible military advisers'?[15] And worst of all, would not countries faced with insoluble domestic problems be tempted to take the gamble of solving them by foreign triumph, especially when their military advisers told them that, since war was certain, the best time for it was now?

This was plainly not the case in Britain and France, in spite of their troubles. It probably was the case in Italy, though fortunately Italian adventurism could not itself set off world war. Was it in Germany? Historians continue to argue about the effect of domestic German politics on its foreign policy. It seems clear that (as in all other powers) grassroots right-wing agitation encouraged and assisted the competitive armaments race, especially at sea. It has been claimed that labour unrest and the electoral advance of Social Democracy made ruling elites keen to defuse trouble at home with success abroad. Certainly there were plenty of conservatives who, like the Duke of Ratibor, thought that a war was needed to get the old order back on its feet, as it had done in 1864–71.[16] Still, probably this amounted to no more than that the civilians would be rather less sceptical of the arguments of their bellicose generals than they might otherwise have been. Was it the case in Russia? Yes, insofar as tsarism, restored after 1905 with modest concessions to political liberalization, probably saw its most promising strategy for revival and reinforcement in the appeal to Great Russian nationalism and the glory of military strength. And indeed, but for the solid and enthusiastic loyalty of the armed forces, the situation in 1913–14 would have been closer to revolution than at any time between 1905 and 1917. Still, in 1914 Russia certainly did not want war. But, thanks to a few years of military build-up, which German generals feared, it was possible for Russia to contemplate a war in 1914, as it patently had not been a few years earlier.

However, there was one power which could not but stake its existence on the military gamble, because it seemed doomed without it: Austria–Hungary, torn since the mid-1890s by increasingly unmanageable national problems, among which those of the southern Slavs seemed to be the most racalcitrant and dangerous for three reasons. First, because not merely were they troublesome as were other politically organized nationalities in the multinational empire, jostling each other for advantages, but they complicated matters by belonging both to the linguistically flexible government of Vienna and to the ruthlessly magyarizing government of Budapest. Southern Slav agitation in Hungary not only spilled over into Austria, but aggravated the always difficult relations of the two halves of the empire with each other. Second, because the Austrian Slav problem could not be disentangled from Balkan politics, and had indeed since 1878 been even more deeply entangled in them by the occupation of Bosnia. Moreover, there already existed an independent south Slav state of Serbia (not to mention Montenegro, a Homeric little highland state of raiding goatherds, gun-fighters and prince-bishops with a taste for blood-feud and the composition of heroic epics) which could tempt southern Slav dissidents in the empire. Third, because the collapse of the Ottoman Empire virtually doomed the Habsburg Empire, unless it could establish beyond any doubt that it was still a great power in the Balkans which nobody could mess about.

To the end of his days Gavrilo Prinčip, the assassin of Archduke Franz Ferdinand, could not believe that his tiny match put the world in flames. The final crisis in 1914 was so totally unexpected, so traumatic and, in retrospect, so haunting, because it was essentially an incident in Austrian politics which, Vienna felt, required 'teaching Serbia a lesson'. The international atmosphere seemed calm. No foreign office expected trouble in June 1914, and public persons had been assassinated at frequent intervals for decades. In principle, nobody even minded a great power leaning heavily on a small and troublesome neighbour. Since then some five thousand books have been written to explain the apparently inexplicable: how, within a little more than five weeks of Sarajevo, Europe found itself at war.* The immediate answer now seems both clear and trivial: Germany decided to give Austria full backing, that is to say not to defuse the situation. The rest followed inexorably. For by 1914 *any* confrontation between the blocs, in which

---

* With the exception of Spain, Scandinavia, the Netherlands and Switzerland, all European states were eventually involved in it, as also Japan and the USA.

one side or the other was expected to back down, brought them to the verge of war. Beyond a certain point the inflexible mobilizations of military force, without which such a confrontation would not have been 'credible', could not be reversed. 'Deterrence' could no longer deter but only destroy. By 1914 *any* incident, however random – even the action of an inefficient student terrorist in a forgotten corner of the continent – could lead to such a confrontation, if any single power locked into the system of bloc and counter-bloc chose to take it seriously. Thus war came, and, in comparable circumstances, could come again.

In short, international crisis and domestic crisis merged in the last years before 1914. Russia, once again menaced by social revolution, Austria, threatened by the disintegration of a politically no longer controllable multiple empire, even Germany, polarized and perhaps threatened with immobilism by her political divisions – all tilted towards their military and its solutions. Even France, united by a reluctance to pay taxes and therefore to find money for massive rearmament (it was easier to extend conscript service again to three years), elected a president in 1913 who called for revenge against Germany and made warlike noises, echoing the generals who were now, with murderous optimism, abandoning a defensive strategy for the prospect of a storming offensive across the Rhine. The British preferred battleships to soldiers: the navy was always popular, a national glory acceptable to Liberals as the protector of trade. Naval scares had political sex-appeal, unlike army reforms. Few, even among their politicians, realized that the plans for joint war with France implied a mass army and eventually conscription, and indeed they did not seriously envisage anything except a primarily naval and trade war. Still, even though the British government remained pacific to the last – or rather, refused to take a stand for fear of splitting the Liberal government – it could not consider staying out of the war. Fortunately the German invasion of Belgium, long prepared under the Schlieffen Plan, provided London with a morality cover for diplomatic and military necessity.

But how would the masses of Europeans react to a war which could not but be a war of the masses, since all belligerents except the British prepared to fight it with conscript armies of enormous size? In August 1914, even before hostilities broke out 19 million, and potentially 50 million, armed men faced each other across the frontiers.[17] What would the attitude of these masses be when called to the colours, and what would the impact of war be on civilians especially if, as some military men shrewdly suspected – though taking little account of it in their planning – the war would not be over quickly? The British were particularly alive to this problem, because they relied exclusively on volunteers to reinforce their modest professional army of 20 divisions (compared with 74 French, 94 German and 108 Russian ones), because their working classes were fed mainly by food shipped from overseas which was extremely vulnerable to a blockade, and because in the immediate pre-war years government faced a public mood of social tension and agitation unknown in living memory, and an explosive situation in Ireland. 'The atmosphere of war', thought the Liberal minister John Morley, 'cannot be friendly to order in a democratic system that is verging on the humour of [18]48.'* But the domestic atmosphere of the other powers was also such as to disturb their governments. It is a mistake to believe that in 1914 governments rushed into war to defuse their internal social crises. At most, they calculated that patriotism would minimize serious resistance and non-cooperation.

In this they were correct. Liberal, humanitarian and religious opposition to war had always been negligible in practice, though no government (with the eventual exception of the British) was prepared to recognize a refusal to perform military service on grounds of conscience. The organized labour and socialist movements were, on the whole, passionately opposed to militarism and war, and the Labour and Socialist International even committed itself in 1907 to an international general strike against war, but hard-headed politicians did not take this too seriously, though a wild man on the right assassinated the great French socialist leader and orator Jean Jaurès a few days before the war, as he desperately tried to save the peace. The main socialist parties were against such a strike, few believed it to be feasible, and in any case, as Jaurès recognized, 'once war has broken out, we can take no further action'.[20] As we have seen, the French Minister of the Interior did not even bother to arrest the dangerous anti-war militants of whom the police had carefully prepared a list for this purpose. Nationalist dissidence did not prove to be a serious factor immediately. In short, the governments' calls to arms met with no effective resistance.

But governments were mistaken in one crucial respect: they were taken utterly by surprise, as were the opponents of the war, by the extraordinary wave of patriotic enthusiasm with which their people appeared to plunge into a conflict in which at least 20 millions of them were to be killed and wounded, without counting the incalculable millions of births forgone and excess civilian deaths through hunger and disease. The French authorities had reckoned with 5–13 per cent of deserters: in fact only 1.5 per cent dodged the draft in 1914. In Britain, where political opposition to the war was strongest, and where it was deeply rooted in Liberal as well as Labour and socialist tradition,

* Paradoxically the fear of the possible effects of starvation on the British working class suggested to naval strategists the possibility of destabilizing Germany by a blockade which would starve its people. This was in fact attempted with considerable success during the war.[19]

750,000 volunteered in the first eight weeks, a further million in the next eight months.[21] The Germans, as expected, did not dream of disobeying orders. 'How will anyone be able to say we do not love our fatherland when after the war so and so many thousands of our good party comrades say "we have been decorated for bravery".' Thus wrote a German social democratic militant, having just won the Iron Cross in 1914.[22] In Austria not only the dominant people were shaken by a brief wave of patriotism. As the Austrian socialist leader Victor Adler acknowledged, 'even in the nationalities struggle war appears as a kind of deliverance, a hope that something different will come'.[23] Even in Russia, where a million deserters had been expected, all but a few thousands of the 15 millions obeyed the call to the colours. The masses followed the flags of their respective states, and abandoned the leaders who opposed the war. There were, indeed, few enough left of these, at least in public. In 1914 the peoples of Europe, for however brief a moment, went lightheartedly to slaughter and to be slaughtered. After the First World War they never did so again.

They were surprised by the moment, but no longer by the fact of war, to which Europe had become accustomed, like people who see a thunderstorm coming. In a way its coming was widely felt as a release and a relief, especially by the young of the middle classes – men very much more than women – though less so by workers and least by peasants. Like a thunderstorm it broke the heavy closeness of expectation and cleared the air. It meant an end to the superficialities and frivolities of bourgeois society, the boring gradualism of nineteenth-century improvement, the tranquillity and peaceful order which was the liberal utopia for the twentieth century and which Nietzsche had prophetically denounced, together with the 'pallid hypocrisy administered by mandarins'.[24] After a long wait in the auditorium, it meant the opening of the curtain on a great and exciting historical drama in which the audience found itself to be the actors. It meant decision.

Was it recognized as the crossing of a historical frontier – one of those rare dates marking the periodization of human civilization which are more than pedagogic conveniences? Probably yes, in spite of the widespread expectations of a short war, of a foreseeable return to ordinary life and the 'normalcy' retrospectively identified with 1913, which imbues so many of the recorded opinions of 1914. Even the illusions of the patriotic and militarist young who plunged into war as into a new element, 'like swimmers into cleanness leaping'.[25] had implied utter change. The sense of the war as an epoch ended was perhaps strongest in the world of politics, even though few were as clearly aware as the Nietzsche of the 1880s of the 'era of monstrous [*ungeheure*] wars, upheavals [*Umstürze*], explosions' which had now begun,[26] and even fewer on the left, interpreting it in their own way, saw hope in it, like Lenin. For the socialists the war was an immediate and double catastrophe, as a movement devoted to internationalism and peace collapsed suddenly into impotence, and the wave of national union and patriotism under the ruling classes swept, however momentarily, over the parties and even the class-conscious proletariat in the belligerent countries. And among the statesmen of the old regimes there was at least one who recognized that all had changed. 'The lamps are going out all over Europe,' said Edward Grey, as he watched the lights of Whitehall turned off on the evening when Britain and Germany went to war. 'We shall not see them lit again in our lifetime.'

Since August 1914 we have lived in the world of monstrous wars, upheavals and explosions which Nietzsche prophetically announced. That is what has surrounded the era before 1914 with the retrospective haze of nostalgia, a faintly golden age of order and peace, of unproblematic prospects. Such back projections of imaginary good old days belong to the history of the last decades of the twentieth century, not the first. Historians of the days before the lights went out are not concerned with them. Their central preoccupation, and the one which runs through the present book, must be to understand and to show how the era of peace, of confident bourgeois civilization, growing wealth and western empires inevitably carried within itself the embryo of the era of war, revolution and crisis which put an end to it.

EPILOGUE

Wirklich, ich lebe in finsteren Zeiten!
Das arglose Wort ist töricht. Eine glatte Stirn
Deutet auf Unempfindlichkeit hin. Der Lachende
Hat die furchtbare Nachricht
Nur noch nicht empfangen.

> Bertolt Brecht, 1937–38[1]

Preceding decades were for the first time perceived as a long, almost golden age of uninterrupted, steady forward movement. Just as according to Hegel, we begin to understand an era only as the curtain is rung down on it ('the owl of Minerva only spreads its wings with the falling of dusk'), so can we apparently bring ourselves to acknowledge the positive features only as we enter a subsequent one, whose troubles we now wish to underline by painting a strong contrast with what came before.

> Albert O. Hirschman, 1986[2]

I

If the word 'catastrophe' had been mentioned among the members of the European middle classes before 1913, it would almost certainly have been in connection with one of the few traumatic events in which men and women like themselves were involved in the course of a lengthy, and in general tranquil, lifetime: say, the burning of the Karltheater in Vienna in 1881 during a performance of Offenbach's *Tales of Hoffmann*, in which almost 1500 lives were lost, or the sinking of the *Titanic* with a similar number of victims. The much greater catastrophes which affect the lives of the poor – like the 1908 earthquake in Messina, so much vaster and more neglected than the more modest tremors of San Francisco (1905) – and the persistent risks to life, limb and health which always dogged the existence of the labouring classes, are still apt to attract less public attention.

328

After 1914 it is a safe bet that the word suggested other and greater calamities even to those most immune to them in their personal lives. The First World War did not turn out to be 'The Last Days of Humanity', as Karl Kraus called it in his denunciatory quasi-drama, but nobody who lived an adult life both before and after 1914–18 anywhere in Europe, and increasingly in large stretches of the non-European world, could fail to observe that times had changed dramatically.

The most obvious and immediate change was that world history now appeared to proceed by a series of seismic upheavals and human cataclysms. Never did the pattern of progress or continuous change appear less plausible than in the lifetime of those who lived through two world wars, two global bouts of revolutions following each of the wars, a period of wholesale and partly revolutionary global decolonization, two bouts of massive expulsions of peoples culminating in genocide, and at least one economic crisis so severe as to raise doubts about the very future of those parts of capitalism not already overthrown by revolution, – upheavals which affected continents and countries quite remote from the zone of war and European political upheaval. A person born in, say, 1900 would have experienced all these at first hand, or through the mass media which made them immediately accessible, before he or she reached the age of pensionable retirement. And, of course, the pattern of history by upheaval was to continue.

Before 1914 virtually the only quantities measured in millions, outside astronomy, were populations of countries and the data of production, commerce and finance. Since 1914 we have become used to measuring the numbers of victims in such magnitudes: the casualties of even localized wars (Spain, Korea, Vietnam) – larger ones are measured in tens of millions – the numbers of those driven into forced migration or exile (Greeks, Germans, Moslems in the Indian subcontinent, kulaks), even the number massacred in genocide (Armenians, Jews), not to mention those killed by famine or epidemics. Since such human magnitudes escape precise recording or elude the grasp of the human mind, they are hotly debated. But the debates are about *millions* more or less. Nor are these astronomic figures to be entirely explained, and still less justified, by the rapid growth of the world population in our century. Most of them occurred in areas which were not growing all that fast.

Hecatombs on this scale were beyond the range of imagination in the nineteenth century, and those which actually occurred, took place in the world of backwardness or barbarism outside the range of progress and 'modern civilization', and were surely destined to retreat in the face of universal, if uneven, advance. The atrocities of Congo and Amazon, modest in scale by modern standards, so shocked the Age of

Empire – witness Joseph Conrad's *Heart of Darkness* – just because they appeared as regressions of civilized men into savagery. The state of affairs to which we have become accustomed, in which torture has once again become part of police methods in countries priding themselves on their record of civility, would not merely have profoundly repelled political opinion, but would have been, justifiably, regarded as a relapse into barbarism, which went against every observable historical trend of development since the mid-eighteenth century.

After 1914 mass catastrophe, and increasingly the methods of barbarism, became an integral and expected part of the civilized world, so much so that it masked the continued and striking advances of technology and the human capacity to produce, and even the undeniable improvements in human social organization in many parts of the world, until these became quite impossible to overlook during the huge forward leap of the world economy in the third quarter of the twentieth century. In terms of the material improvement of the lot of humanity, not to mention of the human understanding and control over nature, the case for seeing the history of the twentieth century as progress is actually rather more compelling than it was in the nineteenth. For even as Europeans died and fled in their millions, the survivors were becoming more numerous, taller, healthier, longer-lived. And most of them lived better. But the reasons why we have got out of the habit of thinking of our history as progress are obvious. For even when twentieth-century progress is most undeniable, prediction suggests not a continued ascent, but the possibility, perhaps even the imminence, of some catastrophe: another and more lethal world war, an ecological disaster, a technology whose triumphs may make the world uninhabitable by the human species, or whatever current shape the nightmare may take. We have been taught by the experience of our century to live in the expectation of apocalypse.

But for the educated and comfortable members of the bourgeois world who lived through this era of catastrophe and social convulsion, it seemed to be, in the first instance, not a fortuitous cataclysm, something like a global hurricane which impartially devastated everything in its path. It seemed to be directed specifically at their social, political and moral order. Its probable outcome, which bourgeois liberalism was powerless to prevent, was the social revolution of the masses. In Europe the war produced not only the collapse or crisis of every state and regime east of the Rhine and the western edge of the Alps, but also the first regime which set out, deliberately and systematically, to turn this collapse into the global overthrow of capitalism, the destruction of the bourgeoisie and the establishment of a socialist society. This was the Bolshevik regime brought to power in Russia by the collapse of tsarism.

As we have seen, mass movements of the proletariat dedicated to this aim in theory were already in existence in most parts of the developed world, although politicians in parliamentary countries had concluded that they provided no real threat to the status quo. But the combination of war, collapse and the Russian Revolution made the danger immediate and, almost, overwhelming.

The danger of 'Bolshevism' dominates not only the history of the years immediately following the Russian Revolution of 1917, but the entire history of the world since that date. It has given even its international conflicts for long periods the appearance of civil and ideological war. In the late twentieth century it still dominated the rhetoric of super-power confrontation, at least unilaterally, even though the most cursory look at the world of the 1980s showed that it simply did not fit into the image of a single global revolution about to overwhelm what international jargon called the 'developed market economies', still less one orchestrated from a single centre and aiming at the construction of a single monolithic socialist system unwilling to coexist with capitalism or incapable of doing so. The history of the world since the First World War took shape in the shadow of Lenin, imagined or real, as the history of the western world in the nineteenth century took shape in the shadow of the French Revolution. In both cases it eventually moved out of that shadow, but not entirely. Just as politicians even in 1914, speculated about whether the mood of the pre-war years had recalled 1848, so in the 1980s every overthrow of some regime anywhere in the west or the Third World evokes hopes or fears of 'Marxist power'.

The world did not turn socialist, even though in 1917–20 this was regarded as possible, even in the long run as inevitable, not only by Lenin but, at least for a moment, by those who represented and governed bourgeois regimes. For a few months even European capitalists, or at least their intellectual spokesmen and administrators, seemed resigned to euthanasia, as they faced socialist working-class movements enormously strengthened since 1914, and indeed, in some countries like Germany and Austria, constituting the only organized and potentially state-sustaining forces left in being by the collapse of the old regimes. Anything was better than Bolshevism, even peaceful abdication. The extensive debates (mainly in 1919) on how much of the economies were to be socialized, how they were to be socialized, and how much was to be conceded to the new powers of the proletariats were not purely tactical manoeuvres to gain time. They merely turned out to have been such when the period of serious danger to the system, real or imagined, proved to have been so brief that nothing drastic needed to be done after all.

In retrospect we can see that the alarm was exaggerated. The moment of potential world revolution left behind nothing but a single communist regime in an extraordinarily weakened and backward country whose main asset lay in the vast size and resources that were to make her into a political super-power. It also left behind the considerable potential of anti-imperialist, modernizing and peasant revolution, at that time mainly in Asia, which recognized its affinities with the Russian Revolution, and those parts of the now divided pre-1914 socialist and labour movements which threw in their lot with Lenin. In industrial countries these communist movements generally represented a minority of the labour movements until the Second World War. As the future was to demonstrate, the economies and societies of the 'developed market economies' were remarkably tough. Had they not been, they could hardly have emerged without social revolution from some thirty years of historical gales which might have been expected to wreck unseaworthy vessels. The twentieth century has been full of social revolutions, and there may well be more of them before it ends; but the developed industrial societies have been more immune to them than any others, except when revolution came to them as the by-product of military defeat or conquest.

Revolution thus left the main bastions of world capitalism standing, though for a while even their defenders thought they were about to crumble. The old order fought off the challenge. But it did so – it *had* to do so – by turning itself into something very different from what it had been in 1914. For after 1914, faced with what an eminent liberal historian called 'the world crisis' (Elie Halévy), bourgeois liberalism was entirely at a loss. It could abdicate or be swept away. Alternatively, it could assimilate itself to something like the non-Bolshevik, non-revolutionary, 'reformist' social democratic parties which actually emerged in western Europe as the chief guarantors of social and political continuity after 1917, and consequently turned from parties of opposition into parties of potential or actual government. In short, it could disappear or make itself unrecognizable. But in its old form it could no longer cope.

Giovanni Giolitti (1842–1928) of Italy (see pp. 87, 97, 102 above) is an example of the first fate. As we have seen, he had been brilliantly successful at 'managing' the Italian politics of the early 1900s: conciliating and taming labour, buying political support, wheeling and dealing, conceding, avoiding confrontations. In the socially revolutionary post-war situation of his country these tactics utterly failed him. The stability of bourgeois society was re-established by means of the armed middle-class gangs of 'nationalists' and fascists, literally waging the class war against a labour movement incapable of itself making a revolution. The (liberal) politicians supported them, vainly hoping to be able to integrate them into their system. In 1922 the fascists took over as government, after which democracy, parliament, parties and the old liberal politicians were eliminated. The Italian case was merely one among many. Between 1920 and 1939 parliamentary democratic systems virtually disappeared from most European states, non-communist as well as communist.* The fact speaks for itself. For a generation liberalism in Europe seemed doomed.

John Maynard Keynes, also discussed above (see pp. 177, 184), is an example of the second choice, all the more interesting because he actually remained all his life a supporter of the British Liberal Party and a class-conscious member of what he called his class, 'the educated bourgeoisie'. As a young economist Keynes had been almost quintessentially orthodox. He believed, rightly, that the First World War was both pointless and incompatible with a liberal economy, not to mention with bourgeois civilization. As a professional adviser to wartime governments after 1914, he favoured the least possible interruption of 'business as usual'. Again, quite logically, he saw the great (Liberal) war-leader Lloyd George as leading Britain to economic perdition by subordinating everything else to the achievement of military victory.† He was horrified but not surprised to see large parts of Europe and what he regarded as European civilization collapse in defeat and revolution. Once again correctly, he concluded that an irresponsible politicking peace treaty imposed by the victors would jeopardize what chances of restoring German, and therefore European, capitalist stability on a liberal basis. However, faced with the irrevocable disappearance of the pre-war *belle époque* which he had so much enjoyed with his friends from Cambridge and Bloomsbury, Keynes henceforth devoted all his considerable intellectual brilliance, ingenuity and gifts of style and propaganda to finding a way of saving capitalism from itself.

He consequently found himself revolutionizing economics, the social science most wedded to the market economy in the Age of Empire, and which had avoided feeling that sense of crisis so evident in other social sciences (see pp. 270, 271 above). Crisis, first political and then economic, was the foundation of the Keynesian rethinking of liberal orthodoxies. He became a champion of an economy managed and controlled by the state such as would, in spite of Keynes' evident dedication to capitalism,

---

* In 1939, of the twenty-seven states of Europe, the only ones which could be described as parliamentary democracies were the United Kingdom, the Irish Free State, France, Belgium, Switzerland, the Netherlands and the four Scandinavian states (Finland only just). Of these all but the United Kingdom, the Irish Free State, Sweden and Switzerland soon disappeared temporarily under occupation by or alliance with fascist Germany.

† His attitude to the Second World War, fought against fascist Germany, was naturally very different.

have been regarded as the ante-chamber of socialism by every ministry of finance in every developed industrial economy before 1914.

Keynes is worth singling out because he formulated what was to be the most intellectually and politically influential way of saying that capitalist society could only survive if capitalist states controlled, managed and even planned much of the general shape of their economies, if necessary turning themselves into mixed public/private economies. The lesson was congenial after 1944 to reformist, social democratic and radical-democratic ideologists and governments, who took it up with enthusiasm, insofar as they had not, as in Scandinavia, pioneered such ideas independently. For the lesson that capitalism on the pre-1914 liberal terms was dead was learned almost universally in the period of the two world wars and the world slump, even by those who refused to give it new theoretical labels. For forty years after the early 1930s the intellectual supporters of pure free-market economics were an isolated minority, apart from businessmen whose perspective always makes it difficult to recognize the best interests of their system as a whole, in proportion as it concentrates their minds on the best interests of their particular firm or industry.

The lesson had to be learned, because the alternative in the period of the Great Slump of the 1930s was not a market-induced recovery, but collapse. This was not, as revolutionaries hopefully thought, the 'final crisis' of capitalism, but it was probably the only genuinely system-endangering economic crisis so far in the history of an economic system which operates essentially through cyclical fluctuations.

Thus the years between the start of the First and the aftermath of the Second World War were a period of extraordinary crises and convulsions in history. They can best be regarded as the era when the world pattern of the Age of Empire collapsed under the force of the explosions it had been quietly generating in the long years of peace and prosperity. What collapsed was clear: the liberal world system and nineteenth-century bourgeois society as the norm to which, as it were, any kind of 'civilization' aspired. This, after all, was the era of fascism. What the shape of the future would be remained unclear until the middle of the century, and even then the new developments, though perhaps predictable, were so unlike what people had grown accustomed to in the era of convulsions that they took almost a generation to recognize what was happening.

II

The period which succeeded this era of collapse and transition, and which still continues, is probably, in terms of the social transformations which affect the ordinary men and women of the world – growing in numbers at a rate unprecedented even in the previous history of the industrializing world – the most revolutionary ever experienced by the human race. For the first time since the stone age the world population was ceasing to consist of people who lived by agriculture and livestock. In all parts of the globe except (as yet) sub-Saharan Africa and the southern quadrant of Asia, peasants were now a minority, in developed countries a tiny minority. This happened in a matter of a single generation. Consequently the world – and not only the old 'developed' countries – became urban, while economic development, including major industrialization, was internationalized or globally redistributed in a manner inconceivable before 1914. Contemporary technology, thanks to the internal-combustion engine, the transistor, the pocket calculator, the omni-visible aeroplane, not to mention the modest bicycle, has penetrated the remotest corners of the planet, which are accessible to commerce in a way which few could have imagined even in 1939. Social structures, at least in the developed societies of western capitalism, have been dramatically shaken, including that of the traditional family and household. It is now possible to recognize in retrospect how much of what made nineteenth-century bourgeois society function was in fact inherited and taken over from a past which the very processes of its development were bound to destroy. All this has happened within a, by historical standards, incredibly brief period – within the memory of men and women born during the Second World War – as the product of the most massive and extraordinary boom of world economic expansion ever experienced. A century after Marx's and Engels' *Communist Manifesto* its predictions of the economic and social effects of capitalism seemed to be realized – but not, in spite of the rule of a third of humanity by their disciples, the overthrow of capitalism by the proletariat.

This period is clearly one in which nineteenth-century bourgeois society and all that went with it belong to a past that no longer immediately determines the present, though, of course, both the nineteenth century and the late twentieth are part of the same long period of the revolutionary transformation of humanity – and nature – which became recognizably revolutionary in the last quarter of the eighteenth. Historians may notice the odd coincidence that the super-boom of the twentieth century occurred exactly one hundred years after the great mid-nineteenth-century boom (1850–73, 1950–73), and consequently the late-twentieth-century period of world economic troubles since 1973, began just one hundred years after the Great Depression with which the present book started. But there is no relation between these facts, unless someone were to discover some cyclical mechanism of the economy's movement which would produce such a neat chronological repetition; and this is rather improbable. Most of us do not want to or need to go back to the 1880s to explain what was troubling the world in the 1980s or 1990s.

And yet the world of the late twentieth century is still shaped by the bourgeois century, and in particular by the Age of Empire, which has been the subject of this volume. Shaped in the literal sense. Thus, for instance, the world financial arrangements which were to provide the international framework for the global boom of the third quarter of this century were negotiated in the middle 1940s by men who had been adult in 1914, and who were utterly dominated by the past twenty-five years' experience of the Age of Empire's disintegration. The last important statesmen or national leaders who had been adults in 1914 died in the 1970s (eg. Mao, Tito, Franco, de Gaulle). But, more significantly, today's world was shaped by what one might call the historical landscape left behind by the Age of Empire and its collapse.

The most obvious piece of this heritage is the division of the world into socialist countries (or countries claiming to be such) and the rest. The shadow of Karl Marx presides over a third of the human race because of the developments we have tried to sketch in chapters 3, 5 and 12. Whatever one might have predicted about the future of the land-mass stretching from the China seas to the middle of Germany, plus a few areas in Africa and in the Americas, it is quite certain that regimes claiming to realize the prognoses of Karl Marx could not possibly have been among the futures envisaged for them until the emergence of mass socialist labour movements, whose example and ideology would in turn inspire the revolutionary movements of backward and dependent or colonial regions.

An equally obvious piece of the heritage is the very globalization of the world's political pattern. If the United Nations of the late twentieth century contain a considerable numerical majority of states from what came to be called the 'Third World' (and incidentally states out of sympathy with the 'western' powers), it is because they are, overwhelmingly, the relics of the division of the world among the imperial powers in the Age of Empire. Thus the decolonization of the French Empire has produced about twenty new states, that of the British Empire many more; and, at least in Africa (which at the time of writing consists of over fifty nominally independent and sovereign entities), all of them reproduce the frontiers drawn by conquest and inter-imperialist

336

negotiation. Again, but for the developments of that period, it was hardly to be expected that the great bulk of them would at the end of this century conduct the affairs of their educated strata and governments in English and French.

Somewhat less obvious an inheritance from the Age of Empire is that all these states should be described, and often describe themselves, as 'nations'. This is not only because, as I have tried to show, the ideology of 'nation' and 'nationalism', a nineteenth-century European product, could be used as an ideology of colonial liberation, and was imported as such by members of westernized elites of colonial peoples, but also because, as chapter 6 has argued, the concept of the 'nation-state' in this period became available to groups of *any* size which chose so to describe themselves, and not only, as the mid-nineteenth-century pioneers of 'the principle of nationality' took for granted, to medium or large peoples. For most of the states that have emerged to the world since the end of the nineteenth century (and which have, since President Wilson, been given the status of 'nations') were of modest size and/or population, and, since the onset of decolonization, often of tiny size.* Insofar as nationalism has penetrated outside the old 'developed' world, or insofar as non-European politics have become assimilated to nationalism, the heritage of the Age of Empire is still present.

It is equally present in the transformation of traditional western family relations, and especially in the emancipation of women. No doubt these transformations have been on an altogether more gigantic scale since the mid-century than ever before, but in fact it was during the Age of Empire that the 'new woman' first appeared as a significant phenomenon, and that political and social mass movements dedicated, among other things, to the emancipation of women became political forces: notably the labour and socialist movements. Women's movements in the west may have entered a new and more dynamic phase in the 1960s, perhaps largely as a result of the much increased entry of women, and especially married women, into paid employment outside the home, but it was only a phase in a major historical development which can be traced back to our period, and for practical purposes, not earlier.

Moreover, as this book has tried to make clear, the Age of Empire saw the birth of most of what is still characteristic of the modern urban society of mass culture, from the most international forms of spectator sport to press and film. Even technically the modern media are not fundamental innovations, but developments which have made more

---

* Twelve of the African states in the early 1980s had populations of less than 600,000, two of them of less than 100,000.

universally accessible the two basic devices introduced during the Age of Empire: the mechanical reproduction of sound and the moving photograph. The era of Jacques Offenbach has no continuity with the present comparable to the era of the young Fox, Zukor, Goldwyn and 'His Master's Voice'.

III

It is not difficult to discover other ways in which our lives are still formed by, or are continuations of, the nineteenth century in general and the Age of Empire in particular. Any reader could no doubt lengthen the list. But is this the main reflection suggested by looking back at nineteenth-century history? For it is still difficult, if not impossible, to look back dispassionately on that century which created world history because it created the modern capitalist world economy. For Europeans it carried a particular charge of emotion, because, more than any other, it was the European era in the world's history, and for the British among them it is unique because, and not only economically speaking, Britain was at its core. For North Americans it was the century when the USA ceased to be part of Europe's periphery. For the rest of the world's peoples it was the era when all the past history, however long and distinguished, came to a necessary halt. What has happened to them, or what they have done, since 1914 is implicit in what happened to them between the first industrial revolution and 1914.

It was a century which transformed the world – not more than our own century has done, but more strikingly, inasmuch as such revolutionary and continuous transformation was then new. Looking back, we can see this century of the bourgeoisie and of revolution suddenly heaving into view, like Nelson's battle-fleet getting ready for action, like it even in what we do not see: the kidnapped crews who manned them, short, poor, whipped and drunk, living on worm-eaten rusks. Looking back we can recognize that those who made it, and increasingly those growing masses who participated in it in the 'developed' west, knew that it was destined for extraordinary achievements, and thought that it was destined to solve all the major problems of humanity, to remove all the obstacles in the path of their solution.

In no century before or since have practical men and women had such high, such utopian, expectations for life on this earth: universal peace, universal culture by means of a single world language, science which would not merely probe but actually answer the most fundamental questions of the universe, the emancipation of women from all their past history, the emancipation of all humanity through the emancipation of the workers, sexual liberation, a society of plenty, a world in which each contributed according to their abilities and received what they needed. These were not only dreams of revolutionaries. Utopia through progress was in fundamental ways built into the century. Oscar Wilde was not joking when he said that no map of the world which did not contain Utopia was worth having. He was speaking for Cobden the free trader as well as for Fourier the socialist, for President Grant as well as for Marx (who rejected not utopian aims, but only utopian blue-prints), for Saint-Simon, whose utopia of 'industrialism' can be assigned neither to capitalism nor to socialism, because it can be claimed by both. But the novelty about the most characteristic nineteenth-century utopias was that in them history would *not* come to a stop.

Bourgeois expected an era of endless improvement, material, intellectual and moral, through liberal progress; proletarians, or those who saw themselves as speaking for them, expected it through revolution. But both expected it. And both expected it, not through some historic automatism, but through effort and struggle. The artists who expressed the cultural aspirations of the bourgeois century most profoundly, and became, as it were, the voices articulating its ideals, were those like Beethoven, who was seen as the genius who fought through to victory after struggle, whose music overcame the dark forces of destiny, whose choral symphony culminated in the triumph of the liberated human spirit.

In the Age of Empire there were, as we have seen, voices – and they were both profound and influential among the bourgeois classes – who foresaw different outcomes. But, on the whole, the era seemed, for most people in the west, to come closer than any before to the promise of the century. To its liberal promise, by material improvement, education and culture; to its revolutionary promise, by the emergence, the massed strength and the prospect of the inevitable future triumph of the new labour and socialist movements. For some, as this book has tried to show, the Age of Empire was one of growing uneasiness and fear. For most men and women in the world transformed by the bourgeoisie it was almost certainly an age of hope.

It is on this hope that we can now look back. We can still share it, but no longer without scepticism and uncertainty. We have seen too many promises of utopia realized without producing the expected results. Are we not living in an age when, in the most advanced countries, modern communications, means of transport and sources of energy have abolished the distinction between town and country, which was once thought achievable only in a society that had solved virtually

339

all its problems? But ours demonstrably has not. The twentieth century has seen too many moments of liberation and social ecstasy to have much confidence in their permanence. There is room for hope, for human beings are hoping animals. There is even room for great hopes for, in spite of appearances and prejudices to the contrary, the actual achievement of the twentieth century in material and intellectual progress – hardly in moral and cultural progress – is extraordinarily impressive and quite undeniable.

Is there still room for the greatest of all hopes, that of creating a world in which free men and women, emancipated from fear and material need, will live the good life together in a good society? Why not? The nineteenth century taught us that the desire for the perfect society is not satisfied by some predetermined design for living, Mormon, Owenite or whatever; and we may suspect that even if such a new design were to be the shape of the future, we would not know, or be able today to determine, what it would be. The function of the search for the perfect society is not to bring history to a stop, but to open out its unknown and unknowable possibilities to all men and women. In this sense the road to utopia, fortunately for the human race, is not blocked.

But, as we know, it can be blocked: by universal destruction, by a return to barbarism, by the dissolution of the hopes and values to which the nineteenth century aspired. The twentieth has taught us that these things are possible. History, the presiding divinity of both centuries, no longer gives us, as men and women used to think, the firm guarantee that humanity would travel into the promised land, whatever exactly this was supposed to be. Still less that they would reach it. It could come out differently. We know th at it can, because we live in the world the nineteenth century created, and we know that, titanic though its achievements were, they are not what was then expected or dreamed.

But if we can no longer believe that history guarantees us the right outcome, neither does it guarantee us the wrong one. It offers the option, without any clear estimate of the probability of our choice. The evidence that the world in the twenty-first century will be better is not negligible. If the world succeeds in not destroying itself, the probability will be quite strong. But it will not amount to certainty. The only certain thing about the future is that it will surprise even those who have seen furthest into it.

TABLES

TABLE I

STATES AND POPULATIONS 1880–1914 (MILLIONS OF PERSONS)

		1880	1914
E/K	*UK	35.3	45
R	*France	37.6	40
E	*Germany	45.2	68
E	*Russia	97.7	161 (1910)
E/K	*Austria	37.6	51
K	*Italy	28.5	36
K	Spain	16.7	20.5
K, 1908R	Portugal	4.2	5.25
K	Sweden	4.6	5.5
K	Norway	1.9	2.5
K	Denmark	2.0	2.75
K	Netherlands	4.0	6.5
K	Belgium	5.5	7.5
R	Switzerland	2.8	3.5
K	Greece	1.6	4.75
K	Roumania	5.3	7.5
K	Serbia	1.7	4.5
K	Bulgaria	2.0	4.5
K	Montenegro	–	0.2
K	Albania	0	0.8
E	Finland (in Russia)	2.0	2.9
R	USA	50.2	92.0 (1910)
E	Japan	c. 36	53
E	Ottoman Empire	c. 21	c. 20
E	China	c.420	c.450

Other states, orders of magnitude of population:

Over 10 millions	Brazil, Mexico
5–10 millions	Persia, Afghanistan, Argentina
2–5 millions	Chile, Colombia, Peru, Venezuela, Siam
Below 2 millions	Bolivia, Cuba, Costa Rica, Domin. Republic, Ecuador, El Salvador, Guatemala, Haiti, Honduras, Nicaragua, Panama, Paraguay, Uruguay

E = empire, K = kingdom, R = republic.
* The great powers of Europe.

TABLE 2

URBANISATION IN NINETEENTH-CENTURY EUROPE, 1800–1890

	Number of cities (10,000 and over)			Total urban population (percentage)		
	1800	1850	1890	1800	1850	1890
Europe	364	878	1709	10	16.7	29
N. and W.*	105	246	543	14.9	26.1	43.4
Central†	135	306	629	7.1	12.5	26.8
Mediterranean‡	113	292	404	12.9	18.6	22.2
Eastern§	11	34	133	4.2	7.5	18
England/Wales	44	148	356	20.3	40.8	61.9
Belgium	20	26	61	18.9	20.5	34.5
France	78	165	232	8.8	14.5	25.9
Germany	53	133	382	5.5	10.8	28.2
Austria/Bohemia	8	17	101	5.2	6.7	18.1
Italy	74	183	215	14.6	20.3	21.2
Poland	3	17	32	2.4	9.3	14.6

* Scandinavia, UK, Netherlands, Belgium
† Germany, France, Switzerland
‡ Italy, Spain, Portugal
§ Austria/Bohemia, Poland

Source: Jan deVries, *European Urbanisation 1500–1800* (London, 1984), Table 3.8.

TABLE 3

EMIGRATION TO LANDS OF EUROPEAN SETTLEMENT 1871–1911 (MILLIONS OF PERSONS)

Years	Total	Britain/ Ireland	Spain/ Portugal	Germany/ Austria	Others
1871–80	3.1	1.85	0.15	0.75	0.35
1881–90	7.0	3.25	0.75	1.8	1.2
1891–1900	6.2	2.15	1.0	1.25	1.8
1901–11	11.3	3.15	1.4	2.6	4.15
	27.6	10.4	3.3	6.4	7.5

IMMIGRATION TO (MILLIONS OF PERSONS):

Years	Total	USA	Canada	Argentina/ Brazil	Australia/ N.Z.	Others
1871–80	4.0	2.8	0.2	0.5	0.2	0.3
1881–90	7.5	5.2	0.4	1.4	0.3	0.2
1891–1900	6.4	3.7	0.2	1.8	.45	0.25
1900–11	14.9	8.8	1.1	2.45	1.6	0.95
	32.8	20.5	1.9	6.15	2.5	1.7

Based on A. M. Carr Saunders, *World Population* (London, 1936). The difference between the totals for immigration and emigration should warn readers about the unreliability of these calculations.

TABLE 4

ILLITERACY

1850	Countries of low illiteracy: below 30% adults	Medium illiteracy 30–50%	High illiteracy over 50%
	Denmark Sweden Norway Finland Iceland Germany Switzerland Netherlands Scotland USA (whites)	Austria Czech lands France England Ireland Belgium Australia	Hungary Italy Portugal Spain Rumania all Balkans & Greece Poland Russia USA (non-whites) rest of world
1913	Countries of low illiteracy: below 10%	Medium 10–30%	High above 30%
	(As above) France England Ireland Belgium Austria Australia New Zealand	N. Italy N.W. Yugoslavia (Slovenia)	Hungary Centr. & S. Italy Portugal Spain Rumania all Balkans & Greece Poland Russia USA (non-whites) rest of world

TABLE 5

UNIVERSITIES (NUMBER OF INSTITUTIONS)

	1875	1913
North America	c.360	c.500
Latin America	c.30	c.40
Europe	c.110	c.150
Asia	c.5	c.20
Africa	0	c.5
Australasia	2	c.5

MODERNITY

Newsprint used in different parts of the world, *c.* 1880

(Source: calculated from M. G. Mulhall, *The Progress of the World Since the Beginning of the Nineteenth Century* (London, 1880, reprinted 1971), p. 91.)

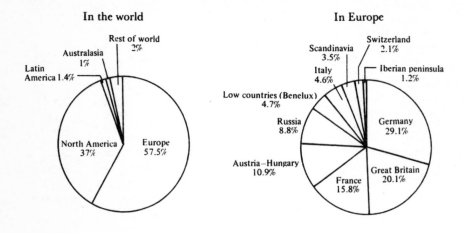

In the world

In Europe

Telephones in the world in 1912

(Source: *Weltwirtschaftliches Archiv*, 1913, I/ii, p. 143.)

World total (in 000s)	12,453
USA	8,362
Europe	3,239

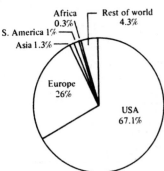

TABLE 6

THE PROGRESS OF THE TELEPHONE: SOME CITIES (PHONES PER 100 INHABITANTS

	1895	Rank	1911	Rank
Stockholm	4.1	1	19.9	2
Christiania (Oslo)	3	2	6.9	8
Los Angeles	2	3	24	1
Berlin	1.6	4	5.3	9
Hamburg	1.5	5	4.7	10
Copenhagen	1.2	6	7	7
Boston	1	7	9.2	4
Chicago	0.8	8	11	3
Paris	0.7	9	2.7	12
New York	0.6	10	8.3	6
Vienna	0.5	11	2.3	13
Philadelphia	0.3	12	8.6	5
London	0.2	13	2.8	11
St Petersburg	0.2	14	2.2	14

Source: *Weltwirtschaftliches Archiv*, 1913, I/ii, p. 143.

TABLE 7

% OF WORLD'S AREA IN INDEPENDENT STATES IN 1913

North America	32%
Central & South America	92.5%
Africa	3.4%
Asia	70% excluding Asiatic Russia
	43.2% including Asiatic Russia
Oceania	0%
Europe	99%

Source: calculated from *League of Nations International Statistical Yearbook* (Geneva, 1926).

TABLE 8

BRITISH INVESTMENTS ABROAD:% SHARE

	1860–70	1911–13
British Empire	36	46
Latin America	10.5	22
USA	27	19
Europe	25	6
Other	3.5	7

Source: C. Feinstein cited in M. Barratt Brown, *After Imperialism* (London 1963), p. 110.

TABLE 9

WORLD OUTPUT OF PRINCIPAL TROPICAL COMMODITIES, 1880–1910 (IN 000 TONS)

	1880	1900	1910
Bananas	30	300	1,800
Cocoa	60	102	227
Coffee	550	970	1,090
Rubber	11	53	87
Cotton fibre	950	1,200	1,770
Jute	600	1,220	1,560
Oil Seeds	–	–	2,700
Raw sugar cane	1,850	3,340	6,320
Tea	175	290	360

Source: P. Bairoch, *The Economic Development of the Third World Since 1900* (London, 1975), p. 15.

TABLE 10

WORLD PRODUCTION AND WORLD TRADE,
1781–1971 (1913 = 100)

	Production	Trade	
1781–90	1.8	2.2	(1780)
1840	7.4	5.4	
1870	19.5	23.8	
1880	26.9	38	(1881–5)
1890	41.1	48	(1891–5)
1900	58.7	67	(1901–5)
1913	100.0	100	
1929	153.3	113	(1930)
1948	274.0	103	
1971	950.0	520	

Source: W. W. Rostow, *The World Economy: History and Prospect* (London, 1978), Appendices A and B.

TABLE 11

SHIPPING: TONNAGE (VESSELS OVER 100 TONS ONLY) IN 000 TONS

	1881	1913
World total	18,325	46,970
Great Britain	7,010	18,696
USA	2,370	5,429
Norway	1,460	2,458
Germany	1,150	5,082
Italy	1,070	1,522
Canada	1,140	1,735*
France	840	2,201
Sweden	470	1,047
Spain	450	841
Netherlands	420	1,310
Greece	330	723
Denmark	230	762
Austria–Hungary	290	1,011
Russia	740	974

* British dominions.

Source: Mulhall, *Dictionary of Statistics* (London, 1881) and League of Nations, *International Statistics Yearbook 1913*, Table 76.

THE ARMAMENTS RACE

Military expenditure by the great powers (Germany, Austria–Hungary, Great Britain, Russia, Italy and France) 1880–1914

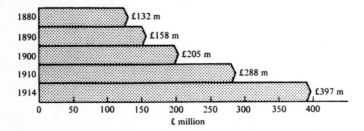

(Source: *The Times Atlas of World History* (London, 1978), p. 250.)

TABLE 12

ARMIES (IN 000s)

	1879		1913	
	Peacetime	Mobilized	Peacetime	Mobilized
Great Britain	136	*c*.600	160	700
India	*c*.200	–	249	
Austria–Hungary	267	772	800	3,000
France	503	1,000	1,200	3,500
Germany	419	1,300	2,200	3,800
Russia	766	1,213	1,400	4,400

TABLE 13

NAVIES (IN NUMBER OF BATTLESHIPS)

	1900	1914
Great Britain	49	64
Germany	14	40
France	23	28
Austria–Hungary	6	16
Russia	16	23

MAPS

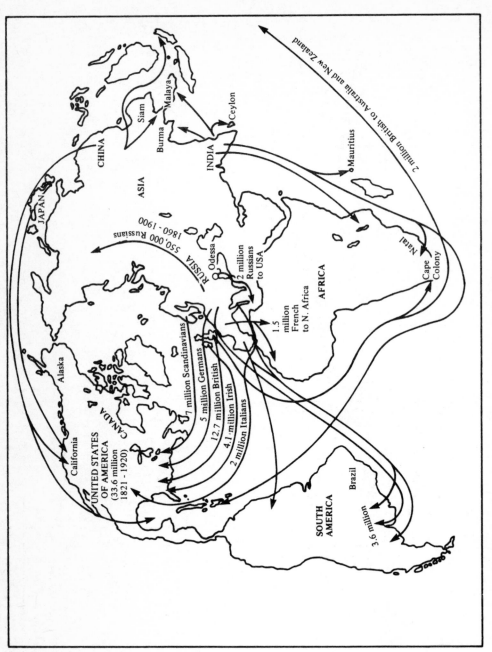

Map 1. International migrations 1820–1910 (Source: *The Times Atlas of World History*)

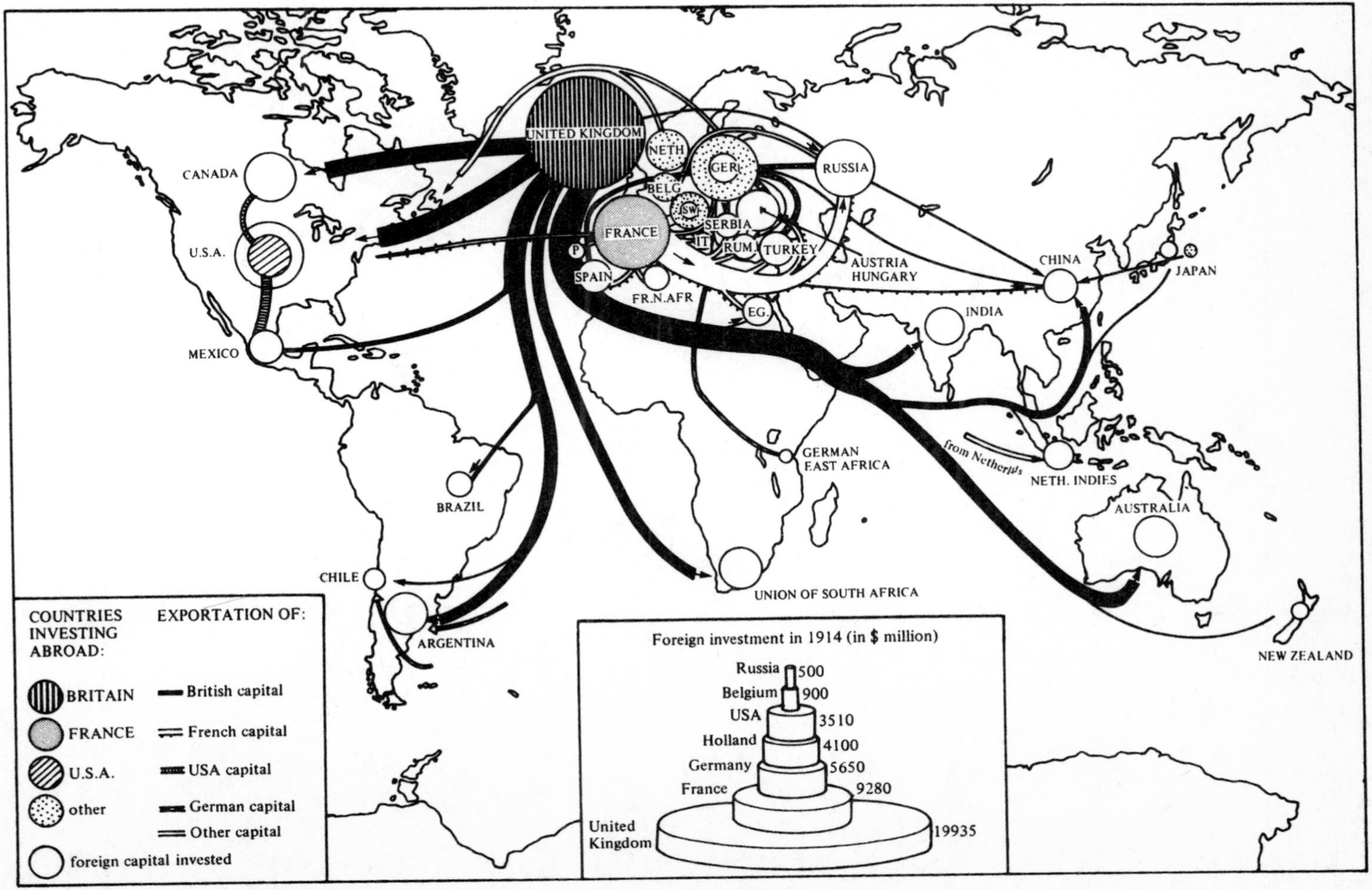

Map 2. Movements of capital 1875–1914

COUNTRIES
INVESTING
ABROAD:
BRITAIN
FRANCE
U.S.A.
other
○ foreign capital invested

EXPORTATION OF:
━━ British capital
══ French capital
▦ USA capital
▨ German capital
≡ Other capital

Foreign investment in 1914 (in $ million)

Russia 500
Belgium 900
USA 3510
Holland 4100
Germany 5650
France 9280
United Kingdom 19935

CANADA
U.S.A.
MEXICO
BRAZIL
CHILE
ARGENTINA
NEW ZEALAND
AUSTRALIA
NETH. INDIES
JAPAN
CHINA
INDIA
RUSSIA
AUSTRIA HUNGARY
GERMAN EAST AFRICA
UNION OF SOUTH AFRICA
UNITED KINGDOM
NETH
BELG
SW
GER
FRANCE
SPAIN
P
FR.N.AFR
EG
TURKEY
RUM
SERBIA
IT
from Netherpts

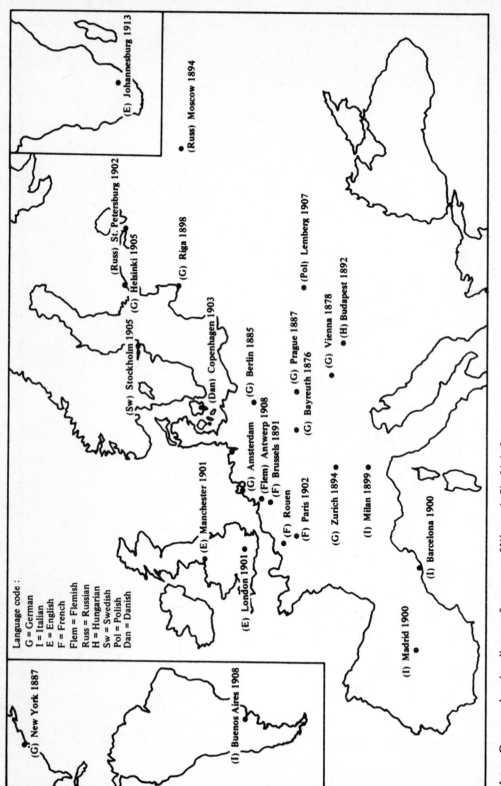

Map 3. Opera and nationalism: performances of Wagner's *Siegfried* 1875–1914

Language code :
G = German
I = Italian
E = English
F = French
Flem = Flemish
Russ = Russian
H = Hungarian
Sw = Swedish
Pol = Polish
Dan = Danish

(E) Johannesburg 1913

(Russ) Moscow 1894

(Russ) St. Petersburg 1902

(G) Helsinki 1905

(G) Riga 1898

(Pol) Lemberg 1907

(Sw) Stockholm 1905

(Dan) Copenhagen 1903

(G) Berlin 1885

(G) Prague 1887

(G) Vienna 1878

(H) Budapest 1892

(G) Amsterdam

(Flem) Antwerp 1908

(F) Brussels 1891

(G) Bayreuth 1876

(E) Manchester 1901

(F) Rouen

(F) Paris 1902

(G) Zurich 1894

(I) Milan 1899

(E) London 1901

(I) Barcelona 1900

(I) Madrid 1900

(G) New York 1887

(I) Buenos Aires 1908

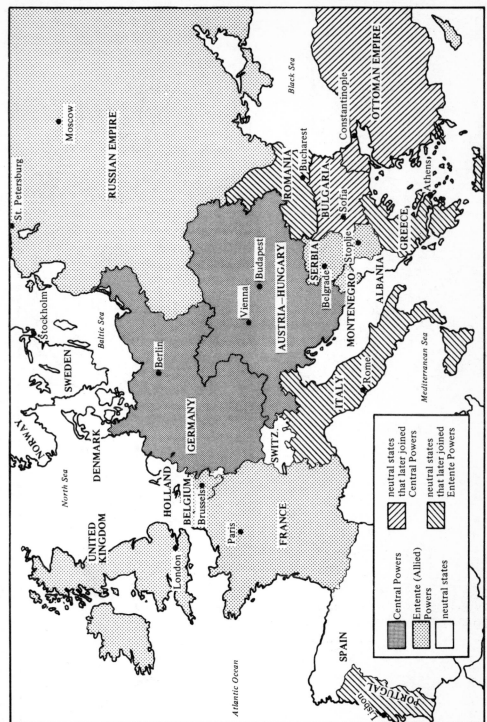

Map 4. Europe in 1914

Map 5. The world divided: empires in 1914

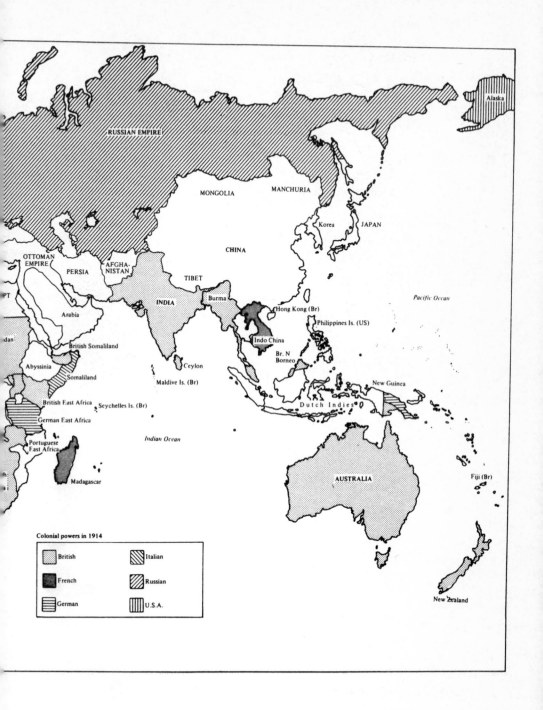

Colonial powers in 1914

British   Italian

French   Russian

German   U.S.A.

NOTES

OVERTURE

1 P. Nora in Pierre Nora (ed.), *Les lieux de la mémoire*, vol. I: *La République* (Paris 1984), p. XIX.
2 G. Barraclough, *An Introduction to Contemporary History* (London 1964), p. 1.

CHAPTER 1: THE CENTENARIAN REVOLUTION

1 Finlay Peter Dunne, *Mr Dooley Says* (New York 1910), pp. 46–7.
2 M. Mulhall, *Dictionary of Statistics* (London 1892 edn), p. 573.
3 P. Bairoch, 'Les grandes tendances des disparités économiques nationales depuis la Révolution Industrielle' in *Seventh International Economic History Congress, Edinburgh 1978: Four 'A' Themes* (Edinburgh 1978), pp. 175–86.
4 See V. G. Kiernan, *European Empires from Conquest to Collapse* (London 1982), pp. 34–6; and D. R. Headrick, *Tools of Empire* (New York 1981), *passim*.
5 Peter Flora, *State, Economy and Society in Western Europe 1815–1975: A Data Handbook*, I (Frankfurt, London and Chicago 1983), p. 78.
6 W. W. Rostow, *The World Economy: History and Prospect* (London 1978), p. 52.
7 Hilaire Belloc, *The Modern Traveller* (London 1898), vi.
8 P. Bairoch *et al.*, *The Working Population and Its Structure* (Brussels 1968) for such data.
9 H. L. Webb, *The Development of the Telephone in Europe* (London 1911).
10 P. Bairoch, *De Jéricho à Mexico: Villes et économie dans l'histoire* (Paris 1985), partie C, *passim* for data.
11 *Historical Statistics of the United States, From Colonial Times to 1957* (Washington 1960), census of 1890.
12 Carlo Cipolla, *Literacy and Development in the West* (Harmondsworth 1969), p. 76.
13 Mulhall, *op. cit.*, p. 245.
14 Calculated on the basis of *ibid.*, p. 546; *ibid.*, p. 549.
15 *Ibid.*, p. 100.

16 Roderick Floud, 'Wirtschaftliche und soziale Einflüsse auf die Körpergrössen von Europäern seit 1750', *Jahrbuch für Wirtschaftsgeschichte* (East Berlin 1985), II, pp. 93–118.

17 Georg v. Mayr, *Statistik und Gesellschaftslehre*, II: *Bevölkerungsstatistik*, 2 (Tübingen 1924), p. 427.

18 Mulhall, *op. cit.*, 'Post Office', 'Press', 'Science'.

19 *Cambridge Modern History* (Cambridge 1902), I, p. 4.

20 John Stuart Mill, *Utilitarianism, On Liberty and Representative Government* (Everyman edn, 1910), p. 73.

21 John Stuart Mill, 'Civilisation' in *Dissertations and Discussions* (London, n.d.), p. 130.

CHAPTER 2: AN ECONOMY CHANGES GEAR

1 A. V. Dicey, *Law and Public Opinion in the Nineteenth Century* (London 1905), p. 245.

2 Cited in E. Maschke, 'German Cartels from 1873–1914' in F. Crouzet, W. H. Chaloner and W. M. Stern (eds.), *Essays in European Economic History* (London 1969), p. 243.

3 From 'Die Handelskrisen und die Gewerkschaften', reprinted in *Die langen Wellen der Konjunktur. Beiträge zur Marxistischen Konjunktur- und Krisentheorie von Parvus, Karl Kautsky, Leo Trotski und Ernest Mandel* (Berlin 1972), p. 26.

4 D. A. Wells, *Recent Economic Changes* (New York 1889), pp. 1–2.

5 *ibid.*, p. vi.

6 Alfred Marshall, *Official Papers* (London 1926), p. 98–9.

7 C. R. Fay, *Cooperation at Home and Abroad* (1908; London 1948 edn), I, pp. 49 and 114.

8 Sidney Pollard, *Peaceful Conquest: The Industrialization of Europe 1760–1970* (Oxford 1981), p. 259.

9 F.X. v. Neumann-Spallart, *Übersichten der Weltwirthschaft*, *Jg. 1881–82* (Stuttgart 1884), pp. 153 and 185 for the basis of these calculations.

10 P. Bairoch, 'Città/Campagna' in *Enciclopedia Einaudi*, III (Turin 1977), p. 89.

11 See D. Landes, *Revolution in Time* (Harvard 1983), p. 289.

12 *Harvard Encyclopedia of American Ethnic Groups* (Cambridge, Mass. 1980), p. 750.

13 Williams' book was originally a series of alarmist articles published in the imperialist W. E. Henley's *New Review*. He was also active in the anti-aliens agitation.

14 C. P. Kindleberger, 'Group Behavior and International Trade', *Journal of Political Economy*, 59 (Feb. 1951), p. 37.

15 P. Bairoch, *Commerce extérieur et développement économique de l'Europe au XIXe siècle* (Paris–Hague 1976), pp. 309–11.

16 (Folke Hilgerdt), *Industrialization and Foreign Trade* (League of Nations, Geneva 1945), pp. 13, 132–4.

17 H. W. Macrosty, *The Trust Movement in British Industry* (London 1907), p. 1.

18 William Appleman Williams, *The Tragedy of American Diplomacy* (Cleveland and New York 1959), p. 44.

19 Bairoch, *De Jéricho à Mexico*, p. 288.

20 W. Arthur Lewis, *Growth and Fluctuations 1870–1913* (London 1978), appendix IV.

21 *Ibid.*, p. 275.

22 John R. Hanson II, *Trade in Transition: Exports from the Third World 1840–1900* (New York, 1980), p. 55.

23 Sidney Pollard, 'Capital Exports 1870–1914: Harmful or Beneficial?' *Economic History Review*, XXXVIII (1985), p. 492.

24 They were *Lloyd's Weekly* and *Le Petit Parisien*.

25 P. Mathias, *Retailing Revolution* (London 1967).

26 According to the estimates of J. A. Lesourd and Cl. Gérard, *Nouvelle Histoire Économique I: Le XIXe Siècle* (Paris 1976), p. 247.

CHAPTER 3: THE AGE OF EMPIRE

1 Cited in Wolfgang J. Mommsen, *Max Weber and German Politics 1890–1920* (Chicago 1984), p. 77.

2 Finlay Peter Dunne, *Mr Dooley's Philosophy* (New York 1900), pp. 93–4.

3 V. I. Lenin, 'Imperialism, the Latest Stage of Capitalism', originally published in mid-1917. The later (posthumous) editions of the work use the word 'highest' instead of 'latest'.

4 J. A. Hobson, *Imperialism* (London 1902), preface; (1938 edn), p. xxvii.

5 Sir Harry Johnston, *A History of the Colonization of Africa by Alien Races* (Cambridge 1930; first edn 1913), p. 445.

6 Michael Barratt Brown, *The Economics of Imperialism* (Harmondsworth 1974), p. 175; for the vast and, for our purposes, oversophisticated debate on this subject, see Pollard, 'Capital Exports 1870–1914', *loc. cit.*

7 W. G. Hynes, *The Economics of Empire: Britain, Africa and the New Imperialism, 1870–1895* (London 1979), *passim*.

8 Cited in D. C. M. Platt, *Finance, Trade and Politics: British Foreign Policy 1815–1914* (Oxford 1968), pp. 365–6.

9 Max Beer, "Der neue englische Imperialismus', *Neue Zeit*, XVI (1898), p. 304. More generally, B. Semmel, *Imperialism and Social Reform: English Social–Imperial Thought 1895–1914* (London 1960).

10 J. E. C. Bodley, *The Coronation of Edward VII: A Chapter of European and Imperial History* (London 1903), pp. 153 and 201.

11 Burton Benedict *et al.*, *The Anthropology of World's Fairs: San Francisco's*

Panama Pacific International Exposition of 1915 (London and Berkeley 1983), p. 23.

12 *Encyclopedia of Missions* (2nd edn New York and London 1904), appendix IV, pp. 838–9.

13 *Dictionnaire de spiritualité* (Paris 1979), x, 'Mission', pp. 1398–9.

14 Rudolf Hilferding, *Das Finanzkapital* (Vienna 1909; 1923 edn), p. 470.

15 P. Bairoch, 'Geographical Structure and Trade Balance of European Foreign Trade from 1800 to 1970', *Journal of European Economic History*, 3 (1974), pp. 557–608; *Commerce extérieur et développement économique de l'Europe au XIXe siècle*, p. 81.

16 P. J. Cain and A. G. Hopkins, 'The Political Economy of British Expansion Overseas, 1750–1914', *Economic History Review*, XXXIII (1980), pp. 463–90.

17 J. E. Flint, 'Britain and the Partition of West Africa' in J. E. Flint and G. Williams (eds.), *Perspectives of Empire* (London 1973), p. 111.

18. C. Southworth, *The French Colonial Venture* (London 1931), appendix table 7. However, the average dividend for companies operating in French colonies in that year was 4.6 per cent.

19 M. K. Gandhi, *Collected Works*, I: 1884–96 (New Delhi 1958).

20 For the unusually successful, for a while, incursion of Buddhism into western milieux, see Jan Romein, *The Watershed of Two Eras* (Middletown, Conn. 1978), pp. 501–3, and the export of Indian holy men abroad, largely via champions drawn from among Theosophists. Among them Vivekananda (1863–1902) of 'Vedanta' can claim to be the first of the commercial gurus of the modern West.

21 R. H. Gretton, *A Modern History of the English People*, II: 1899–1910 (London 1913), p. 25.

22 W. L. Langer, *The Diplomacy of Imperialism, 1890–1902* (New York 1968 edn), pp. 387 and 448. More generally, H. Gollwitzer, *Die gelbe Gefahr: Geschichte eines Schlagworts: Studien zum imperialistischen Denken* (Göttingen 1962).

23 Rudyard Kipling, 'Recessional' in *R. Kipling's Verse, Inclusive Edition 1885–1918* (London n.d.), p. 377.

24 Hobson, *op. cit.* (1938 edn), p. 314.

25 See H. G. Wells, *The Time Machine* (London 1895).

26 H. G. v. Schulze-Gaevernitz, *Britischer Imperialismus und englischer Freihandel zu Beginn des 20. Jahrhunderts* (Leipzig 1906).

CHAPTER 4:   THE POLITICS OF DEMOCRCY

1 Gaetano Mosca, *Elementi di scienza politica* (1895), trs. as *The Ruling Class* (New York 1939), pp. 333–4.

2 Robert Skidelsky, *John Maynard Keynes*, I (London 1983), p. 156.

3 Edward A. Ross, 'Social Control VII: Assemblage', *American Journal of Sociology*, II (1896–7), p. 830.

4 Among the works which then appeared, Gaetano Mosca (1858–1941), *Elementi di scienza politica;* Sidney and Beatrice Webb, *Industrial Democracy* (1897); M. Ostrogorski (1854–1919), *Democracy and the Organization of Political Parties* (1902); Robert Michels (1876–1936), *Zur Soziologie des Parteiwesens in der modernen Demokratie (Political Parties)* (1911); Georges Sorel (1847–1922), *Reflexions on Violence* (1908).

5 Hilaire Belloc, *Sonnets and Verse* (London 1954), p. 151: 'On a General Election', Epigram XX.

6 David Fitzpatrick, ''The Geography of Irish Nationalism', *Past & Present*, 78 (Feb. 1978), pp. 127–9).

7 H.-J. Puhle, *Politische Agrarbewegungen in kapitalistischen Industriegesellschaften* (Göttingen 1975), p. 64.

8 G. Hohorst, J. Kocka and G. A. Ritter, *Sozialgeschichtliches Arbeitsbuch: Materialien zur Statistik des Kaiserreichs 1870–1914* (Munich 1975), p. 177.

9 Michels, *op. cit.* (Stuttgart 1970 edn), part VI, ch. 2.

10 R. F. Foster, *Lord Randolph Churchill, a Political Life* (Oxford 1981), p. 395.

11 C. Benoist, *L'Organisation du suffrage universel: La crise de l'état moderne* (Paris 1897).

12 C. Headlam (ed.), *The Milner Papers* (London 1931–3), II, p. 291.

13 T. H. S. Escott, *Social Transformations of the Victorian Age* (London 1897), p. 166.

14 Flora, *op. cit.*, ch. 5.

15 Calculated from Hohorst, Kocka and Ritter, *op. cit.*, p. 179.

16 Gary B. Cohen, *The Politics of Ethnic Survival: Germans in Prague 1861–1914* (Princeton 1981), pp. 92–3.

17 Graham Wallas, *Human Nature in Politics* (London 1908), p. 21.

18 David Cannadine, 'The Context, Performance and Meaning of Ritual: The British Monarchy and the "Invention of Tradition" *c.* 1820–1977' in E. J. Hobsbawm and T. Ranger (eds.), *The Invention of Tradition* (Cambridge 1983), pp. 101–64.

19 The distinction comes from Walter Bagehot's *The English Constitution*, first published in the *Fortnightly Review* (1865–67), as part of the debate on the Second Reform Bill, i.e. on whether to give workers the vote.

20 Rosemonde Sanson, *Les 14 Juillet: fête et conscience nationale, 1789–1975* (Paris 1976), p. 42, on the motives of the Paris authorities in combining popular amusements and public ceremony.

21 Hans-Georg John, *Politik und Turnen: die deutsche Turnerschaft als nationale Bewegung im deutschen Kaiserreich von 1870–1914* (Ahrensberg bei Hamburg 1976), pp. 36–9.

22 'I believe it will be absolutely necessary that you should prevail on our future masters to learn their letters' (Debate on the Third Reading of the

Reform Bill, *Parliamentary Debates*, 15 July 1867, p. 1549, col. 1). This is the original version of the phrase which, shortened, became familiar.

23 Cannadine, *op. cit.*, p. 130.

24 Wallace Evan Davies, *Patriotism on Parade* (Cambridge, Mass. 1955), pp. 218–22.

25 Maurice Dommanget, *Eugène Pottier, membre de la Commune et chantre de l'Internationale* (Paris 1971), p. 138.

26 V. I. Lenin, *State and Revolution* part I, section 3.

CHAPTER 5: WORKERS OF THE WORLD

1 The labourer Franz Rehbein, remembering in 1911. From Paul Göhre (ed.), *Das Leben eines Landarbeiters* (Munich 1911), cited in W. Emmerich (ed.), *Proletarische Lebensläufe*, I (Reinbek 1974), p. 280.

2 Samuel Gompers, *Labor in Europe and America* (New York and London 1910), pp. 238–9.

3 *Mit uns zieht die neue Zeit: Arbeiterkultur in Österreich 1918–1934* (Vienna 1981).

4 Sartorius v. Waltershausen, *Die italienischen Wanderarbeiter* (Leipzig 1903), pp. 13, 20, 22 and 27. I owe this reference to Dirk Hoerder.

5 Bairoch, *De Jéricho à Mexico*, pp. 385–6.

6 W. H. Schröder, *Arbeitergeschichte und Arbeiterbewegung: Industriearbeit und Organisationsverhalten im 19. und frühen 20. Jahrhundert* (Frankfurt and New York 1978), pp. 166–7 and 304.

7 Jonathan Hughes, *The Vital Few: American Economic Progress and its Protagonists* (London, Oxford and New York 1973), p. 329.

8 Bairoch, 'Città/Campagna', p. 91.

9 W. Woytinsky, *Die Welt in Zahlen*, II: *Die Arbeit* (Berlin 1926), p. 17.

10 *Warum gibt es in den Vereinigten Staaten keinen Sozialismus?* (Tübingen 1906).

11 Jean Touchard, *La Gauche en France depuis 1900* (Paris 1977), p. 62; Luigi Cortesi, *Il Socialismo Italiano tra riforme e rivoluzione: Dibatti congressuali del Psi 1892–1921* (Bari 1969), p. 549.

12 Maxime Leroy, *La Coutûme ouvrière* (Paris 1913), I, p. 387.

13 D. Crew, *Bochum: Sozialgeschichte einer Industriestadt* (Berlin and Vienna 1980), p. 200.

14 Guy Chaumel, *Histoire des cheminots et de leurs syndicats* (Paris 1948), p. 79, n. 22.

15 Crew, *op. cit.*, pp. 19, 70 and 25.

16 Yves Lequin, *Les Ouvriers de la région lyonnaise*, I: *La Formation de la classe ouvrière régionale* (Lyon 1977), p. 202.

17 The first recorded use of 'big business' (*OED* Supplement 1976) occurs in 1912 in the USA; '*Grossindustrie*' appears earlier, but seems to become common during the Great Depression.

18 Askwith's memorandum is cited in H. Pelling, *Popular Politics and Society*

in Late Victorian Britain (London 1968), p. 147.

19   Maurice Dommanget, *Histoire du Premier Mai* (Paris 1953), p. 252.
20   W. L. Guttsman, *The German Social-Democratic Party 1875–1933* (London 1981), p. 96.
21   *Ibid.*, p. 160.
22   *Mit uns zieht die neue Zeit: Arbeiterkultur in Österreich 1918–1934: Eine Ausstellung der Österreichischen Gesellschaft für Kulturpolitik und des Meidlinger Kulturkreises*, 23 Jänner–30 August 1981 (Vienna), p. 240.
23   Constitution of the British Labour Party.
24   Robert Hunter, *Socialists at Work* (New York 1908) p. 2.
25   Georges Haupt, *Programm und Wirklichkeit: Die internationale Sozialdemokratie vor 1914* (Neuwied 1970), p. 141.
26   And perhaps even more popular, the anti-clerical Corvin's *Pfaffenspiegel* (H.-J. Steinberg, *Sozialismus und deutsche Sozialdemokratie: Zur Ideologie der Partei vor dem ersten Weltkrieg* [Hanover 1967], p. 139). The SPD Congress (Parteitag) 1902 observes that only anti-clerical party literature really sells. Thus in 1898 the Manifesto is issued in an edition of 3000, Bebel's *Christenthum und Sozialismus* in 10,000 copies; in 1901–4 the Manifesto was issued in 7000 copies, Bebel's *Christenthum* in 57,000 copies.
27   K. Kautsky, *La Questione Agraria* (Milan 1959 edn), p. 358. The quotation is at the start of Part II, l.c.

CHAPTER 6:   WAVING FLAGS: NATIONS AND NATIONALISM
 1   I owe this quotation from the Italian writer F. Jovine (1904–1950) to Martha Petrusewicz of Princeton University.
 2   H. G. Wells, *Anticipations* (London 5th edn 1902), pp. 225–6.
 3   Alfredo Rocco, *What Is Nationalism and What Do the Nationalists Want?* (Rome 1914).
 4   See Georges Haupt, Michel Lowy and Claudie Weill, *Les Marxistes et la question nationale 1848–1914: études et textes* (Paris 1974).
 5   E. Brix, *Die Umgangsprachen in Altösterreich zwischen Agitation und Assimilation: Die Sprachenstatistik in den zisleithanischen Volkszählungen 1880–1910* (Vienna, Cologne and Graz 1982), p. 97.
 6   H. Roos, *A History of Modern Poland* (London 1966), p. 48.
 7   Lluis Garcia i Sevilla, 'Llengua, nació i estat al diccionario de la reial academia espanyola', *L'Avenç*, Barcelona (16 May 1979), pp. 50–5.
 8   Hugh Seton-Watson, *Nations and States* (London 1977), p. 85.
 9   I owe this information to Dirk Hoerder.
10   *Harvard Encyclopedia of American Ethnic Groups*, 'Naturalization and Citizenship', p. 747.
11   Benedict Anderson, *Imagined Communities: Reflections on the Origins and Spread of Nationalism* (London 1983), pp. 107–8.
12   C. Bobinska and Andrzej Pilch (eds.), *Employment-seeking Emigrations of the*

Poles World-Wide XIX and XX C. (Cracow 1975) pp. 124–6.

13 Wolfgang J. Mommsen, *Max Weber and German Politics 1890–1920* (Chicago 1984), pp. 54 ff.

14 Lonn Taylor and Ingrid Maar, *The American Cowboy* (Washington DC 1983), pp. 96–8.

15 Hans Mommsen, *Nationalitätenfrage und Arbeiterbewegung* (Schriften aus dem Karl-Marx-Haus, Trier 1971), pp. 18–19.

16 *History of the Hungarian Labour Movement. Guide to the Permanent Exhibition of the Museum of the Hungarian Labour Movement* (Budapest 1983), pp. 31 ff.

17 Marianne Heiberg, 'Insiders/Outsiders; Basque Nationalism', *Archives Européennes de Sociologie*, XVI (1975), pp. 169–93.

18 A. Zolberg, 'The Making of Flemings and Walloons: Belgium 1830–1914', *Journal of Interdisciplinary History*, V (1974), pp. 179–235; H.-J. Puhle, 'Baskischer Nationalismus im spanischen Kontext' in H. A. Winkler (ed.), *Nationalismus in der Welt von Heute* (Göttingen 1982), especially pp. 60–5.

19 *Enciclopedia Italiana*, 'Nazionalismo'.

20 Peter Hanak, 'Die Volksmeinung während den letzten Kriegsjahren in Österreich-Ungarn' in R. G. Plaschka and K. H. Mack (eds.), *Die Auflösung des Habsburgerreiches: Zusammenbruch und Neuorientierung im Donauraum* (Vienna 1970), pp. 58–67.

CHAPTER 7: WHO'S WHO OR THE UNCERTAINTIES OF THE
BOURGEOISIE

1 William James, *The Principles of Psychology* (New York 1950), p. 291. I owe this reference to Sanford Elwitt.

2 H. G. Wells, *Tono-Bungay* (1909; Modern Library edn), p. 249.

3 Lewis Mumford, *The City in History* (New York 1961), p. 495.

4 Mark Girouard, *The Victorian Country House* (New Haven and London 1979), pp. 208–12.

5 W. S. Adams, *Edwardian Portraits* (London 1957), pp. 3–4.

6 This is a basic theme of Carl E. Schorske, *Fin-de-Siècle Vienna* (London 1980).

7 Thorstein Veblen, *The Theory of the Leisure Class: An Economic Study of Institutions* (1899). Revised edition New York 1959.

8 W. D. Rubinstein, 'Wealth, Elites and the Class Structure of Modern Britain', *Past & Present*, 76 (Aug. 1977), p. 102.

9 Adolf v. Wilke, *Alt-Berliner Erinnerungen* (Berlin 1930), pp. 232 f.

10 W. L. Guttsman, *The British Political Elite* (London 1963), pp. 122–7.

11 Touchard, *op. cit.*, p. 128.

12 Theodore Zeldin, *France, 1848–1945* (Oxford 1973), I, p. 37; D. C. Marsh, *The Changing Social Structure of England and Wales 1871–1961* (London 1958), p. 122.

13 G. A. Ritter and J. Kocka, *Deutsche Sozialgeschichte. Dokumente und Skizzen. Band II 1870–1914* (Munich 1977), pp. 169–70.

14 Paul Descamps, *L'Éducation dans les écoles Anglaises* (Paris 1911), p. 67.

15 Zeldin, *op. cit.*, I, pp. 612–13.

16 *Ibid.*, II, p. 250; H.-U. Wehler, *Das deutsche Kaiserreich 1871–1918* (Göttingen 1973), p. 126; Ritter and Kocka, *op. cit.*, pp. 341–3.

17 Ritter and Kocka, *op. cit.*, pp. 327–8 and 352; Arno Mayer, *The Persistence of the Old Regime: Europe to the Great War* (New York 1981), p. 264.

18 Hohorst, Kocka and Ritter, *op. cit.*, p. 161; J.J. Mayeur, *Les Débuts de la IIIe République 1871–1898* (Paris 1973), p. 150; Zeldin, *op. cit.*, II, p. 330. Mayer, *op. cit.*, p. 262.

19 Ritter and Kocka, op. cit., p. 224.

20 Y. Cassis, *Les Banquiers de la City à l'époque Edouardienne 1890–1914* (Geneva 1984).

21 Skidelsky, *op. cit.*, I p. 84.

22 Crew, *op. cit.*, p. 26.

23 G. v. Schmoller, *Was verstehen wir unter dem Mittelstande? Hat er im 19. Jahrhundert zu- oder abgenommen?* (Göttingen 1907).

24 W. Sombart, *Die deutsche Volkswirthschaft im 19. Jahrhundert und im Anfang des 20. Jahrhunderts* (Berlin 1903), pp. 534 and 531.

25 Pollard, 'Capital Exports 1870–1914', pp. 498–9.

26 W. R. Lawson, *John Bull and His Schools: A Book for Parents, Ratepayers and Men of Business* (Edinburgh and London 1908), p. 39. He estimated the 'middle class proper' at *c.* half a million.

27 John R. de S. Honey, *Tom Brown's Universe: The Development of the Victorian Public School* (London 1977).

28 W. Raimond Baird, *American College Fraternities: a descriptive analysis of the Society System of the Colleges of the United States with a detailed account of each fraternity* (New York 1890), p. 20.

29 Mayeur, *op. cit.*, p. 81.

30 Escott, *op. cit.*, pp. 202–3.

31 *The Englishwoman's Year-Book* (1905), p. 171.

32 Escott, *op. cit.*, p. 196.

33 As can be verified from the Victoria County History for that county.

34 *Principles of Economics* (London 8th edn 1920), p. 59.

35 Skidelsky, *op. cit.*, pp. 55–6.

36 P. Wilsher, *The Pound in Your Pocket 1870–1970* (London 1970), pp. 81, 96 and 98.

37 Hughes, *op. cit.*, p. 252.

38 Cited in W. Rosenberg, *Liberals in the Russian Revolution* (Princeton 1974), pp. 205–12.

39 A. Sartorius v. Waltershausen, *Deutsche Wirtschaftsgeschichte 1815–1914* (2nd edn Jena 1923), p. 521.

40 E.g. in *Man and Superman, Misalliance.*

41 Robert Wohl, *The Generation of 1914* (London 1980), pp. 89, 169 and 16.

CHAPTER 8: THE NEW WOMAN

1 H. Nunberg and E. Federn (eds.), *Minutes of the Vienna Psychoanalytical Society,* I: 1906–1908 (New York 1962), pp. 199–200.

2 Cited in W. Ruppert (ed.), *Die Arbeiter: Lebensformen, Alltag und Kultur* (Munich 1986), p. 69.

3 K. Anthony, *Feminism in Germany and Scandinavia* (New York 1915), p. 231.

4 *Handwörterbuch der Staatswissenschaften* (Jena 1902 edn), 'Beruf', p. 626, and 'Frauenarbeit', p. 1202.

5 *ibid.,* 'Hausindustrie', pp. 1148 and 1150.

6 Louise Tilly and Joan W. Scott, *Women, Work and Family* (New York 1978), p. 124.

7 *Handwörterbuch,* 'Frauenarbeit', pp. 1205–6.

8 For Germany: Hohorst, Kocka and Ritter, *op. cit.,* p 68, n. 8; for Britain, Mark Abrams, *The Condition of the British People 1911–1945* (London 1946), pp. 60–1; Marsh, *op. cit.,* p. 127.

9 Zeldin, *op. cit.,* II, p. 169.

10 E. Cadbury, M. C. Matheson and G. Shann, *Women's Work and Wages* (London 1906), pp. 49 and 129. The book describes conditions in Birmingham.

11 Margaret Bryant, *The Unexpected Revolution* (London 1979), p. 108.

12 Edmée Charnier, *L'Évolution intellectuelle féminine* (Paris 1937), pp. 140 and 189. See also H.-J. Puhle, 'Warum gibt es so wenige Historikerinnen?' *Geschichte und Gesellschaft,* 7 Jg. (1981), especially p. 373.

13 Rosa Leviné-Meyer, *Leviné* (London 1973), p. 2.

14 First translated into English in 1891.

15 Caroline Kohn, *Karl Kraus* (Stuttgart 1966), p. 259, n. 40; J. Romein, *The Watershed of Two Eras,* p. 604.

16 Donald R. Knight, *Great White City, Shepherds Bush, London: 70th Anniversary, 1908–1978* (New Barnet 1978), p. 26.

17 I owe this point to a student of Dr S. N. Mukherjee of Sydney University.

18 Claude Willard, *Les Guesdistes* (Paris 1965), p. 362.

19 G. D. H. Cole, *A History of the Labour Party from 1914* (London 1948), p. 480; Richard J. Evans, *The Feminists* (London 1977), p. 162.

20 Woytinsky, *op. cit.,* II, provides the basis for these data.

21 Calculated from *Men and Women of the Time* (1895).

22 For conservative feminism, see also E. Halévy, *A History of the English People in the Nineteenth Century* (1961 edn), VI, p. 509.

23 For these developments see S. Giedion, *Mechanisation Takes Command* (New

York 1948), *passim*; for the quotation, pp. 520–1.

24   Rodelle Weintraub (ed.), *Bernard Shaw and Women* (Pennsylvania State University 1977), pp. 3–4.

25   Jean Maitron and Georges Haupt (eds.), *Dictionnaire biographique du mouvement ouvrier international: L'Autriche* (Paris 1971), p. 285.

26   T. E. B. Howarth, *Cambridge Between Two Wars* (London 1978), p. 45.

27   J. P. Nettl, *Rosa Luxemburg* (London 1966), I, p. 144.

CHAPTER 9: THE ARTS TRANSFORMED

1   Romain Rolland, *Jean Christophe in Paris* (trs. New York 1915), pp. 120–1.

2   S. Laing, *Modern Science and Modern Thought* (London 1896), pp. 230–1, originally published 1885.

3   F. T. Marinetti, *Selected Writings*, ed. R. W. Flint (New York 1971), p. 67.

4   Peter Jelavich, *Munich and Theatrical Modernism: Politics, Playwriting and Performance 1890–1914* (Cambridge, Mass. 1985), p. 102.

5   The word was coined by M. Agulhon, 'La statuomanie et l'histoire', *Ethnologie Française* 3–4 (1978).

6   John Willett, 'Breaking Away', *New York Review of Books*, 28 May 1981, pp. 47–9.

7   *The Englishwoman's Year-Book* (1905), 'Colonial journalism for women', p. 138.

8   Among the other series which cashed in on the thirst for self-education and culture in Britain, we may mention the Camelot Classics (1886–91), the 300-odd volumes of Cassell's National Library (1886–90 and 1903–7), Cassell's Red Library (1884–90) Sir John Lubbock's Hundred Books, published by Routledge (also publisher of Modern Classics from 1897) from 1891, Nelson's Classics (1907–) – the 'Sixpenny Classics' only lasted 1905–7 – and Oxford's World's Classics. Everyman (1906–) deserves credit for publishing a major modern classic, Joseph Conrad's *Nostromo*, in its first fifty titles, between Macaulay's *History of England* and Lockhart's *Life of Sir Walter Scott*.

9   Georg Gottfried Gervinus, *Geschichte der poetischen Nationalliteratur der Deutschen*, 5 vols. (1836–42).

10   F. Nietzsche, *Der Wille zur Macht* in *Sämtliche Werke* (Stuttgart 1965), IX, pp. 65 and 587.

11   R. Hinton Thomas, *Nietzsche in German Politics and Society 1890–1918* (Manchester 1984), stresses – one might say overstresses – his appeal for libertarians. Nevertheless, and in spite of Nietzsche's dislike of anarchists (cf. *Jenseits von Gut und Böse* in Sämtliche Werke, VII, pp. 114, 125), in French anarchist circles of the 1900s 'on discute avec fougue Stirner, Nietzsche et surtout Le Dantec' (Jean Maitron, *Le Mouvement anarchiste en France* [Paris 1975] I, p. 421).

12 Eugenia W. Herbert, *Artists and Social Reform: France and Belgium 1885–1898* (New Haven 1961), p. 21.

13 Patrizia Dogliani, *La 'Scuola delle Reclute': L'Internazionale Giovanile Socialista dalla fine dell'ottocento, alla prima guerra mondiale* (Turin 1983), p. 147.

14 G. W. Plechanow, *Kunst und Literatur* (East Berlin 1955), p. 295.

15 J. C. Holl, *La Jeune Peinture contemporaine* (Paris 1912), pp. 14–15.

16 'On the spiritual in art', cited in *New York Review of Books*, 16 Feb. 1984, p. 28.

17 Cited in Romein, *Watershed of Two Eras*, p. 572.

18 Karl Marx, *The Eighteenth Brumaire of Louis Bonaparte*.

19 Max Raphael, *Von Monet zu Picasso. Grundzüge einer Aesthetik und Entwicklung der modernen Malerei* (Munich 1913).

20 The role of countries with a strong democratic and populist press, and lacking a large middle-class public, in the evolution of the modern political cartoon is to be noted. For the importance of pre-1914 Australia in this connection, see E. J. Hobsbawm, Introduction to *Communist Cartoons* by 'Espoir' and others (London 1982), p. 3.

21 Peter Bächlin, *Der Film als Ware* (Basel 1945), p. 214, n. 14.

22 T. Balio (ed.), *The American Film Industry* (Madison, Wis. 1985), p. 86.

23 G. P. Brunetta, *Storia del cinema italiano 1895–1945* (Rome 1979), p. 44.

24 Balio, *op. cit.*, p. 98.

25 *Ibid.*, p. 87; *Mit uns zieht die Neue Zeit*, p. 185.

26 Brunetta, *op. cit.*, p. 56.

27 Luigi Chiarini, 'Cinematography' in *Encyclopedia of World Art* (New York, London and Toronto 1960), III, p. 626.

CHAPTER 10:   CERTAINTIES UNDERMINED: THE SCIENCES

1 Laing, *op. cit.*, p. 51.

2 Raymond Pearl, *Modes of Research in Genetics* (New York 1915), p. 159. The passage is reprinted from a 1913 lecture.

3 Bertrand Russell, *Our Knowledge of the External World as a Field for Scientific Method in Philosophy* (London 1952 edn), p. 109.

4 Carl Boyer, *A History of Mathematics* (New York 1968), p. 82.

5 Bourbaki, *Éléments d'histoire des mathématiques* (Paris 1960), p. 27. The group of mathematicians publishing under this name were interested in the history of their subject primarily in relation to their own work.

6 Boyer, *op. cit.*, p. 649.

7 Bourbaki, p. 43.

8 F. Dannemann, *Die Naturwissenschaften in ihrer Entwicklung und ihrem Zusammenhange* (Leipzig and Berlin 1913), IV, p. 433.

9 Henry Smith Williams, *The Story of Nineteenth-Century Science* (London and New York 1900), p. 231.

10 *Ibid.*, pp. 230–1.

11 *Ibid.*, p. 236.

12 C. C. Gillispie, *The Edge of Objectivity* (Princeton 1960), p. 507.

13 Cf. Max Planck, *Scientific Autobiography and Other Papers* (New York 1949).

14 J. D. Bernal, *Science in History* (London 1965), p. 630.

15 Ludwig Fleck, *Genesis and Development of a Scientific Fact* (Chicago 1979; orig. Basel 1935), pp. 68–9.

16 W. Treue and K. Mauel (eds.), *Naturwissenschaft, Technik und Wirtschaft im 19. Jahrhundert*, 2 vols. (Göttingen 1976), I, pp. 271–4 and 348–56.

17 Nietzsche, *Der Wille zur Macht, book IV*, e.g. pp. 607–9.

18 C. Webster (ed.), *Biology, Medicine and Society 1840–1940* (Cambridge 1981), p. 225.

19 *ibid.*, p. 221.

20 As is suggested by the titles of A. Ploetz and F. Lentz, *Deutsche Gesellschaft für Rassenhygiene* (1905: 'German Society for Racial Hygiene'), and the Society's journal *Archiv für Rassen- und Gesellschaftsbiologie* ('Archives of Racial and Social Biology'); or G. F. Schwalbe's *Zeitschrift für Morphologie und Anthropologie, Erb- und Rassenbiologie* (1899: 'Journal for Morphology, Anthropology, Genetic and Racial Biology'). Cf. J. Sutter, *L'Eugénique: Problèmes-Méthodes-Résultats* (Paris 1950), pp. 24–5).

21 Kenneth M. Ludmerer, *Genetics and American Society: A Historical Appraisal* (Baltimore 1972), p. 37.

22 Cited in Romein, *op. cit.*, p. 343.

23 Webster, *op. cit.*, p. 266.

24 Ernst Mach in *Neue Österreichische Biographie*, I (Vienna 1923).

25 J. J. Salomon, *Science and Politics* (London 1973), p. xiv.

26 Gillispie, *op. cit.*, p. 499.

27 Nietzsche, *Wille zur Macht*, Vorrede, p. 4.

28 *Ibid.*, aphorisms, p. 8.

29 Bernal (*op. cit.*, p. 503) estimates that in 1896 there were perhaps 50,000 persons in the world carrying on 'the whole tradition of science', of whom 15,000 did research. The number grew: from 1901 to 1915 there were in the USA alone *c.* 74,000 first degrees or bachelors in the natural sciences and 2577 doctoral degrees in natural sciences and engineering (D. M. Blank and George J. Stigler, *The Demand and Supply of Scientific Personnel* [New York 1957], pp. 5–6).

30 G. W. Roderick, *The Emergence of a Scientific Society* (London and New York 1967), p. 48.

31 Frank R. Pfetsch, *Zur Entwicklung der Wissenschaftspolitik in Deutschland 1750–1914* (Berlin 1974), pp. 340 ff.

32 The prizes have been taken to 1925 so as to allow for some lag in recognizing achievements of the brilliant young in the last pre-1914 years.

33 Joseph Ben-David, 'Professions in the Class Systems of Present-Day Societies', *Current Sociology*, 12 (1963–4), pp. 262–9.

34 Paul Levy, *Moore: G. E. Moore and the Cambridge Apostles* (Oxford 1981), pp. 309–11.

CHAPTER 11: REASON AND SOCIETY

1 Rolland, *op. cit.*, p. 222.

2 Nunberg and Federn, *op. cit.*, II, p. 178.

3 Max Weber, *Gesammelte Aufsätze zur Wissenschaftslehre* (Tübingen 1968), p. 166.

4 Guy Vincent, *L'École primaire française: Étude sociologique* (Lyon 1980), p. 332, n. 779.

5 Vivekananda, *Works*, part IV, cited in *Sedition Committee 1918: Report* (Calcutta 1918), p. 17 n.

6 Anil Seal, *The Emergence of Indian Nationalism* (Cambridge 1971), p. 249.

7 R. M. Goodridge, 'Nineteenth Century Urbanisation and Religion: Bristol and Marseille, 1830–1880', *Sociological Yearbook of Religion in Britain*, I (London 1969) p. 131.

8 'La bourgeoisie adhère au rationnalisme, l'instituteur au socialisme' – Gabriel Le Bras, *Études de sociologie réligieuse*, 2 vols. (Paris 1955–6), I, p. 151.

9 A. Fliche and V. Martin, *Histoire de l'Église. Le pontificat de Pie IX* (2nd edn Paris 1964), p. 130.

10 S. Bonnet, C. Santini and H. Barthélemy, 'Appartenance politique et attitude réligieuse dans l'immigration italienne en Lorraine sidérurgique, *Archives de Sociologie des Réligions* 13 (1962), pp. 63–6.

11 R. Duocastella, 'Géographie de la pratique réligieuse en Espagne', *Social Compass*, XII (1965), p. 256; A. Leoni, *Sociologia e geografia religiosa di una Diocesi: saggio sulla pratica religiosa nella Diocesi di Mantova* (Rome 1952), p. 117.

12 Halévy, *op. cit.*, V, p. 171.

13 Massimo Salvadori, *Karl Kautsky and the Socialist Revolution* (London 1979), pp. 23–4.

14 Not to mention the sister of the socialist leader Otto Bauer who, under another name, figures prominently in Freud's case-book. See Ernst Glaser, *Im Umfeld des Austromarxismus* (Vienna 1981), *passim*.

15 For this episode see *Marx-Engels Archiv*, ed. D. Rjazanov (reprint Erlangen 1971), II, p. 140.

16 The fullest discussions of the expansion of Marxism are not available in English.; cf. E. J. Hobsbawm, 'La diffusione del Marxismo, 1890–1905', *Studi Storici*, XV (1974), pp. 241–69; *Storia del Marxismo, II: Il marxismo nell'età della seconda Internazionale* (Turin 1979), pp. 6–110, articles by F. Andreucci and E. J. Hobsbawm.

17 E. v. Böhm-Bawerk, *Zum Abschluss des Marxschen Systems* (Berlin 1896), long remained the most powerful orthodox critique of Marx. Böhm-

Bawerk held cabinet office in Austria three times during this period.

18 Walter Bagehot, *Physics and Politics*, originally published in 1872. The 1887 series was edited by Kegan Paul.

19 Otto Hintze, 'Über individualistische und kollektivistische Geschichts auffassung', *Historische Zeitschrift*, 78 (1897), p. 62.

20 See in particular the long polemic of G. v. Below, 'Die neue historische Methode', *Historische Zeitschrift*, 81 (1898), pp. 193–273.

21 Schorske, *op. cit.*, p. 203.

22 William MacDougall (1871–1938), *An Introduction to Social Psychology* (London 1908).

23 William James, *Varieties of Religious Belief* (New York 1963 edn), p. 388.

24 E. Gothein, 'Gesellschaft und Gesellschaftswissenschaft' in *Handwörterbuch der Staatswissenschaften* (Jena 1900), IV, p. 212.

CHAPTER 12: TOWARDS REVOLUTION

1 D. Norman (ed.), *Nehru, The First Sixty Years*, I (New York 1965), p. 12.

2 Mary Clabaugh Wright (ed.) *China in Revolution: The First Phase 1900–1915* (New Haven 1968), p. 118.

3 *Collected Works*, IX, p. 434.

4 *Selected Works* (London 1936), IV, pp. 297–304.

5 For a comparison of the two Iranian revolutions, see Nikki R. Keddie, 'Iranian Revolutions in Comparative Perspective', *American Historical Review*, 88 (1983), pp. 579–98.

6 John Lust, 'Les sociétés secrètes, les mouvements populaires et la révolution de 1911' in J. Chesneaux *et al.* (eds.), *Mouvements populaires et sociétés secrètes en Chine aux XIXe et XXe siècles* (Paris 1970), p. 370.

7 Edwin Lieuwen, *Arms and Politics in Latin America* (London and New York 1961 edn), p. 21.

8 For the transition, see chapter 3 of *M. N. Roy's Memoirs* (Bombay, New Delhi, Calcutta, Madras, London and New York 1964).

9 Friedrich Katz, *The Secret War in Mexico: Europe, The United States and the Mexican Revolution* (Chicago and London 1981), p. 22.

10 Hugh Seton-Watson, *The Russian Empire 1801–1917* (Oxford 1967), p. 507.

11 P. I. Lyashchenko, *History of the Russian National Economy* (New York 1949), pp. 453, 468 and 520.

12 *Ibid.*, pp. 528–9.

13 Michael Futrell, *Northern Underground: Episodes of Russian Revolutionary Transport and Communication Through Scandinavia and Finland* (London 1963), *passim*.

14 M. S. Anderson, *The Ascendancy of Europe 1815–1914* (London 1972), p. 266.

15 T. Shanin, *The Awkward Class* (Oxford 1972), p. 38 n.

16 I follow the arguments of L. Haimson's pathbreaking articles in *Slavic*

Review, 23 (1964), pp. 619–42 and 24 (1965), pp. 1–22, 'Problem of Social Stability in Urban Russia 1905–17'.

CHAPTER 13:   FROM PEACE TO WAR

1   Fürst von Bülow, *Denkwürdigkeiten,* I (Berlin 1930), pp. 415–16.
2   Bernard Shaw to Clement Scott, 1902: G. Bernard Shaw, *Collected Letters, 1898–1910* (London 1972), p. 260.
3   Marinetti, *op. cit.,* p. 42.
4   *Leviathan,* part I, ch. 13.
5   *Wille Zur Macht, loc. cit.,* p. 92.
6   Georges Haupt, *Socialism and the Great War: The Collapse of the Second International* (Oxford 1972), pp. 220 and 258.
7   Gaston Bodart, *Losses of Life in Modern Wars* (Carnegie Endowment for International Peace, Oxford 1916), pp. 153 ff.
8   H. Stanley Jevons, *The British Coal Trade* (London 1915), pp. 367–8 and 374.
9   W. Ashworth, 'Economic Aspects of Late Victorian Naval Administration', *Economic History Review,* XXII (1969), p. 491.
10   Engels to Danielson, 22 Sept. 1892: Marx–Engels *Werke,* XXXVIII (Berlin 1968), p.467.
11.   Clive Trebilcock, ' "Spin-off" in British Economic History: Armaments and Industry, 1760–1914', *Economic History Review,* XXII (1969), p. 480.
12   Romein, *op. cit.,* p. 124.
13   Admiral Raeder, *Struggle for the Sea* (London 1959), pp. 135 and 260.
14   David Landes, *The Unbound Prometheus* (Cambridge 1969), pp. 240–1.
15   D. C. Watt, *A History of the World in the Twentieth Century* (London 1967), I, p. 220.
16   L. A. G. Lennox (ed.), *The Diary of Lord Bertie of Thame 1914–1918* (London 1924), pp. 352 and 355.
17   Chris Cook and John Paxon, *European Political Facts 1848–1918* (London 1978), p. 188.
18   Norman Stone, *Europe Transformed 1878–1918* (London 1983), p. 331.
19   A. Offner, 'The Working Classes, British Naval Plans and the Coming of the Great War', *Past & Present,* 107 (May 1985), pp. 204–26, discusses this at length.
20   Haupt, *op. cit.,* p. 175.
21   Marc Ferro, *La Grande Guerre 1914–1918* (Paris 1969), p. 23.
22   W. Emmerich (ed.), *Proletarische Lebensläufe* (Reinbek 1975), II, p. 104.
23   Haupt, *op. cit.,* p. 253 n.
24   *Wille zur Macht,* p. 92.
25   Rupert Brooke, 'Peace' in *Collected Poems of Rupert Brooke* (London 1915).
26   *Wille zur Macht,* p. 94.

EPILOGUE
1 Bertolt Brecht, 'An die Nachgeborenen' in *Hundert Gedichte 1918–1950* (East Berlin 1955), p. 314.
2 Albert O. Hirschman, *The Political Economy of Latin American Development: Seven Exercises in Retrospection* (Center for US-Mexican Studies, University of California, San Diego, December 1986), p. 4.

FURTHER READING

'A shilling life will give you all the facts,' wrote the poet W. H. Auden about the subject of his reflections. It costs more today, but anyone who wishes to find out, or to be reminded of, the main events and personalities of nineteenth-century history should read this book together with one of the many basic school or college texts, such as Gordon Craig's *Europe 1815–1914* (1971), and may usefully also consult such reference works as Neville Williams, *Chronology of the Modern World* (1969), which gives the main events under various subjects for each year since 1763. Among textbooks on the period covered in this book, the early chapters in James Joll, *Europe Since 1870* (various editions) and Norman Stone, *Europe Transformed 1878–1918* (1983) are to be recommended. D. C. Watt, *History of the World in the Twentieth Century*, vol. I: 1890–1918 (1967) is strong on international relations. The present author's *The Age of Revolution 1789–1848* and *The Age of Capital 1848–1875* provide the background to this volume, which continues the survey of the nineteenth century begun in the earlier volumes.

There are by now numerous more or less impressionistic or rather pointillist pictures of Europe and the world in the last decades before 1914, among which Barbara Tuchman's *The Proud Tower* (1966) is the most widely distributed. Edward R. Tannenbaum, *1900, The Generation Before the Great War* (1976) is less well known. The one I like best, partly because I have drawn heavily on its encyclopaedic erudition, partly because I share an intellectual tradition and historical ambition with the author, is the late Jan Romein's *The Watershed of Two Eras: Europe in 1900* (1976).

There are a number of collective or encyclopaedic works, or reference compendia, which cover subjects in our period as well as much else. The relevant volume (XII) of the *Cambridge Modern History* is not to be recommended, but those of the *Cambridge Economic History of Europe* (vols. VI and VII) contain excellent studies. The *Cambridge History of the British Empire* represents an obsolete and useless style of history, but the histories of Africa, China and especially Latin America belong properly to the historiography of the late twentieth century. Among historical atlases the *Times Atlas of World History* (1978), compiled under the direction of an original and imaginative historian, G. Barraclough, is outstanding, the Penguin *Atlas of Modern History* is very useful. *Chambers Biographical Dictionary* contains brief data on a surprising number of persons of all periods up to the present in a single volume. Michael Mulhall's *Dictionary of Statistics* (1898 edition reprinted 1969) remains indispensable for the nineteenth century. B. Mitchell's *European Historical Statistics* (1980) is the essential modern compendium, primarily economic. Peter Flora (ed.), *State, Economy and Society in Western Europe 1815–1975* (1983) contains a mass of information on political, institutional and administrative, educational and other matters. Jan Romein's *The Watershed of Two Eras* is not designed as a work of reference, but can be consulted as such, especially on matters of culture and ideas.

On a subject of special interest for the period, I. Ferenczi and W. F. Wilcox (eds.), *International Migration*, 2 vols (1929–31) is still the best source. On a topic of permanent interest, C. McEvedy and R. Jones, *An Atlas of World Population History* (1978) is convenient. Some works of reference on more specialized subjects are mentioned under separate headings. Anyone who would like to know how the nineteenth century saw itself just before the First World War should consult the 11th edition of the *Encyclopaedia Britannica* (the last British one, 1911), which, because of its excellence, is still available in many good reference libraries.

ECONOMIC HISTORY

On the economic history of the period, brief introductions are W. Woodruff, *Impact of Western Man: A Study of Europe's Role in the World Economy 1750–1960* (1966) and W. Ashworth, *A Short History of the International Economy Since 1850* (various editions). The *Cambridge Economic History of Europe* (vols. VI and VII) and C. Cipolla (ed.), *The Fontana Economic History of Europe* (vols. IV and V, parts 1 and 2) (1973–5), are co-operative ventures ranging in quality from the good to the outstanding. Paul Bairoch's *The Economic Development of the Third World Since 1900* (1975) extends the range. Of the many useful works of this author, unfortunately only some of them translated, P. Bairoch and M. Levy-Leboyer (eds.), *Disparities in Economic Development Since the Industrial Revolution* (1981) contains relevant material. A. Milward and S. B. Saul, *The Economic Development of Continental Europe 1780–1870* (1973) and *The Development of the Economies of Continental Europe 1850–1914* (1979) are much more than just college texts. S. Pollard and C. Holmes (eds.),

Documents of European Economic History, vol. II: *Industrial Power and National Rivalry 1870–1914* (1972) concern our period. D. S. Landes, *The Unbound Prometheus* (various editions) is much the best and most exciting treatment of technological developments. Sidney Pollard, *Peaceful Conquest* (1981) integrates the history of British and continental industrialization.

On economic themes of importance for this period, see the discussions on theme B9 ('From Family Firm to Professional Management') at the Eighth International Economic History Congress (Budapest 1982). Alfred D. Chandler, *The Visible Hand: The Management Revolution in American Business* (1977) and Leslie Hannah, *The Rise of the Corporate Economy* (1976) are to the point. A. Maizels, *Industrial Growth and World Trade*, W. Arthur Lewis, *Growth and Fluctuations 1870–1913* (1978), Herbert Feis, *Europe, the World's Banker* (repr. from 1930) and M. de Cecco, *Money and Empire: The International Gold Standard 1890–1914* (1974) discuss other topics relevant to the economy of the times.

SOCIETY

Most of the world consisted of peasants, and T. Shanin (ed.), *Peasants and Peasant Societies* (1971) is an excellent introduction to their world; the same author's *The Awkward Class* (1972) deals with the Russian peasantry; Eugene Weber, *Peasants into Frenchmen* (1976) throws much light on the French; Max Weber's 'Capitalism and Rural Society in Germany' (in H. Gerth and C. Wright Mills, *From Max Weber*, numerous editions, pp. 363–85) is broader than its title suggests. The old petty-bourgeoisie is discussed in G. Crossick and H. G. Haupt (ed.), *Shopkeepers and Master Artisans in 19th Century Europe* (1984). There is by now an immense literature on the working class, but almost always confined to one country, occupation or industry. Peter Stearns, *Lives of Labor* (1971), Dick Geary, *European Labor Protest 1848–1939* (1981), Charles, Louise and Richard Tilly, *The Rebellious Century 1830–1930* (1975) and E. J. Hobsbawm, *Labouring Men* (1964 and other editions) and *Worlds of Labour* (1984) cover a wider area, at least in part. Even fewer studies see workers in the context of their relation to other classes. David Crew, *Town in the Ruhr: A Social History of Bochum 1860–1914* (1979) is one. The classic study of the transformation from peasants to workers is F. Znaniecki and W. I. Thomas, *The Polish Peasant in Europe and America* (1984, originally published 1918).

There are even fewer comparative studies of the middle classes or bourgeoisies, though national histories or studies are now, fortunately, more common. Theodore Zeldin's *France 1848–1945*, 2 vols. (1973) contains much material on this as on other aspects of society, but no analysis whatever. The early chapters of R. Skidelsky, *John Maynard*

Keynes, vol. 1, 1880–1920 (1983) constitute a case-study of social mobility by a combination of accumulation and examination-passing; and various studies by William Rubinstein, mainly in *Past & Present*, throw a more general light on the British bourgeoisie. The general topic of social mobility is authoritatively discussed in Hartmut Kaelble, *Social Mobility in the 19th and 20th Centuries: Europe and America in Comparative Perspective* (1985). Arno Mayer, *The Persistence of the Old Regime* (1982) is widely comparative, and contains valuable material, notably on the relations between middle and upper classes, embedded in a controversial thesis. As always, in the nineteenth century novels and plays are the best presentations of the worlds of aristocracy and bourgeoisie. Culture and politics as the illumination of a bourgeois predicament are beautifully used in Carl E. Schorske, *Fin-de-Siècle Vienna* (1980).

The great movement for the emancipation of women has produced a large quantity of historical literature of varying quality, but there is no single book about the period which is satisfactory. Though it is neither historical nor primarily concerned with the developed world, Ester Boserup, *Women's Role in Economic Development* (1970) is important. Louise Tilly and Joan W. Scott, *Women, Work and Family* (1978) is basic; see also the section 'Sexual division of labor and industrial capitalism' in the excellent review of women's studies *Signs*, (Winter 1981). T. Zeldin, *France 1848–1945*, vol. 1 has a chapter on women. Few national histories have. On feminism there is a great deal. Richard J. Evans (who has written a book on the German movement) covers the ground comparatively in *The Feminists: Women's Emancipation Movements in Europe, America and Australia 1840–1920* (1977). However, many of the unpolitical ways in which the situation of women changed, usually for the better, and their relation to movements other than those of the secular left, have not been systematically investigated. On the main demographic changes see D. V. Glass and E. Grebenik, 'World Population, 1800–1950' in *Cambridge Economic History of Europe*, vol. IV (1965) and C. Cipolla, *The Economic History of World Population* (1962). D. V. Glass and D. E. C. Eversley (eds.), *Population in History* (1965) contains a crucial paper by J. Hajnal on the historic differences between the west European marriage pattern and the others.

Anthony Sutcliffe, *Towards the Planned City 1780–1914* (1981) and Peter Hall, *The World Cities* (1966) are modern introductions to nineteenth-century urbanization; Adna F. Weber, *The Growth of Cities in the Nineteenth Century* (1897, and recent reprints) is a contemporary survey, which remains important.

On religion and churches Hugh McLeod, *Religion and the People of Western Europe* (1974) is brief and lucid. D. E. Smith, *Religion and Political Development* (1970) is more geared to the non-European world, for which W. C. Smith, *Islam in Modern History* (1957), though old, is still important.

EMPIRE

The basic contemporary text on imperialism is J. A. Hobson's *Imperialism* (1902, many subsequent editions). For the debate on the subject, Wolfgang Mommsen, *Theories of Imperialism* (1980) and R. Owen and B. Sutcliffe (eds.), *Studies in the Theory of Imperialism* (1972). The conquest of colonies is illuminated by Daniel Headrick, *Tools of Empire: Technology and European Imperialism in the Nineteenth Century* (1981) and V. G. Kiernan, *European Empires from Conquest to Collapse 1815–1960* (1982). V. G. Kiernan's marvellous *The Lords of Human Kind* (1972) is much the best survey of 'European attitudes to the outside world in the imperial age' (its subtitle). On the economics of imperialism, see P. J. Cain, *Economic Foundations of British Overseas Expansion 1815–1914* (1980), A. G. Hopkins, *An Economic History of West Africa* (1973) and the old but valuable Herbert Feis, already mentioned, as well as J. F. Rippy, *British Investments in Latin America 1822–1949* (1959) and – on the American side – Charles M. Wilson's study of United Fruit, *Empire in Green and Gold* (1947).

On the views of policy-makers, J. Gallagher and R. F. Robinson, *Africa and the Victorians* (1958) and D. C. M. Platt, *Finance, Trade and Politics in British Foreign Policy 1815–1914* (1968). On the domestic implications and roots of imperialism, Bernard Semmel, *Imperialism and Social Reform* (1960) and, for those unable to read German, H.-U. Wehler, 'Bismarck's Imperialism 1862–1890' *Past & Present*, 48 (1970). On some of the effects of empire in the receiving countries, Donald Denoon, *Settler Capitalism* (1983), Charles Van Onselen, *Studies in the Social and Economic History of the Witwatersrand 1886–1914*, 2 vols. (1982) and – a neglected corner – Edward Bristow, *The Jewish Fight Against White Slavery* (1982). Thomas Pakenham, *The Boer War* (1979) is a vivid picture of the biggest of the imperial wars.

POLITICS

The historical problems of the coming of popular politics can only be studied country by country. Still, a few general works may be useful. Some contemporary enquiries are indicated in notes to chapter 4. Among these Robert Michels' *Political Parties* (various editions) is still interesting, because based on hard looks at the subject. Eugene and Pauline Anderson's *Political Institutions and Social Change in Continental Europe in the Nineteenth Century* (1967) is useful on the growth of the state apparatus; Andrew McLaren, *A Short History of Electoral Systems in Western Europe* (1980) is just what it says; Peter Köhler, F. Zacher and

Martin Partington (eds.), *The Evolution of Social Insurance 1881–1981* (1982) unfortunately only covers Germany, France, Britain, Austria and Switzerland. Much the fullest collection of data for reference on all relevant matters is Peter Flora, *State, Economy and Society in Western Europe*, mentioned above. E. J. Hobsbawm and T. Ranger (eds.), *The Invention of Tradition* (1983) deals with non-institutional reactions to the democratization of politics, especially in the essays by D. Cannadine and E. J. Hobsbawm. Hans Rogger and Eugen Weber (eds.), *The European Right: A Historical Profile* (1965) is a guide to that part of the political spectrum which is not discussed in the text, except incidentally in connection with nationalism.

On the emergence of the labour and socialist movements the standard work of reference is G. D. H. Cole, *A History of Socialist Thought*, III, parts 1 and 2, 'The Second International' (1956). James Joll, *The Second International 1889–1914* (1974) is briefer. W. Guttsman, *The German Social-Democratic Party 1875–1933* (1981) is the most convenient survey of a classical 'mass party'; Georges Haupt, *Aspects of International Socialism 1889–1914* (1986) and M. Salvadori, *Karl Kautsky and the Socialist Revolution* (1979) are good introductions to expectations and ideologies. J. P. Nettl, *Rosa Luxemburg*, 2 vols. (1967) and Isaac Deutscher's *Life of Trotsky*, vol. 1: *The Prophet Armed* (1954) see socialism through the eyes of prominent participants.

On nationalism, the relevant chapters in my *Age of Revolution* and *Age of Capital* may be consulted. Ernest Gellner, *Nations and Nationalism* (1983) is a recent analysis of the phenomenon and Hugh Seton-Watson, *Nations and States* (1977) is encyclopaedic. M. Hroch, *Social Preconditions of National Revival in Europe* (1985) is fundamental. On the relationship between nationalism and labour movements see my essay 'What is the Workers' Country?' in *Worlds of Labour* (1984). Though apparently of only specialized interest, the Welsh studies in D. Smith and H. Francis, *A People and a Proletariat* (1980) are extremely relevant.

CULTURAL AND INTELLECTUAL HISTORY

H. Stuart Hughes, *Consciousness and Society* (numerous editions) is the best-known introduction to the transformations of ideas in this period; George Lichtheim, *Europe in the Twentieth Century* (1972), though published as a general history, is essentially about intellectual developments. Like all this author's work, it is dense but immensely rewarding. Jan Romein, *The Watershed of Two Eras* (already mentioned) provides endless material. For the sciences, C. C. Gillispie, *On the Edge of Objectivity* (1960), which covers a much more extensive period, is a sophisticated introduction. The field is too vast for a brief survey – C. C. Gillispie (ed.), *Dictionary of Scientific Biography*, 16 vols. (1970–80) and

Philip P. Wiener (ed.), *Dictionary of the History of Ideas*, 4 vols. (1973–4) are excellent for reference; and W. F. Bynum, E. J. Browne and Roy Porter (eds.), *Dictionary of the History of Science* (1981) and the *Fontana Dictionary of Modern Thought* (1977) are good and brief. On the crucial areas of physics, Ronald W. Clark, *Einstein, the Life and Times* (1971) may be supplemented by R. McCormmach (ed.), *Historical Studies in the Physical Sciences* vol. II (1970) for the reception of relativity. The same author's novel *Night Thoughts of a Classical Physicist* (1982) is a fine evocation of the average conventional scientist and, incidentally, of German academics. C. Webster (ed.), *Biology, Medicine and Society 1840–1940* (1981) may introduce readers to the worlds of genetics, eugenics, medicine and the social dimensions of biology.

Reference works for the arts, usually without much historical sense, abound: the *Encyclopedia of World Art* is very useful for the visual arts; the *New Grove Dictionary of Music*, 16 vols. (1980) is too much written by experts for other experts. The general surveys of Europe in and around 1900 usually contain much about the arts of the period (e.g. Romein). General histories of the arts are a matter of taste unless pure chronicles. Arnold Hauser, *The Social History of Art* (1958) is a fairly inflexible Marxist version. W. Hofmann, *Turning-Points in Twentieth-century Art 1890–1917* (1969) is interesting but also debatable. The link between William Morris and modernism is stressed in N. Pevsner, *Pioneers of the Modern Movement* (1936). Mark Girouard, *The Victorian Country House* (1971) and *Sweetness and Light: The Queen Anne Movement 1860–1900* (1977) are good on the links between architecture and class lifestyles. Roger Shattuck, *The Banquet Years: The Origins of the Avantgarde in France 1885 to World War One* (rev. edn. 1967) is instructive and fun. Camilla Gray, *The Russian Experiment in Art 1863–1922* (1971) is quite excellent. For theatre, and indeed the *avant garde* of a major European centre, P. Jelavich, *Munich and Theatrical Modernism* (1985). Roy Pascal, *From Naturalism to Expressionism: German Literature and Society 1880–1918* (1973) is to be recommended.

Among books seeking to integrate the arts with contemporary society and other intellectual trends, Romein and Tannenbaum are, as usual, to be consulted. Stephen Kern, *The Culture of Time and Space 1880–1918* (1983) is adventurous and exciting. Readers must judge whether it is also convincing.

On the major trends in the social and human sciences, J. A. Schumpeter, *History of Economic Analysis* (various editions since 1954) is encyclopaedic and tart: for reference only. G. Lichtheim, *Marxism* (1961) repays attentive reading. Sociologists, always inclined to ruminate about what their subject is, have also investigated its history. The articles under the heading 'Sociology' in the *International Encyclopedia of the Social Sciences* (1968), vol. xv, are a guide. The history of historiography in our period is not easily surveyed, except in George Iggers, *New Directions in European Historiography* (1975). However, the article 'History' in the *Encyclopaedia of the Social Sciences*, ed. E. R. A. Seligman (1932) – which has in many respects not been superseded by the *International Encyclopedia* of 1968 – gives a good picture of its debates. It is by Henri Berr and Lucien Febvre.

NATIONAL HISTORIES

A bibliography confined to the English language is adequate for countries using this language, and (thanks largely to the strength of East Asian studies in the USA) is not inadequate for the Far East, but it inevitably omits most of the best and authoritative works on most European countries.

For Britain R. T. Shannon, *The Crisis of Imperialism 1865–1915* (1974) is a good text, strong on cultural and intellectual themes, but George Dangerfield, *The Strange Death of Liberal England* (originally 1935), some fifty years old and wrong on most details, is still the most exciting way to start looking at the nation's history during this period. Elie Halévy, *A History of the English People in the Nineteenth Century*, (1895–1915), vols. iv and v, is even older, but the work of a remarkably intelligent, erudite and perceptive contemporary observer. For readers totally ignorant of British history R. K. Webb, *Modern Britain from the Eighteenth Century to the Present* (1969) is ideal.

Fortunately some excellent French manuals have been translated. J. M. Mayeur and M. Reberioux, *The Republic from its Origins to the Great War 1871–1914* (1984) is the best short history there is; Georges Dupeux, *French Society 1789–1970* (1976) is also to be recommended. T. Zeldin, *France 1848–1945* (1973) is encyclopaedic (except on economic matters) and quirky; Sanford Elwitt, *The Third Republic Defended: Bourgeois Reform in France 1880–1914* (1986) analyses the ideology of the republic's rulers; Eugene Weber's notable *Peasants into Frenchmen* analyses one of the republic's major achievements.

German works have been less translated, though H.–U. Wehler, *The German Empire 1871–1918* (1984) is fortunately available; it may still usefully be supplemented by an old book by a very able Weimar Marxist, Arthur Rosenberg, *The Birth of the German Republic* (1931). Gordon Craig, *German History 1867–1945* (1981) is comprehensive. Volker Berghahn, *Modern Germany, Society, Economics and Politics in the Twentieth Century* (1986) provides more general background. J. J. Sheehan, *German Liberalism in the Nineteenth Century* (1974), Carl Schorske, *German Social Democracy 1905–1917* (1955) – old but perceptive – and Geoffrey Eley, *Reshaping the German Right* (1980) – polemical – help to understand German politics.

For Austria–Hungary C. A. Macartney, *The Habsburg Empire* (1968) is the most convenient general account; R. A. Kann, *The Multinational Empire: Nationalism and National Reform in the Habsburg Monarchy 1848–1918*, 2 vols. (1970) is exhaustive and sometimes exhausting. For those who can get hold of it, H. Wickham Steed, *The Habsburg Monarchy* (1913) is what a gifted and informed journalist would have seen at the time: Steed was *Times* correspondent. Carl Schorske's *Fin-de-Siècle Vienna* is about politics as well as culture. Various writings by Ivan Berend and George Ranki, two excellent Hungarian economic historians, survey and analyse Hungary in particular and east-central Europe in general to good effect.

Our period in Italy is not particularly well covered for those who do not read Italian. There are some general histories such as Denis Mack-Smith, *Italy: A Modern History* (1969) by an author whose major work falls into earlier and later periods. Christopher Seton-Watson, *Italy from Liberalism to Fascism 1871–1925* (1967) is less lively than the great philosopher Benedetto Croce's old but relevant *History of Italy 1871–1915* (1929), which, however, omits most of what does not interest an idealist thinker and much of what interests a modern historian. For Spain, on the other other hand, English readers have two outstanding general works: Raymond Carr's dense but immensely rewarding *Spain 1808–1939* (1966) and Gerald Brenan's marvellous if 'unscientific' *The Spanish Labyrinth* (1950). The history of the Balkan peoples and states is covered in various works by J. and/or B. Jelavich, e.g. Barbara Jelavich, *History of the Balkans*, vol. II on the twentieth century (1983), but I cannot resist drawing attention to Daniel Chirot, *Social Change in a Peripheral Society: The Creation of a Balkan Colony* (1976), which analyses the tragic fate of the Rumanian people, and Milovan Djilas' *Land Without Justice* (1958) which recreates the world of the brave Montenegrins. Stanford J. Shaw and E. K. Shaw, *History of the Ottoman Empire and Modern Turkey*, vol. II: 1808–1975 (1977) is authoritative but not exactly exciting.

It would be misleading to suggest that the general histories of other European countries available in English are really satisfactory, though monographic work (e.g. in the *Scandinavian Economic History Review* or other journals) is quite another matter.

The Cambridge Histories of Africa, Latin America and China – all available for our period – are good guides to their respective continents or regions. John K. Fairbank, Edwin O. Reischauer and Albert M. Craig, *East Asia: Tradition and Transformation* (1978) deals with all the countries of the Far East, and incidentally provides (chapters 17–18, 22–23) a useful introduction to modern Japanese history, for which, more generally, see J. Whitney Hall, *Japan: From Prehistory to Modern Times* (1986 edn), John Livingston *et al.*, *The Japan Reader*, vol. 1: 1800–1945 (1974) and Janet E. Hunter, *A Concise Dictionary of Modern Japanese History* (1984). Non-orientalists interested in Japanese life and culture may enjoy Edward Seidensticker's *Low City, High City: Tokyo from Edo to Earthquake . . . 1867–1923* (1985). The best introduction to modern India is Judith M. Brown, *Modern India* (1985), with a good bibliography.

Some works on China, Iran, the Ottoman Empire, Mexico, Russia and other regions in ferment are indicated under the heading of 'Revolutions'.

For some reason there is a shortage of good introductions to the history of the twentieth-century USA, though there is no shortage of college manuals of all kinds, or of ruminations on the nature of being an American, and there is a mountain of monographs. The updated version of an old standby, S. E. Morison, H. S. Commager and W. E. Leuchtenberg, *The Growth of the American Republic* (6th edn 1969) is still better than most. However, George Kennan, *American Diplomacy 1900–1950* (1951, expanded edn 1984) is to be recommended.

REVOLUTIONS

For comparative perspectives on twentieth-century revolutions, Barrington Moore's *The Social Origins of Dictatorship and Democracy* (1965) is a classic, and has inspired Theda Scocpol, *States and Revolutions* (1978). Eric Wolf, *Peasant Wars of the Twentieth Century* (1972) is important; E. J. Hobsbawm 'Revolution' in Roy Porter and M. Teich (eds.), *Revolution in History* (1986) is a brief comparative survey of the problems.

The historiography of tsarist Russia, its collapse and revolution, is too vast for even a cursory shortlist. Hugh Seton-Watson, *The Russian Empire 1801–1917* (1967), easier to refer to than read, and Hans Rogger, *Russia in the Age of Modernisation 1880–1917* (1983) provide the data. T. G. Stavrou (ed.), *Russia under the Last Tsar* (1969) contains essays by various hands on a variety of topics. P. Lyashchenko, *History of the Russian National Economy* (1949) should be supplemented by the relevant parts of the *Cambridge Economic History of Europe*. On the Russian peasantry Geroid T. Robinson, *Rural Russia under the Old Regime* (1932 and often reprinted since), is the best way to start, though it is out of date. Teodor Shanin's *Russia as a Developing Society*, vol 1: *Russia's Turn of Century* (1985) and vol. II: *Russia 1905–07: Revolution as a Moment of Truth* (1986), an extraordinary and not easy work, tries to see the revolution both from below and in the light of its influence on subsequent Russian history. L. Trotsky's *History of the Russian Revolution* (various editions) provides a participant's communist view full of intelligence and brio.

The English edition of Marc Ferro's *The Russian Revolution of February 1917* contains a convenient bibliography.

The English bibliography of the other great revolution, the Chinese, is also lengthening, though by far the greatest part of it deals with the period since 1911. J. K. Fairbank, *The United States and China* (1979) is really a short modern history of China. The same author's *The Great Chinese Revolution 1800–1985* (1986) is even better. Franz Schurmann and Orville Schell (eds.), *China Readings 1: Imperial China* (1967) provides background; F. Wakeman, *The Fall of Imperial China* (1975) lives up to its title. V. Purcell, *The Boxer Rising* (1963) is the fullest account of this episode. Mary Clabaugh Wright (ed.), *China in Revolution: the First Phase 1900–1915* (1968) may introduce readers to more monographic studies.

On the transformations of other ancient eastern empires, Nikki R. Keddie, *Roots of Revolution: An Interpretive History of Modern Iran* (1981) is authoritative. On the Ottoman Empire, Bernard Lewis, *The Emergence of Modern Turkey* (1961, revised 1969) and D. Kushner, *The Rise of Turkish Nationalism 1876–1908* (1977) may be supplemented by N. Berkes, *The Development of Secularism in Turkey* (1964) and Roger Owen, *The Middle East in the World Economy* (1981).

For the only actual revolution erupting out of imperialism in our period, the Mexican, two works may serve as an introduction: the early chapters of Friedrich Katz, *The Secret War in Mexico* (1981) – or the same author's chapter in the *Cambridge History of Latin America* – and John Womack, *Zapata and the Mexican Revolution* (1969). Both authors are superb. There is no equally good introduction to the much-disputed history of Indian national liberation. Judith Brown's *Modern India* (1985) provides the best start, A. Maddison, *Class Structure and Economic Growth in India and Pakistan Since the Mughals* (1971) the economic and social background. For those who want a taste of the more monographic, C. A. Bayly, *The Local Roots of Indian Politics: Allahabad 1880–1920* (1975) is by a brilliant Indianist; L. A. Gordon, *Bengal: The Nationalist Movement 1876–1940* (1974) is about the most radical region.

On the Islamic region outside Turkey and Iran, there is not much to recommend. P. J. Vatikiotis, *The Modern History of Egypt* (1969) may be consulted, but the famous anthropologist E. Evans-Pritchard's *The Sanusi of Cyrenaica* (1949) (on Libya) is more fun. It was written to inform the British commanders who found themselves fighting in these deserts in the Second World War.

PEACE AND WAR

A good recent introduction to the problems of the origin of the First World War is James Joll, *The Origins of the First World War* (1984). A. J. P. Taylor, *The Struggle for Mastery in Europe* (1954) is old but excellent on the complications of international diplomacy. Paul Kennedy, *The Rise of the Anglo-German Antagonism 1860–1914* (1980), Zara Steiner, *Britain and the Origins of the First World War* (1977), F. R. Bridge, *From Sadowa to Sarajevo: The Foreign Policy of Austria–Hungary 1866–1914* (1976) and Volker Berghahn, *Germany and the Approach of War* (1973) are fine examples of recent monographs. Geoffrey Barraclough's *From Agadir to Armageddon: The Anatomy of a Crisis* (1982) is the work of one of the most original historians of his time. For war and society in general, William H. McNeil, *The Pursuit of Power* (1982) is stimulating; for the specific period of the present book, Brian Bond, *War and Society in Europe 1870–1970* (1983); for the pre-war arms race, Norman Stone, *The Eastern Front 1914–1917* (1978), chapters 1–2. Marc Ferro, *The Great War* (1973) is a good conspectus of the impact of war. Robert Wohl, *The Generation of 1914* (1979) discusses some of those who looked forward to war; Georges Haupt, *Aspects of International Socialism 1871–1914* (1986) discuss those who did not – and, with special brilliance, Lenin's attitude to war and revolution.

Note: This guide to further reading has assumed that readers are in command only of English. Unfortunately today this is likely to be the case in the Anglo-Saxon world. It also assumes that, if sufficiently interested, they will consult the numerous specialist academic journals in the historical field.

INDEX

391